Binge-Watching and Contemporary Television Studies

Binge-Watching and Contemporary Television Studies

Edited by Mareike Jenner

EDINBURGH
University Press

Edinburgh University Press is one of the leading university presses in the UK. We publish academic books and journals in our selected subject areas across the humanities and social sciences, combining cutting-edge scholarship with high editorial and production values to produce academic works of lasting importance. For more information visit our website: edinburghuniversitypress.com

© editorial matter and organisation Mareike Jenner, 2021, 2023
© the chapters their several authors, 2021, 2023

Edinburgh University Press Ltd
The Tun – Holyrood Road
12 (2f) Jackson's Entry
Edinburgh EH8 8PJ

First published in hardback by Edinburgh University Press 2021

Typeset in 11/13 Ehrhardt MT by
IDSUK (DataConnection) Ltd

A CIP record for this book is available from the British Library

ISBN 978 1 4744 6198 6 (hardback)
ISBN 978 1 4744 6199 3 (paperback)
ISBN 978 1 4744 6200 6 (webready PDF)
ISBN 978 1 4744 6201 3 (epub)

The right of the contributors to be identified as authors of this work has been asserted in accordance with the Copyright, Designs and Patents Act 1988 and the Copyright and Related Rights Regulations 2003 (SI No. 2498).

Contents

Notes on Contributors   vii
Acknowledgements   x

1. Introduction   1
   Mareike Jenner

Part I Bingeing Fans

2. Historical Binge-Watching: Marathon Viewing on Videotape   23
   E. Charlotte Stevens
3. 'A small Christmas for me': A Study of Binge-Watching and Fan Engagement on Reddit   40
   Rhiannon Bury
4. Binge-Watching and Fandom: Conclusion   59
   Rhiannon Bury and E. Charlotte Stevens

Part II Binge-Watching Audiences

5. Commercial Constructions of Binge-Viewers: A Typology of the New and Improved Couch Potato as Seen on TV   65
   Emil Steiner
6. Binge-Watching Conditions and Multitasking: The Enjoyable Ephemeral   82
   Lisa Glebatis Perks
7. What Defines a Binge? Elapsed Time versus Episodes   98
   Ri Pierce-Grove
8. Binge-Watching and the Organisation of Everyday Life   112
   Lothar Mikos and Deborah Castro
9. Binge-Watching Audience Typologies: Conclusion   131
   Lisa Perks, Emil Steiner, Ri Pierce-Grove and Lothar Mikos

Part III Transnational Bingeing

10 National, Transnational, Transcultural Media:
    Netflix – The Culture-Binge   145
    B. G.-Stolz

11 National TV as Transnational 'Cinematic' Object:
    How Binge-Consumption Frames the Critical Vocabulary   162
    Robert Watts

12 Transnationalising Genre: Netflix, Teen Drama and
    Textual Dimensions in Netflix Transnationalism   183
    Mareike Jenner

13 Transnational Bingeing: Conclusion   201
    B. G.-Stolz, Robert Watts and Mareike Jenner

Part IV Binge-Watching Narratives

14 Digressions and Recaps: The Bingeable Narrative   207
    Lynn Kozak and Martin Zeller-Jacques

15 'Next Episode in 5 . . .' – Binge-Watching and Narrative in
    Streaming Television Comedy   224
    Tom Hemingway

16 The Bingeable Ms Gilmore: A Comparative Analysis of Narrative
    Structure in Broadcast TV Show *Gilmore Girls* and Netflix
    Original Show *Gilmore Girls: A Year in the Life*   236
    Orcun Can

17 Netflix Feminism: Binge-Watching Rape Culture in
    Unbreakable Kimmy Schmidt and *Unbelievable*   250
    Júlia Havas and Tanya Horeck

18 Bingeing Narratives: Conclusion   274
    *Lynn Kozak and Martin Zeller-Jacques, Tom Hemingway,
    Orcun Can, Júlia Havas and Tanya Horeck*

Index   278

Notes on Contributors

Rhiannon Bury is Professor of Women's and Gender Studies at Athabasca University, Canada's Open University. Her most recent book, *Television 2.0: Viewer and Fan Engagement with Digital TV*, was published in 2017. Her research has been published in journals such as *New Media & Society*; *Convergence: The International Journal of Research into New Media Technologies* and *Critical Studies in Television*.

Orcun Can is a writer and filmmaker, currently writing up his PhD at King's College London, Department of Culture, Media and Creative Industries. His research focuses on Netflix Originals' narrative forms. Utilising a formal analytical tool, the STNA Model, Can's research maps out different narrative possibilities facilitated by SVOD platforms. He teaches various modules on Media and Creative Industries in different universities, including King's College London and the University of Bedfordshire.

Deborah Castro is Marie Skłodowska-Curie Research Fellow at the Department of Arts and Culture Studies at Erasmus University Rotterdam (The Netherlands) and a research fellow at ITI-LARSyS (Portugal). Castro's main research interests lie in the fields of audience and television studies. Her research has been published in peer-reviewed journals such as *Convergence: The International Journal of Research into New Media Technologies* (2019), *Television & New Media* (2020) and *Addictive Behaviors Reports* (2021).

B. G.-Stolz is programme director of Media and Communications and Research Fellow at the Center for Arts, Memory and Communities at Coventry University. She investigates storytelling in the post-digital age through universal themes, global media brands and affective cultural engagement.

Júlia Havas is Lecturer in Media and Communication at De Montfort University (Leicester). Her research focuses on Anglo-American television, gender and race in popular media, streaming cultures, Hungarian film and TV, and the transcultural flow of Anglo-American media. Her monograph *Feminist Quality Television* is forthcoming. She has published in the journals *Television and New Media* and *Animation Studies*, and contributed chapters to the anthologies *Hysterical! Women in American Comedy* (2017) and *The Routledge Companion to European Cinemas* (forthcoming).

Tom Hemingway is a doctoral candidate at the University of Warwick, writing on the aesthetics of post-broadcast comedy television. His research interests include contemporary film and television comedy, and post-broadcast television programming.

Tanya Horeck is Associate Professor in Film, Media & Culture at Anglia Ruskin University. A feminist media studies scholar, she has published widely on popular TV and film. She is the author of the books *Justice on Demand: True Crime in the Digital Streaming Era* (2019) and *Public Rape: Representing Violation in Fiction and Film* (2004), and is the co-editor of two anthologies, *The New Extremism in Cinema* (2011) and *Rape in Stieg Larsson's Millennium Trilogy and Beyond* (2013).

Mareike Jenner is a Senior Lecturer in Media Studies at Anglia Ruskin University.

Lynn Kozak is Associate Professor in Classics at McGill University. Current research focuses on serial poetics in ancient epic and in contemporary North American television, building on their monograph on this subject, *Experiencing Hektor: Character in the Iliad* (Bloomsbury Academic 2016). They have also published on Homeric fandom in Greek tragedy and the politics of horror in FOX's *The Exorcist*, and they have forthcoming chapters and articles on epic strategies in television, characterisation in *iZombie*, genre hybridity in *Lucifer*, and Homeric intimacy in NBC's *Hannibal*, as well as continuing work on Homer's *Iliad*, following their 2018 serial performance of the entire *Iliad*, available on YouTube.

Lothar Mikos is Professor of Television Studies in the Department of Media Studies at the Filmuniversity Babelsberg in Potsdam, Germany. He founded the Television Studies Section of the European Communication Research and Education Associaten (ECREA) in which he served as Chair from 2010 until 2016. His main areas of work are global television and platform economy, television formats worldwide, digital distribution, transmedia storytelling, (de-)convergence culture, popular television genres and formats, and qualitative audience studies.

Lisa Glebatis Perks is Associate Professor and Department Chair in the Department of Communication and Media at Merrimack College. Her work focuses on audience responses to contemporary television cultures and includes the monograph *Media Marathoning: Immersions in Morality* (2015).

Ri Pierce-Grove is a PhD candidate in Communications, Columbia University, USA.

Emil Steiner is Assistant Professor of Journalism at Rowan University. His research explores how and why people enjoy sports, binge-watch, and stream esports. Prior to joining the academy, he was a reporter and editor at *The Washington Post* and a member of the newsroom awarded the 2008 Pulitzer Prize for Breaking News Reporting.

E. Charlotte Stevens is Lecturer in Media and Communications at Birmingham City University. She is the author of *Fanvids: Television, Women, and Home Media Re-Use* (2020). She has also published on videogame fan histories, screen vampires and poetic television documentaries on the BBC. She is currently working on television fans' viewing practices found in 1980s media fanzines.

Robert Watts is an early career researcher and associate lecturer in media at the University of Salford. His research interests are in television aesthetics and discourses of authorship and prestige in contemporary media cultures. His PhD thesis, completed in 2019 at the University of Manchester, was titled *Transnational Television Aesthetics: National Culture and the 'Global' Prestige Drama*.

Martin Zeller-Jacques is a former Senior Lecturer in Film and Television at Queen Mary University. He recently left academia to go to culinary school.

Acknowledgements

With many thanks to Gillian Leslie and Richard Strachan from EUP for guiding me through this process with invaluable advice.

This collection is the result of a workshop on binge-watching, which was financed by a British Academy Small Grant. This collection is the result of the hard work of these scholars, who all deserve a massive THANK YOU for making the workshop a success.

This workshop was geared to bring together Early Career Researchers and more senior scholars. Understandably, some ECRs and more senior researchers had to leave academia before this collection could be published. We wish them good luck and all the best in their future endeavours and are particularly grateful to other contributors whose research could be usefully integrated here.

Mareike Jenner

CHAPTER I

Introduction

Mareike Jenner

In 2018 and 2019 a group of scholars came together in Cambridge, UK at Anglia Ruskin University to discuss the various implications of binge-watching for the discipline of television studies. The aim was to get researchers collaborating on differing ideas regarding binge-watching, dividing them into four groups. The themes of these groups were guided by research approach and consisted of: fandom and identity constructions; audience and reception studies; transnational television; and narratology and narrative structures. This collection is the result of these discussions, of contributors exchanging ideas and the ability to relate to each other's work, even where we might disagree on approaches or definitions. These four research branches determine the various parts of this book. Not all of these parts may strike the reader as automatically part of a broader discourse of binge-watching. After all, the term binge-watching seems to describe, first and foremost, an audience practice and as such appears to be best addressed from the perspective of audience and reception studies (as done in Part II). Yet, more questions need to be asked: Is it also a mode of narratology visible in the narrative structures of 'bingeable' texts? If so, what makes a text bingeable, and how can this be assessed? How do texts travel around the world within these structures? And how does this shift influence industrial and textual models, never mind ideas of what 'transnational television' is? How does binge-watching determine representational modes? How do audiences relate to these texts in fan practices or other modes of audience behaviour? And how is binge-watching rooted in a history of fandom? To some, many of these questions may be better encompassed by the descriptors 'contemporary television' or 'TV IV' rather than 'binge-watching'. Yet approaching developments via the perspective of binge-watching allows us to think about the wider consequences of audience behaviours on the structures of contemporary television. Thus, binge-watching is understood here as an issue of audience practices and a structural and conceptual issue that influences narratology and the structures of television that are historical, cultural, industrial and technological. Admittedly, Netflix looms large in these discussions. This is not because Netflix is the only contribution to the various ways in which binge-watching functions, but because it is the platform that has incorporated the assumed desires and ambitions of binge-watching audiences most successfully in its marketing, the structure of its interface, and algorithm. In order to contextualise the debates in this volume, it is important to position them in the context of media history, predominantly television history, for Netflix has often understood and conceptualised itself as part of this medium.

Before outlining the structure of this volume, this introduction aims to draw out some of the important debates surrounding binge-watching to show why it is so difficult to arrive at a common definition of the term. It does so by first highlighting the way in which audience practices have interacted with the technologies of television throughout its history. To gain a broad understanding of what binge-watching means, it is important to consider it in relation to contemporary television and its relationship with previous eras. Television studies has broadly divided the history of the medium into four phases (see, for example, Ellis 2002; Jenner 2016). TV I refers to early television up until roughly the mid-1970s, in which the main changes to the television set were the addition of colour and the remote control. TV II describes the phase from the mid-1970s to the mid-to-late 1990s, which has seen some of the most significant changes to television: cable channels with their increased competition and 24-hour broadcasting; remote controls that, at once, became more accurate than previous models and so cheap to manufacture that they were quickly included as a matter of course with a majority of consumer electronics (see Benson-Allott 2015, 81); the VCR and, along with it, a whole industry that would radically transform home viewing (see Greenberg 2008); and, finally, video gaming consoles for the home that would transform the television set into a more interactive medium (see Newman 2017). To respond to these developments, television's bid for audience attention changed through aesthetic shifts that John T. Caldwell describes as 'televisuality' (1995). TV III describes shifts towards digital television through the introduction of technologies such as DVD players and digital recording technologies such as TiVo, as many broadcasting systems changed to digital. Perhaps most visibly, this era describes the era of 'quality' TV in the US: HBO started to invest in talent to create original drama, often by breaking the supposed 'rules' of broadcast television. The much-discussed marketing slogan 'it's not TV, it's HBO' may encompass this best.[1] These phases or eras are, of course, simplifications and, as Derek Kompare argues:

... technology, industry and culture are not autonomous domains: each is shaped by the other in particular ways, helping construct particular media forms and practices in particular contexts. (2005, 198)

Furthermore, these eras are relatively America-centric, though many of these shifts took place in other Western countries with only a few years delay. Yet the timeline changes for most former USSR countries and parts of Asia as well as Africa. More recently, the term TV IV has emerged to describe how television has moved online and the various changes to viewing practices, narrative structures and technologies that have influenced the way contemporary television culture is structured. The difficulties in defining TV IV and how this era interlinks with problems in defining binge-watching will be discussed in more depth in this introduction. Thus, the aim here is to grasp some of the complexities pertaining to binge-watching and provide an overview of how this is understood within different sub-disciplines of the field. To use Kompare's vocabulary, TV IV is a *reconception* of television (2005, 199). Reconceptions are discursive shifts that are often linked to how media habits change, which is a central idea with regard to how we can conceptualise binge-watching's shift from 'rogue' audience practice to the mainstream. As Wendy Hui Kyong Chun argues,

> Habit frames change as persistence, as it habituates: it is a reaction to change – to an outside sensation or action – that remains beyond that change within the organism. (2016, Kindle location 336)

In other words, changes in media habits build on the habits that already exist and become part of the same 'structure of feeling', to borrow Raymond Williams's phrase. Thus, these shifts in habits often *feel* less radical than they are. Binge-watching is a central way in which media habits linked to television have changed. This is not a sudden shift, but one that is linked to slow-moving changes in technologies and the behaviours these technologies foster. In other words, binge-watching is the most convenient way to watch DVD box sets and was, thus, already part of the discourses surrounding viewing practices when streaming was introduced. This is elaborated upon in more detail below. Netflix introduced the model to publish all episodes of a season at once and its interface privileges binge-watching through the post-play function. Yet, when it published its first original series, *House of Cards* (Netflix 2013–18), it also mobilised a vast marketing effort in the US to explain what binge-watching is and how to do it (Jenner 2018, 161–82). This highlights that the change in media habits is not 'natural', but guided through industry practices and marketing language, even if it may tie in with (some) viewer desires (see Bury 2017, 86–7).

To understand what binge-watching is, then, it is crucial to bear in mind, as John Hartley argues in *Uses of Television* (1999, 15–27), that television studies looks and feels different depending on the many possible approaches that can be taken. In line with this, binge-watching may be impossible to encompass in just one definition, as different research perspectives and questions emphasise different points. As such, the various articles in this volume do not subscribe to one fixed definition of binge-watching but rather embrace a diversity in definitions and research approaches. One way of grasping what binge-watching is lies in exploring its history, particularly in relation to television's ancillary technologies.

HISTORICISING BINGE-WATCHING: 'ROGUE' AUDIENCES, CONTROL AND CHOICE

One important element of the discourse of binge-watching has been the way in which autonomous scheduling is highlighted. This has moved more to the forefront with the supposedly 'un-scheduled' nature of Netflix and other platforms. As I have explored elsewhere, this language aims to hide how structured viewing on Netflix actually is (see Jenner 2018, 119–37). But these discourses have a long history in the marketing language and academic accounts of the various ancillary technologies to television throughout television history. Max Dawson's PhD *TV Repair* (2008) emphasises that concepts of subverting the schedule by allowing viewers to exert more control or autonomy go back to the remote control within American discourse. Unlike in most European systems, where often only one or two national channels existed, several national and local channels were available in the US from the early days of the medium. Dawson uses the language of 'repairing' television to describe how ancillary technologies have been used to (supposedly) counteract the assumed negative effects traditionally associated with television (physical and mental illnesses, anti-social behaviours). Yet, one element central to the successful ancillary technologies both in the US and across Europe has been the ability to give viewers control over 'their own schedule' through time-shifting technologies. This control is limited to the individual's immediate environment, so is much more limited and individualised than what critics such as Gilles Deleuze (1992) or David Harvey (2005) theorise as control governments or private capital exercise. As theorists such as Renata Salecl (2010) or Michel Feher (2009) argue, this idea of control over consumption is closely linked with neoliberalism and ideologies of 'self-improvement'. The control the individual exercises does not equal power, though it does allow for the building of cultural capital if it is used to access culturally elevated 'quality' television (Jenner 2019). There are two important elements to the way in which new technologies are often marketed and viewing practices develop, both linked to concepts of 'choice' and 'control': on the one hand, viewer desire to design their own schedules instead of being dictated one by broadcasters and, on the other, viewer desire to revisit television (either individual episodes or whole programmes). Both overlap significantly, as autonomous scheduling (control over the schedule) often involves revisiting programmes (choice of available programmes). Different practices relating to the various ways in which audiences consume television started out as 'rogue' practices until industry found a way to put them into more desirable forms. The idea of taking control over television, meaning the television schedule rather than the object, has often dominated the marketing language associated with these technologies. The introduction of technologies like the remote control in the late 1940s suggests that discourses surrounding viewer control over the television schedule were in circulation before the term neoliberal was even coined. In fact, Dawson argues that the task of 'repairing' television falls more urgently to the viewer in the 'digital era' of TV III and TV IV when online safety and privacy become issues that sit squarely outside of the remit of the television industries or linked government agencies (2008, 199–200). As such, it would be simplistic to argue that discourses surrounding narratives of self-improvement and control over television are solely linked to the rise of neoliberalism. Yet, the way viewing practices have developed since the 1980s in the US and other Western countries suggests a strong linkage in which a complex formation of technology, marketing, 'rogue' viewing practices and capitalist discourses work to shape television culture.[2] This does not mean a nostalgia for eras of television where viewing was essentially prescribed through the schedule, but a critical engagement with the way in which television culture has developed to increasingly highlight the control viewers can exercise. The fact that, for many viewers, more or less self-scheduled platform television exists in parallel to linear television already highlights that streaming mostly implies more choice, including over the kind of control viewers can exercise. Choice is, of course, its own problematic concept. Salecl, for example, argues that the large amount of choice available to consumers only increases pressure to make the 'right' one. This could potentially lead to paralysis in the face of 'too much' choice. Benson-Allott argues:

> Beginning in the mid-1950s advertisers exploited the portability of wireless remote controls, rebranding 'control' as 'freedom' – what Sony would one day call the 'freedom of total control'. (2015, 46)

Benson-Allott highlights the terms 'freedom' and 'power' here, though, as the quote above implies, these terms belong to the same marketing vocabulary as control and choice:

> In fact, the terms *freedom* and *power* became almost interchangeable in late twentieth-century ads for consumer electronics. They helped

> convince us that remote control was the same thing as active engagement with the media. Remotes do offer many conveniences, but the 'freedom' to sit back passively and choose is not the same thing as cultural intervention. (2015, 46, italics in the original)

Choice and control, the freedom to make choices and the power to control what programming is played on the TV set, remain intrinsically linked. The more choice viewers are presented with, the more they are supposed to be able to exercise control over their own experience. Both control and choice have extended massively over television's history and binge-watching is the current culmination of both.

Various technologies to extend choice and increase viewer control have been introduced since the beginning of the history of the medium, though many have remained unsuccessful. In the US, the first main addition to the television set in the TV I era was the remote control, which became available in 1948. As Benson-Allott argues, the first 'hit' remote control was Zenith's Lazy Bones, a wired remote which came out in 1950 with two buttons: 'one black, the other white – that adjusted the tuner clockwise or counterclockwise by a single station' (2015, 33). As Dawson (2008, 60) and Benson-Allott (2015, 34) point out, Zenith founder Eugene F. McDonald Jr saw himself as fighting the ad-financed television system that developed in the US. He positioned the remote control as part of this 'battle' by emphasising in marketing material that it could be used to mute advertising or change channels.[3] Dawson points to two myths dominant in US society: that ads were played at a louder volume than other programming and that advertising has 'bad' effects on audiences (2008, 44–113). This indicates annoyance with, and even fear of, advertising, which could be easily controlled via the remote control. At the same time, remote controls were expensive, adding $30 to the cost of the television set, which, according to Benson-Allott (2015, 33), adjusted for inflation, amounted to $300 in 2015. Additionally, as Louise Benjamin (1993) outlines, the technology was prone to failure. Matt Hills and Joanne Garde-Hansen (2017, 161) point to further ways in which viewers in the (late) TV I era could gain control over their experience. They find in researching fan memories of *Doctor Who* (BBC 1963–) that some of their interview subjects used audio recording equipment to revisit older episodes before VCRs made this into a wider practice. This suggests that later technologies built on these 'rogue' practices.

Though Kompare outlines the various advantages that reruns had for the television industry in late 1950s America (2005, 80), he also points out that the audience welcomed reruns, with ratings staying virtually the same as for the original broadcasts. This went against the industry expectation that audiences would watch repeats only if they had missed the first run:

By 1955 [. . .] the ratings evidence established that reruns were more than a cheap substitute for new programmes. The 'new audience' rationale had been only partially accurate; instead, repeat programs were also consistently drawing repeat viewers, to an extent that had not been foreseen, but would soon be relied upon. (2005, 52)

Thus, though reruns were provided by the US television industry (primarily local stations) within the parameters of the schedule, this was driven by ratings. Kompare even goes on to point out that audience shares in reruns were, in some cases, greater than on first airing. Thus, embracing the choice of watching repeats was a somewhat 'rogue' audience practice, though the parameters of repetition were defined by the industry. In terms of textual politics, the conditions of seriality invite the desire to re-experience episodes, in itself not an inherent function of the schedule. Whether in stories that rely on narrative closure or soaps that rely on cliffhangers, most TV series are repetitive enough in terms of themes and central narrative conflicts to allow for episodes to be revisited as stand-alone artefacts. As Lynn Kozak and Martin Zeller-Jacques point out in their article in this volume, episodes also tend to include recapping mechanisms that allow audiences to find their place in broader storylines when watching episodes out of sequence. This does not mean that narratives have not grown increasingly complex the more recording technologies have become available, and access to them has become easier, as discussed below. It does mean, however, that revisiting episodes has been part of television culture – whether recognised and catered to by industry or not – from the 1950s onwards. In fact, Kompare's central argument in *Rerun Nation: How Repeats Invented American Television* is that 'repetition is [. . .] the primary structural factor of commercial television in the United States' (2005, xi).

Much changed in the period outlined as TV II, which coincided with periods of neoliberal politics in most Western countries, led by Ronald Reagan as US president from 1980 until 1988. In 1980, Viewstar introduced the first infrared TV remote in the US market, marking a moment for remote controls in which they became both cheaper to manufacture and more accurate (Benson-Allott 2015, 80–1). Around the same time, the introduction and, in some parts of the US, extension of cable (see Lotz 2018) meant that their necessity also increased as more channels could be 'sampled' before making a choice about which programme to watch. As the number of available channels increased, channel-surfing became a more common, even necessary, practice to control the increased choice offered by the medium. It is difficult now to accurately trace the emergence of channel-surfing as a term, as search engines usually treat it as synonymous with linear television. This fact alone, however, is telling as it indicates how much the practice has become interlinked with the medium. Channel-surfing as a term encompasses different practices, such as grazing (sampling different channels to end on one), advertising avoidance, or parallel viewing (Walker and Bellamy 1993, 4). Yet, the medium was also extended in other ways throughout the TV II era: the VCR and video gaming consoles were introduced to add new versions of control over what was displayed on the television screen. It was the VCR, in particular, that allowed viewers to control and experience television differently through time-shifting. Wasser points to the differences in what 'choice' actually means in different media landscapes:

> In Western Europe, the state-controlled systems often had austere collections of various forms of popular entertainment. In other regions, government censorship frustrated the desires of local residents to see the kinds of movies and programs they had become familiar with on their travels. Therefore, the choice these purchasers sought with their VCRs was a larger selection of programs. Japanese and American locals suffered relatively less from these frustrations; rather they suffered from time constraints. (2001, Kindle location 1853)

As a solution to these constraints, the possibility of recording and time-shifting television would be provided by the VCR. Allowing viewers to record programmes offered more choice (recording one programme while watching another, for example), but it also extended the control viewers could take over the schedule. The elements of choice and control, however, would prove to be even more complex than suggested above, as regimes of re-viewing content varied. Julia Dobrow (1990) points to how frequent re-viewing of a variety of content on tapes was, including educational material, children's programming, films and serialised formats. The wave of aerobics videos following the massive success of *Jane Fonda's Workout* (Galanty, 1982) as well as the emergence of 'how-to' tapes (including cooking or DIY tapes) clearly intended for repeat viewing also evidences this. Kompare points to the impractical nature of the VHS tape for the publication of entire TV series for the sell-through market (2005, 204). Yet, it is difficult to assess how common the recording and archiving of TV episodes was in the TV II era. Ann Gray's research on women and VHS culture in Britain (1992) suggests that the recording of television episodes was common, even though, as she points out, it was mostly films that were archived, and TV episodes mostly time-shifted and then recorded over. E. Graham McKinley mentions, in passing, young female viewers of *Beverly Hills 90210* (Fox 1990–2000) recording and re-watching episodes, though the practice is not explored further (1997, 1). Kim Bjarkman (2004) points to a small community of fans collecting VHS recordings of TV episodes. Thus, it is difficult to ascertain how common the recording, archiving and 'saving up' of episodes for binge-watching actually was. Yet, Hills and Garde-Hansen's research (2017) indicates that, at least among fans, this would not have been an uncommon occurrence. E. Charlotte Stevens's contribution in this volume is crucial to understanding how fans binge-watch in the TV II era. Her archival research on *Starsky and Hutch* (ABC 1975–9) fanzines even finds the use of the term 'binge' as early as 1985. Versions of binge-watching provided by linear television in the form of marathons also indicate the industry's recognition of viewer desire to watch several episodes of a series in a row. In the UK, the omnibus of the week's soap opera episodes on weekends is a powerful reminder of the importance of reruns as a way to offer viewers a possibility to 'catch up' on missed episodes. In the 1980s and 1990s, there was a growing dominance of soap and flexi-narratives (Nelson 1997, 31) on US TV, following the critical and commercial success of *Hill Street Blues* (NBC 1981–7) and programmes like *St. Elsewhere* (NBC 1982–8) or *Twin Peaks* (ABC 1990–1) with their reliance on cliffhangers and deferred closure of storylines. These conditions of seriality suggest the rewards for viewers watching (and re-watching) more than one episode in a row. Additionally, though not common, some VHS tapes of TV series were published: this was often in the form of a 'best of' tape. Only a few series like fan favourites *Friends* (NBC 1994–2004) or *The X-Files* (Fox 1993–) were published as season box sets towards the end of the TV II and beginning of the TV III era, shortly before DVD box sets became available. The 'official' versions of TV series on VHS, provided in the form of sell-through tapes and marathons or other scheduling practices, indicate that viewer desire to watch several episodes of a TV programme in a row is well established by the 1990s.

The TV III era saw a range of changes to how television series became understood as bingeable and the various ways in which industry catered to viewer desires. A number of US broadcast and cable channels would get involved in the development of original series that pushed the envelope on what television programmes could be. However, no channel is as associated with this period, the re-invigoration of the term 'quality' TV, and the industrial practices that developed at this time as HBO. Central features of the way in which texts became bingeable were the focus on writing and narrative complexity, the shortening of seasons to 12 or 13 episodes, the high investment in cast and the creation of 'cinematic' aesthetics. The 18-month hiatus between seasons that was once given to the writers of *The Sopranos* (HBO 1999–2007) to develop stories for the next season would remain a rarity, but the story highlights the importance that was assigned to creative processes and how much HBO aimed to market itself as purveyor of this kind of creativity. Of course, it helped that the series was already successful and the anticipation built during the hiatus was an effective marketing strategy. Furthermore, this also gave viewers time to re-watch episodes through reruns and DVD box sets, while also allowing new viewers to catch up. In fact, box sets did prove important to HBO's strategy for 'quality' television, especially as narratives grew increasingly complex. Arguably, DVD box sets were also driving concepts like bingeability, making binge-watching an increasingly common mode of viewing. Even though self-directed recording and viewing of several episodes of television in a row was possible with the VHS, it is difficult to imagine that binge-watching would have ever become common to contemporary television cultures without series as complex as *Lost* (ABC 2004–10) or *The Wire* (HBO 2002–8). Kathrin Rothemund argues that narrative complexity can be conceptualised via the following factors: number of and variety in storylines (both can be summarised under the term diversity); an emerging sense of connection between the different storylines; non-linearity; openness (polysemic meanings of the narration as intertextual and multi-platform storytelling); and contingency (2013, 55–78). This narrative complexity rewards attentive viewing, something more easily guaranteed by autonomous scheduling rather than linear schedules. Industry may not have expected the force with which binge-watching of DVD box sets became common, as indicated by the lack of the 'play all' functions on many box sets in the first decade of the 2000s (including most HBO series, cult series like *Firefly* [Fox 2002–3], and even early seasons of *CSI: Crime Scene Investigation* [CBS 2000–15]). Yet, the delivery system made binge-watching not only easier but even preferable for audiences who did not want to switch back to linear television or box sets of other series after viewing one episode. Further delivery systems that made binge-watching easier were the DVR (digital video recorder), particularly prominent in North America, the first online platforms, such as the BBC iPlayer, which launched in 2007 in the UK or Hulu, launched the same year in the US, or illegal downloads.[4] What these delivery systems suggest is an extension of choices to watch TV and control over the way it is watched. Perhaps more importantly, binge-watching remained a somewhat 'rogue' practice, only (somewhat) inadvertently catered to by industry. Helped by these developments, binge-watching has become more of a 'mainstream' practice over the last decade or so (Jenner 2016, 2019). As the discussions in this volume show, Netflix has played a central role, using the term in its marketing, as publishing model and designing texts specifically for binge-watching. Thus, it is hardly surprising that a volume on binge-watching features so many articles on Netflix texts, their reception or the company's role in transnational markets.

The history of binge-watching can, therefore, be read as a history of control, choice and 'rogue' viewing practices slowly becoming part of the 'mainstream' of television discourse via different technologies that are adopted as part of television culture (remote control, VCR, DVD, etc.). This control can be read and understood in different ways: being able to integrate media better into our daily lives may be part of neoliberal narratives of 'self-improvement', but the desire for control over the schedule aligns with television's ancillary technologies since the 1950s. Yet, as the discussions in this book will show, this is only one perspective of binge-watching that privileges its place within a specific national history of television's ancillary technologies. More perspectives will emerge here, as different research approaches emphasise the broad variety of themes, structures and histories linked to binge-watching.

DEFINING BINGE-WATCHING

As in previous eras, different perspectives on texts, structures and viewing behaviours dominate the current TV IV era. As outlined above, binge-watching is tied to different delivery systems of television. Bury argues in a study of fan behaviour in the current TV environment that viewers continue to rely on a variety of authorised and unauthorised delivery systems of content (2017, 111–17). Netflix, and the way it privileges binge-watching as a mode of consumption, serves here as a starting point for grasping its centrality to TV IV.

Netflix was initially a DVD-rental service, which introduced digital streaming as an add-on for US customers in 2007. Lotz points out that 'predictions of web TV began in 1995, which was well before most [US] homes even had internet access' (2017, Kindle location 218). Netflix, of course, extended the idea of streaming by offering its own in-house productions from 2013, focusing on serialised programmes with *House of Cards* or *Orange is the New Black* (Netflix 2013–19). Importantly, these series were published in the form of complete seasons, rather than the one-episode-per-week format common for linear television. Together with its interface, which privileges binge-watching through the post-play function, Netflix nudges viewers towards binge-watching. Additionally, marketing discourses in the form of promotional appearances of writers or cast members of original series often highlight the control that audiences gain via binge-watching by deciding what is watched when and where and for how long (see Jenner 2018, 161–78). As I have argued elsewhere, the Netflix interface and its algorithm 'orders' the experience and strongly privileges binge-watching in a way similar to the television schedule (Jenner 2018, 119–37). Yet, though the discussions in this volume often highlight Netflix and its linkage with binge-watching, the viewing structures that interfaces enable are important for digital media platforms beyond Netflix. Catherine Johnson points out that one of the functions of online TV interfaces is to:

> . . . encourage viewing-related activities over other forms of engagement [which computers, in particular, allow for], despite the fact that the convergence of television and the internet makes it possible to offer a wide range of activities within one service. (2019, 119)

Johnson highlights the various ways in which interfaces compete for viewer attention within a media landscape where the concept of 'buzz' has become a highly valued commodity.

Binge-watching builds on previous media practices and is a media practice many viewers have engaged in since recording technologies have allowed for more self-directed viewing. I have previously understood binge-watching as a practice of watching more than one episode of a serialised programme on a device that allows for self-scheduling (computers, but also DVD players, DVRs, VCRs, etc.). This privileges what Jason Jacobs (2011) terms the 'pure text', meaning an avoidance of the 'pollutions' of broadcast television: ads, idents, teasers, etc. This understanding is based on a survey of existing definitions in journalistic and academic texts, emphasising their commonalities (see Jenner 2018, 109–18). Yet, as pointed out in relation to the various concepts and vocabularies mobilised to understand TV IV, other definitions are in circulation. One of the major points omitted in this definition is the question of how many episodes viewers are likely to watch. Audience definitions have varied widely, depending on whether the audiences surveyed are used to binge-watching on DVD or digital media or not. A particular focus here has often been the number of episodes necessary to constitute a binge: a 2013 Harris Interactive study commissioned by Netflix set the number at two episodes watched in a row, other audience research has found a number of five or six episodes (Steiner and Xu 2020).

Concepts of binge-watching that are too focused on episode numbers are bound to be nationally specific, dominated by existing television cultures and attitudes towards screen time. As Graeme Turner recently argued, current definitions tend to ignore the fields' efforts at de-Westernisation through a focus on the US and Western Europe (2019). Existing definitions are also likely to be highly momentary, with the culture and technologies surrounding binge-watching constantly in flux. Furthermore, the question of how many hours need to be watched to constitute a binge is likely influenced by how many leisure hours an individual has at their disposal at their current life stage. Overall, it seems impossible to define something that, ultimately, is a viewing practice, without taking into account what audiences have to say about their understandings, practices and motivations. Yet it must be accepted that definitions vary widely among different demographics, which makes it highly difficult to arrive at a (relatively) stable definition. Lisa Glebatis Perks argues for the understanding of binge-watching as 'media marathoning'. For audience studies, this language is highly useful as it highlights the 'ultimate goal' of watching: finishing the text. Charlotte Brunsdon highlights binge-watching's links with addiction metaphors:

> The metaphors [of addiction implied in the term binge] demonstrate the shift from something that is rationed temporally (broadcast television), and which you must therefore get a fix from regularly, to

something more like a box of chocolates which you purchase and consume in your own time. (2010, Kindle location 1626)

This understanding, importantly, from a period when binge-watching was largely relegated to the viewing of DVD box sets, highlights that there appears to be no number of episodes that need to be consumed, as long as there is a 'fix' of as much as you want, whenever you want. Though the metaphors used by Perks and Brunsdon are almost in opposition to each other in the way they are linked to broader discourses of health, they highlight something similar: marathons can be run at a different pace, and there can be huge differences in how long it might take someone to finish a box of chocolates or at what intervals a 'fix' is necessary in cases of addiction. This changeability is highly important for an understanding of binge-watching and makes it almost impossible to reach a clear idea of how long a binge is or *should* be.

Understandings of binge-watching often highlight different aspects. Viewer autonomy and control, interface structures, modes of storytelling, or audience behaviour and understanding are certainly some of these aspects, but hardly all of them. Depending on the research approach, different aspects are emphasised by different researchers. Thus, this collection does not aim to impose one single definition of what binge-watching is. In fact, this would be counterproductive in a collection that brings together a range of approaches.

THE STRUCTURE OF THIS BOOK

As divergent and often diffuse as understandings of binge-watching may be, the term remains a central concept in researching and understanding contemporary television cultures. This collection embraces the complex nature of the term and seeks to explore a diversity in understandings, rather than work with a strict definition.

This collection starts out with a view of binge-watching that highlights its role within different media environments and 'phases' of television. The concept of binge-watching is often linked to fan practices and fan cultures. Initial discussions of binge-watching often draw on fan studies to understand the practice (Jenner 2017; Perks 2015). In line with this, E. Charlotte Stevens's article on fan conventions and binge-watching in fanzine descriptions of the 1980s works to set up binge-watching as historical practice, while Rhiannon Bury's work on fandom in contemporary television culture on Reddit takes us into the current era. Between Stevens's and Bury's work, Part I serves to introduce the reader to the way in which fan studies is central to understanding both the history and the present of binge-watching research.

Part II aims to understand who binge-watchers are and writes a typology of binge-watching. The part opens with Emil Steiner's chapter on how different typologies of binge-watching are developed in advertising campaigns. The chapter is concerned with how binge-watching is represented in broader media discourses. This is then linked to the findings of audience research. The marketing typology serves as a jumping-off point to explore audience behaviours in Lisa Glebatis Perks's chapter on immersive and distracted viewing, Ri Pierce-Grove's chapter on the perception of time while binge-watching and Lothar Mikos and Deborah Castro's chapter on the comparison between German and Dutch binge-watchers. Steiner, Perks, Pierce-Grove and Mikos then return to the question of typologies to develop their own typology of binge-watching, based on their findings. The part, thus, productively links media representation to the findings of audience research.

The next part ties in with Mikos's and Castro's chapter by exploring the new environment of binge-watching and transnational television. Part III deals with the re-formulation and renegotiation of the 'national' in the context of transnational television and publication models that make texts available in many markets at the same time. Netflix is particularly dominant here, as it has built a company structure that positions it explicitly as transnational broadcaster. B. G.-Stolz's model of the 'transcultural' frames this part. The transcultural serves to explain cultural exchange in contemporary television, where new publication models dictate different ways in which texts operate. Robert Watts and Mareike Jenner both explore how these shifts are formulated by different stakeholders. Watts's article compares the reception of British texts in newspaper and magazine reviews in the context of British and American discourses. Thereby, he explores how 'the local' is coded and understood in transatlantic television discourse. Jenner discusses how Netflix uses genre as part of a grammar of transnationalism. Focusing on the teen genre on Netflix, using *Sex Education* (Netflix 2019–) and *How to Sell Drugs Online (Fast)* (Netflix 2019–) as examples, Jenner debates the textual politics of transnationalism on the platform. The authors then move on to reflect together on how the 'national' is negotiated in the contemporary television landscape.

The last part, Part IV, ties in with many of the discourses touched upon in previous articles: the importance of the text and narrative structures as part of the concept of 'bingeability'. This goes beyond issues of autonomous scheduling or control that viewers can exercise to look at questions of how narratives implicitly formulate an invitation to binge-watch. In their introductory chapter to this part, Lynn Kozak and Martin Zeller-Jacques explore how narrative structures have changed with platforms that explicitly invite viewers to binge-watch. Of major concern in this article are the different strategies of 'recapping' used in *Stranger Things* (Netflix 2016–). Thus, the authors explore how series designed to be watched in quick succession recap information to remind viewers of previous events. Next, Tom Hemingway considers the role of bingeability and comedy. His argument focuses on the shift in narrative structures, specifically in relation to narrative time, as the comedy genre moves from broadcast television to streaming. Orcun Can compares the narrative structures of the CW series *Gilmore Girls* (The CW 2000–7) and its revival on Netflix in the form of *Gilmore Girls: A Year in the Life* (Netflix 2016). To do this, he develops an original analytical model he terms the Serialised Televisual Narrative Analysis Model (STNA), which conceptualises narrative on a micro-level. Tanya Horeck and Júlia Havas focus in more closely on the narrative strategies used to tell stories of rape. The authors, thus, describe how Netflix enables feminist storytelling. Overall, the part on narratology brings together different perspectives to consider the micro-levels of narrative structures in the TV IV era, guided and shaped by ideas of bingeability.

CONCLUSION

The individual parts of this book were developed together by contributors, and each part ends with a co-authored conclusion, which brings the various perspectives together. The strength of this edited collection is that it is based on close collaboration between authors. Furthermore, having the structure based on two separate workshops, one year apart, has enabled each contributor to interact with other contributors, allowing for an awareness of the broader project during the writing, peer reviewing and editing of individual articles. This development of arguments influenced and guided by an interaction with a breadth of research approaches has produced a collection framed by collaboration. In this spirit, we embrace the complexity of the term binge-watching and the broad variety of research linked to it. Yet, this volume has its limitations. As such, reality TV as bingeable fare remains unexplored, despite the fact that this is a major genre for Netflix and many other platforms.[5] The role of self-scheduling in children's television viewing also remains unexplored. This is not because these topics are viewed as unimportant (in fact, contributors have discussed cooking shows, in particular, at length). However, this collection remains indebted to the spirit of collaboration among workshop participants, which is the main reason for these exclusions.

The Covid-19 pandemic and the response of national lockdowns in 2020 and 2021 has brought new attention to binge-watching and the various texts designed for binge-watching on different platforms. The articles in this volume were largely written before the Covid-19 pandemic, though some authors still managed to integrate relevant material. Debates surrounding binge-watching have intensified as people are asked to spend more time at home.

This makes critical discussion on binge-watching more urgent, but not substantively different from what it was pre-pandemic. Discourses surrounding 'quality' television and 'othered', supposedly low-brow, reality TV became no less relevant in view of the popularity of the Netflix series *Tiger King* (Netflix 2020), which was published at a time that marked the first few weeks of national lockdown in various western European countries and several states in the US. Perhaps more than other TV programmes, *Tiger King* illuminated the importance of a communal television experience, despite autonomous scheduling, and the comforts of 'spectacular' reality television. Yet, as transnational television designed for transnational audiences, its textual structures are often not fundamentally different to those of *Stranger Things* or other programming discussed in Part IV. But perhaps these first few weeks of viewing in lockdown also point us to the importance of concepts like distracted viewing in stressful times (as explored in Perks's chapter), different versions of communal viewing when viewers can't be in the same physical space (as explored by Mikos and Castro), or even perceptions of time while bingeing (as Pierce-Grove analyses). Further, the importance of Netflix and the idea of a transnational communal viewing that brings the citizens of different countries in lockdown together is usefully addressed by G.-Stolz in her article on the transcultural as well as by other articles in Part III that grapple with the meanings of the local, the national and the transnational. This does not mean that the pandemic does not shift our television cultures in the long run; only that the shifts that are currently visible suggest that the discourse is merely intensified, not different.

The debates surrounding binge-watching in times of Covid-19 do illuminate the importance of the practice, its function in revisiting and reframing content, and even the way it can enable communication about communal viewing and shared social values – despite the fact that audiences are given more autonomy in deciding *how* to binge-watch. This collection represents various approaches to grappling with the concept and its role in contemporary television cultures.

NOTES

1. Among other sources, discussions are included in the edited collections *It's Not TV: Watching HBO in the Post-Television Era* (2008, edited by Cara Louise Buckley, Marc Leverette, Brian L. Ott), *The Essential HBO Reader* (2008, edited by Gary R. Edgerton) or *Quality TV: Contemporary American Television and Beyond* (2007, edited by Kim Akass and Janet McCabe).
2. This is not to argue that the technologies and 'subversive' viewing practices were not present in communist countries. Douglas A. Boyd (1989) has researched VCR use in the USSR, particularly pointing to the viewing of American fare. Anecdotally, one of the researchers featured in this volume, Júlia Havas, has shared her viewing in communist

Hungary of a VHS tape of *Dirty Dancing* (Ardolino 1987), dubbed into German with a Hungarian voice-over, pointing to the vast linguistic and technological complexity of 'rogue' viewing and control in USSR countries.

3. Of course, McDonald's more likely motive was to wrest power over the medium away from advertisers and avoid the kind of monopoly that Marconi had established over radio a few decades earlier.
4. Piracy was never conceptualised as a 'threat' to the medium of television in the way it was for film, which means viewing practices remain relatively under-researched. One exception to this is Michael Strangelove's *Post-TV: Piracy, Cord-Cutting and the Future of Television* (2015), which describes television piracy largely in relation to cord-cutting. Rhiannon Bury's *Television 2.0* (2017) engages productively with issues of piracy from a fan studies perspective.
5. In fact, contributors who wanted to write on reality TV, specifically cooking shows, were often hindered by the structures of contemporary academia, which forced them to leave the sector altogether.

REFERENCES

Benjamin, L. (1993). 'At the Touch of a Button: A Brief History of Remote Control Devices'. In R. V. Bellamy and J. R. Walker (eds), *The Remote Control in the New Age of Television*. London: Praeger, pp. 15–22.
Benson-Allott, C. A. (2015). *Remote Control*. New York: Bloomsbury Academic.
Bjarkman, K. (2004). 'To Have and to Hold: The Video Collector's Relationship with an Ethereal Medium'. *Television and New Media* 5(3): 217–46.
Boyd, D. A. (1989). 'The Videocassette Recorder in the USSR and Soviet-Bloc Countries'. In M. Levy (ed.), *The VCR Age: Home Video and Mass Communication*. London: Sage, pp. 252–70.
Brunsdon, Charlotte (2010). 'Bingeing on Box-Sets: The National and the Digital in Television Crime Drama'. In J. Gripsrud (ed.), *Relocating Television: Television in the Digital Context*. London: Routledge, pp. 61–75.
Buckley, C. L., M. Leverette and B. L. Ott (eds) (2008a). *It's Not TV: Watching HBO in the Post-Television Era*. London: Routledge.
Bury, R. (2017). *Television 2.0: New Perspectives on Digital Convergence, Audiences and Fans*. New York: Peter Lang.
Chun, W. H. K. (2016). *Updating to Remain the Same: Habitual New Media*. Cambridge, MA: The MIT Press.
Dawson, M. (2008). *TV Repair: New Media Solutions to Old Media Problems*. Ph.D. Dissertation, Illinois: Northwestern University.
Deleuze, G. (1992). 'Postscript on the Societies of Control'. *October* 59 (Winter): 3–7.
Dobrow, J. (1990). 'The Rerun Ritual: Using VCRs to Re-View'. In J. Dobrow (ed.), *Social and Cultural Aspects of VCR Use*. Hillsdale, NJ: L. Erlbaum Associates, pp. 181–94.
Edgerton, G. R. and J. P. Jones (eds) (2008). *The Essential HBO Reader*. Lexington, KY: University Press of Kentucky.
Ellis, J. (2002). *Seeing Things: Television in the Age of Uncertainty*. London: I. B. Tauris.
Feher, Michel. (2009). 'Self-Appreciation: Or, the Aspirations of Human Capital'. *Public Culture* 21(1): 21–41.
Gray, A. (1992). *Video Playtime: The Gendering of a Leisure Technology*. London: Routledge.
Hartley, J. (1999). *Uses of Television*. London: Routledge.

Harvey, D. (2005). *A Brief History of Neoliberalism*. Oxford; New York: Oxford University Press.
Hills, M. and J. Garde-Hansen (2017). 'Fandom's Paratextual Memory: Remembering, Reconstructing, and Repatriating "Lost" Doctor Who'. *Critical Studies in Media Communication* 34(2): 158–67.
Jacobs, J. (2011). 'Television, Interrupted: Pollution or Aesthetic?' In J. Bennett and N. Strange (eds), *Television as Digital Media*. Durham, NC: Duke University Press. Kindle location 3065–399.
Jenner, M. (2016). 'Is this TVIV?: On Netflix, TVIII and Binge-Watching'. *New Media & Society* 18(2): 257–73.
Jenner, M. (2018). *Netflix and the Re-Invention of Television*. Basingstoke: Palgrave Macmillan.
Jenner, M. (2019). 'Control Issues: Binge-Watching, Channel-Surfing and Cultural Value'. *Participations* 16(2): 298–317.
Johnson, C. (2019). *Online Television*. London: Routledge.
Kompare, D. (2005). *Rerun Nation: How Repeats Invented American Television*. New York: Routledge.
Lin, C. A. and D. J. Atkin (2007). *Communication Technology and Social Change: Theory and Implications*. Mahwah, NJ; London: Lawrence Erlbaum Associates.
Lotz, A. D. (2017). *Portals: A Treatise on Internet-Distributed Television*. Ann Arbor, MI: Maize Books.
Lotz, A. D. (2018). *We Now Disrupt this Broadcast: How Cable Transformed Television and the Internet Revolutionised it All*. Cambridge, MA: The MIT Press.
McCabe, J. and K. Akass (2007). *Quality TV: Contemporary American Television and Beyond*. London: I. B. Tauris.
McKinley, E. Graham (1997). *Beverly Hills, 90210 Television, Gender, and Identity*. Philadelphia, PA: University of Pennsylvania Press.
Nelson, R. (1997). *TV Drama in Transition: Forms, Values and Cultural Change*. Basingstoke: Macmillan.
Newman, M. Z. (2017). *Atari Age: The Emergence of Video Games in America*. Cambridge, MA: MIT Press.
Perks, L. G. (2015). *Media Marathoning: Immersions in Morality*. Lanham, MD: Lexington Books.
Rothemund, K. (2013). *Komplexe Welten: Narrative Strategien in US-Amerikanischen Fernsehserien*. Berlin: Bertz + Fischer.
Salecl, R. (2010). *Choice*. London: Profile Books.
Steiner, Emil and K. Xu (2020). 'Binge-Watching Motivates Change: Uses and Gratifications of Streaming Video Viewers Challenge Traditional TV Research'. *Convergence: The International +Journal of Research into New Media Technologies* 26(1) 82–101.
Strangelove, M. (2015). *Post-TV: Piracy, Cord-Cutting, and the Future of Television* Toronto: University of Toronto Press.
Turner, G. (2019). 'Television Studies, We Need to Talk About Binge-Viewing'. *Television and New Media*. OnlineFirst, 1–13.
Walker, J. R. and R. V. Bellamy (1993). 'The Remote Control Device: An Overlooked Technology'. In J. R. Walker and R. V. Bellamy (eds), *The Remote Control in the New Age of Television*. Westport, CN; London: Praeger, pp. 3–14.
Wasser, F. (2001). *Veni, Vidi, Video: The Hollywood Empire and the VCR*. Austin, TX: University of Texas Press.

TV

Beverly Hills 90210 (1990–2000), USA: Fox
CSI: Crime Scene Investigation (2000–15), USA: CBS
Doctor Who (1963–), UK: BBC
Firefly (2002–3), USA: Fox
Friends (1994–2004), USA: NBC
Gilmore Girls (2000–7), USA: The CW
Gilmore Girls: A Year in the Life (2016), USA: Netflix
Hill Street Blues (1981–7), USA: NBC
House of Cards (2013–18), USA: Netflix
Lost (2004–10), USA: ABC
Orange is the New Black (2013–19), USA: Netflix
Sopranos, The (1999–2007), USA: HBO
St. Elsewhere (1982–8), USA: NBC
Starsky and Hutch (1975–9), USA: ABC
Stranger Things (2016–), USA: Netflix
Tiger King: Murder, Mayhem, and Madness (2020), USA: Netflix
Twin Peaks (1990–1), USA: ABC
Wire, The (2004–8), USA: HBO
X-Files, The (1993–), USA: Fox

FILM

Ardolino, E. (1987) *Dirty Dancing*. USA: Vestron Pictures
Galanty, S. (1982) *Jane Fonda's Workout*, USA: Karl Video Corporation

PART I

Bingeing Fans

CHAPTER 2

Historical Binge-Watching: Marathon Viewing on Videotape

E. Charlotte Stevens

In September 2019, *The Guardian* covered news of the launch of the Disney+ streaming service by asking whether 'the age of bingewatching may finally be over' (Heritage 2019). This followed the announcement that the service would release episodes weekly, rather than a full season at a time. Aside from the fact that weekly episodes have been part of radio broadcasting since the 1920s, notable here is the presentation of binge-watching as industry-led, and not an audience-led practice. As this chapter points out, television audiences have been recording weekly episodes to (binge-)watch at their own convenience since the 1970s when VCRs entered the domestic market (Gauntlett and Hill 1999; Gray 1992; Newman 2014). The archived fan letters I consulted for this chapter arguably date the start of 'the age of bingewatching' to 1979 at the latest, many decades before 'the Netflix model' which supposedly initiated this period (Heritage 2019). Furthermore, Disney+'s weekly episodes will presumably accumulate to allow catch-up viewing once word-of-mouth builds around each new series. What makes a television series bingeable is perhaps not how it is broadcast or released, or its inherent narrative properties, but how its audience chooses to consume it.

This chapter looks back to television's network era, and analyses how compressed or 'marathon' viewing events were narrativised for fellow fans. It presents findings arising from archival research into fans' accounts of watching off-air television recordings, as found in early-1980s letterzines about series such as *Star Trek* (NBC 1967–9), *Starsky & Hutch* (ABC 1975–9) and *Simon & Simon* (CBS 1981–9). The discussions in media fandom letterzines capture a time when multi-channel broadcasting and video recorders offered a challenge to how television was watched before DVD box sets delivered full seasons of TV to consumers (Brunsdon 2010; Kompare 2016; Williams 2015), and prior to the digital platforms and VOD capabilities associated with binge-watching (Jenner 2017; Jenner 2018; Mikos 2016). The letterzines also capture a predominantly female perspective, as media fandom is generally understood to be a gendered space; the typically female names of the letter-writers bears this out. My purpose is to recover some of those contemporary conversations about watching television alone, with friends, and in fan convention programming organised around group viewings of off-air recordings.

Therefore, in this chapter, I explore how methods of watching television were discussed by female television audiences before 'binge-watching' became mainstream. Convention reports and letters of comment (LOCs) in the letterzines include lists of episodes watched, contextual information and discussion of reactions to key moments. Exploring these primary documents allows access to fans' accounts of watching several episodes of a series in a shared space over a limited time. This is not always a binge-watch of sequential episodes, but a 'marathon' (Bacon-Smith 1992; Perks 2015) of re-watching on videotape. This chapter works through how fans narrativise their non-broadcast viewing at fan conventions and at home, with particular attention paid to the language used to discuss their activity and to signal their participation in the wider fan community.

By the mid-1970s, domestic videotape technology allowed audiences to record programmes off the air to watch later (time-shifting) and to rent or buy pre-recorded video cassettes. The story of historical binge-watching starts with VCRs, which enabled time-shifting and behaviour that expanded the definition of 'watching television'. In Jason Jacobs's words, the VCR was 'the earliest domestic weapon against the interruption and chronological authority of the broadcast schedule' (2011, 259). Recent work on audiences' use of television (Bury 2017; Perks 2015) reminds us that early fan studies scholarship describes marathon viewing practices enabled by VCRs. When presented with copies of an entire season or series, then as now, viewers take advantage of the freedom from a weekly broadcast schedule to watch in 'short bursts of compressed multiple-episode viewing' (Bacon-Smith 1992, 130). One key example is Henry Jenkins's experience of watching *Blake's 7* (BBC1, 1978–81) at a rate of 'as many as three or four episodes in a row' (1992, 73) across a couple of weeks of intensive consumption. Another is a brief mention in Mary Ellen Brown's work about soap opera fans, one of whom makes an off-hand mention of taking 'the day off' to watch 'two tapes' of episodes recorded by a friend (1994, 108). Descriptions like this are familiar today, particularly in how we watch to catch up on a show that others have recommended.

Cassandra Amesley argued that fans watching TV together leads to discussion while watching, from which arise agreed interpretations and meanings specific to each group of fans, where 'meaning is not so much negotiated between text and audience as it is *among* audience members and text' (1989, 337, emphasis in original). The letterzines created an interpretive community, which involves sharing descriptions of conversations had while watching with friends in one's home. In the 1980s letterzines discussed here, the regularity with which videotape and re-viewing practices are mentioned bears out Jenkins's assertion that sharing videotape is 'a central ritual of fandom' that makes it a 'distinctive community' (1992, 51). With this chapter, I am reaching back to archival sources originating in the sorts of communities that Amesley (1989), Jenkins and Bacon-Smith (1992) describe in their work. Amid the discussions of series themselves – which established an interpretive community – are fans' accounts of videotape, group viewing and experiences of television consumption beyond a broadcast schedule. Vitally, the fans contributing to letterzines not only talked about the shows they watched but *how* they watched these series.

METHOD

In this research, I consulted two archives among the respectable number of science fiction collections and archives around the world (Latham et al. 2010). The first was the Merril Collection of Science Fiction, Speculation & Fantasy, which is a special collection of the Toronto Public Library (Canada) and is not digitised. Their fanzine holdings are indexed in two card catalogue drawers, and are mostly examples of science fiction amateur press association (APA) publications (see Hartwell 1984, 160–9; Latham 2006; Lymn 2018), but also include some media fandom letterzines. An average APA zine would contain articles, news items, fiction and a section for letters of comment (LOCs). In contrast, letterzines are almost entirely LOCs: reader contributions that address individuals or the broader readership, respond to prompts from zine editors and otherwise participate in an ongoing conversation with fellow fans. The second archive I consulted was the Cushing Memorial Library and Archives at Texas A&M University (USA), where two collections, The Media Fanzine Collection and The Sandy Hereld Memorial Digitized Media Fanzine Collection, hold a significant number of digitised media fanzines, including some letterzines amongst the fanfiction zines.

This project began with a day at the Merril Collection, where I was guided more by curiosity than by any specific project, but with the time to browse the fanzine index and get a sense of their print-only holdings. It was fortunate that the first item in the S section – where I expected to find zines about *Star Trek* and *Star Wars* – was an index card for *S&H Letterzine* (1979–83, also known as *S and H*; 'S and H' 2016), a fanzine dedicated to the action/detective show *Starsky & Hutch*. While this might be a surprising holding for a science fiction and fantasy collection, the fannish women who may have met because of a shared love for *Star Trek* or *Star Wars* also enjoyed media in other genres, and were similarly productive in producing zines around those other sources as well. For clarity of in-text citation, I have assigned abbreviations to each letter cited: for example, the first *S&H* letter becomes SH1, and so forth. A table with full references is provided at the end of the chapter (Table 2.1).

The media letterzines are reflections on fan practice written by women active in what became known as 'media' fandom, so named to signal their difference from male (and misogynist) fans of *literary* science fiction who looked down on those who embraced *Star Trek* and other television science fiction (Coppa 2006). I found evidence of this attitude throughout the general APA zines, for example, a disparaging reference to 'Star Drek' (HTT1 1984, 105) or lamentations that a convention video room was empty but 'about 20 people [were] watching the pathetic *Babylon 5* in the fan lounge' (TASF1 1994, 7). I had hoped *S&H* might discuss making song tapes, which were variously spelled 'songtapes' (Penley 1991, 145) or 'song-tapes' (Gillilan 1999, 42) and were my primary research focus (Stevens 2017, 2020), because the zine was started by the innovators of that form (Coppa 2009, 108 n3). Instead, the zines contained tantalising mentions of what might now be called binge-watching. Based on these findings, I reached out to Cushing Memorial Library and Archives to access their digital collection, and also returned to the Merril Collection in early 2019 for more in-depth research. When the dust settled, I had research copies of nearly fifty individual zine titles, often with multiple issues. These zines largely reflect an American experience, though there are occasional contributions from Canadian, British and Australian fans.

Most of my examples in this chapter come from three of those fifty titles, published between 1982 and 1986, which focus on two different shows: the *Starsky & Hutch* letterzines *S&H* and its successor *Between Friends* (1984–5), and the *Simon & Simon* letterzine *Details at 11* (1983–7). The *Starsky & Hutch* letterzines respond to a series that had finished airing, with reruns and videotape recordings the only way to watch. In contrast, *Simon & Simon* was broadcast and syndicated as the zine was in publication, meaning *Details at 11* documents how fans of an ongoing television series in the 1980s discussed the object of their fandom as the show was airing. Also, *Simon & Simon* began just as VCRs started to penetrate the home market, meaning that *Details at 11* documents how this group of fans integrated the new capacity for in-home off-air recording into their viewing practice. Descriptions of how and where fans went about watching these series are woven throughout these letters.

Letterzines were routinely signed with full name and mailing address to facilitate individual communication. Whereas today fans know each other through screen names and pseudonyms, this use of so-called 'wallet names' (Busse 2018, 11) raises an ethical issue about citation, which is also reflected in the complexities of copyright and metadata in archiving fanworks as fans may not consent to having their identities attached to their work (Brett 2013; see also Lee 2011). In writing up my findings, I have followed a convention in fan studies of protecting the identities of individuals who may not have imagined their works being used in this way. I borrow Jenkins's (1992) approach of identifying fans by their initials, in what I hope is a middle ground between adequate historical citation and the ethical considerations of fan studies research. Therefore, as part of a larger project based in these letterzines, in this chapter I am taking the opportunity to examine the contemporary discussions fans had around pre-digital non-broadcast ways of consuming television episodes.

CONVENTION VIEWING

Film and video screenings have long been one of the many kinds of programming at fan conventions, with films and television episodes being shown alongside other programming such as panel discussions, workshops, special guest Q&A sessions, awards presentations, masquerades, and so forth. Marathon screenings can take place as part of the scheduled programming, sometimes running twenty or even twenty-four hours. One such track at an event from 1979 is memorialised in a poem detailing the convention's history: 'Well the video room, it ran all night – we watched with bleary eyes' (SH1 1982, 40). In this instance, the exact screening list is not provided, presumably because its readers had been there themselves, or would know which episodes the fan community valued and could imagine the schedule and the experience.

However, some convention reports do list the episodes watched, alongside commentary about attendees' reactions. One report from a UK-based fan, written about a *Starsky & Hutch* convention held in Wales (SH2 1982), seems to signal to the zine's primarily American readership that the British fans were watching key episodes and enjoying them in an appropriate manner. The report names eight specific *Starsky & Hutch* episodes screened over a weekend between blooper reels and interviews, with other programming including a charity auction of fan art and other paraphernalia. The letter-writer notes the screenings were curtailed on the Friday evening by mutual agreement after screening the third-season episode 'Murder Ward', since 'all 39 of us were glazed around the eyes---either from the Starsky-in-bondage scene or from sheer exhaustion' (SH2 1982, 38). The weekend's programming also included one episode, 'The Fix', that was new to the majority of attendees (and 'it had an electrifying effect on the audience', SH2 1982, 38) due to it having been banned by the BBC. It seems the episode was not shown in the UK until 1999; for these fans in 1982, the group screening offered a rare opportunity to complete their first-hand experience of the series. This convention appears to have been motivated in part by a desire to consume as many hours of video on a good-quality copy as possible, the better to participate in the interpretive community arising through discussion of the episodes. Therefore, demonstrating a familiarity with episode titles is more than just an effective shorthand to note what was watched, it is an articulation of participation in transatlantic fandom.

Other convention marathons were organised around an actor rather than a series, in which the marathon event used stardom (rather than a programme) as a focal point. For example, the Third Leonard Nimoy Convention was devoted to discussing Nimoy's career and appeal, and significantly, to watching the *Star Trek* actor in his other roles. The convention report in an issue of the zine *Communicator* describes it thus: 'the main interest centred on the video room where, from 3pm on Friday until 2:30am on Monday, videos and films were show in an impressive flow, pausing only for meals and sleep' (CM1 1984, 21). This weekend was oriented around consuming new, rare, and familiar performances in a variety of formats (some in 'glorious tech[nicolor]' and others in 'crackling, flickering b&w'; CM1 1984, 21) covering non-*Trek* performances across Nimoy's career. The weekend's final event was a cut-down version of the 10-hour *Marco Polo* series (NBC/RAI 1982), 'which featured a ferociously aristocratic & dangerous Achmet, Lord of the Armies who had the audience wilting in their seats' (CM1 1984, 21). It is notable that this desire for the actor on screen is presented without guilt or shame, and indeed ends with a plea for a repeat screening at a future event, were there to be one.

Marathons would also happen outside of the schedule, as fans brought personal tape collections and VCRs to set up in hotel rooms; for example, letters often note a named fan attended 'with her VCR and most of her tapes' (DAE1 1985, 53). This would occasionally divert attention from scheduled events: one report laments low attendance at panels one afternoon, but an editorial intervention in the letter confesses that attendees had actually been watching 'song tapes' (later known as fanvids, a kind of found footage music video) with the zine's editors in their hotel room (SH3 1982, 8). There were a variety of motivations for these peripheral screenings: the pleasure of watching television with friends, sharing better-quality recordings with those who had poorer-quality tape (Bacon-Smith 1992), and to show episodes to potential recruits for an existing fandom. A domestic iteration of a recruitment party is described by Jenkins (1992, 73). However, given that American zines discussed court cases in which rights-holders asserted their copyright to off-air recordings (CL1 1982, 2), a small fan-run convention might reasonably provide a space for attendees to bring their own kit and share tapes outside of scheduled programming (SH4 1982, 8), and thus allow the convention to avoid liability for any licensing fees that might otherwise be payable.

Whether part of the official schedule or not, convention viewing practices offer a different model to domestic marathon viewing. To attend a fan convention, a fan must take time away from home and/or work commitments and travel some distance to a hotel in order to spend time with fellow fans in pursuit of their fandom. As one con report puts it, the ideal convention is a group of friends 'just getting off on getting together' (SH3 1982, 8), regardless of programming, where one may leave 'short of sleep, with sore bottoms and square eyes but relaxed and happy with pleasant memories to last the long, cold, conless winter' (CM1 1984, 21). The fan convention is a structured interruption from daily routine, albeit without much rest, with one fan reflecting that '[p]art of being in fandom just naturally means you have to learn to live on less sleep than "normal" people do' (BF1 1985, 23). Instead of guilt or remorse at their marathon, fans report 'the long hours gabbing and watching tapes' (BF1 1985, 23) as a marker of a successful event. Frustratingly, this latter example does not list the contents of those tapes or shape of the conversation, suggesting that the letter-writer presumes her readers would already have a sense of the kind of material screened or topics discussed. However, that comment does offer clear evidence of the performance of an interpretive community, one centred around marathon viewing and fellowship, enabled by videotape.

AWAY FROM THE CONVENTION: DOMESTIC MARATHONS WITH FRIENDS

Beyond the programmed disruptions of convention viewing, zine LOCs discuss videotape marathons in domestic settings. There is a striking contrast between the language used in describing watching many episodes of television alone, or in a group. Alone, as described below, there is a tendency toward more negative framings; however, when with others, this activity is much more positive or even boastful. The affordances of videotape might enable an evening of champagne and 'episode after episode' of *Simon & Simon* (DAE2 1983, 3), as one's introduction to the fandom. In later issues of *Details at 11*, fans describe this activity as being 'Simonized' (DAE3 1984, 9), a phrase with a typically fannish semi-ironic cast.

A marathon with friends can be prompted by revisiting favourite episodes, such as a fan's '8,000 calorie video parties', so named for the abundance of 'good food' on offer, wherein 'you watch STAR TREK episodes for six hours or until your eyes quit' (IS1 1979, 13). These 1970s parties are the earliest mention of a television marathon in my sample, which alone would make it a notable comment to highlight: evidently, the 'era of bingewatching' (Heritage 2019) began over forty years ago. However, I also want to draw attention to the twinned excesses of television and food, with both consumed in abundance. In contrast to a 'binge', this description evokes satisfaction, or satiation, rather than shame or guilt at overdoing either kinds of consumption (see also Brunsdon 2010). Indeed, the language shifts between compliments and self-aware teasing, with the letter-writer lauding her host's 'beautiful home' and the delight of 'meet[ing] other normal people like yourself' in *Star Trek* fandom (IS1 1979, 13).

As a whole, domestic viewing is framed as positive and celebratory, with fans positioning the act of watching with friends as a key social activity. In another case that may be familiar to a contemporary reader, one letter-writer thanks friends for visiting for a marathon, as it provided a rare excuse for her to re-watch her taped episodes (DAE4 1985). This is particularly poignant as this is the same letter-writer who, two years earlier, had celebrated being newly 'blessed (cursed?) with a VCR' (DAE5 1983). Evidently her leisure time had not allowed as many chances to explore her hobby as she had wished. Letter-writers publicly thank and acknowledge fellow fans who have lent tapes to enable catch-up viewing or a return to episodes not seen since broadcast; in both convention and domestic group marathons, the activity compensates for a scarcity, be it of tapes or of a community with which to watch.

Somewhat less ambiguous is a LOC co-written by five fans which endeavours to list all moments in *Starsky & Hutch* where the leads are barefoot. Rather than re-watching every episode, they confess they wrote from a prompt list of episode titles, 'with an occasional run to the television to verify a fact', and accompanied by 'several bottles of champagne' (SH5 1982, 9). The tongue-in-cheek framing in this LOC positions this discussion as research, aimed at answering a previous LOC's question on the topic with accuracy and objectivity. While this is not a *viewing* marathon, it is time taken with friends for sustained engagement with a television text, with a licence to appreciate (or, to fetishise) the actors on display. Indeed, the commentary that runs throughout the LOC makes the letter-writers' desiring gaze very clear. What is significant here is that these fans, armed with their 1980s video technology, gather without the excuse of a fan convention to enact a kind of marathon in relation to a series that had finished production, but which was still present for them because of the enduring fan community and the affordances of videotape.

WATCHING ALONE: PERFORMING A SHARED ADDICTION

When fans describe their individual consumption of television, away from conventions or other social events, the metaphors used in the letterzines turn pathological. This highlights tensions in how fans narrativise their relationship with television at a time when it became possible to choose to watch many episodes in a row, outside of a broadcast schedule. It also suggests the letterzines are a space of fannish discussion in which individuals perform their participation in a community through the language of a shared addiction to television series. The level of elevated language is not unusual for media fandom; for example, in fans' descriptions of their 'poor quality video taped episodes which we guard with our lives' (SH6 1982, 15), or in the explicit framing of their relationship with zines as 'my primary addiction, even though I am lusting after a VCR' (BF4 1985, 11). Indeed, videotape is the mechanism through which the addiction is realised, occasionally to the exclusion of watching full episodes. One *Simon & Simon* fan notes that she copies favourite parts of episodes on to a separate tape, which she used 'for a quick fix' (DAE6 1985, 7).[1]

As Charlotte Brunsdon has pointed out, 'addiction metaphors [. . .] have always been used to characterize the consumption of television drama' (2010, 65), as for example when soap fans refer to a morning spent watching taped episodes as an 'overdose' (Brown 1994, 108), and the letterzines bear this out in fan usage. The earliest such comment in my sample is of 'withdrawal symptoms' following the six-hour *Star Trek* party mentioned above (IS1 1979, 13), where the success of the event is measured in terms of its hangover. Since I am working from written text alone, rather than interviews, I can only speculate about motivations for this framing. It may be that these fans are humorously reclaiming a persistent pathologising of fans and of the female television audience by using hyperbolic language. They might also be giving voice to an internalised sense of shame (Busse 2013; Zubernis and Larsen 2012), or the excesses are being used to mask or defray guilt (Perks 2015).

Universal Translator (1980–6), a cross-fandom catalogue of fanzines, contains personal ads from fans asking for help from the community to feed their addiction. Across the zines, the word 'desperate' crops up regularly when fans are seeking off-air recordings, as when one is 'desperate for good copies' of *Simon & Simon* after buying a VCR (UT1 1986, 38), and another is 'desperate' (UT2 1986, 45) for select episodes of *Shadow Chasers* (ABC 1985–6) that were only broadcast on American overseas military networks ('*Shadow Chasers*' 2019). Desperation may be apt, as a fan presumably would only place an ad and appeal to the community once she had exhausted her existing networks. Declarations of desperation are not limited to videotape: fans were occasionally 'frantic' for a particular zine back issue (UT3 1983, 35), or 'desperate' for a missing piece of a licensed board game (UT4 1983, 29). However, across the zines there is a regular link made between access to videotape and the implied viewing marathon to follow; for example, when the editors of *S&H* report that their tapes of second-season *Starsky & Hutch* episodes were returned with a 'frantic' note asking for the third season, with their correspondent confessing, 'I'm in desperate need of a fix' (SH7 1982, 2). This could also manifest through desire for the technology itself, which was quickly becoming central to this expression of fandom: a fan writes that a previous LOC 'triggered me yet again on a "craving" for a VCR. I'm going nutso, trying to get involved in Professionals [ITV 1977–83] fandom without one' (BF4 1985, 11).

Rather than 'marathon', or the much later 'binge', several *Starsky & Hutch* fans use 'overdose', abbreviated to OD, to frame the experience of watching many taped episodes:

> I think eighty-seven episodes over one weekend sounds like an O.D. When did you sleep? Well, of course you didn't. Wait a minute—eighty-seven? Oh, it was a three-day weekend . . . (SH8 1982, 2)
>
> My husband bought us a VCR for Christmas and I've been ODing on [redacted]'s tapes ever since. (SH9 1983, 10)
>
> Right off, I want to make a public thank-you to [redacted] for all her time and patience in copying off thirteen of my favorite S&H shows and sending same to me. I have been OD'ing on the tapes ever since. (BF2 1985, 15)

This usage galvanises the language of addiction, desperation, and wanting a fix. In two of the above examples, the letter-writers are reflecting on how the consummated anticipation for tapes or a VCR lead to an outcome of excessive consumption. This echoes Mareike Jenner's speculation about later binge-watching, namely that the long wait and high cost of a DVD box set means that 'watching the whole box set in only one or two sittings might also contribute to a feeling of excess' (2017, 308). The videotape overdose comes about at the end of a kind of scarcity, in which the access to an abundant resource is evidently overwhelming. One *Between Friends* contributor uses the word 'mainlining' to describe watching a lot of episodes and then jokes about not being able to find the word in the dictionary to know whether to hyphenate it (BF3 1985, 29). It is interesting to note that these are not marathons to be trained for, with achievement commended, but an addiction, communicated through a (boastful) confession to fellow addicts. Speaking from my own experience, in online fan communities in the 1990s/2000s I did see 'OD' and 'mainline' used in this way, but these seem to have dropped off as 'binge' entered mainstream usage.

This first decade of discussion of videotaped television is rife with an elevated language that reads as self-deprecatingly confessional or outright pathological. I was hard-pressed to find mention of solo videotape marathoning that did not have some performance of membership in a community of fellow addicts, playfully excusing their excessive consumption in these terms.

LABOUR, LEISURE AND LETTERS OF COMMENT

In this final section, I focus on two compelling phrases used by fans to describe their practice, that together highlight a contradiction in what it means to participate in media fandom. The tension here is between thinking of fandom as a hobby, and recognising the effort, time and money that goes into the parallel culture industry of fandom (Penley 1991): editing and publishing fanzines, organising conventions and writing LOCs for publication. The functioning of fandom depends on productive fans (Fiske 1992; Hills 2013), as Derek Kompare puts it, 'to produce, reproduce, curate and distribute those materials. Without that labor there would be no fandom' (2018, 108). To reiterate: the leisure time of fandom is underpinned by a considerable amount of fannish labour. LOCs will regularly make references to canon details – dialogue, costuming, narrative points – which have been fact-checked through re-watching episodes on videotape, occasionally in a marathon. The very detailed LOCs enact the labour of fandom, as they are based on repeat viewings of a text to verify elements of the canon and report these discoveries back to the community of zine readers. The level of detail is offered in a format that is useful for fans without the time or capacity to do this research themselves.

Excitingly, given the purpose of this collection, one LOC from 1985 does use the word 'binge' to refer to a compressed engagement with media. This is the only such instance in my sample, though it refers to binge-reading rather than binge-watching. Rather than watching television, the context of the comment concerns the effort needed to complete a fan awards ballot, with the letter-writer re-reading many fanzines to make her choice: 'yes, "binge" could describe what followed. Or constructive indulgence?' (BF5 1985, 10). The phrase 'constructive indulgence' rather wonderfully exposes some of the tensions around time, labour and shame with regard to fannish leisure activities, including watching television and related pursuits.

In this instance, the pleasure of re-reading back issues is framed as an indulgence, and by implication an unnecessary activity presumably because the zines have already been read once, and there are 'better' uses of this fan's time than revisiting older fanworks. Doing the work of reading to fill out the ballot, again presumably, might be otherwise directed toward more 'useful' activity: reading new zines, writing a letter of comment for inclusion in a future zine, or even non-fannish domestic or leisure activity that might occupy one's time outside paid employment. The modifier 'constructive' is fascinating since this active participation in a fan community – a pleasurable leisure activity – appears to be excused because it has some value. The indulgence is not just for one's own benefit, or put another way, the 'binge' is not an 'involuntary, non-cerebral reaction to the medium' (Brunsdon 2010, 65), but is instead a useful pursuit that helps this letter-writer make an informed decision when filling out her ballot. She is, in a sense, indulging in the practice of fannish good citizenship. The use of 'binge' here elides the work that goes into making a fandom happen.

A second instance of the tension between labour and leisure in fandom is in the 'exquisite torture' of watching every episode of *Starsky & Hutch* over a weekend (SH10 1982, 13), a comment that introduces a five-page concordance of facts about Hutch derived from a meticulous re-watching of the series. As leisure activity, this is exquisite because it is the chance to spend time with something with which you have a strong affective connection; as labour it is torture for the volume of material to review, its variable interest, the bodily discomfort of sitting to watch so much and the time pressure to complete the task. The footnotes across this LOC reference episode titles and dialogue, as well as an unproduced script for the series (of the sort which would be auctioned at a convention). One footnote also references a single-page 'biography' of Hutch from an earlier issue, contributed by another fan (SH11 1982, 3); this concordance expands and annotates that previous contribution. However, and as discussed above, a viewing marathon is not necessary for research: the group that contributed the champagne-fuelled research report about bare feet in SH5, which included the author of SH10, demurred that they did not have time to review all the episodes and instead worked from memory. Presumably, however, this was not memory formed in a single viewing, but was knowledge built up through enough repeat viewings that an actual re-watch would be redundant.

These performances of verification signal the letter-writers' competence and available leisure time to perform this labour, but also provide a record and reference point for other fans who offer their own analyses and reflections on elements of the series, or simply use the descriptions as a proxy for revising the episodes themselves. These also appear to be valuable reference points for fanfiction writers who want to verify that their characterisation and background details stay within the parameters of the canon. These activities are an 'indulgence' in that immersing oneself in a fannish activity takes away from other tasks that one might be doing, but 'constructive' in that they contribute to a community that only exists through production of commentaries and paratexts, and through participation in activities such as awards. These productive marathons are excused by the letter-writers as being for the benefit of the community, where the language used enacts an ambivalence around the shame and pleasure of contributing fannish labour.

CONCLUSION

One of the most striking parts of this research, speaking for myself, has been how familiar I find these fans' descriptions of their viewing practice. Current fannish binge-watching still involves visiting a friend to spend a day (or more!) watching recorded episodes, for the pleasure of watching together and for the purpose of sharing favourite series with a fresh pair of eyes. While videotape collections have become scarce, streaming libraries complement fans' own digital collections. Far from being an artefact of the analogue age, peripheral screenings happen at conventions today, with fans arriving equipped to use time between (or alongside, or after) a scheduled programming track for social watching. Over the years this has involved bringing audio/video cables from home to use the hotel room television as a laptop's external monitor, plugging an external hard drive directly into the USB port on the television, and – lately – going wireless by using a streaming device such as Roku or Chromecast. There is an absolute continuity of experience between the ways of watching television on videotape described in the letterzines and current strategies of taking advantage of being in the same location and using available spaces and technologies to watch television together.

The contents of letterzines occasionally describe watching together in person, as discussed in this chapter, but the majority of the letters work to create a shared community, with fans initiating and continuing conversations about what they were (re-)watching on their own. Currently, social media allows fans to watch together in real time or at a delay, via public live-tweeting (Pittman and Tefertiller 2015; Stewart 2019), through direct messaging with friends who have hit play at the same time (or who are currently offline and will backread the viewer's reactions), or by contributing to conversations on sites such as Reddit (Bury, this volume). The asynchronous affordance of live-tweeting enables fans to write a thread while watching several episodes of a series, both to document a minute-by-minute experience for a live audience responding in real time and to leave a record of their unfolding experience for fellow fans to engage with after the fact. These Twitter threads, as an iteration of conversations on internet message boards and live-blogging, echo the back-and-forth of the LOCs in letterzines in the ways that Twitter users comment on a thread through replies and quote-Tweets.

This chapter provides a brief but significant overview of some of the discussions around marathon viewing of television episodes enabled by videotape in the first decade of domestic VCRs. While none of this activity was called 'binge-watching', proximate modes of watching were described by fans in the late 1970s, through letters of comment in contemporary fannish letterzines. With a few exceptions (e.g. Gillilan 1998, 1999), letterzines are an untapped resource for television and fandom historians. Therefore, this chapter is an examination of what I read in these collections, and also a call for more attention to be paid to this documentation. As a research method, reading fans' letters about their engagement with television texts enables access to discussions of textual elements – narrative, characterisation, performance – and also the contexts in which fans watched the episodes themselves. The fans who contributed to letterzines have left many conversations about their viewing practice, their experience of fandom and the pleasures they found in these varied storyworlds. My analysis of fannish viewing at conventions and in domestic spaces reveals not just evidence of historical marathon viewing, but also the texture of language used to recount these activities to the wider fandom community.

ACKNOWLEDGEMENTS

My thanks to the staff at the Merril Collection and at the Cushing Memorial Library and Archives, for in-person and digital support. This work was supported by the Birmingham Centre for Media and Cultural Research, and through Birmingham City University's Go Global fund. Finally, my thanks to Anita Slater, who provided valuable research assistance.

Table 2.1 Table of letters

Key	Reference
BF1	MJB (1985) Letter of comment. *Between Friends* 9 (May), pp. 23–5. CMLA[1]. <http://hdl.handle.net/1969.1/159440>
BF2	CLB (1985) Letter of comment. *Between Friends* 7 (January), pp. 15–17. CMLA. <http://hdl.handle.net/1969.1/159438>
BF3	NG (1985) Letter of comment. *Between Friends* 9 (May), pp. 28–31. CMLA. <http://hdl.handle.net/1969.1/159440>
BF4	AT (1985) Letter of comment. *Between Friends* 8 (March), pp. 11–12. CMLA. <http://hdl.handle.net/1969.1/159439>
BF5	TD (1985) Letter of comment. *Between Friends* 11 (September), pp. 8–10. CMLA. <http://hdl.handle.net/1969.1/159436>
CL1	REG (1982) Editorial. *Comlink* 7, p. 2. MCSFSF[2].
CM1	RW (1984) 'CONVENTION REPORT: THE THIRD LEONARD NIMOY CONVENTION.' *Communicator* 15 (January), p. 21. MCSFSF.
DAE1	MLC (circa 1985) Letter of comment. *Details at 11* 10, pp. 52–3. CMLA. Media Fanzine Collection, id. 00/C000150
DAE2	CS (circa 1983) Editorial. *Details at 11* 1, p. 3. CMLA. Media Fanzine Collection, id. 00/C000150
DAE3	CJ (circa 1984) Letter of comment. *Details at 11* 6, pp. 9–17. CMLA. Media Fanzine Collection, id. 00/C000150
DAE4	RK (circa 1985) Letter of comment. *Details at 11* 10, pp. 52–3. CMLA. Media Fanzine Collection, id. 00/C000150
DAE5	RK (circa 1983) Letter of comment. *Details at 11* 1, p. 6. CMLA. Media Fanzine Collection, id. 00/C000150
DAE6	BKA (circa 1985) Letter of comment. *Details at 11* 10, pp. 7–10. CMLA. Media Fanzine Collection, id. 00/C000150
HTT1	IC (1984) Letter of comment. *Holier Than Thou* 20, p. 105. MCSFSF.
IS1	AC (1979) 'Ann's Last Words'. *Interstat* 16 (February), p. 13. CMLA. <http://hdl.handle.net/1969.1/153044>
SH1	BoPeep (1982) 'HOW DOTH OUR LITTLE ZEBRA CON or Look Back In Confusion or Look Forward In Confusion'. *S&H* 37 (December), p. 40. MCSFSF.
SH2	TB (1982) 'DOBEYCON 3 – 'OFFICIAL' REPORT', *S&H* 32 (April), p. 38. MCSFSF.
SH3	KB (1982) Letter of comment. *S&H* 37 (December), pp. 8–10. MCSFSF.

SH4	KB (1982) Letter of comment. *S&H* 33/34 (June), pp. 7–8. MCSFSF.
SH5	NH, CS, SO, DB, and KH (1982) *S&H* 36 (October), pp. 9–10. MCSFSF.
SH6	BS (1982) Letter of comment. *S&H* 32 (April), pp. 15–16. MCSFSF.
SH7	DB and KH (1982) Editorial. *S&H* 33/34 (June), pp. 2 and 56. MCSFSF.
SH8	TB (1982) *S&H* 36 (October), pp. 2–3. MCSFSF.
SH9	RK (1983) Letter of comment. *S&H* 38 (January), p. 10–11. MCSFSF.
SH10	KH (1982) Letter of comment. *S&H* 35 (September), pp. 13–17. MCSFSF.
SH11	MR (1982) Letter of comment. *S&H* 33/34 (June), p. 3. MCSFSF.
TASF1	CM (1994) 'Constantinople '94'. *Thyme: The Australasian SF News Magazine* 97, pp. 6–9. MCSFSF.
UT1	SL (1986) Advertisement in 'The Saurian Grapevine'. *Universal Translator* 31, pp. 36–9. MCSFSF.
UT2	LF (1986) Advertisement in 'The Saurian Grapevine'. *Universal Translator* 32, pp. 44–6. MCSFSF.
UT3	Letterpress (1983) Advertisement in 'The Saurian Grapevine'. *Universal Translator* 18, p. 35. MCSFSF.
UT4	JP (1983) Advertisement in 'The Saurian Grapevine'. *Universal Translator* 16, p. 29. MCSFSF.

[1] CMLA: Cushing Memorial Library and Archives, Texas A&M University.
[2] MCSFSF: Merril Collection of Science Fiction, Speculation & Fantasy, Toronto Public Library

NOTE

1. An editorial insertion mid-LOC points out that this tape of so-called 'most memorable moments' is close to being a 'song tape' (fanvid) and all it lacks is an appropriate soundtrack (DAE6 1985: 7).

REFERENCES

Amesley, C. (1989). 'How to Watch *Star Trek*'. *Cultural Studies* 3(3): 323–39.

Bacon-Smith, C. (1992). *Enterprising Women: Television Fandom and the Creation of Popular Myth*. Philadelphia, PA: University of Pennsylvania Press.

'Between Friends (Starsky and Hutch zine)' (2019). *Fanlore.org*. 18 February 2019. Available at: <https://fanlore.org/wiki/Between_Friends_(Starsky_and_Hutch_zine)> (last accessed 22 August 2019).

Brett, J. (2013). 'Preserving the Image of Fandom: The Sandy Hereld Digitized Media Fanzine Collection at Texas A&M University', *Texas Digital Library*. 28 June 2013. Available at: <https://tdl-ir.tdl.org/handle/2249.1/64291> (last accessed 23 August 2019).

Brown, M. E. (1994). *Soap Opera and Women's Talk: The Pleasure of Resistance*. London: Sage Publications.

Brunsdon, C. (2010). 'Bingeing on Boxsets: The National and the Digital in Television Crime Drama'. In J. Gripsrud (ed.), *Relocating Television: Television in the Digital Context*. Abingdon: Routledge, pp. 63–75.

Bury, R. (2017). *Television 2.0: Viewer and Fan Engagement with Digital TV*. New York: Peter Lang.
Bury, R. (this volume). '"A small Christmas for me": A Study of Binge-Watching and Fan Engagement on Reddit'. In M. Jenner (ed.), *Binge-Watching and Contemporary Television Research*. Edinburgh: Edinburgh University Press, pp. 40–58.
Busse, K. (2013). 'Geek Hierarchies, Boundary Policing and the Gendering of the Good Fan'. *Participations: Journal of Audience & Reception Studies* 10(1): 73–91.
Busse, K. (2018). 'The Ethics of Studying Online Fandom'. In M. A. Click and S. Scott (eds), *The Routledge Companion to Media Fandom*. New York and Abingdon: Routledge, pp. 9–17.
Coppa, F. (2006). 'A Brief History of Media Fandom'. In K. Hellekson and K. Busse (eds), *Fan Fiction and Fan Communities in the Age of the Internet: New Essays*. Jefferson, NC: McFarland & Company, Inc., pp. 44–60.
Coppa, F. (2009). 'A Fannish Taxonomy of Hotness'. *Cinema Journal* 48(4): 107–13.
'Details at 11' (2019). *Fanlore.org*. 16 July 2009. Available at: <https://fanlore.org/wiki/Details_at_11> (last accessed 22 August 2019).
Fiske, J. (1992). 'The Cultural Economy of Fandom'. In L. A. Lewis (ed.), *The Adoring Audience: Fan Culture and Popular Media*. London and New York: Routledge, pp. 30–49.
Gauntlett, D. and A. Hill (1999). *TV Living: Television, Culture and Everyday Life*. London: Routledge.
Gillilan, C. (1998). '*WAR OF THE WORLDS*: Richard Chaves, Paul Ironhorse, and the Female Fan Community'. In C. Harris and A. Alexander (eds), *Theorizing Fandom: Fans, Subculture and Identity*. Cresskill, NJ: Hampton Press, pp. 131–52.
Gillilan, C. (1999). *Zine Fans, Zine Fiction, Zine Fandom: Exchanging the Mundane for a Woman-Centred World*. PhD Thesis, University of Colorado.
Gray, A. (1992). *Video Playtime: The Gendering of a Leisure Technology*. London: Routledge.
Hartwell, D. (1984). *Age of Wonders: Exploring the World of Science Fiction*. New York: Walker and Company.
Heritage, S. (2019). 'Make them wait! Why the age of bingewatching may finally be over'. *The Guardian*. 2 September 2019. Available at: <https://www.theguardian.com/tv-and-radio/2019/sep/02/why-the-age-of-bingewatching-may-be-over-disney-plus-netflix> (last accessed 3 September 2019).
Hills, M. (2013). 'Fiske's "Textual Productivity" and Digital Fandom: Web 2.0 Democratization Versus Fan Distinction?'. *Participations: Journal of Audience & Reception Studies* 10(1): 130–53.
Jacobs, J. (2011). 'Television, Interrupted: Pollution or Aesthetic?'. In J. Bennett and N. Strange (eds), *Television as Digital Media*. Durham, NC and London: Duke University Press, pp. 255–80.
Jenkins, H. (1992). *Textual Poachers: Television Fans and Participatory Culture*. London: Routledge.
Jenner, M. (2017). 'Binge-Watching: Video-On-Demand, Quality TV and Mainstreaming Fandom'. *International Journal of Cultural Studies* 20(3): 304–20.
Jenner, M. (2018). *Netflix and the Re-invention of Television*. Basingstoke: Palgrave Macmillan.
Kompare, D. (2016). 'Publishing Flow: DVD Box Sets and the Reconception of Television', *Television & New Media*, 7(4): 335–360.
Kompare, D. (2018). 'Fan Curators and Gateways into Fandom'. In M. A. Click and S. Scott (eds), *The Routledge Companion to Media Fandom*. New York and Abingdon: Routledge, pp. 107–13.
Latham, R. (2006). '*New Worlds* and the New Wave in Fandom: Fan Culture and the Reshaping of Science Fiction in the Sixties'. *Extrapolation* 47(2): 296–315.

Latham, R., M. Conway, L. Yaszek, W. W. Wilson, J. Brett, C. McKitterick, K. Beckler, P. Weaver, G. Bundy, K. Quinlivan, M. Combs, N. Down., T. M. Whitehead, T. Samuelson, C. Coker, M. Brodsky, S. Hilder, M. Boyd, L. Toolis, A. Sawyer, M. Bonacker, M. Barceló, P. T. Gyger, and J-M. Margot (2010). 'SFS Showcase: Library Collections and Archives of SF and Related Materials'. *Science Fiction Studies* 37(2): 161–90.

Lee, R. Y. (2011). 'Textual Evidence of Fandom Activities: The Fanzine Holdings at UC Riverside's Eaton Collection'. *Transformative Works and Cultures*, 6, no page. Available at: <http://dx.doi.org/10.3983/twc.2011.0271> (last accessed 23 April 2018).

Lymn, J. (2018). 'Looking in on a Special Collection: Science Fiction Fanzines at Murdoch University Library', *Australasian Journal of Popular Culture* 7(1): pp. 23–39.

Mikos, L. (2016). 'Digital Media Platforms and the Use of TV Content: Binge Watching and Video-on-Demand in Germany'. *Media and Communication* 4(3): 154–61.

Newman, M. Z. (2014). *Video Revolutions: On the History of a Medium*. New York: Columbia University Press.

Penley, C. (1991). 'Brownian Motion: Women, Tactics, and Technology'. In C. Penley and A. Ross (eds), *Technoculture*, Minneapolis, MN: University of Minnesota Press, pp. 135–61.

Perks, L. G. (2015). *Media Marathoning: Immersions in Morality*. Lanham, MD: Lexington Books.

Pittman, M. and A. C. Tefertiller (2015). 'With or Without You: Connected Viewing and Co-viewing Twitter Activity for Traditional Appointment and Asynchronous Broadcast Television Models'. *First Monday* 20(7): no page.

'S and H (Starsky and Hutch letterzine)' (2016). *Fanlore.org*. 23 August 2016. Available at: <https://fanlore.org/wiki/S_and_H_(Starsky_and_Hutch_letterzine)> (last accessed 22 August 2019).

'Shadow Chasers' (2019). *Wikipedia.com*. 28 June 2019. Available at: <https://en.wikipedia.org/wiki/Shadow_Chasers> (last accessed 29 August 2019).

Stevens, E. C. (2020). *Fanvids: Television, Women, and Home Media Re-Use*. Amsterdam: Amsterdam University Press.

Stevens, E. C. (2017). 'On Vidding: The Home Media Archive and Vernacular Historiography'. In J. Wroot and A. Willis (eds), *Cult Media: Re-packaged, Re-released and Restored*. London: Palgrave Macmillan, pp. 143–59.

Stewart, M. (2019). 'Live tweeting, Reality TV and the Nation'. *International Journal of Cultural Studies*, online first, 1–16.

'Universal Translator' (2019). *Fanlore.org*. 10 September 2019. Available at: <https://fanlore.org/wiki/Universal_Translator> (last accessed 3 December 2019).

Williams, R. (2015). *Post-Object Fandom: Television, Identity and Self-narrative*. London and New York: Bloomsbury Academic.

Zubernis, L. and K. Larsen (2012). *Fandom at the Crossroads: Celebration, Shame and Fan/Producer Relationships*. Newcastle upon Tyne: Cambridge Scholars Publishing.

TV

Blake's 7 (1978–82), UK, BBC1
Marco Polo (1982) USA/Italy: NBC/RAI
Professionals, The (1977–83), UK: ITV
Shadow Chasers (1985–6), USA: ABC
Simon & Simon (1981–9), USA: CBS
Star Trek (1967–9), USA: NBC
Starsky & Hutch (1975–9), USA: ABC

CHAPTER 3

'A small Christmas for me': A Study of Binge-Watching and Fan Engagement on Reddit

Rhiannon Bury

There can be no question that Netflix is one affordance of what Amanda Lotz (2014) describes as the post-network era of TV. Mareike Jenner (2016) concluded that the changes engendered by Netflix with regard to production, distribution and reception may be significant enough to warrant a new categorisation of TV. Similarly, I have discussed the subscription streaming service in relation to *Television 2.0* (Bury 2017a); as a result of Web 2.0-era downloading and streaming technologies, television is no longer exclusively tied to the almost 100-year-old national broadcast model of centralised transmission (Williams 1975). That said, it is important to heed the caution by Matt Hills (2007) that any 'new' period of television effectively functions to solidify and homogenise the periods that preceded it. Binge-watching is a case in point. Although the nomenclature is bound up with Netflix, the history of the practice and its connection to the network era and participatory culture is often overlooked. According to Mark Poster, periodisation needs to be understood in terms of *complexification*: 'Periods or epochs do not succeed but implicate one another, do not replace but supplement one another, are not consecutive but simultaneous' (1995, 69).

At its broadest, this paper sets out to complexify the relationship between broadcast TV (BTV) and Internet Protocol TV (IPTV) in relation to fannish binge-watching. To this end, I conducted a discourse analysis of fan discussion about eight Netflix 'Originals' on Reddit. First, I offer a theoretical conceptualisation of television as a tele-technological assemblage, one which allows me to trace *rhizomatic* connections between subscription streaming and fannish binge-watching. After providing background about the study and methods, I critically discuss the themes that emerged from data analysis. I will present data from the study to demonstrate that the practice of binge-watching is both driven and limited by affective relations to the televisual text as well as domestic relations and the routines of every life.

NETFLIX AND THE TELE-TECHNOLOGICAL ASSEMBLAGE

Roger Silverstone (1994) defines television as a tele-technological system, articulated into the household as both an object and a medium. Through the broadcast schedule and programming on offer, members are tied into broader public discourses and mobilise some of these to fashion a private domestic culture. Writing in the early 1990s, Silverstone may not have anticipated downloading and streaming technologies and the decentralised systems of transmission they engender. He did, however, recognise that the tele-technological system is not static or isolated and that the convergence of televisual, computer and internet technologies would result in 'an increasingly complex environment from within which to make sense of television in everyday life' (1994, 82). Drawing on Deleuze and Guattari (1987), I find it more fruitful to talk about television as a *tele-technological assemblage*, a conceptualisation which foregrounds instability and heterogeneity over structure and homogeneity. It places emphasis on processes of 'becoming and unbecoming, combining and recombining' (323). Moreover, assemblage/reassemblage is not a linear process but rhizomatic, extending in ways that are uneven and not contained within recognised channels of production, distribution and consumption. Given this understanding of television, discussions about the displacement of BTV by IPTV are misleading. BTV and IPTV are *intra-assemblages* (Deleuze and Guattari 1987), which overlap in the contemporary middle-class household in developed countries (Bury 2017a). This conceptualisation also allows us to examine and take account of the ways in which engagement with television extends from the site of reception into sites of participation and fandom and in doing so recombines various aspects of the assemblage.

When Netflix was set up in 1998, it was a DVD rental company, and as such, it was more closely connected to the film assemblage than that of television. According to Jenner (2016), it had a film library of 90,000 titles. This is understandable given that until the invention of the DVD and the establishment of industry standards (Frankel 2007), television had only a tentative connection to what Kompare refers to as 'the publishing model of media production and distribution' (2006, 338). The number of VHS tapes required for a single season of a television series made the enterprise commercially unviable. Opportunities to create what Jani Merikivi et al. (2019) refer to as continuous flow of a single serialised narrative, however, date back even further to the analogue era of BTV. Syndication of post-run network content was part of the spread of cable and the expansion of smaller networks in the US context. Reruns were often broadcast in blocks in non-prime time slots, for example, *Star Trek* (NBC 1967–9) on UPN (Pearson 2011). Marathon broadcasts became a promotional strategy for some networks: for example, AMC scheduled marathons of previous seasons of *Breaking Bad* (AMC 2008–13) or *The Walking Dead* (AMC 2010-) close to the premiere of a new season. It was the advent of home recording that afforded opportunities for the creation of viewer-centred flow (Uricchio 2004) and the opportunity to build an archive of content for repeat viewing. In *Textual Poachers*, Henry Jenkins (1992) provides several examples of marathoning events for fan favourites such as *Star Trek* at a local host's home (see also Stevens, this volume). Whether organised around the broadcast schedule or those of fans, marathon viewing was exclusively associated with either repeat viewing or 'catch-up' viewing for a series that was part-way through or after completion of its first run.

When it began its limited streaming service as an add-on for its mail-order customers in 2007, Netflix did not alter established repeat or catch-up viewing practices. In 2010, Abigail de Kosnik described the limits of Netflix as follows: 'all of the television episodes available via Watch Instantly are from past seasons of currently airing shows or from classic shows; new TV episodes are not viewable, with the exception of (US)Starz cable network's original programs' (2010, 4). Beginning with *House of Cards* (Netflix 2013–18), Netflix began to produce its own brand of 'original' series. By breaking with the established network practice of releasing new episodes on a weekly basis, its subscribers could simultaneously access an entire season of new content across borders and time zones and for the first time, engage in a binge-watch of new content if they so choose.

BINGE-WATCHING AS FAN PRACTICE

The association of binge-watching with fandom has been considered in recent scholarship. Matt Hills (2019) cites Lisa Perks, who states that marathoners are not necessarily fans but 'temporarily adopt fan practices' (2015, 8). He also cites Jenner (2017), who claims that binge-watching is synonymous with watching video-on-demand, independent of whether those engaging in the practice identify as fans or not. Both claims raise questions as to the definition of the fan. The distinction between a fan and a non-fan, and between a participatory fan and a non-participatory fan, can be traced back to Jenkins (1992), one which is reflected in the literature's focus on fan community and creativity. While this focus has cast a light on meaningful cultural activities and social relationships, particularly those associated with female fans, the effect, even if unintentional, has been to render invisible those fans who have an emotional investment in a text but are not involved in participatory culture. In my TV 2.0 study, I found no connection between levels of investment in a text and levels of involvement in fandom (Bury 2017a). While I don't classify viewing as a participatory practice, I classify all attentive viewing informed by an affective relationship to the text as fannish. If this relationship is intense, then viewing is highly anticipated. With BTV, this means watching a new episode live or as close to the original airdate as possible. If the content is not available in a global region, then fans are more likely to engage in unauthorised downloading to gain timely access (Bury 2017a). Combining anticipatory viewing with binge-watching is an affordance of the subscription streaming release model of IPTV.

Although Merikivi et al. (2019) do not mention fans or fandom, they suggest that the desire for completion is a factor in the decision to binge-watch content. Over thirty years ago, John Fiske (1989) argued that popular television series evoke a sense of 'nowness' that works to deny closure. They are 'open, reverberating, and ready for reactivation . . . Television's tension between the forces of closure and of openness, between authorial and viewer authority, still remains central to the experience they offer' (69). Series produced by Netflix or any other streaming service are no different in this regard: the episodes are still doled out in discrete seasons. Reactivation is a feature of the narrative that stokes anticipation alongside platform activation with a featured 'countdown' until the next episode automatically loads. Finally, the risk of being spoiled in terms of plot or character development is an additional pressure placed upon participatory fans to consume new content as soon as possible (Bennett 2014). Binge-watching becomes the most viable viewing option for uninterrupted participation on social media platforms and discussion forums.

Based on the above, the fannish binge-watch, driven by an emotional commitment to the text, anticipation, a desire for completion, and an involvement in participatory culture might be expected to comprise more than two or three episodes in a row, the minimum number to define viewing as a binge (Merikivi et al. 2019). A press release from Netflix (2016) suggests that the minimum is the norm:

> Netflix examined global viewing of more than 100 serialized TV series across more than 190 countries and found when members are focused on finishing a series, they watch a little over two hours a day to complete a season.

Rather than assume that these viewers are not fans, another factor needs to be considered: constraints on time due to personal, professional and family commitments. While fans will strive to organise their schedules around the viewing of new content, doing so is of course not always possible or desirable. After all, the binge of a Netflix original series in one sitting requires 'the luxury of time'

(Jenner 2017, 317). The length of binge is therefore dependent on not only affective but domestic relations as well.

BACKGROUND AND METHODS

Reddit may seem at first glance an odd site to conduct a study on binge-watching as a fan practice, given its strong association with gaming and STEM cultures (Massanari 2015). When compared to Reddit's most popular forums – r/gaming (23.2 million subscribers) and r/science (22.1 million) – r/television, as it turns out, is not far behind, with 15.6 million subscribers at the time of writing. In addition, fans come to the forums (known as subreddits) dedicated to specific series (e.g., r/strangerthings) to share memes and reactions as well as to engage in collective interpretation. As was the case with the web-based discussion boards such as Television Without Pity (1998–2014), Reddit offers a space for a subset of participatory fans who do more than seek information or read reviews or recaps, but who cannot be assumed to be involved in creative practices (e.g., production of fanfiction or fan videos). Given that fan studies scholarship has tended to focus on the latter (see Booth 2017; Gray, Sandvoss and Harrington 2017; Hellekson and Busse 2006; Jenkins 2006), Reddit also provides an opportunity to cast a light on those fans whose practices I place in the middle range of a continuum of participation (Bury 2017b). Indeed, there are but two studies that focus on fandom and Reddit (see Hills 2019; Pearson 2018).

Reddit is also a logical choice of site for my study given that almost two-thirds of its members are in the 18–29 cohort (Sattelberg 2019). This cohort is more likely to eschew traditional live or time-shifted modes of viewing television content for online viewing (Bury 2017a). People under 30 are also more likely to be cable cutters or cable 'nevers' and therefore do not have access to or watch BTV (Bury 2017a). By extension, they are more likely to binge-watch a favourite series than older cohorts and they are also likely to have more flexibility to binge-watch for longer periods of time. Reddit thus affords an interesting opportunity to conduct a discourse analysis of talk about new seasons of Netflix original series shortly after their release, with specific attention paid to both affective and domestic relations.

From September 2018 to July 2019, I reviewed eleven series in total and selected eight for data collection and discourse analysis. Although this selection was largely determined by the Netflix release schedule, I wanted to ensure that the titles analysed were reasonably representative with regard to genre, popularity, as well as length and number of episodes, and length of series run.

To get a sense of the time frame for completion of a single season and to get a snapshot of the popularity of binge-watching, I recorded the number of comments (Reddit conveniently provides a current tally at the bottom of each post)

Table 3.1 Netflix Original Series released September 2018 – July 2019

Title	Season	Number of Episodes
Big Mouth (BMth)	2 (ongoing)	10 (30 minutes)
Black Mirror (BM)	5 (ongoing)	3 (1 hour to 1.5 hours)
BoJack Horseman (BJH)	5 (ongoing)	12 (30 minutes)
Daredevil (DD)	3 (cancelled)	13 (1 hour or less)
House of Cards (HoC)	6 (complete)	8 (1 hour)
Maniac	1 (limited series)	10 (30–50 minutes)
Russian Doll (RD)	1 (ongoing)	8 (30 minutes or less)
Stranger Things (ST)	3 (ongoing)	8 (50–80 minutes)

made to the general season discussion thread or 'hub' for each of the eight series listed above, over a series of intervals during the 21-day post-release period and then again at the time of writing or time of archive (generally the moderators closed the season discussion hubs after six months). As Hills (2019) points out, talk about television remains primarily structured around individual episodes and seasons. My assumption was that the comments would almost exclusively be made by those who had finished viewing the series. For each series, I manually saved comments made to either the hub or to the series finale within one week of release that made direct or indirect reference to binge-watching. I then coded and organised them into broad themes related to affective and domestic relations. Once those themes reached saturation, I stopped collecting data; as a result, the samples presented in the paper are made primarily in reference to the shows with seasons released earlier in the data collection period. In presenting the data samples, I have removed the Reddit username and replaced it with an acronym based on the series (see Table 3.1).

BINGE-WATCH TALK ON REDDIT

Based on the average of the comment tallies, the majority of comments were made within the first 48–72 hours of release, confirmation that the Redditors who made them had binge-watched the series; with the exception of *Black Mirror* (Channel 4, 2011–13; Netflix 2016–19), one would be required to watch more than two episodes at a time in order to complete the series and participate in the discussion. Of the 1,300 comments made for the third season of *Daredevil* (Netflix 2015–18) for example, in the first two weeks of release, two-thirds were made in the first 48 hours. The final count at archive six months later was almost the same at 1,400. Similarly, for Season Five of *BoJack Horseman* (Netflix 2015–20), 3,800 comments were made within

17 days after release of the fifth season, with 1,200 made within the first 24 hours. Only 200 more were added almost one year later. The length of episode (30 minutes x 12 vs 60 minutes x 13) was not a factor. The time period was slightly more extended for *Black Mirror*: 561 comments in 24 hours, with the largest growth taking place in the 3–5 day span for a total of 3,900. After that, numbers increased slowly but steadily from 4.2k after seven days to 4.6k after 14 days. Although the third season has only three episodes, *Black Mirror* is also an anthology and is not structured around a serial narrative. *Stranger Things* (Netflix 2016–) is one of Netflix's most popular series and after its third season was reported to have the highest TV series viewership of all its 'original' series in 2019 (Lee 2019). There were almost 9,000 comments made to the Series 5 'discussion hub' within 48 hours after its release. The numbers jumped to 15, 200 at 72 hours. Growth slowed but was steady: 19.6k at five days and 22.6k at 14 days.

KEEPING ME WAITING

While a new season of episodes may be dropped at any time of year, Netflix released all eight series included in the study on a Thursday at midnight Pacific Time (PT; US & Canada). As such, there is still a time and date around which fans can engage in anticipatory practices. In the case of the six returning series, Redditors expressed excitement not just for the return of the series but for a binge-watch immediately upon release.

> ST-1: I tried to get a nap in for before the binging but I was too excited to sleep
> BMth-1: We have to wait till it's midnight in LA. I was so excited. I thought Netflix shows dropped on EST time :((((Welp, back to sleep!

For those in locations many hours ahead of PT, there was frustration with the long wait:

> BMth-2: Yea, I'm in Australia and it's 10:20am on the fifth and I'm just sitting here all day waiting for California to catch up!!
> BMth-3: Dude are you watching on Netflix cos I'm in QLD [Queensland] and it's not showing on Netflix and I'm about to RAGE!
> BMth-2: Melbourne! I'll get it at 6pm
> BMth-3: God damn . . . don't think I can do it. Cheers for the heads up.

Some fans who were poised to start watching at the moment of drop ran into technical issues as per the exchange below:

DD-1: WHY WON'T IT LOAD I sat here counting down the seconds and netflix Daredevil episodes haven't been refreshed
DD-2: I'm watching it right now. It's pretty hype!!
DD-3: Ahhhh it's still not loading for me! :

While the 1,200 comments on the BoJack subreddit made within the first 24 hours provide evidence of the desire to share reactions and interpretations while the content is fresh in viewers' minds, this Redditor was parked on the thread eagerly waiting for others to join in.

BJH-1: I really want to see the thread traffic on this one because it is exactly the amount of time that it takes to finish the show right now and I'm sensing a spike in posts

Anticipation of discussion post-binge was not limited to returning series:

Maniac-1: Just did the same [completed a binge-watch] and came here to see some discussions. I am blown away!

GETTING TO KNOW YOU

The next set of samples indicate that a complete binge-watch need not be anticipated or planned. This was the case with the two new series included in data collection period: *Maniac* (Netflix 2018) and *Russian Doll* (Netflix 2019). Pathways to becoming a fan were similar to those of a new network series: internal and external promotion, sometimes combined with familiarity with the previous work of producers or actors associated with the new series (Bury 2017a):

RD-1: Netflix was like, here's this thing, and I was like, alright, I like Natasha Lyonne, why not. However many hours later, I was sitting there having watched the entire thing and was just blown away by how good it was.

The actor/producer named above was a main character in Netflix's series, *Orange is the New Black* (Netflix 2013–19), and the main draw for this Redditor. A 'trial-watch' led to a binge once an intensive relationship with the text was established. The next set of data samples illustrate the same shift:

Maniac-2: For once I am glad that those intrusive Netflix previews introduced me to this show. Ended up binge watching the whole thing in one day.

> Maniac-3: Same here. Remembered watching a trailer and being slightly intrigued a while back, but forgot most of the details and went in more or less blind. 10 episodes later and my head is spinning.
> Maniac-4: Just binge watched the entire thing on a whim. The part of the trailer where she is yelling at the people and trying to go down the stairs is what made me click play.

Based on these responses, it would appear that Netflix's internal marketing of new series is effective. Perks's (2015) notion of the tourist who becomes a resident is evident in the sample below: a participatory fan not just new to the series but new to the practice:

> RD-2: I have never binge watched a whole season of anything . . . rural, new to wifi . . . and I couldn't stop watching this! I loved the grittiness and raunchiness.

DAY FOR NIGHT

For North American fans, binge-watching the entire season of a returning series in one sitting immediately upon release resulted in disruption to their sleep routines (see also Perks 2015):

> BJH-2: I love this show. Just finished it. I'm tired, but it was worth it.
> RD-3: My only regret is that I put on the first episode at midnight. Once it started, I was IN. Flop into bed 4 hours later, brain full.
> RD-4: I stayed up way too late to finish the show in one go. Well worth it. What a ride! Spiraled from comedy to straight up existential dread-filled thriller and came right back around with an uplifting ending.
> RD-5: This was a damned delight! I really didn't need to be staying up 'til 3, but whatever, I'll take it.

The intensity of experience clearly outweighed its discontents, even when the post-binge was described as akin to a hangover from excessive partying and/or drinking:

> RD-6: This morning. I'm going to feel like shit
> RD-7: It's this morning for me. Definitely feel like shit. No regrets!

Others directly referenced having to go to work the next morning:

> BJH-3: Eastern US – went to bed at 8pm so I could wake up at 3am and binge before work – I did it!

BJH-4: I binged the entire season the night it came out cause it's what I always do. I have an interview at 9:30 am and it is currently 4:50. I have no regrets. It was amazing.

The first Redditor described his strategy to mitigate the lack of sleep while the second just soldiered on sleep-deprived. For those in the UK or Europe, binge-watching immediately meant doing so during the day:

DD-4: Asked for the day off just to binge in one day.

Given that the best time for most people to watch television is in the evening after work, the Netflix 'prime time release zone' falls in Australia:

BJH-5: So glad I live in Australia. It's only 6pm here.
BJH-6: Binging a show non stop and finishing it at 10pm? That feels good

BINGE-WATCHING AND EVERYDAY LIFE

Not everyone, however, had the flexibility to engage in the practice in line with the release time and date:

BMth-4: drops here at 5pm and I have work at 9pm I'm devastated!

Due to work and life commitments, some were forced to delay or pace out their binge-watch:

BMth-5: The only way I could stop watching was falling asleep, but then I woke up to go to work and I felt the urge to watch one more episode before heading to work.
BJH-7: I just woke up at 8:30am in the UK just as the episodes have gone live, I need to watch as many as I can before therapy later . . .

The next sample was the only one of its kind in the sample set but noteworthy for casting light on the integration of binge-viewing with domestic and other leisure activities, a practice primarily associated with distracted or background viewing of live TV:

Maniac-5: It's my birthday and I'm having people over for homemade ramen, lychee martinis, and crab Rangoon in four hours, and I'm so disappointed. I may just bring my laptop into the kitchen while I finish up the cooking so I can binge as long as possible.

In the final sample, this *BoJack* fan decided to engage in mobile binge-viewing to fit with their travel schedule:

> BJH-8: I have a cross-country flight tomorrow morning and all 12 unwatched episodes of season 5 downloaded to my phone. What a great way to make a long flight go by quickly.

The responses, however, point to the complications of watching certain types of television content outside the privacy of one's home.

> BJH-9: Beware the little kids trying to watch it with you. I was on an 8 hr long bus trip yesterday and I noticed that the little girl behind me was watching it with me when I was watching that scene where BoJack and Diane were arguing.
> BJH-10: enjoy having a depressive episode in public!
> BJH-11: I tried something similar on my long about 20 hours flight. And you just burn out in the middle and just want to sleep

These comments point to not only privacy but also the level of comfort of the home that affords attentive and intense viewing. In sum, the samples above clearly illustrate the ways in which fan engagement with television both regulates and is regulated by everyday life.

THE DEVIL MADE ME DO IT

Regardless of whether the emotional attachment to the text was established or newly formed, overtures of binge-watching as an addiction run through the data. Redditors regularly referred to being 'hooked' and/or incapable of stopping viewing:

> BMth-6: The trailer for the second season started playing before I could do anything to stop it and I got hooked. The lines delivered in that trailer sold me immediately and oh, boy . . . The only way I could stop watching it was falling asleep.

That said, Perks (2015) cites survey data that suggest that that the negative connotations that surround the practice are disappearing. Similarly, Jenner states that binge-watching 'signifies a socially legitimised excess' (2017, 317). My data analysis supports these claims. The positive comments about the experience far outnumbered the negatives of excess. That said, a few Redditors still framed their responses in terms of a temptation that should be resisted:

Maniac-6: So far so good, trying to resist binge watching but I badly want the story to unravel . . . and failing

Maniac-7: This is where I take a break. This show is excellent I don't want to watch it all in one go. Update: I have watched it all in one go. Totally worth it

This *BoJack* fan expressed disappointment in themselves for succumbing to the temptation:

BJH-12: ugh I finished it in one sitting. I have no self control and I hate myself. Now I have to wait for another year.

Others eschewed discourses of excess and temptation completely:

BJH-13: Congrats on everyone who made it through the night/day/ other-6-hour-time-span on release! I've said this every new season (at least since 3) but this seems to be my favorite season so far.

This Redditor emphasised the endurance and stamina required to complete a 'real-life' marathon and as such completion in a single sitting was framed as a source of pride. In discussing similar comments made in relation to an earlier season of *Black Mirror*, Hills (2019) argues that the discourse of toughness mobilised is gendered, 'treating bingeing as a culturally masculinized test' (228).

A more unusual upside of the binge-watch is captured below:

BJH-14: The new season of Bojack came out and I binged, hard. I have no idea why, but it helped. It seriously turned my attitude towards my progress around. Life was getting really hard, existence was extremely painful, but for some reason I found a reason to continue trying in spite of all this. I too have decided to finally seek professional help. I've been looking for a therapist that best fits my needs and I feel hopeful about it.

Finding the binge-watching experience therapeutic and cathartic needs to be understood in relation to the narrative arc of the season and the sixth episode, 'Free Churro', in particular. This fan's lengthy response captures the power of the episode as experienced mid-way through the binge on the night of release:

BJH-15: I sat glued to my TV screen at 4:15 am watching a cartoon horse eulogize his recently deceased mother, and talk about his blossoming addiction, lack of any semblance of a real relationship with either of his deeply flawed, more-(wo)man-than-horse-or-more-horse-than-(wo)man parents, and realize that the one positive aspect of his entire life spent with his mother, this one tiny moment with his dying mother that was kind of actually pretty much just okay, was actually just a dementia-stricken mare flashing in and out of memories of debutante balls and emotional abuse at the hands of an alcoholic failed novelist . . . and she was just reading a sign, indicating which wing of the hospital in which she was currently residing . . . What a fucking amazing episode/show/actor/profound sense of sadness.

The simultaneous release of two returning series, *American Vandal* (reviewed but not included in the study) and *BoJack* on the same date led to a case of a 'double binge' for anticipatory fans of both series. Expressions of both extreme pleasure but also of personal failing are recounted in responses to a post entitled, 'Who decided to release [American Vandal] and BoJack at the same time!:

BJH-16: being released on the same day was a small Christmas for me.
BJH-17: I finished both seasons in the same night/following day. Send help, I have no life.

TO BINGE OR NOT TO BINGE

The question of 'binge-worthiness' was a related theme that surfaced in the data. Although scholars such as Jenner (2017) and Hills (2019) link the quality drama to binge-watching, Netflix (2016) offers the opposite interpretation of its data. Dividing its series into the categories of 'devour' and 'savour', quality dramas are placed in the latter. The following stand-alone post, entitled 'A Case Against Binging Season 5', sparked debate on the *Black Mirror* Season Five thread around this divide:

BM-1: I learned what Black Mirror was pretty much exactly a year ago, and since then have gone through and watched all 20 episodes of the series. During that time, I never watched two new episodes back-to-back. As you are all aware: there is so much to analyze in each episode, and I feel like they pack a bigger punch when you have a day or two (or even a week) to soak in.

I know many of you have your alarms set for the middle of the night tonight and will watch all three by the time I wake up tomorrow. **Don't do it!** Watch one episode tomorrow. Then another this weekend. Then the third a couple days later. Don't waste them all in one night!

This Redditor is a 'catch-up' fan who is firmly in the savour camp but, interestingly, not because of the anthology structure of the series and its ensuing lack of what Hills calls 'immersive potential' (2019, 228). Instead, this poster makes explicit the assumption that underlies the devour/savour distinction, namely that binge-watching forecloses the possibility to engage in close reading of the text. In the past, critical analysis of the so-called quality text required the 'quality' fan to not 'sit too close' as Jenkins (1992) puts it; one maintains critical distance by not allowing an affective relationship to cloud one's judgement. With the Netflix release model, the 'quality' fan must disavow anticipation and desire for completion by manually inserting temporal distance between episodes through use of the stop and exit commands. Indeed, the post above even suggests a schedule for viewing the three episodes. Some Redditors agreed with this position:

> BM-2: Absolutely. This is not a 'binge-worthy' type of show at all, for exactly the reasons you stated. One episode at a time.
> BM-3: Watching them all, there's no time to reflect on them or let your mind wander to creep you out when you don't expect it.

Others, however, chimed in with a counter-argument:

> BM-4: I like a deep dive all at once too; sometimes there are references set in the episodes that seem to reward binge watchers. (Or long range watchers with excellent visual/verbal memories). I'll know what I wanna come back to.

This comment is in line with Perks's (2015) finding about the rewards of the binge for close readers. The last sentence, however, suggests an alternative approach that enables fans to have their cake (the pleasures of the binge) and eat it too (the pleasures of close reading and analysis). The following comment makes the approach explicit:

> BM-5: I always binge shows out of excitement of it being out then go back and re watch at a slower pace to really take the episodes in.

BINGE IT AGAIN, SAM

Fans have been re-watching television content since the first repeat broadcasts of the early television era. Fans go back to pick up details that they may have missed in previous viewing (Bury 2017a; Perks 2015). In this study the practice was mentioned mostly in the context of *Black Mirror* and *Maniac*, both science fiction series with narrative structures that deliberately conceal before they reveal.

> Maniac-8: I really enjoyed this show. Going to spend the next week slow watching it since I consumed it all in about 24 hours this time around.
> Maniac-9: I finished the series last night and even before it was over I knew I would need to watch them all again to catch the little things I missed. I actually stopped reading other posts on r/maniac so I wouldn't spoil anything.
> BM-6: Just finished binge watching all three. This is the only season where I actually want to rewatch all of the episode instead of maybe just one or two.

One interesting finding was mention of the 'repeat binge'.

> Maniac-10: Now it's 1 am and my mind is doubling back on earlier episodes. Will definitely have to *binge it again* [italics added]!

In a similar vein, the following post was entitled, 'I've finished the series twice in the past 48 hours'. The poster then added the following comment:

> Maniac-11: This quickly became my favorite show of all time. It checks every box for me: Mental health focus, dark comedy, 80's sci-fi. Jonah and Emma's performance were incredible, but Jonah's was especially impressive. May re-watch for a third time.

The suggestion based on this critical assessment was that quality dramas do not need to be savoured, but they do warrant, or demand even, repeat viewing.

BREAKING THE BINGE

There was also evidence that fans may commit to a binge-watch but do not follow through for reasons other than constraints imposed by daily life. One reason that emerged from the analysis was related to depressing or distressing content. Hills (2019), for example, claims that binge-viewing of a previous season of *Black Mirror* was interrupted or discontinued due to emotional intensity, a claim supported by my data:

> BM-7: I find the post episode sense of dread too much to process 3x over lol. It's not exactly a feel good show that makes you want to keep watching haha

This was also the case with *BoJack*. In contrast to the fans who stayed glued to their screens, others needed to take a break:

> BJH-18: I literally had to pause every two episodes watching this. Some episodes are just too heavy to watch. And I'm the type who usually binges 5 eps in one sitting on other animated shows
> BJH-19: The creators have obviously done a great job, to make someone feel so uncomfortable with a character, but it truly is hard for me to watch too much of in a row

The first comment is noteworthy in that it casts into relief the ways in which content can reinforce or disrupt regular viewing practices, including binge-watching.

The next sample points to a different reason for interrupting a binge – difficulty in following the storyline. This Redditor came to the *Maniac* subreddit to seek advice from other viewers as to whether to continue:

> Maniac-12: Halfway through And I have zero idea what's going on lmao. I was expecting something completely different when I first started the show. Excited to see where things go – hoping everything comes together at the end.
> Maniac-13: what are you confused about ill explain it without ruining the show
> Maniac-12: I'm pretty sure I'm following along I was just caught off guard by where the story went. [plot details deleted]. Am I close? Or completely wrong with my take? Lmao
> Maniac-14: You're absolutely spot on . . . While what you've seen so far has all been important, it's really episodes 7–10 that are the real meat and potatoes IMO. If you're hoping the show gets less [more?] straight forward down the line, believe me it does!
> Maniac-12: Awesome! Thank you for helping me out. Throwing on ep 7 now. I'll be back . . .

This exchange also demonstrates the value that the opinion of other fans holds and the role that forums such as Reddit play in facilitating collective interpretation.

Perks suggest that the failure of a new season to live up to past expectations can induce 'marathon regret' (2015, 58). As illustrated by the final sample below, displeasure with the text was the main reason cited for terminating the binge and not completing the series.

> HoC-1: I outright spoiled this season for myself. Turns out, I dodged a bullet. Saved 8 hours of my life.

HoC-2: I was about to start watching the new season of Castlevania when I saw HOC Season 6 came out. That was a mistake. This season is garbage. I watched 2 episodes, made it about 20 minutes into the 3rd and just gave up.

Interestingly, the only series of the eight with these negative reactions was the final season of *House of Cards*. It had the fewest number of comments with only 72 after 24 hours and less than 300 at the time of archive.

CONCLUSION

In this paper, I set out to discuss fannish binge-watching of new content. A convergence of technologies from the film, television and internet assemblages gave rise to IPTV and the rhizome of the DVD extended to subscription streaming. Binge-watching in relation to BTV and early IPTV was an intensive form of repeat and catch-up viewing. Committed fans did not wait for a season of a serialised narrative to come out on DVD or let episodes pile up on tapes or hard drives; rather they anticipated the broadcast of each new weekly episode and made every effort to view it live or as soon as possible. As I hope to have demonstrated, fannish binge-watching functions as a technologically enabled but not technologically determined node around which previously separate viewing practices coalesce. Emotional commitment, anticipation and a desire for completion without being spoiled work in tandem, motivating fans to binge-watch an entire new season of a Netflix series upon release or in very short order after release, regardless of the number or length of episodes. Although some expressed regret for giving in to the 'lure' of the binge, the majority felt the pleasures of the experience outweighed inconveniences such as sleep deprivation. Contrary to the Netflix data, the majority of anticipatory, participatory fans do not 'savour' narratives, complex or not. They 'devour' and then re-watch and/or come to forums on sites such as Reddit to enrich their viewing experience. The binge was broken when the text itself failed to live up to expectations. Of course, fannish binge-watching, like all fan practices and leisure activities, does not stand outside of everyday life. As such, a complete binge may be desired but is not achievable due to work, travel or other commitments.

There are, of course, limitations to this study. The comment tallies I reported are also indicative that numbers of Redditors are 'savouring' a series or are binge-watching at their convenience within the first couple of weeks of release before coming to the forums (e.g., 'I've finally got some time so I'm about to binge watch season 3 of daredevil'). Second, the method itself can only indicate broad patterns of binge-watching and fan engagement. Survey and interview data would be required to tease out the relationship between affective and domestic relations. Finally, while Reddit skews young, it also skews male and white (Sattelberg 2019). Most of its members are also based in the US. Therefore, empirical investigation that collects demographic information about the participants is required in order to understand the ways in which fannish binge-watching is gendered and raced or how it is taken up in a global context.

NOTE

1. In the past, I have been reluctant to use 'binge-watch' given its negative connotations of excess and addiction (see also Jenner 2017; Perks 2015). Given that the term has become firmly established in the vernacular and is becoming so in television scholarship, as indicated by the title of this collection, I will henceforth use it in relation to marathon viewing.

REFERENCES

Bennett, L. (2014). 'Tracing Textual Poachers: Reflections on the Development of Fan Studies and Digital Fandom'. *Journal of Fandom Studies* 2(1): 5–20.
Booth, P. (2017). *Digital Fandom: 2.0 New Media Studies* (2nd edition). New York: Peter Lang.
Bury, R. (2017a). *Television 2.0: Viewer and Fan Engagement with Digital TV*. New York: Peter Lang.
Bury, R. (2017b). 'We're Not There': Fans, Fan Studies and the Participatory Continuum'. In M. A. Click and S. Scott (eds), *The Routledge Companion to Media Fandom*. New York: Routledge, pp. 123–31.
De Kosnik, A. (2010). 'Piracy is the future of television'. 1–17. Available at: <http://convergenceculture.org/research/c3-piracy_future_television-full.pdf> (last accessed 17 August 2019).
Deleuze, G. and F. Guattari (1987). *A Thousand Plateaus: Capitalism and Schizophrenia* (B. Massumi, trans.). Minneapolis, MN: University of Minnesota Press.
Fiske, J. (1989). 'Moments of Television: Neither the Text nor the Audience'. In E. Seiter, H. Borchers, G. Kreutzner and E. M. Warth (eds), *Remote Control: Television, Audiences, and Cultural Power*. New York: Routledge, pp. 56–78.
Frankel, D. (2007). 'DVD timeline: looking back at the format's history'. Available at: <http://variety.com/2007/digital/features/dvd-timeline-1117963613> (last accessed 17 October 2016).
Gray, J., C. Sandvoss and C. L. Harrington (eds). (2017). *Fandom: Identities and Communities in a Mediated World* (2nd edition). New York: New York University Press.
Hellekson, K. and K. Busse (eds). (2006). *Fan Fiction and Fan Communities in the Age of the Internet: New Essays*. Jefferson, NC: McFarland & Co.
Hills, M. (2007). 'From the Box in the Corner to the Boxset on the Shelf'. *New Review of Film and Television Studies* 5(1): 41–60.
Hills, M. (2019). 'Black Mirror as a Netflix Original: Program Brand "Overflow" and the Multidiscursive Forms of Transatlantic TV Fandom'. In M. Hills, M. Hilmes and R. Pearson (eds), *Transatlantic Television Drama: Industries, Programs & Fans*. Oxford: Oxford University Press, pp. 213–38.
Jenkins, H. (1992). *Textual Poachers: Television Fans & Participatory Culture*. New York: Routledge.

Jenkins, H. (2006). *Convergence Culture: Where Old and New Media Collide*. New York: New York University Press.

Jenner, M. (2016). 'Is this TVIV? On Netflix, TVIII and Binge-Watching'. *New Media & Society* 18(2): 257–73.

Kompare, D. (2006). 'Publishing Flow: DVD Box Sets and the Reconception of Television'. *Television & New Media* 7(4): 335–60.

Lee, B. (2019). 'Netflix has revealed its most-watched content. You might be surprised'. *The Irish Times*. 23 October 2019. Available at: <https://www.irishtimes.com/culture/tv-radio-web/netflix-has-revealed-its-most-watched-content-you-might-be-surprised-1.4060255> (last accessed 15 November 2019).

Lotz, A. (2014). *The Television will be Revolutionized* (2nd edition). New York: New York University Press.

Massanari, A. L. (2015). *Participatory Culture, Community, and Play: Learning from Reddit*: New York: Peter Lang.

Merikivi, J., J. Bragge, E. Scornavacca and T. Verhagen (2019). 'Binge-Watching Serialized Video Content: A Transdisciplinary Review'. *Television & New Media* 21(7): 697–711.

Netflix (2016). 'Netflix & binge: New binge scale reveals TV series we devour and those we savor'. 30 July 2016. Available at: <https://media.netflix.com/en/press-releases/netflix-binge-new-binge-scale-reveals-tv-series-we-devour-and-those-we-savor-1> (last accessed 20 July 2019).

Pearson, R. (2011). 'Cult Television as Digital Television's Cutting Edge'. In J. Bennett and N. Strange (eds), *Television as Digital Media*. Durham, NC: Duke University Press, pp. 105–31.

Pearson, R. (2018). '"You're Sherlock Holmes, Wear the Damn Hat!": Character Identity in a Transfiction'. In P. Brembilla and I. A. De Pascalis (eds), *Reading Contemporary Serial Television Universes: A Narrative Ecosystem Framework*. New York: Routledge, pp. 144–65.

Perks, L. G. (2015). *Media Marathoning : Immersions in Morality*. Lanham, MD: Lexington Books.

Poster, M. (1995). *The Second Media Age*. Cambridge, MA: Polity Press.

Sattelberg, W. (2019). 'The demographics of Reddit: who uses the site?' Available at: <https://www.techjunkie.com/demographics-reddit/> (last accessed 3 December 2019).

Silverstone, R. (1994). *Television and Everyday Life*. New York: Routledge.

Uricchio, W. (2004). 'Television's Next Generation: Technology/Interface/Culture/Flow'. In L. Spigel and J. Olsson (eds), *Television after TV: Essays on a Medium in Transition* (Durham NC: Duke University Press, pp. 163–82).

Williams, R. (1975). *Television: Technology and Cultural Form*. New York: Schocken Books.

TV

Black Mirror (2011–19), UK: Channel 4, Netflix
BoJack Horseman (2015–20), USA: Netflix
Breaking Bad (2008–13), USA: AMC
Daredevil (2015–18), USA: Netflix
House of Cards (2013–18), USA: Netflix
Maniac (2018), USA: Netflix
Orange is the New Black (2013–19), USA: Netflix
Russian Doll (2019–), USA: Netflix
Star Trek (1967–9), USA: NBC
Stranger Things (2016–), USA: Netflix
Walking Dead, The (2010–), USA: AMC

CHAPTER 4

Binge-Watching and Fandom: Conclusion

Rhiannon Bury and E. Charlotte Stevens

The study of fans and the study of how fans engage with television and each other pre-dates binge-watching as either a mainstream concept or an object of scholarly attention. In this section, we have taken the opportunity to share two narratives that are part of a body of work about fandom and technology. Stevens points to early evidence of what would now be called binge-watching in fans' letters dating back to 1979; Bury analyses Reddit conversations about binge-watching in relation to Netflix series that were released in 2019. In the intervening 40 years, live viewing of television content has been upended by subscription service streaming and subscription viewing on demand (SVOD). Analogue home recording gave way to digital recording, and VHS collections were replaced by DVD box sets. Similarly, letters in print fanzines are largely supplanted by conversations on internet message boards and social sites like Reddit and Twitter.

As both chapters demonstrate, however, fans use the technologies available to them to shape and then share an experience of television viewing beyond a traditional terrestrial broadcast model based on single episodic viewing. For fans in the videotape era, making and sharing off-air recordings allowed for individuals and groups to time-shift and marathon television episodes. The results of this fannish viewing – both for catch-up and repeat viewing – was communicated in letters of comment to amateur fanzines, which were then circulated to fellow zine subscribers. Since the advent of the Netflix release model in 2013, fans have been able to binge-watch an entire season of new content and then come to the popular platform of Reddit to share reactions and engage in collective interpretation. Taken together, our chapters demonstrate that binge-watching has a greater duration than might otherwise be apparent from the conventional narrative about the novelty of the practice. As such, this represents a mainstreaming of fannish modes of engagement with television: it certainly appears as if audiences are finally catching up to fans.

Two additional themes related to binge-watching and fandom arise from and overlap in our research. The first is related to the temporality of engagement. As Stevens notes, media fandoms can endure over many years. Here a community of zine fans is sustained through ongoing connections in text and via conventions even after the original text has gone off air. For example, new fans were able to join the *Starsky & Hutch* fandom because the affordances of videotape meant they did not have to wait for syndication or reruns to access the series. The complementary practices of marathon viewing in person and at conventions perpetuated a fandom past a show's cancellation; this community articulated itself via the enduring but small circulation of letterzines. The subreddits dedicated to original Netflix series, in contrast, can have hundreds of thousands of subscribers. Yet participation waxes and wanes with release. Bury's data shows that the bulk of discussion takes place within the first three days after the drop of a new season, suggesting that binge-watching is the preferred mode of viewing for these fans. This short window of engagement is suggestive of a fandom 'on demand', with strong ties to the text and weak ties to community members.

The second theme raised in both chapters is one of fandom as a port of welcome/refuge. The strong connection to a particular television text and the binge-watching associated with it may not be shared by family and friends or, worse, deemed to be unhealthy or obsessive. While the fans studied by Stevens associated marathoning with obsessive behaviour, the pervasive semi-serious jokes about addiction were made in the safety of a small community of likeminded strangers/pen-pals. The strong ties of the community are arguably seen in how letterzine contributions were almost always published under fans' wallet names, with mailing addresses included as a matter of course, a practice that is unthinkable today. Zines' modest circulation evidently contributed to a sense of safety whereby one could share one's full name and address alongside candidly expressed desires for characters/actors, and spending hours on end re-watching favourite episodes. Even though fannish interests and intensities have become more mainstream and attract less of an immediate stigma, there is something liberating about the affordances of pseudonymity provided by platforms such as Reddit, in contrast to Facebook where one is required to use one's real name (Van der Nagel and Frith 2015). Bury found no evidence that the posters were ashamed of their decisions to stay up half the night or take a day off work to binge-watch an entire season immediately upon release. The few expressions of regret or self-flagellation were recounted in a light-hearted tone. At the very least, these Redditors knew that they could share feelings about the pleasures of the binge and joke about their lack of self-control with like-minded fans.

Despite differences in the types of communities studied, we employed similar methods and returned similar results in our research. Both chapters study similar levels of textual productivity, not taking an ethnographic or case study approach, but performing discourse analysis of traces of conversation, in print and online. Thus, the thousands of paper pages held at the Merril Collection and the digitisations of print holdings at the Cushing Memorial Library contain rare glimpses of *how* fans watched television. While public digital forums such as Reddit render television talk more visible and therefore more accessible to researchers, the thousands of posts made to each forum make for slow and methodical sifting in order to find mentions of specific practices such as binge-watching (Reddit's search function is very limited). As a result of close textual analysis, we were able to find a range of narrativisations of marathon and/or binge-watching as outlined in our respective chapters.

Taken together, our chapters resist periodisation and complicate previous narratives about binge-watching. We make a strong case that a determination as to whether a show is 'binge-worthy' or not cannot be based on the quality or genre of the content. Nor can binge-watching be aligned with a particular era and technology. It is the connection to the text and the set of affective relations that it engenders which drive a particular mode of binge-watching, whether it be related to anticipation of new content or repeat viewing of an old favourite.

REFERENCES

Van der Nagel, E. and J. Frith (2015). 'Anonymity, Pseudonymity and the Agency of On-line Identity: Examining the Social Practices of r/gonewild'. *First Monday* 20(3). Available at: <http://firstmonday.org/ojs/index.php/fm/article/view/5615> (last accessed 25 January 2020).

PART II

Binge-Watching Audiences

CHAPTER 5

Commercial Constructions of Binge-Viewers: A Typology of the New and Improved Couch Potato as Seen on TV

Emil Steiner

Who are binge-viewers? Research on contemporary television audiences has revealed complex, nuanced and at times contradictory depictions of these elusive yet ubiquitous consumers of contemporary media (Castro et al. 2021; Flayelle et al. 2019; Merikivi et al. 2019). At times gluttons at times epicures, binge-viewers consume more voraciously and specifically than any audience in television history. To understand their delicate degustation of control, researchers have examined binge-viewer uses and gratifications (Merrill and Rubenking 2019; Steiner and Xu, 2020), the potential health impacts (Perks 2019; Tefertiller and Maxwell 2018), the role of viewer attentiveness on mood and content selection (Pittman and Steiner 2019; Walton-Pattison, Dombrowski and Presseau 2018), as well as antecedents and outcomes of their binges (Gangadharbatla, Ackerman and Bamford 2019; Pittman and Steiner 2021). The variety and scope of audience studies seeking to identify binge-viewers and their traits and types continues to grow (see Chapter 9 on Typology, which concludes this part).

However, with so many willing human subjects (see Chapter 8 by Lothar Mikos and Deborah Castro and Chapter 6 by Lisa Perks in this part) creating windfalls of user data (as discussed by Ri Pierce Grove in Chapter 7), mediated depictions of binge-viewers have received scant academic attention. Pierce-Grove (2017) and Steiner (2018) chronicled journalistic articulations of binge-watching, but the fictional representations of binge-viewers remain largely unexplored. In part, this may be because there are so few. Couch potatoes were a common trope of twentieth-century TV, but binge-viewers seldom appear in shows being binge-watched. When the term began to catch cultural traction around 2012–14, there were a number of comedic depictions, the most famous of which was *Portlandia*'s (IFC 2011–18) Claire (Carrie Brownstein) and Doug (Fred Armisen) in 'One Moore Episode' (2012). However, unlike Archie Bunker (Carroll O'Connor, *All in the Family*, CBS 1971–9), Al Bundy (Ed O'Neill, *Married . . . with Children*, Fox 1987–97), and Beavis and Butt-Head (*Beavis and Butt-Head*, MTV 1993–2011), all prominent channel-surfers, binge-viewer characters all but disappeared once the practice mainstreamed. Nearly all Americans will binge-watch at some point in their lives (Westcott et al. 2018), but the experience itself does not, as they say, make for good TV. Characters across media today may be binge-viewers, occasional or regular, in their backstories, and they may even mention bingeing, but rarely if ever are they shown in the act and rarely is it described as a defining characteristic. Mediated portrayals of binge-viewers today may be as rare as real-life binge-viewers are common.

How remarkable that in less than a decade, the mass consumption of television has gone from unhealthy to edgy to cool to mainstream to common? Along the way, the popular perception of television itself as both culture and technology has evolved from fuzzy idiot box to high-definition high art. While scholars note that the TV has gone through at least four significant changes over the last 50 years (Jenner 2018, 9–20), viewers tend to associate television's new 'golden age' with Netflix, streaming video technology and binge-watching (Steiner 2018). With that 'evolution', the couch potato trope became extinct, and the binge-viewer became the everyman. But that magical transformation narrative was not simply a matter of new technology, improved content and viewer empowerment. It was also part of a marketing campaign to promote the idea of improved television watching, from streaming video companies seeking to disrupt commercial television through a new kind of ambivalent audience control (Steiner 2017; Tryon 2015).

It is in the commercials of those new media stakeholders during the early years of that campaign where we find actual portrayals of the illusive binge-viewer. Following the satirical model of *Portlandia* and other viral binge-watching spoofs from 2012–14, these commercial binge-viewer portrayals came from streaming media companies and ancillary technology services corporations just as the term binge-watching was surging from obscurity to mainstream usage (Steiner 2018). While absurd, they became part of the cultural discourse on the emerging media practice. How those media companies constructed binge-viewers is remarkable for its perversion of traditional advertising norms and important to our understanding of contemporary audiences.

This chapter attempts to catalogue and organise those articulations as objects of commercial rhetoric. To do so, I conducted a close reading of twenty-five widely viewed, English language commercials from six large corporate players in contemporary media. I analysed those texts through the lens of narrative and social memory theory, discovering how these campaigns used twentieth-century fears of television and hyperbolic depictions of couch potatoes in mock public service announcements (PSAs) to construct binge-viewers (and their companies) as savvy, agentic and self-aware. Through their satirical depictions of binge-viewers in PSAs and the paternalism associated with network broadcast television (their competition), I argue that these companies positioned the users of their products as disrupters of low-quality mainstream mass media who were improving television through their mass consumption of it. These mediated articulations subversively embody the improvements in audience taste and television culture through technological affordances (that these companies offer), a narrative frequently reported by real-life viewers in the growing body of binge-watching literature (Perks 2015; Steiner and Xu 2020).

LITERATURE REVIEW

Advertising, nostalgia and identity

I approached the unpacking of these commercials from the perspective that the media facilitates the social construction of technology through media (Zelizer 1995). Social memories that shade contemporary understandings are co-produced (Jasanoff 2004) by individuals and groups, through artefacts, who diffuse understandings that are adopted through networks of interaction (Latour 2005). The advertising of media corporations creates cultural artefacts that serve to educate the public on the use and understanding of new technologies and media practices while simultaneously branding them for profit (Marchand 1985).

A core contention of collective memory theory is that social ideas of the past can be exploited by contemporary stakeholders for economic gain. Journalism may be the first draft of history, but advertising has long exploited nostalgia to appeal to viewers (Grainge 2000). 'Personal and historical nostalgia advertisements are linked to the consumer effects of, respectively, empathy and idealization of the self' (Stern 1992, 11). In advertising, though, 'the past that is vivified is one that never existed, for it is so idealized that any negative traces are screened out' (Stern 1992, 11). However, Grainge (2000) argues that nostalgia is more complex than commodification, and is 'a new kind of engagement with the past ... based fundamentally on its cultural mediation and textual reconfiguration of the present' (33). As Lizardi points out, nostalgia 'can function in a comparative sense, revealing the odd difference between then and now' (2014, 15). Following this logic, personal habits like TV watching may be capable of being reconstructed as 'branded space' (Banet-Weiser 2012, 14) in the personal and shared nostalgia of the binge-viewer, whose own identity is a co-mediated construction through advertising. These commercial depictions of binge-viewers are, therefore, vital artefacts in our understanding of how audiences identify themselves and how they view television. For Netflix and other streaming companies, 'binge-watching has become a structuring concept' (Jenner 2018, 115) vital to the flow of its content and how audiences are positioned by technology to experience it. Exploring their commercial rhetoric as for-profit instruction can help us better understand the reimagining of television and audiences in the second decade of the twenty-first century.

Rebranding moonshot: a PSA

In 2013, binge-watching presented something of a branding dilemma (Wallenstein 2013). Media companies, content producers and internet providers had a direct incentive for promoting binge-watching and celebrating the binge-viewer. As one celebrity in an *Entertainment Weekly* mock-PSA points out: 'The more you binge-watch, the more we binge-make' (*Entertainment Weekly* 2014). If media corporations profit from the mass consumption of streaming video properties, then it stands to reason that they would want their advertisements of the services that binge-watching facilitates to depict binge-viewers in an attractive fashion. But how do you make a couch potato on steroids desirable? As Tryon notes, '[p]opular discourse has historically treated television as a "vast wasteland," a drug, or junk food' (2015, 104). While that began changing gradually in the 1990s, the prevailing perceptions of TV, particularly large amounts of TV, were less than positive in 2012. No matter how new and improved a recipe might be, a food company rarely advertises how addictive its products are or promotes the negative consequences of gluttony. Cigarette companies may sell more cigarettes if everyone chain smokes, but they have yet to create a chain-smoking spokesperson. Alcohol companies have depicted their consumers doing just about everything in ads, everything except binge-drinking.

The easiest strategy would have been to drop the word 'binge', as Netflix founder Reed Hastings attempted at first (Seward 2013). But by 2013, when the Oxford Dictionary named 'binge watch' one of its Words of the Year (Oxford 2013), it was clear the term was firmly entrenched in the Western zeitgeist. 'Binge' had captured a delicious linguistic ambivalence: On the one hand, mainstream perceptions of TV watchers remained stubbornly tied to the unhealthy, slovenly couch potato trope. On the other, there was a growing underground movement of self-labelled binge-viewers who for years had used technology in attempts to cut the cord on corporate commercial control of their video consumption. By 2012, the press was beginning to report on these TV superfans (Pierce-Grove 2017) whose binge-watching practices were, much like remote controls 40 years early, 'subvert[ing] commercial television by allowing viewers to change channels during ad breaks' (Jenner 2019, 299). Media companies wishing to brand themselves as disruptors of commercial television were facing the advertising equivalent of the moon landing: How do you create a commercial that rebrands couch potatoes as cool, smart and in control for people who hate commercials? To do so, advertisers need a strawman that would be an immediately recognisable embodiment of why 'old TV' was uncool – cheap production, stock characters, tone-deafness, paternalism – a cultural object that could unite disruptor viewers with disruptor corporations and against the common enemy of commercial television. For this theme, they chose the most didactic of all mass media products, the public service announcement (PSA).

The more you know about PSAs

By the middle of the twentieth century, public service announcements (PSAs) began appearing across American televisions. These earnest attempts to raise awareness for issues of concern to the general public were aired on the major networks who 'donated' airtime as required by the Federal Communications Commission (FCC). Like most television of that time, PSAs contained low production values and simplistic stories aimed at a wide audience (Lloyd-Kolkin and Tyner 1991, 157). As Sopkin described it, '[t]he networks really don't want quality. They do *schlock* so much better, anyhow, why should they bother with quality? The audiences don't watch it – at least not in economically feasible numbers' (1968, 283; italics in the original).

Because of the fears associated with children's use of television (Himmelweit, Oppenheim and Vince, 1958), PSAs were seen as an opportunity to enhance the content of young American viewers through wholesome educational spots tucked in between commercial entertainment. If 1960s TV was 'schlock' (Sopkin 1968, 283), 1960s PSAs were low-budget, medicinal schlock. Commercial TV might have entertained at least, but PSAs nagged the viewers with officious messages and scare tactics from groups who, sometimes overtly, had other interests in mind than the public's well-being (Gregory 2004): Encouraging children to 'drink milk' at school may seem beneficial, but the fine print at the end of such ads revealed that American dairy interest groups were sponsoring the messages.

The obvious irony of PSAs is that the messages were meant to serve the public, but they were created by interest groups whose economic and political power allowed them to decide who the public was and what the public needed to learn. That determination was an unspoken announcement of authority and conformity over the public – paternalism. What PSAs of the twentieth century lacked was self-awareness in their messaging. They carried an unacknowledged and un-ironic paternalism evident in their constructions, values and assumptions about the audience (Haag 1957). Their patronising missives showed not that audiences of the time were too ignorant to know better, but that they lacked a voice with which to respond. The idea of an unquestionable authority telling you what is in everyone's interest while ignoring individuality and context became the shared understanding of PSAs – simplistic, campy and paternalistic. Comedy shows of the late twentieth century, such as *Saturday Night Live* (NBC 1975–) and *In Living Color* (Fox 1990–4), satirised their obvious hypocrisy. *The Simpsons* load many of their early episodes with PSA parodies. 'Hi, I'm Troy McClure . . .' may be as familiar to Gen Xers as 'Just say no!'. But it would be twenty-first-century advertisers of binge-watching services and technology who raised PSA subversion to a commercial art form. Their absurd depictions of binge-viewer behaviour and outcomes told through the lens of PSAs invited viewers to laugh at the paternalistic voices that called them couch potatoes by unapologetically consuming as much TV as they wanted, wherever and whenever they wanted to. While these commercials unabashedly acknowledge their interest in viewers binge-watching, their articulations also served as instructional artefacts on the uses and perceptions of the audiences they were cultivating.

METHOD

After extensive archival research of cable and streaming media service commercials from 2013–16, I found twenty-five suitable for this study. While search engines provide hundreds of thousands of videos that contain binge-watch or binge-viewer, only a handful are commercials from major media stakeholders. Of them, only twenty-five ads positioned binge-viewers and/or their behaviour as central to the commercial's narrative. These commercials also received significant attention online (shares and views), and they represent a selection of the major streaming video, cable, internet and television content providers in the United States (Amazon, Hulu, Netflix, Comcast, Cox Cable, TV, T-Mobile).

I conducted a close reading of the twenty-five commercials that led to an organisation of the texts through subversive use of twentieth-century PSAs. Adapting Stern's critical methodology, I employed textual and narrative analysis 'to locate manifestations of nostalgia in advertising text' (1992, 12). Since nostalgia in advertising can be a construction of multiple cues (Whalen, 1983), I noted structural, linguistic, musical, cinematic, verbal and thematic indicators during the analytical process (Chou and Lien 2010). I repeatedly viewed the videos, taking notes, coding and memoing until I reached a point of redundancy. I then organised the codes and categorised the data into three overlapping types: 'Deviant Addict'; 'Celebrity Public Service Announcements'; and 'Salvation & Recovery'. I then used these categories and codes to analyse how the commercials exploit social memory of twentieth-century TV to construct the binge-viewer.

FINDINGS

These commercials rely on humour to promote binge-watching and construct the binge-viewer. All of them lampoon the potential effects of binge-watching through absurd depictions of binge-viewers and alarmist, paternalistic warnings reminiscent of twentieth-century PSAs. The promos use mnemonic cues, such as camera angles, narrative structure, voice-over, graphics, sound effects and language to activate memories of PSAs. These devices serve to heighten the tension and fear of outcomes as if binge-watching were akin to drug addiction and mental disorders. This produces irony for any viewer who believes such outcomes are ridiculous. But the verisimilitude employed to recreate the past as both a golden age and a dark age – a simple, Halcyon time that was over-regulated by alarmist digital immigrants – transfers the irony onto the twentieth-century broadcast TV. Furthermore, it unifies those who get the joke against those who don't and organises them by technological acumen. The multi-layered irony separates first by digital native/digital immigrant status around the understanding of TV technology, and second by young/old in terms of perceptions of TV as a cultural object. At the same time, the irony is predicated on a collective memory of what twentieth-century PSAs looked like and a perception that the 'simpler time' was simpler in a closed-minded way. The binge-viewer is thereby cast as an evolved, sophisticated couch potato because of the technology, services and content being advertised.

Many of the promos feature celebrities who offer mock warnings about the dangers of binge-watching, which come across as even more ridiculous because of their uncanny facsimile of actual celebrity PSAs of the twentieth century. They satirise the notion that television could be addictive (Carpenter 1955) by providing polemic depictions of possible effects akin to the anti-marijuana propaganda film *Reefer Madness* (Glasnier 1936). The ironic outcomes of binge-watching are too fantastical to be taken seriously, but through their nostalgic framing and self-deprecation, they serve to other the culture and by proxy the technology of old TV, thereby differentiating and promoting contemporary streaming video products and services. The rhetorical effects are that binge-watching addiction is minimised by *reductio ad absurdum* while cultural criticism of television is othered by association with the strawman of twentieth-century PSA paternalism. Awareness and acknowledgement of the idiot box and couch potato serve as a paromologia. They seem to whisper: 'We know too much TV might not be good, but maybe it's more complicated than what authority figures preached in the twentieth century because we have more choices and better technological resources.' As Jenner writes:

> In the context of these narratives, individual viewers can avoid some of the worst assumed effects of television by choosing to watch 'good'

television. Ancillary technologies of television allow viewers to 'better' themselves by exerting control over the medium and watching 'good' television (2019, 301).

The construction, then, of the binge-viewer is not a direct reflection of these depictions but rather a reflection of the actual viewer who gets the joke by believing that twentieth-century TV and fears of TV addiction are outmoded and outside of contemporary streaming video consumption. Today a binge-viewer, the commercials imply, is savvy, agentic, self-aware, and culturally and technologically evolved. As a result, s/he is not afraid to get lost in a show because, unlike in the dark ages of twentieth-century broadcast television, TV is now so much better. Such a construction creates value for the services and ecosystems of binge-watching via social memory. Through mnemonic cues, it links the un-woke paternalism of PSAs with the exploitative simplicity of twentieth-century TV technology to craft a simplistic instantiation of the past coded in opposition to the complex, ironic present. The ads exploit that simplified past in the furtherance of their sponsors' economic ends. For the savvy binge-viewer, massive TV consumption becomes a counter-authoritarian act, any criticism of which seems as ludicrous and outmoded as PSAs.

Deviant addicts

The commercials in this category were structured around the action of a single character or a single couple and showed their experience of moral and psychological breakdowns as a) a result of a TV binge; or b) in order to facilitate a binge. The 30–60 second vignettes are shot mostly with close-ups and medium shots of the bingers consuming mindlessly. They contain little or no voice-over and focus instead on the ridiculous actions of the binge-viewer characters. The sense of deprivation in them is exaggerated by the playing of dreary minor chord background music reminiscent of PSAs about drug and sexual abuse.

In Hulu's 'No Commercials Plan – Weepy' (2015), a single, young woman becomes so engrossed in an emotional TV show on her tablet that she cries continuously while staring at the screen. Her tears never cease as she wanders about her home attempting normal behaviour – eating, receiving a delivery – without taking her tearful eyes off the tablet. In the process she burns through cases of toilet paper and Kleenex, even going so far as to blow-dry tears from her face, without looking away from the show. Her binge never ends, because, as the concluding voice-over explains, '[o]nce the emotions start they don't stop'. Such single-minded immersion is made possible thanks to Hulu's new commercial-free option.

In the Cox Communications promo 'Delivery Guy' (2015), a female–male couple begins to binge-watch a show on their living room couch after the delivery of a pizza. A series of repetitive close and medium shots shows time passing through the repeated pizza deliveries and the man's growing facial hair. The couple's descent into compulsive viewing is indicated by their neglect of household cleaning and personal hygiene over the days of their binge: mail begins to pile up outside the front door; their living room grows cluttered with old pizza boxes. The extent of their psychological 'downfall' is also reflected by the returning pizza delivery guy character who remains well-groomed but becomes increasingly concerned about the couple's well-being after each delivery. At first, the male viewer tells Delivery Guy that he doesn't want him to spoil the show. As he sinks deeper into the binge, he pleads manically with the delivery man to tell him what happens, presumably so he can break free from the show's grip. The minute-long ad ends with Delivery Guy running away from the home as a voice-over proclaims: 'With a thousand hours of DVR storage and the best of HBO on demand, Cox is the official sponsor of binge watching.'

Xfinity's 2015 spot, 'Cold,' shows a white, female, elementary school teacher eating her student's sandwich, after he sneezes on it, in order to make herself sick so she can stay home and binge during Xfinity Watchathon Week. An on-screen graphic reads: Common Cold Recovery Time: 1 Week. The music remains ominously flat, and the camera angles are similar to others in this category, but the narrative of 'Cold' does not centre on the effects of a single binge. Instead, it focuses on the dangerous and deviant ends 'people who love TV' will go to in order to take advantage of Xfinity's week of free premium on-demand programming.

This category of promos mimics addiction PSAs of the 1980s and 1990s, which depict the progression of a single character's downfall into deviance and the morally questionable choices that addicts make to get their fixes. The simplistic cause-and-effect logic is also reminiscent of Ad Council PSAs and school film strips of the 1940s-1970s, which portray the dangers that bad habits, such as slovenliness, can bring to young Americans (Besco 1952). The first two ads feature a delivery person who serves not only as a foil for the absurdity but as an embodied representation of the on-demand convenience of streaming video culture and post-industrial identity (Banet-Weiser 2012). In 'Cold', that on-demand identity is demonstrated through displays of X1 menus reflecting against the smiling, though still sniffling, countenance of the teacher laid up in bed and surrounded by tissues.

Celebrity Public Service Announcements

These spots are overt parodies of NBC's 'One to Grow On' and 'The More You Know' PSAs, which premiered in 1983 and were often aired during commercial breaks and at the conclusion of children's programming and sitcoms. They featured celebrities, usually actors from the show that just aired, facing the camera against a neutral background and speaking directly to the viewers about avoiding drugs, alcohol or other temptations. Ironically, these PSAs were sometimes part of community service sentences the celebrities had to fulfil to make restitution for crimes committed while under the influence of drugs or alcohol.

Netflix's 'Binge Responsibly' campaign uses nearly identical cinematic and linguistic structures and musical effects as 'The More You Know'. Actors from the streaming service's original content look directly at the viewers and warn them about the dangers of binge-watching. Michael Kelly, political hatchet man Douglas Stamper in *House of Cards* (Netflix 2013–18), advises viewers to 'go outside, take a walk, get some fresh air'. Taylor Schilling, star of *Orange is the New Black* (Netflix 2013–19), implores viewers to remember a time 'before you discovered all these great shows on Netflix . . . You used to have a real life, with real friends you could hug.' Linda Cardellini, of *Bloodline* (Netflix 2015–17), asks knowing rhetorical questions of viewers about their sleep deprivation and poor hygiene. She speaks in a maternal tone that seeks to relieve the pain that she knows binge-viewers are living with. The thirteen spots were streamed on 1 April 2015, to any viewer who watched more than two episodes in a row on Netflix. Online versions were also released, and many viewers shared them through social media. Musically and cinematically they closely mimic NBC's 'The More You Know', including a cheerful bell tone at the end accompanied by a cartoonish 'Binge Responsibly' logo with stars scrolling across the screen during the PSA's final seconds. In 'The More You Know', the celebrities were not participating voluntarily or potentially taking the message seriously, but the assumption was that the audience was ignorant of the motives and receptive to the message. In 'Binge Responsibly', the viewer is rewarded by awareness of the irony, like an inside joke Easter egg, which s/he can share in a demonstration of fandom. At the same time, those who take it seriously are positioned outside the April Fool gag. As a result, the satire minimises the discomfort or isolation of some viewers and the credulity for actual binge-watching side-effects, which some have argued exist (Sung, Kang and Wee 2015).

Because of its Easter egg quality, the 'Binge Responsibly' campaign went viral through the social media of viewers who caught the ads. Its ironic positioning caught the attention of mainstream media as well who shared clips of the commercials on TV and online news sites providing Netflix with a hefty stream of free advertising. It also sparked numerous fan tributes, such as 'PSA for Millennials: The 5 Stages of Binge Watching' and 'The Dangers of Netflix PSA', which further solidified the exaggerated side-effects and consequences for binge-viewers.

Addiction and salvation

Promos in this category contain elements of the other two, but they also offer redemption from the dangerous effects of binge-watching through the embracing of a company's content or technology. As with life choice PSAs, the dangers are not well contextualised, though they are presented as frightful. The solutions are presented as binary choices, as simply achievable as just saying 'no', drinking milk, or switching to an unlimited streaming video plan. Any questions!

Amazon Fire TV's 'Show Hole' (2015) depicts a young woman's trauma at the end of a 58-hour binge. As the 'final, final credits' run, the background music shifts from cheerful to ominous in less than a second. Colour washes out of her living room. The voice-over, provided by Malcolm McDowell (who, as Alex in *A Clockwork Orange* [Kubrick, 1971], was subjected to one of the most memorable forced video binges in cinematic history) proclaims: 'You've fallen in the 'Show Hole'. This fictional malady is an allusion to 'k-hole' a traumatic feeling of dissociation reported by some users of the drug ketamine (Curran and Monaghan 2001). The distraught woman, alone on a couch, is bathed in grey as the foreboding music closes in on her. To compensate, she knits compulsively as McDowell explains: 'The struggle could not be more real. Why even have a TV?' There is a two-second shot of her, still in pyjamas, shovelling dirt onto the grave of her half-buried television set. But before all hope is lost, McDowell proclaims: 'Then you see it! Amazon Fire TV's vast library of best shows ever!'. Instantly the music shifts back to cheerful tones. As the warm lighting returns, the woman's flat affect attempts to smile. 'So long Show Hole', McDowell declares as endless menus of 'high-brow' programming dance across the screen, their glow reflecting off the woman's pale cheeks.

A second 'Show Hole' spot carries over McDowell's voice-over to the story of a white, female–male couple watching TV in bed. The scene opens with an establishing shot of the bedroom with the man holding a remote control as the couple stares at an old cable TV guide screen. McDowell states: 'You've spent more time looking for a show than watching it. She's over it.' We zoom to a close-up of the woman who rolls her eyes disapprovingly and turns over in bed as the music shifts from cheery to dreary. A puff of smoke rolls in the bedroom door and the colour drains from the room. The couple is suddenly lying in a hellish landscape of smoke and rocks. Their bed splits in half. The husband reaches for his sleeping partner as she is pulled along with the bed board, sheets and blanket into the underworld off camera. 'Will you TV drift apart?', McDowell asks sinisterly. 'Will she go back to her TV ex?' The husband now stands in the rain outside their bedroom window as a snarky American football player lies in bed next to the woman who snuggles against his shoulder pad. 'No! You've got Amazon Fire TV'. The man breaks the glass and stands triumphantly over his partner and her paramour as a user interface of premium channel shows scrolls powerfully behind him: 'Its TV brain knows your TV heart.' Cheerful music returns and the couple lie again in each other's arms laughing with the TV show. 'Yes,' McDowell concludes, 'make up binging is the best! So long Show Hole!'

T-Mobile's 'Binge Watchers Anonymous with Aaron Paul' (2015) incorporates addiction nostalgia and a celebrity guide (who happened to portray a meth addict in the often-binged AMC drama *Breaking Bad* [AMC 2008–13]), and plays with the idea of rehabilitation for the over-immersion effects depicted in 'Dangers' (Pratt et al. 2014). The three promos for this campaign are all set in a dark basement at a meeting of 'Binge-Watchers Anonymous', a fictional self-help group run by Paul. In the first promo, Paul encourages a man named Jerry to share. He begins to tell his story, but Paul interrupts him when it becomes obvious that Jerry is describing the life of a character from the first season of *True Detective* (HBO 2014–). Trying again, Jerry adopts a British accent and describes the Stark family from *Game of Thrones* (HBO 2011–19). Frustrated, Paul asks him to 'tell us about the real Jerry'. Jerry takes a deep breath, and then he provides the backstory of Walter White, the main character in Paul's show *Breaking Bad*. As the other attendees begin to complain, Paul quiets them and tells Jerry, 'Go on, I think I like this one'. The screen jumps to a T-Mobile logo with a voice-over introducing T-Mobile's BingeOn: a data plan that allows users to stream unlimited video content.

In the second promo, a woman explains her despair about being on the bus and binge-watching uncontrollably. 'I don't even want to think about the overages!' Paul consoles her, saying 'It's okay, now that T-Mobile has gotten rid of overages for streaming video'. A surprised attendee asks if it's okay that he 'binged an entire season during my kid's piano recital?'. Jerry admits that he has done that too. 'Yup,' Paul assures them before stating, 'I think we've made some real progress today.' Another attendee who had been bingeing looks up from his phone and says 'what?'.

The third promo features Paul welcoming a woman to the group and encouraging her to pull out her phone to watch. When she asks: 'isn't this binge-watchers anonymous?', Paul explains that 'it was. Then T-Mobile started letting people stream all the video they want without the shame of having to pay for extra data.' The shame of binge-watching, and perhaps addiction, has neatly been transferred to a question of economics rather than of culture or health.

Promos in this category treat the absurd side-effects of binge-watching as a reality of modern media culture. They reinterpret those dangers to solve actual technological and economic issues that streaming video users may experience – expensive bandwidth and diffuse content. They also play with the nostalgia of one-dimensional addiction and salvation stories popularised in the after-school special and Movie of the Week genres of twentieth-century TV. Doing so minimises the notion that losing control of one's video consumption is something worth addressing if you can afford to lose control with great content and technology. Actual TV addiction could exist only in our collective memory of twentieth-century TV because today we can choose what and how we are addicted.

DISCUSSION

Through their parody of twentieth-century TV culture's authoritarian and campy PSAs, these promos complicated connotations of the word 'binge' while branding contemporary TV culture, and associated products and services, as other than broadcast television. The producers exploit collective memory in their simplified instantiation of twentieth-century TV to paint criticism of couch potatoes as passé and overly simplistic for today's self-aware binge-viewer. PSAs and broadcast television represent conformity and simple messaging for a homogenous mass known as *audience*. The binge-viewer, by contrast, is individualistic, complex, autonomous.

Through the mnemonic othering of twentieth-century TV, the producers of these ads exploit the irrationality of TV addiction fears to create a technocultural fantasy: We are in what David Bianculli (2016) calls the Platinum Age of TV; binge-watching is cool. This plays against the idiot box identity created by twentieth-century stakeholders – parents, corporations, educators, regulators – preaching the dangers of TV to the masses generally and children specifically (Halpern 1975; Laurent 1957). Doing so identifies past technologies as outmoded along with the alarmist fears they carry. The message implies that culture and technology have evolved and matured and so, too, has the viewer: The couch potato is dead, long live the binge-viewer! In form and function, the commercials evoke memories of a 'simple' past when PSA producers lacked the self-awareness to see how ridiculously ironic their messaging was. The strategy reinforces the contemporary news narrative that TV has evolved through its technology, while celebrities endorse the cultural cool of doing something your parents told you was bad.

Stating that you were a binge-viewer in 2020 was less a confession of addiction than it was a proclamation of your cultural bona fides and technical savvy. Presidents proudly fess up to their binge-watching, as seen on *The Late Show with Stephen Colbert* (2015). Today it is the norm of television; we are all bingeviewers. The term's popularity is partially attributable to its subversive signification and to its rebellious reclamation of that which was once perceived as dangerous and low-brow: excessive TV watching. Today it is so commonplace that some argue it is passé (Jenner 2019). But these early constructions of bingeviewers helped shape the complex and nuanced assemblage of contemporary TV through reflection rather than prescription. Binge-viewers are not the caricatures in the ads; they are the complicated negotiation of culture, technology and memory behind them. Technology empowers the audience to control the time, place and manner of their consumption (Hills 2015); audiences use technology to share and generate culture in ways that influence content producers (Roffman 2016). Corporations use that narrative to capture subscriptions. And TV evolves, or so the post-industrial story goes. Binge-watching is, therefore, a symbolic re-articulation of audience control ironically performed by audiences losing control through the technology they control.

REFERENCES

Banet-Weiser, S. (2012). *Authentic™: The Politics of Ambivalence in a Brand Culture*. New York: New York University Press.
Besco, G. S. (1952). 'Television and its Effects'. *English Journal* 41(3): 151.
Bianculli, D. (2016). *The Platinum Age of Television*. New York: Doubleday.
Braun, K. A., R. Ellis and E. F. Loftus (2002). 'Make My Memory: How Advertising Can Change our Memories of the Past'. *Psychology and Marketing* 19(1): 1–23.
Carpenter, C. R. (1955). 'Psychological Research Using Television'. *American Psychologist* 10(10): 606–10.
Castro, D., J. M. Rigby, D. Cabral and V. Nisi (2019). 'The Binge-Watcher's Journey: Investigating Motivations, Contexts, and Affective States Surrounding Netflix Viewing'. *Convergence* 27(1): 3–20.
Choi, M. (2012). 'Can't Stop Won't Stop: In Praise of Binge TV Consumption'. *Wired* 20(1). Available at: <https://web.archive.org/web/20141024153102/http://www.wired.com/2011/12/pl_column_tvseries/> (last accessed 10 March 2021).
Chou, H. and N. Lien (2010). 'Advertising Effects of Songs' Nostalgia and Lyrics' Relevance'. *Asia Pacific Journal of Marketing and Logistics* 22(3): 314–29.
Curran, H. V. and L. Monaghan (2001). 'In and Out of the K-hole: A Comparison of the Acute and Residual Effects of Ketamine in Frequent and Infrequent Ketamine Users'. *Addiction* 96(5): 749–60.
Flayelle, M., N. Canale, C. Vögele, L. Karila, P. Maurage and J. Billieux (2019). 'Assessing Binge-Watching Behaviors: Development and Validation of the "Watching TV Series Motives" and "Binge-Watching Engagement and Symptoms" questionnaires'. *Computers in Human Behavior* 90, 26–36.
Gangadharbatla, H., C. Ackerman and A. Bamford (2019). 'Antecedents and Consequences of Binge-Watching for College Students'. *First Monday* 24(12).
Genette, G. (1980). *Narrative Discourse: An Essay in Method*. Ithaca, NY: Cornell.
Grainge, P. (2000). 'Nostalgia and Style in Retro America: Moods, Modes, and Media Recycling'. *Journal of American and Comparative Cultures* 23(1): 27–34.
Gregory, D. (2004). *Change your Underwear Twice a Week: Lessons from the Golden Age of the Classroom Filmstrips*. New York: Artisan.
Haag, E. V. D. (1957). *The Menace of Mass Media*. New York: New Leader Publishing Association.
Halpern, W. I. (1975). 'The Effects of Television on Children and Adolescents: Turned-on Toddlers'. *The Journal of Communication* 25(4): 66.
Harlow, J. (2012). 'Hollywood biteback'. *The Sunday Times*. 22 July. Available at: <https://www.thetimes.co.uk/article/hollywood-biteback-3qdkthco9sz> (last accessed 10 March 2021).

Hills, M. (2015). 'The Expertise of Digital Fandom as a "Community of Practice": Exploring the Narrative Universe of Doctor Who'. *Convergence: The International Journal of Research into New Media Technologies* 21(3): 360–74.

Himmelweit, H. T., A. N. Oppenheim and P. Vince (1958). *Television and the Child: An Empirical Study of the Effect of Television on the Young*. New York; London: Published for the Nuffield Foundation by the Oxford University Press.

Jasanoff, S. (2004). *States of Knowledge: The Co-Production of Science and Social Order*. London: Routledge.

Jenner, M. (2018). *Netflix and the Re-invention of Television*. Basingstoke: Palgrave.

Jenner, M. (2019). 'Control Issues: Binge-Watching, Channel-Surfing and Cultural Value'. *Participations* 16(2): 298–317.

Latour, B. (2005). *Reassembling the Social: An Introduction to Actor-Network Theory*. Oxford: Oxford University Press.

Laurent, B. L. (1957, July 12). 'Child's TV addiction follows adult pattern'. *The Washington Post and Times Herald*.

Lizardi, R. (2014). *Mediated Nostalgia: Individual Memory and Contemporary Mass Media*. Washington, DC: Lexington Books.

Lloyd-Kolkin, D. and K. Tyner (1991). *Media & You*. Englewood Cliffs, NJ: Educational Technology Publications.

Lotz, A. (2014). *The Television will be Revolutionized* (2nd edition). New York: New York University Press.

Marechal, A. J. (2013). 'Next level for Netflix: Netcaster Aims to be Considered a Serious Player with Original Programming, but on its Own Terms'. *Daily Variety* 318(4): 1.

Marchand, R. (1985). *Advertising the American Dream: Making Way for Modernity, 1920–1940*. Berkeley: University of California Press.

Mendelsohn, H. (1989). 'Socio-Psychological Construction and the Mass Communication Effects Dialectic'. *Communication Research* 16, 813–23.

Merikivi, J., J. Bragge, E. Scornavacca and T. Verhagen (2019). 'Binge-Watching Serialized Video Content: A Transdisciplinary Review'. *Television & New Media* 21(7): 697–711.

Merrill Jr, K. and B. Rubenking (2019). 'Go Long or Go Often: Influences on Binge Watching Frequency and Duration among College Students'. *Social Sciences* 8(10).

Perks, L. G. (2019). 'Media Marathoning and Health Coping'. *Communication Studies* 70(1): 19–35.

Pierce-Grove, R. (2017). 'Just One More: How Journalists Frame Binge Watching'. *First Monday* 22(1/2): 1.

Pittman, M. and E. Steiner (2019). 'Transportation or Narrative Completion? Attentiveness during Binge-Watching Moderates Regret'. *Social Sciences* 8, 99.

Pittman, M. and E. Steiner (2021). 'Distinguishing Feast-Watching from Cringe-Watching: Planned, Social, and Attentive Binge-Watching Predicts Increased Well-Being and Decreased Regret'. *Convergence*. doi: <10.1177/1354856521999183>

Roffman, M. (2016). 'Social media: how fans do (and don't) impact TV storylines'. *TV Insider*. Available at: <https://www.tvinsider.com/91578/social-media-how-fans-do-and-dont-impact-tv-storylines> (last accessed 10 March 2021).

Sender, K. (2012). *The Makeover: Reality Television and Reflexive Audiences*. New York: New York University Press.

Seward, Z. M. (2013). 'Netflix is doing to TV what steam-powered printing did to books'. *Quartz*. Available at: <https://qz.com/127967/netflix-is-doing-to-tv-what-steam-powered-printing-did-to-books> (last accessed 20 February 2020).

Sopkin, C. (1968). *Seven Glorious Days, Seven Fun-Filled Nights: One Man's Struggle to Survive a Week Watching Commercial Television in America*. New York: Simon and Schuster.

Steiner, E. (2017). 'Binge-Watching in Practice: The Rituals, Motives, and Feelings of Netflix Streaming Video Viewers'. In M. Wiatrowski and C. Barker (eds), *A Netflix Reader: Critical Essays on Streaming Media, Digital Delivery, and Instant Access*. Jefferson, NC: McFarland, pp. 141–61.

Steiner, E. (2018). 'Binge-Watching Killed the Idiot Box: The Changing Identities of Viewers and Television in the Experiential, Streaming Video Age'. Ph.D. dissertation, Temple University, Philadelphia, PA, USA.

Steiner, E. and Xu, K. (2020) 'Binge-Watching Motivates Change: Uses and Gratifications of Streaming Video Viewers Challenge Traditional TV Research'. *Convergence* 26(1): 82–101.

Stern, B. B. (1992). 'Historical and Personal Nostalgia in Advertising Text: The Fin de Siècle Effect'. *Journal of Advertising* 21(4): 11–22.

Sung, Y. H., E. Y. Kang and L. Wee (2015). *A Bad Habit for Your Health? An Exploration of Psychological Factors for Binge-Watching Behavior*. In 65th ICA Annual Conference Puerto Rico.

Tefertiller, A. and L. Maxwell (2018) 'Depression, Emotional States, and the Experience of Binge-Watching Narrative Television'. *Atlantic Journal of Communication* 26(5), 278–90.

Tryon, C. (2015). 'TV Got Better: Netflix's Original Programming Strategies and Binge Viewing'. *Media Industries Journal* 2(2): 104–16.

Wallenstein, A. (2013). 'Breaking Binge: Time to Cook Up New Catch Phrases for Streaming'. *Variety* 321(4): 27.

Walton-Pattison, E., S. U. Dombrowski and J. Presseau, (2018). '"Just one more episode": Frequency and Theoretical Correlates of Television Binge Watching'. *Journal of Health Psychology* 23(1): 17–24.

Westcott, K., J. Loucks, K. Downs and J. Watson (2018). 'Digital media trends survey: A new world of choice for digital consumers'. *Deloitte Insights*. Available at: <https://www2.deloitte.com/uk/en/insights/industry/technology/digital-media-trends-consumption-habits-survey-2018.html> (last accessed 10 March 2021).

Whalen, B. (1983). 'Semiotics: An Art or Powerful Research Tool?' *Marketing News* (17): 8.

Williams, R. (1973). *The Country and the City*. New York: Oxford University Press.

Zelizer, B. (1995). 'Reading the Past against the Grain: The Shape of Memory Studies'. *Critical Studies in Mass Communication* 12(2): 214–39.

TV

All in the Family (1971–9), USA: CBS
Beavis and Butt-Head (1993–2011), USA: MTV
Breaking Bad (2008–13), USA: AMC
Game of Thrones (2011–19), USA: HBO
Late Show with Stephen Colbert, The (2015–), USA: CBS
Married . . . with Children (1987–97), USA: Fox
Portlandia (2011–18), USA: IFC
Saturday Night Live (1975–), USA: NBC
Simpsons, The (1989–), USA: Fox
Sopranos, The (1999–2007), USA: HBO
True Detective (2014–), USA: HBO
Wire, The (2002–8), USA: HBO

ADVERTISEMENTS

Amazon Fire TV (2015). 'Show Hole'. *Amazon*. Available at: <http://www.ispot.tv/ad/Aw_U/amazon-fire-tv-show-hole> (last accessed 16 February 2020).
Cox Communications (2015). 'Delivery Guy'. Available at: <https://www.youtube.com/watch?v=PqwTOs_2xqs> (last accessed 16 February 2020).
Entertainment Weekly (2014). 'Chris Pratt, Amy Poehler, Laura Prepon & More on Dangers of Binge Watching'. Available at: <https://www.youtube.com/watch?v=gfmTcT2cfC8> (last accessed 16 February 2020).
Hulu (2015). No Commercials Plan – Weepy. Available at: <http://www.ispot.tv/ad/AV_b/hulu-no-commercials-plan-weepy-song-by-tobias-jesso-jr> (last accessed 16 February 2020).
Netflix (2015). 'Binge Responsibly'. Available at: <https://www.youtube.com/watch?v=HSVjIU6fzeE> (last accessed 16 February 2020).
T-Mobile (2015). 'Binge Watchers Anonymous with Aaron Paul'. Available at: <https://www.ispot.tv/ad/A2M1/t-mobile-binge-on-binge-watchers-anonymous-featuring-aaron-paul> (last accessed 16 February 2020).
Xfinity (2015). 'Cold'. *Xfinity Watchathon Week*. Available at: <http://www.ispot.tv/ad/7iLX/xfinity-watchathon-week-cold> (last accessed 16 February 2020).

FILM

Gasnier, L. (1936) *Reefer Madness*. USA: G & H Productions.
Kubrick, S. (1971). *A Clockwork Orange*. USA: Warner Bros Entertainment Inc.

CHAPTER 6

Binge-Watching Conditions and Multitasking: The Enjoyable Ephemeral

Lisa Glebatis Perks

A 2013 Netflix survey of binge-watchers revealed that over half of the study population was 'willing to exercise while binge watching' (Netflix 2013). But don't dust off that treadmill just yet: what people are *willing* to do and what they *actually* do can be quite different. Drawing from a survey of 120 people who binge-watched at least two shows in the past 12 months, this chapter presents a picture of the where, when, why, how and with whom of binge-watching. This picture of binge-watching behaviours helps us to more clearly see patterns in multitasking habits, group viewing and genre preferences, as linked (or not) to viewers' levels of cognitive involvement in the narrative. And, spoiler alert: there were no exercising binge-watchers among the survey respondents.

Attentiveness, involvement and immersion have received much attention in binge-watching scholarship. Media engagement can occur along many dimensions, including cognitive, behavioural or affective (see, for example, Merikivi et al. 2018; Nabi and Krcmar 2004; Perks 2015; Tukachinsky and Eyal 2018). But does media engagement through the practice of binge-watching usually involve narrative transportation, immersion or other forms of cognitive engagement? In my 2015 monograph, the majority of media marathoners I interviewed behaved as 'residents' in their text's story world, 'soaking in many engaging [textual] details and nuances' (Perks 2015, 63). A more recent quantitative study by Tukachinsky and Eyal (2018) concluded that, compared to traditional television viewing, 'marathon viewing is associated with active media engagement and more meaningful, reflective, and deeper forms of appreciation' (290). Furthermore, Sun, Kang and Lee (2019, 417) found a significant and positive relationship between the number of episodes viewed and media transportation. Greater attentiveness to a show, Pittman and Steiner (2019, 11) concluded in a test of several hypotheses, had an inverse relationship with 'post-binge regret'.

The rewards (or, perhaps, diminished costs) of an attentive binge-watch have extensive support, yet there are many other ways to be a viewer. In their quantitative research on binge-watchers' cognitive and behavioural involvement, Merikivi et al. found 'support for distracted and somewhat homogeneous' viewing patterns, also noting that viewers do not think 'binge watching requires active cognitive efforts to gain satisfaction' (2018, 118). Steiner and Xu advocate for a Viewer Attentiveness Spectrum rather than a dichotomy because their qualitative study revealed that binge-watcher 'attentiveness varies and sways depending on the genres and plots of the shows they decide to watch' (2020, 96). This spectrum, they argue, can help researchers 'focus on the attention allocation and task switching behavior in the process of media use' (2020, 96). This study furthers that line of research, examining multitasking behaviours in conjunction with other factors such as demographics, viewing conditions, genres, attentiveness and self-reported gratifications. Additionally, this study compares two separate binge-watching experiences (labelled Show I and Show II) from all participants, working to distil situational or more enduring binge-watching behaviours.

The aggregate findings reported in this chapter paint a picture of a binge-watcher who streams content in the late afternoons or evenings, at home, and most often in the bedroom. More often than not, they will complete a full season of the show in a week. There's about a 50% chance that this viewer will multitask during some or all of their binge-watches. If they do multitask (and they're very likely to do so if self-employed), their preferred activities are eating, using the internet, and using social media. The binge-watcher is motived to multitask because the combined activities can make mundane activities more exciting and can lead to a magnified sense of productivity or relaxation. This multitasking happens irrespective of genre or the perceived cognitive effort to process the television content. In sum, the viewer weaves this binge-watch into their everyday domestic experience, adapting it to their location preferences, their activity needs/wants, and their cognitive availability.

After describing the method and participant demographics, this chapter analyses viewing conditions and then multitasking motivations before turning to generic and cognitive involvement factors. The chapter concludes by addressing the implications of binge-watching as a commonly passive, pleasurable and memorable viewing experience.

METHOD

After receiving Institutional Review Board approval for this research, the survey was deployed in 2019 through Amazon's Mechanical Turk (mTurk) human intelligence marketplace. Participants qualified for the study if they had binge-watched at least two separate shows in the 12 months prior to the survey. Two shows were required for comparative purposes – to see whether binge-watcher behaviours were consistent or more situational. Binge-watching was defined as watching three or more episodes in one day. The survey included a mix of open- and closed-ended items that asked about viewing conditions, other activities concurrently with viewing, and viewing/bingeing motivations. Participants were also asked four cognitive involvement scale items, two multitasking items, and demographics questions. The study received 125 responses. One survey was removed for being incomplete, and four were removed for having answers that were not related to the open-ended questions.

Demographics

The final population of 120 respondents had an age range of 21–62, averaging 34.4 with a median of 32. When asked the open-ended question about gender identity, 77 participants typed in 'male', 'man' or 'm' and 37 typed in 'female'. Participants were also asked the following open-ended question: 'What race(s) and/or ethnicity/ethnicities do you identify with?' Eighty-eight participants wrote 'white' or 'caucasian', 11 wrote 'Asian', seven wrote 'black', and four wrote 'African American'. With respect to unique identities, but also to acknowledge their sizeable presence in the data as a collective group, it is worth noting that three participants (one in each category) identified as Latino, Mexican or Hispanic.

In terms of education, the majority of participants reported earning a bachelor's degree ($n = 61$) or having some college education but no degree ($n = 28$). High-school diploma or equivalent was the next most prevalent group ($n = 15$), followed by participants with an associate's degree ($n = 10$) or a graduate degree ($n = 6$). Two people reported 'other' educational attainment. Because living alone or with others could relate to one's binge-watching habits, participants were also asked about their living situation. Living alone was most common ($n = 34$), followed by living with a spouse or partner ($n = 31$), living with a spouse or partner and children/dependents ($n = 27$), living with a roommate/roommates ($n=12$) and living with extended family ($n = 10$). Other participants reported living with their children/dependents ($n = 4$) or another arrangement ($n = 2$).

VIEWING CONDITIONS

Because this study focused on everyday binge-watching experiences, many of the survey's initial questions asked about how people were watching and about their viewing conditions. Some questions had surprisingly homogeneous results that aligned with the image of a typical television viewer who comes home from work and turns on the television in prime time. For example, the majority of respondents were binge-watching in the late afternoon or evening/night (84.1% Show I; 85% Show II), and they were typically viewing in the bedroom (58.8% Show I; 53.3% Show II) or living room (30.8% Show I; 30.8% Show II).

The binge-watch-friendly bedroom was a somewhat surprising finding, considering that many of the other binge-watching conditions were quite traditional. Gauntlett and Hill described the television functioning '*socially*, as a locus of attention and social interaction' in a household (1999, 35, *emphasis in original*). The prevalence of bedroom binge-watching suggests that any screen with television content can now function as a locus of *individualised comfort*, offering the ability to watch in the most private and relaxing place in one's home. Although bedroom TV sets pre-date binge-watching, mobile devices and streaming 'untether' TV, making it even easier to watch a show mere feet from where we lay our heads (Bury 2017, 64). Scholars have highlighted the importance of convenience and agency in the set of practices that comprise and define binge-watching (see Jenner 2018; Steiner 2017). The study findings in this chapter also place *comfort* on that list.

The majority of participants access their content through streaming (85.8% Show I; 82.5% Show II). Despite the portability of streaming and its compatible viewing devices, only three male participants (ages 25, 26 and 33) watched one of their shows on-the-go or in other spaces outside of the home. One contrary example of a mobile binge-watcher is a 26-year-old Asian man who watched *Bigg Boss* (an Indian reality television show modelled on *Big Brother*) (Sony TV 2006–7, Colors TV 2007–) at 'home and office lunch breaks and travel times' on a varied combination of screens: TV screen, laptop, tablet and mobile/cell. 'Entertainment' was his sole motivation to binge. Watching *Game of Thrones* (HBO 2011–19) at home and at the library, a 33-year-old white man noted that he 'always binges' and found the weekly release of new *Game of Thrones* episodes to be 'tough'.

This low number of on-the-go binge-watchers stands in contrast to Bury's finding that a quarter of the 671 TV viewers she surveyed in 2010 'engaged in mobile viewing while traveling' (2017, 64). Neither of the two surveys (this one or Bury's) derives from representative samples; however, the stark difference between the on-the-go rates could indicate that binge-viewers generally prefer domestic sites, that travelling is for watching TV but not binge-watching, *or* that people are increasingly turning to other types of entertainment (for example, audiobooks or podcasts) while on the go.

Even if they were still watching mostly in the home, a convenience of streaming was that it enabled roughly a quarter of participants to binge on a combination of screens, some static and some portable ($n = 32$ [26.6%] Show

I multiple screens; $n = 26$ [21.6%] Show II multiple screens). The ability to bring a laptop, tablet or mobile phone into the bedroom, kitchen, home office, sewing room or other space helped participants to intricately weave the binge-watch through their domestic sphere. Nine participants cited multiple domestic viewing spaces for Show I and three cited multiple domestic viewing spaces for Show II. Of those who binge-watched on multiple screens, the greatest percentage viewed in one room: the bedroom ($n = 13$ Show I; $n = 11$ Show II). These different screens in the same room may have been used to switch from work to binge-watching (on a laptop), to move from binge-watching to reading (on a tablet), to multitask while viewing, or any number of task-switching or multitasking scenarios, depending on one's needs in a given day.

The 'most binged' content from the survey also favoured streaming, with three out of five titles *primarily* available through streaming services (although illegal downloads were certainly possible and some titles were available on DVD): *Stranger Things* (Netflix 2016– ; $n = 23$), *Game of Thrones* ($n = 20$; airing live on HBO and streaming on HBO GO), *Orange is the New Black* (Netflix 2013–19; $n = 14$), *The Boys* (Amazon 2019– ; $n = 8$), *The Office* (NBC 2005–13; $n = 7$; airing in reruns on network and cable television, plus streaming on Netflix in the US). Of note, all but one person who binged *The Office* did so by streaming, only three *Game of Thrones* viewers used a combination of streaming and episode downloads, and only one *Game of Thrones* viewer watched solely on DVD. No participant viewed *Game of Thrones* live, despite the last season airing during this study's time period. These findings bolster Jenner's argument that Netflix has used binge-watching as a way to promote its original content and that streaming has been positioned 'not as an alternative to television, but *as* television' (2018, 4).

In terms of co-viewing (viewing with at least one other person), 36.6% ($n = 44$) of participants watched at least a few episodes of Show I with someone else, and 25.8% ($n = 31$) reported the same for Show II. Much of this co-viewing was intentional. For example, a 29-year-old white man stated, '[m]e and my girlfriend both decided we were going to spend the whole weekend finishing the season [of *Stranger Things*]'. Re-watching favourite content happened intentionally: '[M]y friend and I have been following the series since the beginning and wanted to rewatch' (white woman, 34, *Orange is the New Black*). Couples didn't have set viewing patterns for all shows, but rather made co-binge decisions based on specific content. A 37-year-old white woman binged *Russian Doll* (Netflix 2019–) with her husband 'since we were sucked into the story line', but when it came to *Stranger Things*, her husband only 'watched once or twice with me because he walked into the room'. The comparison of individuals binge-watching two separate shows often pointed to disparate viewing situations and experiences instead of consistent patterns, rituals or viewing traits. These findings dovetail with what Lothar Mikos and Deborah Castro observe in their chapter in this part where they argue: 'a mutual interest in the content is pivotal: the social viewing experience is over as soon as the interests diverge'.

Because binge-watching is 'defined through highly individualized terms and practices' (Jenner 2016, 265), and several scholars have used definitions other than watching three episodes in one day (as done here), participants were asked an additional question about their viewing experiences: 'When you watched at least 3 episodes of a show in a day, did you also complete a whole season of the show in 7 days or less?' Watching a season of a show in a week or less is my (Perks 2015) definition of media marathoning for television, and is a standard that Netflix utilised in a 2018 study (Netflix, Inc. 2018). This timespan also roughly aligns with what Netflix found to be the average time it takes viewers to complete a season: six days (Koblin 2016). The comparison of three episodes per day vs viewing a whole season in a week or less allows us to more clearly see the binge's role in viewers' weekly media diets, as well as their holistic engagement with the season. For Show I, 77.5% ($n = 93$) of participants had finished a season in a week, 18.3% ($n = 22$) had not, and 4.2% ($n = 5$) were not sure. The percentage of participants who finished in a week dropped to 67.5% ($n = 81$) for Show II, with 26.6% ($n = 32$) reporting 'no' and 5.8% ($n = 7$) 'not sure'. This drop in season completion from Show I to Show II was *not* statistically significant: $X^2 (1, n = 228) = 2.66, p = .10$. The completion may be explained by myriad factors, including that participants answered questions on their most engaging binge-watch first in the survey.

MULTITASKING EXPERIENCES AND MOTIVATIONS

Multitasking, and its relationship to both the viewing context and viewer engagement, was a primary focus of this study. As such, participants were asked several questions related to multitasking. The word 'multitasking' is used here to describe the practice of 'engaging in two or more activities at once' (Wang and Tchernev 2012, 493). However, the word 'multitasking' was not used in the survey itself because survey participants may think of multitasking only as using multiple screens (see, for example, Perks, Turner and Tollison 2019).

Participants were given the following prompt (for each of the two shows they reported on): 'Please think carefully about your viewing situation. Were you engaged in any other activities while viewing, such as a hobby, using another screen, doing a chore, eating, caring for a family member, working, etc.?' Although providing examples in the question stem can introduce bias, the authors of this book section dialogued on the subject and decided that the potential benefits outweighed the costs. More specifically, the prompts were expected to elicit more robust and thoughtful answers. In sum, 51.6% (n = 62) of participants did not do anything else while binge-watching, 30.8% (n = 37) engaged in another activity while watching both shows, and 17.5% (n = 21) engaged in another activity while watching *one* of the shows.

Several media scholars have conducted studies on multitasking behaviours as related to gratifications (for example, Leung and Zhang 2016; Wang and Tchernev 2012). And multitasking has been found to be a common behaviour, irrespective of age (see, for example, Voorveld and van der Goot 2013). This study's results yielded a nearly symmetrical chi square when dividing participants into younger and older groups (based on the study's median age of 32) and comparing any reported multitasking (one show or two) to no reported multitasking: $X^2(1, N = 120) = .13, p = .72$. Analysing multitasking (any/none) and educational attainment (divided at Bachelors' degree and above) yielded similar non-significant results: $p = .30$. In sum, we can conclude that multitasking (in general) was not related to age or educational attainment. This finding, however, does not preclude patterns related to life circumstance, setting or *type* of multitasking. Indeed, Wilson (2016) suggests that viewer attention (and consequent use of second screening) 'will vary according to genre, social circumstance, and mood' (187).

The only significant relationship between demographics and multitasking behaviour was for self-employed study participants. Many more self-employed people multitasked than the expected number (Table 6.1).
There are several possible explanations for this trend. First, we should acknowledge that the survey did not capture the *nature* of the self-employment – whether it was full- or part-time, at home or in a different professional space. It is possible that the self-employed binge-watched and multitasked because they had more time on their hands or they were working from home with ready access to their entertainment system and few people around to 'judge' their productivity. The exact opposite is also possible: that the self-employed were multitasking because their earnings depended on working as much as possible and combining activities was how they squeezed in some entertainment. For example, a white 40-year-old man stated that his multitasking was 'always working on my desktop computer' for the express purpose of 'to keep gaining money'. Several other self-employed multitaskers mentioned 'dinner' or 'eating' as their combined binge-watch activities.

Table 6.1 Self-employment and multitasking

	Self-Employed	Not Self-Employed	Total
Any Multitasking	17 (14.2%)	42 (35%)	59
No Multitasking	4 (.03.3%)	57 (47.5%)	61

$X^2(1, N = 120) = 10.29, p = .0013\ p < .005$

Only participants who indicated that they had engaged in another activity were presented with the next two separate questions: 'Please describe any/ all activities you were also doing while viewing.' 'Why do you think you chose to engage in another activity/other activities while watching the show?' The study findings here qualitatively affirm Wang and Tchernev's (2012) relaxation gratifications and dig further into participants' explanations for why multitasking enhanced their enjoyment and sense of productivity. It is important to differentiate between productivity, which is the act of accomplishing tasks, and efficiency, which is the speed with which those tasks are accomplished. In a survey of college students in Taiwan, Chang found that 'High sensation seekers tend to media multitask more frequently to satisfy their high convenience, high social, and low efficient needs to reach optimal level of arousal' (2017, 701). Thus, multitaskers may sacrifice efficiency for arousal – and still feel productive. Table 6.2 lists the ten most common multitasking behaviours distilled from the open-ended responses.

The most common explanations for why study participants multitasked paint a picture of television engagement patterns that are a) woven into the fabric of everyday experience (see Bury 2017; Gauntlett and Hill, 1999); and b) not always meeting viewers' entertainment needs. Bury found that live television viewing 'often involves multitasking in relation to work, domestic chores, and parenting' (2017, 69). Those behavioural patterns were captured in this survey, along with many other multitasking behaviours and their motivations. Participants' reasons for multitasking often interweave emotional and physical needs with some cognitive or engagement deficiencies in the programming. A 36-year-old white man stated that he 'was hungry/thirsty' and ate during his *Chernobyl* (HBO 2019) binge-watch to 'break up the monotony of watching an

Table 6.2 Multitasking activities

Activity	Show I	Show II
Eating	$n = 23$	$n = 17$
Browsing Internet	$n = 9$	$n = 6$
Social Media Use	$n = 7$	$n = 5$
Work	$n = 6$	$n = 5$
Gaming	$n = 5$	$n = 4$
Crafting (includes crocheting, knitting, sewing)	$n = 4$	$n = 5$
Texting	$n = 4$	$n = 4$
Cleaning	$n = 3$	$n = 5$
mTurking[1]	$n = 3$	$n = 4$
Emailing	$n = 3$	$n = 1$

[1] mTurking was separated out from 'work' to clarify any unique findings stemming from conducting the survey through that particular platform.

entire show at once'. The most common multitasking reason (*n*=12 for Show I; *n*=19 for Show II) was that multitasking reduced binge-watchers' boredom. More people said this with Show II, perhaps because they thought of a more engaging show to answer questions about first in the survey. Alternatively, they may have been re-watching their second binged show and thus had more 'mental energy' (see Steiner 2017, 152) for multitasking.

Participants' varying levels of media engagement capture the divergence of 'switched on' versus 'zoning out' binge culture that Horeck, Jenner and Kendall (2018, 502) identified (see also Perks 2019). The same person can emphasise a different side of the spectrum, depending on unique needs. And those individual needs can change *during* engagement with a particular show as well – often based on ebbs and flow in the dramatic sequencing. A 37-year-old white man browsed the internet while binge-watching *Game of Thrones* because it was 'something to do during the slow parts of the show'. Despite having 'slow parts', participants were undeniably drawn to their chosen show, like the 45-year-old white woman who cleaned during *Orange is the New Black*: 'It sometimes start to seem really boring, but I just can't change the show.' A drive toward narrative completion (and the ability to clean as she watched) kept her watching. In the final example, the television content was not the primary entertainment driver; it was a companion. 'I wanted to actually just use my phone but wanted the noise of the show on in the background to make me feel like others were present', recounted a 30-year-old white woman who watched *Stranger Things*. Of note is the fact that the dramatic shows mentioned are typically seen as high involvement shows. Yet, they still did not command full attention from study participants.

Whereas the previous theme was about the value of the media engagement time itself, the next theme focused on 'productivity' and the *overall value of one's time* – how it is used, managed and stored. MTurking while watching *My 600-lb Life* (TLC 2012–) enabled a white woman (age 37) to 'feel more productive'. A 32-year-old man who drew and gamed during *Stranger Things* noted, '[i]t felt like a waste of time if I was just watching'. Also engaged in waste prevention, a 30-year-old man said that eating and watching *House* (Fox 2004–12) 'saves time'. In a more complicated view that took into account the total free time in one's day, a 33-year-old black woman noted that her experience eating and drinking while binge-watching *Russian Doll* 'helps condense home time, allowing space for more quiet/alone time at other hours'. She strategically combined entertainment and sustenance activities to build in room for more peaceful moments. Overall, 13 participants mentioned productivity (or even multitasking) as a motivation for combining activities during their first show and ten said the same about their second show.

Some participants were not concerned with managing the entertainment experience or their time; instead, they were motivated to pair up complementary activities (most of which included eating). Gauntlett and Hill (1999) found that many of the participants in their diary study described eating dinner, or an evening meal, in front of the television. Nearly one-third of their participants even said they would time their meal with a favourite show (Gauntlett and Hill 1999, 25). The need to adapt one's meal schedule to a programming schedule is nearly non-existent in binge-watching practices. Through time-shifting, 'episodes are decontextualized from the media landscape, but recontextualized to fit with the fabric of our lived existence' (Perks 2015, xxix.). Binge-watchers who ate while viewing could choose the timing of *both* tandem activities.

Ten participants found synergy in their multitasking combination for Show I and six said the same about Show II. 'They go together', simply stated a 29-year-old woman who was eating while watching *NOS4A2* (AMC 2019–) with her boyfriend. A 26-year-old Asian man noted that 'both activities can be done at the same time' when asked why he ate while watching *Stranger Things*. Pairing many activities with her binge-watching of *Santa Clarita Diet* (Netflix 2017–), a 28-year-old white woman noted that she will 'respond back to texts, look at discussions about episodes, and I like to eat dinner while watching'. The first two tasks involve communicating with others, and the latter task seems like a more enduring practice as it was the only one she noted 'liking'. This study is not focused on nutrition; however, many people are likely aware of the robust body of research encouraging mindful eating. Distracted eating (such as eating while watching TV) has a significant relationship with eating more, both while distracted and after the distraction is removed (see, for example, the meta-analysis by Robinson et al. 2013). If binge-viewers are more focused on managing their time, tasks and stimulation rather than their nutrition, the combination of activities can prove enjoyable.

A small but significant theme emerged relating relaxation to multitasking (N=2 for Show I; N=3 for Show II). Eating while watching *The Haunting of Hill House* (Netflix 2018–), a 33-year-old black woman noted, added 'to an atmosphere of relaxation and comfort'. Relaxation was also central to a 36-year-old white woman who knitted while watching *Game of Thrones* and *The Handmaid's Tale* (Hulu 2017–). When asked why she did another activity while viewing Show I, she responded, 'because knitting is relaxing'. For Show II, she elaborated about her attentiveness: 'It's relaxing and I don't have to look at it while I'm doing it.' Whereas eating while watching can harm one's memory of the events (thus leading to overeating), knitting while watching can enable one to easily create something perhaps practical and/or artistic while giving full attention (or at least eye contact) to a television show.

Previous media multitasking studies show that 'media multitasking behavior is driven by cognitive needs which are not gratified by the behaviour' (Wang and Tchernev 2012, 509). However, emotional needs (such as entertainment and relaxation) can be met by media-related multitasking (see, for example, Leung and Zhang 2016; Wang and Tchernev 2012). The data presented here offer insight into those mechanisms of relaxation, showing that complementary activities (such as watching TV and eating dinner) can provide a sense of productivity and satisfaction in routine. Although the quality of each might be diminished slightly (less attention on the show, less mindful eating, etc.), the fact that both activities are checked off at the same time can lead to a sense of magnified indulgence and even productivity, because, after all, a person needs to eat and they might as well be entertained while doing it. Various multitasking activities that include additional screens or other forms of entertainment may provide more continuity of engagement (especially in the low-drama or 'boring' parts of a show). Thus, although viewers may be less attentive while viewing, they report being more engaged overall.

Multitasking, genre and cognitive involvement

Previous binge-watching studies have explored the relationship between television viewing practices and cognitive involvement or engagement (for example, Merikivi et al. 2018; Pittman and Steiner 2019; Tukachinsky and Eyal 2018). To dialogue with that body of literature, this survey included two multitasking items drawn from Pittman and Steiner (2019): 'When I binge-watch a show I like, I am often doing other things' and '[w]hen I binge-watch a show I like, I usually have it on in the background'. The results of these two items are referred to as 'multitasking scores' to differentiate between the survey scores and the participants' actual reports of multitasking behaviour. Multitasking composite scores were considered 'high' at a value of 7 and above to ensure that study participants had selected 'somewhat agree' or 'strongly agree' for at least one of the two items.

The survey also included four cognitive involvement measures from Merikivi et al. (2018) (originally adapted from Agarwal and Karahanna 2000; Burton-Jones and Straub 2006): 'When binge-watching, I am able to block out all other distractions', 'When binge-watching, I feel totally immersed in the show', 'When binge-watching, I do not get distracted very easily', and 'When binge-watching, my attention does not get diverted very easily'. These items were assessed with a 5-point Likert scale, anchored by strongly disagree to strongly agree. The data was analysed to provide a composite score for participants (assigned at 1 for strongly disagree up to 5 for strongly agree). Composite cognitive involvement scores could therefore range from 4 to 20, with 20 indicating intense concentration on a show.

Additionally, the participants' two binge-watched programmes were coded according to Pittman and Steiner's (2019) low and high viewer attentiveness spectrum genre classifications (and labelled 'low involvement shows' or 'high involvement shows'). Low involvement shows included shorter comedies (usually under 30 minutes per episode), anime, and reality shows. High involvement shows were generally hour-long dramas (see also Steiner and Xu 2020, 92).

When comparing behavioural self-reports (engaging in another activity while binge-watching one or both shows) to the composite score of the two multitasking survey items, the chi square test results were significant. This significant relationship suggests face validity: the scores for 'often doing other things' or 'having [the show] on in the background' adequately capture binge-watching multitasking behaviour. X^2 (1, N = 120) = 16.01, p = .00, p < .0001 (Table 6.3).

A statistically significant relationship was also revealed when analysing multitasking behaviour and scores on the four cognitive involvement measures. Cognitive involvement composite scores were split at a median score of 16, with 'high' cognitive involvement considered to be 16 and above for the four total cognitive involvement (CINV) measures. Participants who reported *always* multitasking during their bingeing (vs those who sometimes or never reported multitasking) were significantly more likely to score in the lower end of cognitive involvement (Table 6.4).

No associations between genre and multitasking or genre and cognitive involvement were statistically significant. When comparing high and low multitasking scores to the genres binge-watched (only high involvement shows vs only low involvement shows), no statistically significant difference was found (p = .56). Put differently, participants who professed a high affinity for multitasking didn't necessarily binge-watch low involvement content and vice versa. Additionally, when analysing participants who only multitasked during *one* of their reported binge-watching experiences, there was no significant

Table 6.3 Multitasking survey scores and self-reported behaviours

	Reported Multitasking During One or Both Binged Shows	No Reported Multitasking	Total
High Multitasking Score (7+)	28 (14.2%)	9 (35%)	37
Low Multitasking Score	30 (.03.3%)	53 (47.5%)	83

X^2 (1, N = 120) = 16.01, p = .00006, p < .0001

Table 6.4 Multitasking behaviours and cognitive involvement composite survey scores

	Low Cognitive Involvement Score	High Cognitive Involvement Score (16+)	Total
Multitasking Both Shows	24 (20.2%)	13 (10.9%)	37
Multitasking One or No Shows	26 (21.9%)	56 (47.1%)	82

X^2 (1, N = 119) = 11.50, p = .0006, p < .001

relationship between multitasking (yes/no) and genre (high involvement vs low involvement shows): X^2 (1, N = 21) = 1.77, p = .18.

When comparing people who only binged high involvement/low involvement shows and their composite cognitive involvement scores, there was no statistically significant difference (p = .66). The results were also not significant when comparing cognitive involvement scores of people who watched either *all* low involvement or *some* low involvement with those who watched high involvement only (p = .6). In sum, there were no clear, statistically significant associations between the genre of the binge-watched shows and cognitive involvement scores, multitasking affinity, or reported multitasking behaviours while binge-watching.

The lack of genre-associated relationships could be explained in several ways. First, this survey did not ask whether the binge was a re-watch or a re-binge for viewers. As Steiner (2017) notes, a second viewing transforms a high involvement show into a low involvement show. Assessing one's relationship with a show can help parse out a show's cognitive demands. Second, the genre classifications might need refinement. Some comedies, such as those that involve long-running jokes and extensive casts of characters, might ask for higher cognitive involvement than formulaic, hour-long dramas. Thus, the low and high involvement classifications may need to capture and express greater nuance. Alternately, viewers who want to give their full attention to a show (to be immersed and block out distractions) may purposely pick lower involvement or less cognitively complex shows that they can fully master. These findings may also suggest that generic differences of perceived cognitive effort are not nuanced enough to be associative or predictive.

CONCLUSIONS

This study presents several significant insights into binge-watching experiences. Notably, many participants were streaming their content at home at night – using a newer content-delivery technology but in much the same way that television has been watched for decades. One key difference was that streaming was done through both television screens and mobile screens (such as laptops and tablets) to move the binge-watch into domestic spaces beyond the living room. Binge-watching most often took place in the bedroom, suggesting that television viewing plays less of a role as an organiser of domestic space and a site of family power relations than Silverstone (1994) asserted over two decades ago. Instead, binge-watching commonly takes place in an entertainment fiefdom, with no broadcast schedule and no static device in a busy domestic space. The binge-watching form of domestic television viewing functions more as a site of individualised and personalised comfort.

The two-show comparison suggests that binge-watching behaviours such as co-viewing and multitasking were situational rather than ritualistic. Media multitasking involved several different activities, either related to screens (gaming, texting, perusing social media, working on a computer) or unrelated to screens (eating, knitting, drawing). There was no significant relationship between multitasking and age, education or other demographic category except for self-employment. The self-employment/multitasking connection may be rooted in flexibility (of setting one's own schedule and potentially working from home), but more research needs to be conducted to discern those specific details. Although multitasking may diminish the quality of the two coinciding activities, participants reported many multitasking gratifications or benefits. The most common reasons given for multitasking were to alleviate boredom when the show was not engrossing, to be productive, to enjoy complementary activities and to enhance relaxation. No relationship could be discerned between multitasking behaviours and genres, but those who frequently multitasked were significantly more likely to score in the lower end of the cognitive involvement composite measure.

Evans, Coughlan and Coughlan pushed scholars to 'interrogate the value of consciously passive mediated experiences for audiences' (2017, 201). Their research on 'digital estates' (the authors' unique phrase for 'multiscreen experiences') yielded conclusions about 'disconnected, ephemeral and forgettable multiplatform experiences' (197). The findings here present a mixed bag of attentiveness and multitasking, but many experiences seemed memorable and meaningful. Study participants reported passive and fulfilling television engagement experiences that were stitched into the fabric of domestic existence. Television entertainment was at times punctuated with sustenance, artistic creation, computer-mediated communication, paid work and relationship maintenance. These findings gesture toward a view of binge-watching that is irrespective of genre and maximises an entertainment experience in a way that complements rather than replaces other daily activities and rituals.

REFERENCES

Agarwal, R. and E. Karahanna (2000). 'Time Flies When You're Having Fun: Cognitive Absorption and Beliefs about Information Technology Usage'. *Management Information Systems Quarterly* 24(4): 665–94.

Burton-Jones, A. and D. W. Straub (2006). 'Reconceptualizing System Usage: An Approach and Empirical Test'. *Information Systems Research* 17(3): 228–46.

Bury, R. (2017). *Television 2.0: Viewer and Fan Engagement with Digital TV*. New York: Peter Lang.

Chang, Y. (2017). 'Why Do Young People Multitask with Multiple Media? Explicating the Relationships among Sensation Seeking, Needs, and Media Multitasking Behavior'. *Media Psychology* 20(4): 685–703.

Evans, E., T. Coughlan and V. Coughlan (2017). 'Building Digital Estates: Multiscreening, Technology Management and Ephemeral Television'. *Critical Studies in Television: The International Journal of Television Studies* 12(2): 191–205.

Gauntlett, D. and A. Hill (1999). *TV Living: Television, Culture and Everyday Life*. New York: Routledge.

Horeck, T., M. Jenner and T. Kendall (2018). 'On Binge-Watching: Nine Critical Propositions'. *Critical Studies in Media Communication* 13(4): 499–504.

Jenner, M. (2016). 'Is this TVIV? On Netflix, TVIII, and Binge-Watching'. *New Media & Society* 18(2): 257–73.

Jenner, M. (2018). *Netflix and the Re-Invention of Television*. Basingstoke: Palgrave Macmillan.

Koblin, J. (2016). 'Netflix studied your binge-watching habit. That didn't take long'. *The New York Times* [Online] 8th June. Available at: <https://www.nytimes.com/2016/06/09/business/media/netflix-studied-your-binge-watching-habit-it-didnt-take-long.html?module=inline> (last accessed 3 October 2019).

Leung, L. and R. Zhang (2016). 'Predicting Tablet Use: A Study of Gratifications-Sought, Leisure Boredom, and Multitasking'. *Telematics and Informatics* 33(2): 331–41.

Merikivi, J., A. Salovaara, M. Mantymaki and L. Zhang (2018). 'On the Way to Understanding Binge Watching Behavior: The Over-Estimated Role of Involvement'. *Electron Markets* 28: 111–22.

Mikos, L. (2016). 'Digital Media Platforms and the Use of TV Content: Binge Watching and Video-On-Demand in Germany'. *Media and Communication* 4(3): 154–61.

Nabi, R. L. and M. Krcmar (2004). 'Conceptualizing Media Enjoyment as Attitude: Implications for Mass Media Effects Research'. *Communication Theory* 14(4): 288–310.

Netflix (2013). 'Netflix Finds More Than Half of Americans Willing To Trade Their Couches For Treadmills When Binge Watching In 2014'. [Press release], 30th December. Available at: <https://www.marketwatch.com/press-release/netflix-finds-more-than-half-of-americans-willing-to-trade-their-couches-for-treadmills-when-binge-watching-in-2014-2013-12-30> (last accessed 3 October 2019).

Netflix, Inc. (2018). *Do you remember your first time . . . bingeing on Netflix?* [Press release], 7th February. Available at: <https://media.netflix.com/en/press-releases/warning-this-netflix-press-release-is-for-mature-audiences-only> (last accessed 3 October 2019).

Perks, L. G. (2015). *Media Marathoning: Immersions in Morality*. London: Lexington Books.

Perks, L. G. (2019). 'Media Marathoning and Health Coping'. *Communication Studies* 70(1): 19–35.

Perks, L. G., J. S. Turner and A. D. Tollison (2019). 'Podcast Uses and Gratifications Scale Development'. *Journal of Broadcasting and Electronic Media* 63(4): 617–34.

Pittman, M. and E. Steiner (2019). 'Transportation or Narrative Completion? Attentiveness during Binge-Watching Moderates Regret'. *Social Sciences* 8(99): 1–14.

Robinson, E. et al. (2013). 'Eating Attentively: A Systematic Review and Meta-Analysis of the Effect of Food Intake Memory and Awareness on Eating'. *The American Journal of Clinical Nutrition*. 97(4): 728–42.

Silverstone, R. (1994). *Television and Everyday Life*. London: Routledge.

Steiner, E. (2017). 'Binge-Watching in Practice: The Rituals, Motives and Feelings of Streaming Video Viewers'. In C. Barker and M. Wiatrowski (eds), *The Age of Netflix: Critical Essays on Streaming Media, Digital Delivery, and Instant Access*. Jefferson, NC: McFarland, pp. 141–61.

Steiner, E. and K. Xu (2020). 'Binge-Watching Motivates Change: Uses and Gratifications of Streaming Video Viewers Challenge Traditional TV Research'. *Convergence: The International Journal of Research into New Media Technologies* 26(1): 82–101.

Sung, Y. H., E. Y. Kang and W.-N. Lee (2018). 'Why Do We Indulge? Exploring Motivations for Binge Watching'. *Journal of Broadcasting and Electronic Media* 62(3): 408–26.
Tukachinsky, R. and K. Eyal (2018). 'The Psychology of Marathon Television Viewing: Antecedents and Viewer Involvement'. *Mass Communication and Society* 21(3): 275–95.
Voorveld, H. A. M. and M. van der Goot (2013). 'Age Differences in Media Multitasking: A Diary Study'. *Journal of Broadcasting & Electronic Media* 57(3): 392–408.
Wang, Z., and J. M. Tchernev (2012). 'The 'Myth' of media Multitasking: Reciprocal Dynamics of Media Multitasking, Personal Needs, and Gratifications'. *Journal of Communication* 62(3): 493–513.
Wilson, S. (2016). 'In the Living Room: Second Screens and TV Audiences'. *Television and New Media* 17(2): 174–91.

TV

Bigg Boss (2006–7), India: Sony TV
Bigg Boss (2007–), India: Colors TV
Boys, The (2019–), USA: Amazon
Game of Thrones (2011–19), USA: HBO
Handmaid's Tale, The (2017–), USA: Hulu
Haunting of Hill House, The (2018–), USA: Netflix
House (2004–12), USA: Fox
My 600-lb Life (2012–), USA: TLC
NOS4A2 (2019–), USA: AMC
Office, The (2005–13), USA: NBC
Orange is the New Black (2013–19), USA: Netflix
Russian Doll (2019–), USA: Netflix
Santa Clarita Diet (2017–), USA: Netflix
Stranger Things (2016–), USA: Netflix

CHAPTER 7

What Defines a Binge? Elapsed Time versus Episodes

Ri Pierce-Grove

INTRODUCTION

The episode, not the hour, is the unit of the 'binge-watch'. Over and over, in the popular discourse around binge-watching, the excess implied by the word 'binge' is located in the number of narrative units consumed, not the time spent (Pierce-Grove 2016). Many factors combine to make this the case. The legacy of television and video programming structures, marketing, distribution and the storytelling which emerges from economic and technological apparatuses all contribute. This article argues that the prevalence of episodes over time in binge-watching discourse is more than a legacy. It is a live factor in user behaviour. Episode boundaries provide an opportunity for users to decide whether or not to keep watching. The quantitative analysis presented here shows that the more episode boundaries are provided, the more users abandon a season. This suggests that despite the strength of features like auto-play which reduce friction and keep viewers in the 'insulated flow', episode boundaries are still a more pronounced cue to trigger user habits than their internal sense of the passage of time. This is supported by qualitative analysis. Interviews with participants about their binge-watching behaviour confirms that their perception of duration varies, that many of them are aware that binge-watching can affect it and that episode beginnings and endings are often habit cues.

The competing definitions of the 'binge-watch' which have emerged from scholarship and journalism and become enshrined in dictionaries revolve around the consumption of multiple episodes, not multiple hours. Autonomy, continuity, and the episode are fundamental characteristics of the binge-watch (Merikivi et al. 2019; Pierce-Grove 2016).

This continuity has been theorised by Lisa Glebatis Perks, who has characterised the state that sustains a binge-watch once begun as 'insulated flow':

This insulated flow announces itself, making viewers take ownership of their experience, but its automaticity makes it difficult for viewers to escape the insulated flow. They may already envision themselves as moving through a fictive world. Instead of having to opt-in to a marathon, viewers are made to opt-out with technologies like 'post-play'. (Perks 2015, xxvi)

Mareike Jenner has built on Perks's observation that the affordances of the Netflix platform, most notably the auto-play and the option to skip introductory sequences, serve to insulate the viewer further within this flow (Jenner 2018, 119–29). Other platforms have incorporated these features to varying degrees. This creates an environment in which opting out, rather than opting in, is the default for viewers who have begun a binge-watching session on one of these services. The work of habit researchers like Wendy Wood demonstrates how potentially effective these design choices may be since ease and convenience significantly influence habit formation (Wood 2019, 90–1).

A strong preference for continuity and completion has been found in other contexts (see, for example, Steiner and Xu 2020). Participants in other studies were willing to put in more effort on tasks which were perceived as completing a larger 'set' (Barasz et al. 2017; Garland and Conlon 1998). This tendency has been shown to apply to video content as well. Lu, Karmarkar and Venkatraman (2017) performed a series of seven studies designed to test whether viewers derived additional utility from 'completing' a series they saw as a complete set, and found that they did.

And yet, sometimes people do wrest themselves out of insulated flow. They stop viewing for the night, or they abandon viewing altogether. Are there some characteristics intrinsic to the content which could broadly encourage continuity or abandonment? Time is the resource viewers are spending on the binge, and it is time that carries with it an opportunity cost. The episode, by contrast, is a piece of artifice lasting an arbitrary length. Streaming platforms have ensured that episodes' beginning and ending are partially submerged beneath the flow (through post-play or skip intro). So it might be that viewers' choice to abandon a show would correlate more closely with time, and episodes would have little to do with it. And yet, considering the peculiar insistence in binge-watching discourse on the episode, not the hour, might the episode also be worth examining as an exit point from insulated flow?

Although time is the currency a viewer spends in the binge-watch, the brain does not always keep an accurate tally of its outlay. Human beings are quite accurate at estimating time at the level of seconds: it is this which enables them to catch a ball, for example. However, the greater the interval of time, the greater the error in estimation. In addition, any number of factors can distort human perception of duration (Noreika, Falter and Wagner 2014). Sylvia

Droit-Volet (2014) has demonstrated that pleasant film clips cause viewers to underestimate duration, and unpleasant ones cause them to overestimate it. Familiarity causes duration to be underestimated; novelty causes it to be overestimated. Mark Wittman (2014) argues that the speed of the body's internal processes creates a kind of internal clock. This clock can be speeded up or slowed with metabolism. People with fevers think far more time has passed than healthy people (Hoagland 1933; Noreika, et al. 2014). All these factors have potential bearing on binge-watching, since viewers may be sick or well, enjoying content or not, watching for longer sessions or shorter ones. Therefore, this study was designed to investigate which would be more closely correlated with failure to complete a show: episode or time.

METHODOLOGY

Data-gathering for this study took place in two contexts. Both of these were approved by the Institutional Review Board at Columbia University. First, a large set of viewing records was obtained from a commercial service designed for people who wanted to create and preserve records of their own viewing histories. This dataset has been updated at intervals since 2017, with the most recent update being in February 2020. Viewing histories could be recorded by users of this service in one of two ways. First, they could install a variety of third-party software plug-ins which copied information automatically from their content services of choice to their viewing history database. Second, they could supplement this by manually entering in records of what they watched.

The affordances of the manual history recording seemed likely to lead to overly high completion estimates since by far the easiest thing to select was 'watched entire season'. Pilot analysis of the database and interviews with users both confirmed that entering in each individual episode, accompanied by the date and time of watching for each one, was not a popular practice. Manual entries were therefore excluded. Only automatically recorded viewer histories are included in the data analysed here.

The sample for this study was the viewing histories of users who had watched the first episode of the first season of at least one of the 50 shows rated most highly on the commercial service (see Figure 7.1). The 'most popular' shows were selected for two reasons. First, choosing shows with similar popularity rankings was an effort to reduce the impact of varying pleasurability on results. Since pleasure makes time seem to pass more quickly, if time were the determining variable, shows which were not equally enjoyable would present different impressions of the passage of time. Second, choosing the most popular shows ensured a large sample size.

For each show, the percentage of users who watched all the episodes in the first season was calculated. These percentages were then analysed to see if they correlated with any of the three following variables: run-time of a single episode, number of minutes in a season as a whole, and number of episodes in a season as a whole. This was done with a Kendall's Tau B rank correlation analysis.

In addition, a smaller group of people consented to an interview in person or over the phone. Most of these people also contributed their viewing histories associated with one or more of the services for self-tracking, Netflix or YouTube. In total 55 such interviews took place between 2016 and 2019.

The quantitative data was supplemented by a novel method for studying binge-watching: data-prompted interviews. Data-prompted interviewing is a method in which participants are given the opportunity to reflect on their own behavioural data in the company of an interviewer. It is ideally suited for studying habitual media consumption behaviours because the habitual often sinks below conscious awareness. Habitual behaviours, almost by definition, are not novel, and thus lay down fewer memories. The advantages of a mixed-methods approach that includes Netflix data in the study of binge-watching has been demonstrated by Castro et al. (2021).

In addition, remembering events falls into the category of episodic memory. The weakness of this kind of memory has been ably demonstrated by generations of researchers, most notably in research on eye-witness testimony (Loftus 1975). Although remembering how to do something rarely fades (procedural memory), events leave a much more fleeting impression (Loftus 1974). Often, people simply cannot remember what they watched or how much. The details fade into the background of everyday life. But because recognition is easier than unprompted recall, looking at their own behavioural data helps participants remember circumstances which they might otherwise have forgotten. In addition, the interviewer then has access to a trove of behavioural data more accurate than a time diary and far less trouble for the interviewee. In concert with the interviewee's memory (which they are invited to jog with their own calendars, photo rolls, emails, and so on, as needed), this method allows the researcher to approximate the depth of a longitudinal study in a much more rapid timeframe.

Data-prompted interviews are an inherently mixed method and can be used by quantitative and qualitative researchers alike. The result is more robust than either qualitative or quantitative approaches would be alone: people often cannot remember what they did, but behavioural data alone can't give much insight into why.

For this project, data-prompted interviews were performed both with participants who used the tracking service which provided the larger dataset and with users of Netflix and YouTube. In addition, JavaScript was used to export viewers' behavioural data from Netflix and YouTube into CSV files. The users ran the scripts themselves, so no password information was ever transmitted to the research team. The interviewer then sat down with participants, in person, over video chat or phone and asked them to recount the circumstances surrounding the watch histories provided.

DEMOGRAPHICS

Recording their age was optional for the users of the commercial service, and a minority of them chose to do so. The mean age of those viewers who chose to record it was mid-30s. Users were based in North America, Europe, South America, South Asia, South Africa, Russia and Australia, with a high concentration of users in Europe and the east and west coasts of the United States. Interviewees ranged in age from 18 to 66 and were primarily highly educated white-collar migrants. Interviewees were recruited via social media and snowball sampling, with clusters in Europe, the Middle East and North America. Interviews were conducted in English.

RESULTS

The analysis was run three times on three slightly different datasets. First, a pilot analysis was run in 2017 for the top 25 shows up to the date of the analysis and 100,000 users. A second analysis was performed in January 2020 for the top 49 shows at that time and 150,000 users. The third analysis was performed in February 2020 for the top 50 shows at that time and approximately 200,000 users. All three showed a very strong negative correlation between number of episodes per season and season completion, and a less strong but nevertheless significant negative correlation between total number of minutes per season and season completion.

Results for the two analyses in 2020 are as follows: In the January 2020 analysis, the run-time of an individual episode did not have a significant correlation with completion of the first season (tau = 0.1196, n = 49, p-value = 0.246). Minutes per season proved to have a strong negative relationship to completion (tau = -0.5603, n = 49, p < .0001, see Figure 7.1). The strongest relationship was between number of episodes and completion (tau = -0.6526, n = 49, p < .0001, see Figure 7.2). In the February 2020 analysis, the minutes per season proved to have a strong negative relationship to completion (tau = -0.4675, n = 50, p < .0001). The strongest relationship was between number of episodes and completion (tau = -0.6918, n = 50, p < .0001).

The results from the January 2020 analysis show that the correlation between the number of episodes a season has and the percentage of users who

WHAT DEFINES A BINGE? 103

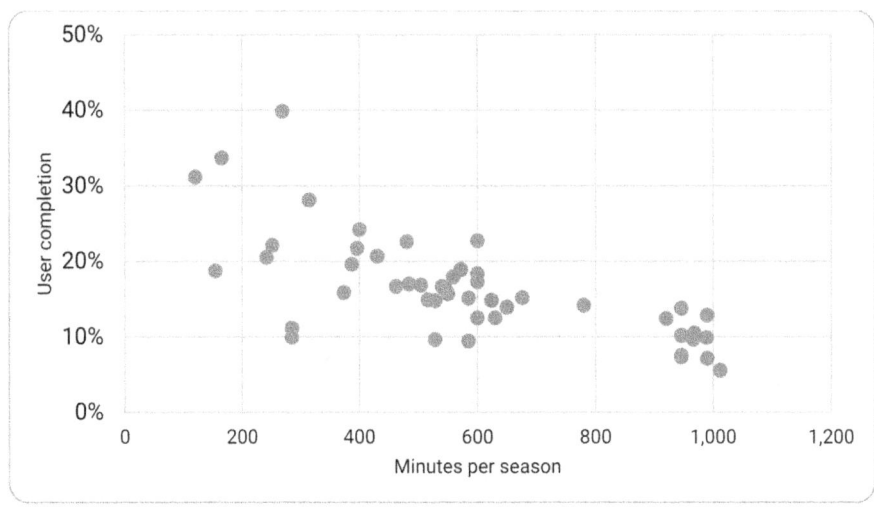

Figure 7.1 Percentage of users who completed first seasons by season duration (minutes).

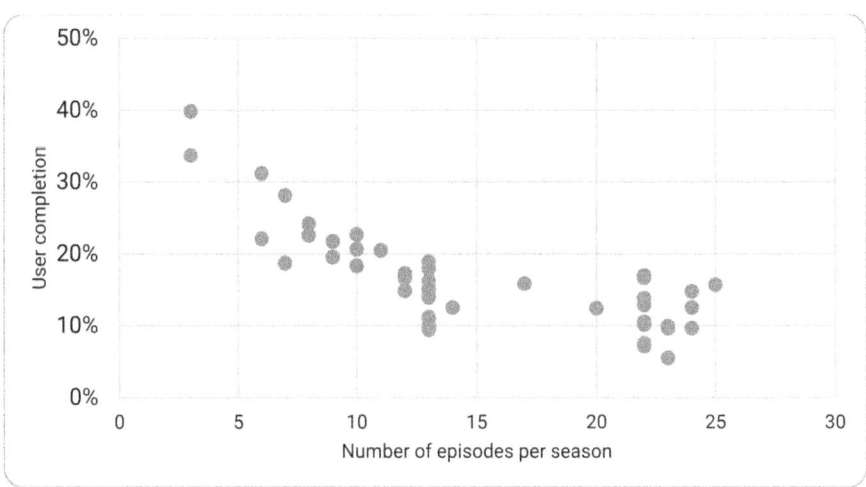

Figure 7.2 Percentage of users who completed first seasons by season duration (episodes).

watched all of the episodes is very strong. The more episodes in the first season, the less likely a viewer is to watch them all. Shows with very few episodes but comparatively long episode run-times are much more likely to be completed than shows with the same number of total minutes per season broken into more episodes. The most-completed show was *Sherlock* (BBC 2010–), a show whose first season had only three episodes, each of which ran for a stunning 90 minutes.

The three shows whose first seasons had the highest completion rates are not all tightly constructed serial dramas. In order, they are: *Sherlock* (detective drama, three episodes); *Black Mirror* (Channel 4 2011–4; Netflix 2014–) (science fiction thriller with an anthology structure, three episodes); and *The Office* (BBC 2001–3) (serial comedy, six episodes). Completion rates did not align with how much a show was liked by viewers. *Sherlock* was the 5th most popular show, *Black Mirror* the 28th, and *The Office* the 42nd. The two least-completed shows, *Supernatural* (The CW 2005–) and *The Flash* (The CW 2014–), were ranked as more popular than either *Black Mirror* or *The Office* (Table 7.1).

Table 7.1 Most popular shows and percentage of users who completed first seasons of those shows

Popularity Rank	TV Series	User Completion
1	*Game of Thrones*	22.70%
2	*Breaking Bad*	28.12%
3	*The Walking Dead*	22.10%
4	*The Big Bang Theory*	15.85%
5	*Sherlock*	39.84%
6	*How I Met Your Mother*	16.99%
7	*Dexter*	17.28%
8	*Arrow*	9.62%
9	*Friends*	9.64%
10	*Stranger Things*	24.18%
11	*House*	10.50%
12	*Homeland*	16.67%
13	*House of Cards*	13.93%
14	*Supernatural*	7.14%
15	*Fringe*	12.41%
16	*Suits*	16.83%
17	*The Flash*	5.53%
18	*Modern Family*	12.50%
19	*Orange Is the New Black*	14.15%
20	*Vikings*	21.71%
21	*The Simpsons*	9.97%
22	*Doctor Who*	9.43%
23	*Mr. Robot*	20.66%
24	*True Detective*	22.58%
25	*Marvel's Agents of S.H.I.E.L.D.*	10.14%
26	*American Horror Story*	14.89%
27	*Prison Break*	12.86%
28	*Black Mirror*	33.69%

WHAT DEFINES A BINGE? 105

29	Marvel's Daredevil	15.18%
30	Westworld	18.33%
31	Firefly	12.50%
32	South Park	11.16%
33	Family Guy	18.72%
34	Community	15.69%
35	Rick and Morty	20.50%
36	Person of Interest	9.89%
37	True Blood	14.81%
38	Sons of Anarchy	15.11%
39	The 100	17.93%
40	The Blacklist	10.20%
41	Once Upon a Time	7.29%
42	The Office	31.16%
43	New Girl	14.76%
44	Battlestar Galactica	18.89%
45	Brooklyn Nine-Nine	16.68%
46	The Vampire Diaries	13.79%
47	Gotham	7.52%
48	Hannibal	16.30%
49	Grey's Anatomy	19.56%

The percentage of users who completed Season 1 may seem surprisingly low for such popular shows. This study can only offer a conjecture about this, which is that the completion records may represent re-watches rather than first-time watches, and that re-watching produces lower completion rates than watching for the first time. The possibility of re-watches is present because the bulk of users joined this commercial service for self-trackers well after the first seasons of the 49 most popular shows were aired. They had, in many cases, several years' opportunity to watch these shows before they installed self-tracking software. A more granular look at watcher behaviour in the first and the latest seasons of *Game of Thrones* (HBO 2011–19) and *Stranger Things* (Netflix 2016–) is supportive of this conjecture. For both, the percentage of watchers completing the season was higher for the most recent season (at the moment of study) than the older one, although for *Stranger Things*, the absolute number of watchers drops between seasons. In addition, for both shows, a considerable percentage of watchers watch only one episode before abandoning the first season – that number is reduced for the recent season. Providing a decisive answer is beyond the scope of this study. Therefore, the completion percentages will not be discussed in absolute terms, but only relative to each other. Further research should investigate the difference between completion rates in first-time and re-watch binge-watching.

Interview results

A number of interviewees reported that they were aware of a change in their perception of duration while binge-watching. Many interviewees reported that some genres made time seem to pass faster than others. Some used binge-watching instrumentally for this reason – to make plane flights or sessions at the gym seem to go faster. Others delayed their binges until they were past a particularly busy time in their schedule because they were concerned that binge-watching would make them lose their awareness of the passage of time. They therefore waited for what Lisa Glebatis Perks has termed 'floating holidays' (Perks 2015, 27).

Interviews show considerable variance in users' subjective sense of duration. The most extreme individual in the sample always stopped after exactly 20 minutes of YouTube content. He explained this by saying he had exhausted the supply of relevant videos. For others, the internal sense of duration Wittman describes as emerging from body processes (Wittman 2014) was not perceptible until fatigue forced itself on their attention. Viewers described themselves as realising how much time had passed when they felt 'exhausted'. Individuals also had stronger or weaker external time cues in their environment. Interviewees with young children, for example, remarked that it was much harder for them to become immersed in narrative time and outside of clock time when there were so many calls on their attention.

Viewers almost uniformly described their viewing in terms of episodes, not time. Very few participants said they would watch 20 minutes of *Family Guy* (Fox 1999–) or 45 minutes of *Game of Thrones*, for example. When discussing their viewing behaviour in connection with others, viewers said things like '[i]t's amazing – he can stop after just one episode', or '[s]he can never stop after just one episode' or '[w]e always watch two episodes in the evening' or 'I watch a couple of episodes after she has gone to bed'.

Negotiation with partners for binge-watching time was consistently described in terms of episodes, not time. For example, one couple agreed to watch two episodes together every week night. Their Netflix data showed that, when they concluded a show with 40-minute episodes and changed to a show with 22-minute episodes, their number of evening episodes did not rise. They continued to watch two episodes each week night, even though their watching time was reduced by almost half.

Duration sometimes factored into users' choices of which show to watch. Some chose an episode of anime to pair with lunch because episodes of anime are short. One switched from watching long episodes to short episodes when he was procrastinating because it was harder to justify taking the time to watch a long episode.

It might be possible to explain this by suggesting that episodes are proxies for time here. A second, and more plausible explanation, is that episodes are not proxies for 'clock time', but take place in what Robert Levine has called 'event time' (Levine 1998, 81–100). Clock time, Levine says, is when people use the hour on the clock to schedule the beginning or the end of activities. In event time, people use their 'activities to mark time, rather than the other way around' (Levine 1998). Levine argues that some cultures run predominantly on event time, others in clock time, and a few in a hybrid. Perhaps agreeing to go to bed 'when this episode is over' is an agreement based in event time, rather than agreeing to go to bed 'at 10 pm', which is an agreement based in clock time.

Completism, and a preference for a 'set', surfaced in interviews. Interviewees showed various degrees of desire to finish a show even if they had lost interest in it. Users of the tracking service felt this impulse more strongly than people who did not use it. Several remarked that they felt nagged by the progress bar in their tracking service, and they would invest hours watching a show they no longer liked simply to see the progress bar completed. One participant remarked that she was sick of the show, but the uncompleted progress bar 'drives me nuts'.

In contrast, one interviewee abandoned a show he was enjoying on hearing that the show had not been renewed. Although he still had several seasons to go, he concluded that the show's abrupt cancellation meant there would be no eventual narrative payoff, no final resolution, and thus no purpose in continuing with the show.

DISCUSSION

What is an episode? It need not be a complete narrative unit; for dramas that use a cliff-hanger structure, for example, plot threads are tied up three-quarters of the way through, leaving the remaining quarter of the episode to trigger suspense intended to entice the viewer across the gap between episodes, as discussed elsewhere in this volume.[1]

And there is a gap, however small: some platforms allow the viewer to skip the opening sequence and go straight to the plot, but the gap still exists. There is a pleasant ritual element to the introductory sequence, which can be associated with emotions of anticipation and relaxation. One can speculate that the opening sequence benefits from both the mere exposure effect (in which familiarity breeds affection) (Tom et al. 2007) and the 'pleasure gloss' in which a stimulus becomes associated with a pleasant experience so strongly that it comes to be pleasurable itself (Aldridge and Berridge 2010). The psychologist Kelly McGonigal supplies examples in which the stimulus itself does not seem inherently delightful – the click of a VCR for someone who had learned to love working out to aerobics videos, or the rubbery smell of an exercise mat for a yoga fan – but elicits delight, nonetheless (McGonigal 2019, 48–9). Jenner points out that title sequences are 'a remnant of linear television' and an 'aesthetic rupture' which now operate more as a signal of prestige than a guidepost (Jenner 2018, 155–7). They sometimes do not arrive until the show has already begun and the viewer is already submerged in the narrative. For example, episodes of the Noelle Stevenson reboot of *She-Ra* (Netflix 2018–) displays logos of DreamWorks and Netflix in the show's thematic colours and then cuts right to the chase, sometimes literally. Only after the show has begun and the plot has advanced does the introductory sequence with theme song display. Children are known to take pleasure in repetition, but the same pattern is visible in adult shows like *Hannibal* (NBC 2013–15). The opening sequence plays a few minutes into the show, once the viewer has comfortably surrendered to the narrative. Both the strategies of varying the opening sequence within the plot and providing a 'skip intro' option serve to reduce friction, reduce the opening sequence's potential as a decision point for exiting a show, and insulate the flow.

What, then, of the end of an episode? It is difficult to make a blanket statement about this since different platforms behave differently, and platforms change their own behaviour. Netflix France, for example, tweeted in January 2019 that it would be changing the auto-play time between episodes from 15 seconds to less than 6. They added: 'Désolés, c'est juste pour tester ta rapidité à retrouver la télécommande' ['Sorry, it's just to test how fast you can find your remote control']. This joke supports the notion of the episode as the unit of the binge-watch, rather than 'clock time' or the completed season. The implication is that if you cannot find your remote control before the 6 seconds are up, it will be too late. Further research should investigate at which point viewers who abandon a season stop – at the end of an episode or at the beginning of another?

LIMITATIONS OF THIS STUDY

The participants in this study used a diverse set of technological assemblages to watch the shows in question. Their experience of moving from episode to episode ranged from the comparatively seamless transitions offered by Netflix to the relatively choppy and effortful process of searching for clean copies of episodes to download illegally: An early interviewee from Pakistan remarked that for him and his peers, access to serialised dramas was not about subscribing to streaming services but about keeping their anti-virus software cutting-edge and up-to-date. Their experience changed with the platforms used. One Israeli participant had switched to legal streaming services but was nostalgic about her past practices of streaming and downloading illegally. She had succeeded in creating the unpredictable rewards which are key to habit formation, and visibly relished the satisfaction of finding an episode of good quality outside a paywall. Several other interviewees described changes in their habits associated with moving from a country with a strong copyright enforcement regime to one with a weak regime, or vice versa. Other users shifted in and out of the use of services like Kodi and Plex. This variety means that stable conclusions cannot be drawn about how marked a boundary the end of an episode was for participants.

It is conceivable that the drop-off in completion rates associated with larger numbers of episodes is affected by the possibility that viewers may have watched an episode outside their usual contexts, somewhere unconnected to the tracking software they installed. They may, for example, have watched an episode at a friend's house or on a device without the plug-in which automatically recorded user watch histories. Interviews did not reveal this as a tendency, but nevertheless the possibility cannot be ruled out.

CONCLUSION

Tendencies towards completionism are present in the viewer population, the accuracy of subject time estimation varies, and binge-watching may take place in 'event time,' not clock time. Notwithstanding the disappearance of functional limitations on episode length for streaming video, episode endings remain cues for viewer decisions. The prevalence of the episode in discourse around binge-watching extends to user behaviour. The episode, not the hour, does indeed seem to be the conceptual unit of the binge-watch.

ACKNOWLEDGEMENTS

This paper would not exist without the tireless help and ingenuity of Armagan Amcalar, Colette Berbesque, Ece Caliskan, Brendan Gautier, Marion Le Mière, Kaya Pierce-Grove, Sharon Ringel and Steve R. White. Invaluable comments were provided by Deborah Castro, Ödül Gürsimsek, Mareike Jenner and Michael Schudson.

NOTE

1. Novelty also leads to more memories being laid down, which means that duration is remembered as longer.

REFERENCES

Aldridge, J. and K. Berridge (2010). 'Neural Coding of Pleasure: Rose-Tinted Glasses of the Ventral Pallidum'. In M. Kringlebachj and K. Berridge (eds), *Pleasures of the Brain*. New York: Oxford University Press.

Barasz, K., L. John, E. Keenan and M. Norton (2017). 'Pseudo-Set Framing'. *Journal of Experimental Psychology: General* 146(10): 1460–77.

Castro, D., J. Rigby D. Cabral and V. Nisi (2019). 'The Binge-Watchers' Journey: Investigating Motivations, Contexts, and Affective States Surrounding Netflix Viewing'. *Convergence* 27(1): 3–20.

Droit-Volet, S. (2014). 'What Emotions Tell Us About Time'. In V. Arstila and D. Lloyd (eds), *Subjective Time: The Philosophy, Psychology, and Neuroscience of Temporality*. Cambridge, MA: MIT Press, pp. 477–506.

Garland, H. and D. Conlon (1998). 'Too Close to Quit: The Role of Project Completion in Maintaining Commitment'. *Journal of Applied Social Psychology* 28(22): 2025–48.

Hoagland, H. (1933). 'The Physiological Control of Judgments of Duration: Evidence for a Chemical Clock'. *The Journal of General Psychology* 9(2): 267–87.

Jenner, M. (2018). *Netflix and the Re-invention of Television*. Cham: Palgrave Macmillan.

Levine, R. (1998). *A Geography of Time: The Temporal Misadventures of a Social Psychologist*. New York: Basic Books.

Loftus, E. (1974). 'Activation of Semantic Memory'. *American Journal of Psychology* 86: 331–7.

Loftus, E. (1975). 'Leading Questions and the Eyewitness Report'. *Cognitive Psychology* 7: 560–72.

Lu, J., U. Karmarkar and V. Venkatraman (2017). 'Planning to Binge: How Consumers Choose to Allocate Time to View Sequential Versus Independent Media Content'. Unpublished, cited with permission.

McGonigal, K. (2019). *The Joy of Movement*. New York: Avery.

Merikivi, J., J. Bragge, E. Scornavacca and T. Verhagen (2019). 'Binge-Watching Serialized Video Content: A Transdisciplinary View'. *Television & New Media* 21(7): 697–711.

Noreika, V., C. Falter and T. Wagner (2014). 'Variability of Duration Perception: From Natural and Induced Alterations to Psychiatric Disorders'. In V. Arstila and D. Lloyd (eds), *Subjective Time: The Philosophy, Psychology, and Neuroscience of Temporality*. Cambridge, MA: The MIT Press.

Perks, L. G. (2015). *Media Marathoning: Immersions in Morality*. London: Lexington Books.

Pierce-Grove, R. (2016). 'Just One More: How Journalists Frame Binge Watching'. *First Monday* 22(1).

Pittman, M. and E. Steiner (2019). 'Transportation or Narrative Completion? Attentiveness during Binge-Watching Moderates Regret'. *Social Sciences* 8(3): 99.

Steiner, E. and K. Xu (2020). 'Binge-Watching Motivates Change: Uses and Gratifications of Streaming Video Viewers Challenge Traditional TV Research'. *Convergence: The International Journal of Research into New Media Technologies* 26(1) 82–101

Tom, G., C. Nelson, T. Srzentic and R. King (2007). 'Mere Exposure and the Endowment Effect on Consumer Decision Making'. *The Journal of Psychology* 141(2): 117–25.

Wittman, M. (2014). 'Embodied Time: The Experience of Time, the Body, and the Self'. In V. Arstila and D. Lloyd (eds), *Subjective Time: The Philosophy, Psychology, and Neuroscience of Temporality*. Cambridge, MA: The MIT Press.

Wood, W. (2019). *Good Habits, Bad Habits: The Science of Making Positive Changes that Stick*. London: Macmillan.

TV

Black Mirror (2011–), UK: Channel 4, Netflix
Family Guy (1999–), USA: Fox
Flash, The (2014–), USA: The CW
Game of Thrones (2011–19), USA: HBO
Hannibal (2013–15), USA: NBC
Office, The (2001–3), UK: BBC
Sherlock (2010–), UK: BBC
She-Ra (2018–), USA: Netflix
Stranger Things (2016–), USA: Netflix
Supernatural (2005–), USA: The CW

CHAPTER 8

Binge-Watching and the Organisation of Everyday Life

Lothar Mikos and Deborah Castro

INTRODUCTION

Watching television is a cultural activity that is an integral part of the practices and routines of everyday life (see also Bury 2017). In this context, the binge-watching phenomenon illustrates a trend from mass communication to massive personalisation (Bolin 2014). The algorithms of video-on-demand (VoD) services confront users with a personalised offer that is not only about personalised content and recommendation systems, but also about, for example, the design of the start screen when users access Netflix.

Despite the growing numbers of academic publications on binge-watching, the concept lacks a standardised definition (see Introduction to this volume). Moreover, the term co-exists with more 'comprehensive' concepts like 'media marathoning', which refers to a type of media engagement that 'captures viewers' and reader's engrossment, effort, and sense of accomplishment surrounding their media interaction' (Perks 2015, ix). By means of a literature review, Merikivi et al. concluded that binge-watching could be defined as the 'consumption of more than one episode of the same serialized video content in a single sitting at one's own time and pace' (2019, 6). This definition not only links a pretty low (and therefore controversial) number of episodes in its definition, but it also misses the reference to a key aspect on the studied phenomenon: the technological development. A definition suggested by Mikos in 2016 emphasises it, when he says that binge-watching could be defined 'as a form of television consumption which only became possible with certain technological and commercial developments in the media market, and at the same time was promoted by certain aesthetic and narrative developments in the television series market' (Mikos 2016, 157). Taking into account that people may have differing personal understandings of what a bingeing experience is (Jenner 2016) according to factors such as age, occupation, family situation (Horeck, Jenner and Kendall 2018), one could argue that technological developments, self-determination of the viewer, viewer autonomy and the focus on serialised TV fiction are key variables when defining this mode of viewing.

This chapter looks at the integration of binge-watching as a consumption practice into everyday lives. Back in 2010, Brunsdon connected this mode of viewing with domestic life. Six years later, Chambers concluded that most media and television consumption takes place at home. This aligns with recent data that suggested that 70% of Netflix subscribers watch content on TV screens at home (Richter 2018). Drawing on this, the aim of this chapter is to explore how young audiences integrate the consumption practice of binge-watching television fiction into the rhythms and routines of their everyday lives. Binge-watching has become both a 'me time' and 'us time' activity (with a partner or friends) that, as we will discuss, is critically approached by some young viewers.

The following section presents a brief overview of the theoretical framework where we refer to studies on patterns of everyday television use, television consumption at home and the structures of everyday life. It has been shown that television consumption is also an 'escape attempt' from the constraints of everyday life and creates free space for viewers; 'it is an escape route to other areas and the force that charges up our fantasy batteries' (Cohen and Taylor 1992, 139). Here we suspect a similarity to the practice of binge-watching. The literature review is followed by the results of an empirical qualitative study based on in-depth interviews in two countries, Germany and the Netherlands, whose viewing cultures are also introduced. The presentation of the results concentrates on viewing preferences, the integration of binge-watching into everyday life with a focus on communal watching, and on the self-perception of viewers in relation to their media consumption. It is worth noting that we do not seek to establish a comparison between the results of the two selected countries. By replicating a study originally conducted in Germany (in 2015) in a neighbouring country, i.e., the Netherlands (in 2019), we wanted to get an in-depth view and a richer image of binge-watching patterns as well as to emphasise the need to conduct cross-national research. Finally, the conclusions summarise the findings and contextualise them with current trends in media communication.

THEORETICAL FRAMEWORK

VoD platforms such as Netflix have tried to adapt to the emerging on-the-go watching habits by, for example, allowing offline viewing. However, most of the media consumption of television content still takes place at home (Chambers 2016). For instance, 40% of the global sign-ups on Netflix happen on PCs, 30%

on smartphones and 25% on TV sets. However, six months after subscription, viewers tend to move from their smaller screens to bigger ones, resulting in 70% of Netflix viewing happening on TV sets, 15% on PCs and 10% on smartphones (Peter 2018). The significance of the home as an environment in which to consume television content, even on platforms that facilitate personalised viewing, also in terms of location, justifies the need to review the existing academic literature that deals with domestic television consumption and everyday lives. In this section, domestic viewing, leisure time, motivation to consume television content, and contextual viewing factors will be discussed.

DOMESTIC VIEWING, LEISURE TIME AND EVERYDAY LIFE

The role of everyday life in television consumption has been highlighted by a diverse number of scholars in the last decades. As early as 1982, for instance, Dorothy Hobson noted in her study on the soap opera *Crossroads* (ITV 1964–88): 'Watching television is part of the everyday life of viewers. It is not, as sometimes suggested, a separate activity undertaken in perfect quiet in comfortable surroundings' (Hobson 1982, 110). In the 1980s and 1990s, watching television was considered not only a part of the social organisation of family's homes (Gauntlett and Hill 1999; Lull 1990; Morley 1986) but also a structural and a relational aspect (Lull 1990, 39). Silverstone highlighted that television has a place 'in the visible and hidden ordering of everyday life; in its special and temporal significance; in its embeddedness in quotidian patterns and habits' (Silverstone 1994, 19) and therefore contributes to people's ontological security, mainly in the evenings. Gauntlett and Hill argued 'that the evening schedule is the most significant space in relation to television and leisure time' (1999, 49).

Leisure time cannot be separated from working, because work, leisure and private life 'make up a dialectical system, a global structure' (Lefebvre 2014, 62). And this global structure is the totality of everyday life in which people are integrated and to which they are bound. This totality of everyday life is characterised by 'routines, rituals, tradition, myths [. . .] the stuff of social order and everyday life' (Silverstone 1994, 18). Nevertheless, while work is alienated, leisure activities such as hobbies, holidays, media consumption 'lead us back towards the feeling of presence, towards nature and the life of the senses (or, as the experts would say, towards an audio-visual milieu revitalized by modern techniques)' (Lefebvre 2014, 63–4). At the same time, leisure activities support our recreation, finally to get fit for another day of alienated work.

According to Cohen and Taylor (1992), mass culture can serve as an escape from everyday life. Going to the movies, reading a novel, watching television or binge-watching a drama series can become a daily routine or ritual that allows some comfort time in which the pressures (and the totality) of everyday life disappear. The escape attempts of media consumption take us into a 'liminal period'. In his work on rituals and theatre, Victor Turner explained it as follows: 'The liminal period is that time and space betwixt and between one context of meaning and action and another' (Turner 1982, 113). Media consumption is a time and space between leisure time and the totality of everyday life, it's a free area in which viewers can experience in a fictional world 'a sense of alternative realities' (Cohen and Taylor 1992, 139). Bury compared TV consumption to other leisure activities in the sense that it is 'constrained by professional, personal and family responsibilities' (2017, 61).

The domestic consumption of television was eased by the integration of the TV set into the living room. In the 1970s, remote controls and portable TV sets changed the media arrangement at homes and 'liberated' the TV set 'from its permanent place in the living room' (Chambers 2016, 36). With digitalisation and the advent of the internet, new technical devices allowed the consumption of TV content. As Chambers has noted: 'Despite the allure of second screens, the large TV screen continues to be a social screen: the focal point of the living room in terms of viewing time' (2019, 8).

TELEVISION VIEWING IN THE DIGITAL ERA

That television content is a 'part of the grain of everyday life' (Silverstone 1994, 22) is a claim that has survived the advent and popularisation of newer mediums and entertainment forms. In fact, television is still the world's favourite medium (Zenith Media 2019). In the current digital and hyper-connected world, the ways through which viewers get to know about cultural products have increased greatly and take multiple forms. For example, today's viewers can become acquainted with a cultural product via worth-of-mouth, algorithms or a combination of both. This is what Perks has conceptualised as the 'entrance flow' (Perks 2015, xxiii). In the viewing experience, the entrance to a narrative world can be followed by what she calls the 'insulated flow', which refers to a person's 'extended and focused attention on one text' (Perks 2015, xxiv). In the current context of television consumption, creators of complex television drama (Mittell 2015) and, most importantly, digital developments, have seduced audiences to binge-watch.

For years, one of the aspects that has caught academic attention in the field of media consumption is that of viewing motivations. In the specific context of binge-watching, several international scholars have explored viewers' motivations to engage in this specific type of viewing. Empirical research suggests that these motivations seem to imitate those identified for regular television audiences but transformed, to some extent, by technological developments.

For instance, a study conducted in Portugal by Castro et al. (2021) connects the motivations to watch TV series on Netflix with the period of the day at which this consumption took place. Relaxation seemed to be the main motivation at the end of the day, whilst boredom relief seemed to be the main factor in the afternoon. Catching up, relaxation, a sense of completion, cultural inclusion and improved viewing experiences are the binge-watchers' main motivations identified by Steiner (2017) and Steiner and Xu (2020) in their empirical studies conducted in the US. Panda and Pandey (2017) stated that social interaction, escape from reality, easy accessibility of content and advertising effectiveness of content providers (e.g., through viral content trailers) motivated US college students to spend more time binge-watching.

Viewer autonomy has also been identified as a strong motive to binge-watch (Merikivi et al. 2019, 3–4). Nonetheless, it is worth noting that viewer autonomy has its origin in the 1980s when the VCR allowed people to record TV programmes (McDonald 2007). In the late 1990s, Gauntlett and Hill (1999, 143) explained that viewers would pre-record broadcast programmes to watch the shows at a more convenient time. The commercial use of home entertainment with VHS and more likely DVD box sets underpinned viewer autonomy (Hills 2007; Kompare 2006). Home entertainment became, therefore, an important revenue stream for broadcasters, cable channels and distribution companies. The development of new technical devices changed viewer habits, from dependency on the flow of TV programmes (Williams 1974) to more autonomy and self-determination, culminating with the advent of streaming services.

The contextual factors of the binge-watching experience have also received international scholarly attention, with studies showing similarities in space and time. Young viewers in the Netherlands, for example, tend to binge-watch alone at home, with the living room and the bedroom being the most popular spaces (De Feijter, Khan and van Gisbergen 2016). In the US, 'most binge-watching takes place at home, in the evenings of workdays, and on weekends' (Steiner 2017, 150). Similarly, a study conducted in Portugal suggests that, among young people, binge-watching is considered as an individual activity performed primarily on weekdays, at night (in the bedroom) and in the evening (in the living room) (Castro et al. 2021). The domestic context is thus placed at the centre of the binge-watcher experience on streaming platforms and its practice is integrated into the rhythms of everyday life, as was (and partly still is) television.

All in all, there is a clear intersection point between the different modes of media use and the rhythms and routines of everyday life. People are not able to overcome the dialectical system, the global structure of quotidian life, meaning that watching television and using streaming services mainly takes place in the evenings during times of recreation, allowing escape attempts from everyday pressures. This is the reason our empirical study focuses on binge-watching in the context of domestic life. Our study shows how this integration takes place and how viewers themselves perceive these activities.

VIEWING CULTURE IN GERMANY AND THE NETHERLANDS

In Germany, streaming services began receiving increased attention in 2014, when Amazon Prime Video (known as Amazon Instant Video back then) landed in the country. Seven months later, the popular streaming service Netflix was also made available. In 2018, Amazon Prime Video and Netflix were the main players in the German streaming market. In fact, by the third quarter of 2018, Amazon Prime had 9.9 million subscribers and Netflix had 5.1 million (Rumbucher 2018). Other streaming services such as Dazn, Maxdome, Sky Ticket, and Magenta TV, some of which are focused on special areas like arthouse movies, children's movies and sports, complete the complex VoD landscape.

Despite the growing popularity of these new services, Germany still watches classical linear television. Nonetheless, the number of minutes of daily use decreased from an average of 225 minutes per day in 2011 to 217 minutes per day in 2018 (Zubayr and Gerhard 2019, 91). Young people aged 14 to 29, the generation that first socialised with digital media, watch less and less linear television, spending only 94 minutes per day in front of the TV set. Whereas in 2018 only 31% of adult Germans used streaming services, 67% of youngsters aged between 14 and 29 used Amazon Prime, Netflix and other streaming services, and 96% of this cohort watched videos online (including YouTube, media libraries of public service broadcasters, etc.) compared to 60% of German adults (Frees and Koch 2018, 408).

In the Netherlands, the over-the-top (OTT) market is a 'fast-growing consumer revenue line' (Scheffer and Oemar 2018, 14). In 2017, there were more than 20 different OTT TV video providers in the country, such as Netflix (which arrived in September 2013), Amazon Prime Video, and HBO Go, but also local platforms such as RTL's Videoland. Despite this being a crowded market, Netflix became the most dominant player (PWC n.d.). Netflix penetration has, in fact, increased rapidly, as the following data illustrate: at the end of December 2018, Netflix was present in 39% of Dutch households, 5% more than in December 2017.[1] Due to its high penetration, Netflix growth seems to have slowed down in the second quarter of 2019.[2] In fact, the local player, Videoland, seems to be 'winning ground with penetration of 40% and over 10% of households, respectively' (PWC n.d.).[3] With regard to television viewing consumption, linear television viewing is also decreasing in the under-35 segment 'although at a slower rate than initially expected' (Dhaliwal et al. 2018: 24). As explained by these authors, sports and live shows like *The*

Voice of Holland (RTL4 2010–) still work well in linear television (Dhaliwal et al. 2018: 24).

METHOD

This book chapter presents the results of 26 semi-structured in-depth interviews conducted in Germany and in the Netherlands. The study population ranged in age from 19 to 36, with an average age of 27. The gender breakdown was skewed toward women, with 18 females and eight males. A combination of purposive sampling and snowball sampling was used to recruit the 26 interviewees. To qualify for the study, participants had to a) be television fiction viewers; b) hold German or Dutch nationality and/or be living in the two selected countries at the moment the data was collected; c) be young adults up to 36 years; and d) be able to express themselves in either German or English.

In Germany, 14 participants (10 female and four male) with a median age of 29 were interviewed from October to November 2015. All held German nationality. Four participants had a university entrance diploma (Abitur) at the moment of the interview, three had finished an undergraduate programme and seven a Master's programme. In the Netherlands, 12 interviewees (8 female and four male) with a mean age of 25 participated in the study from April to June 2019. Ten participants were Dutch, one was Lithuanian and one Ukrainian. With regard to educational level, seven had obtained a Master's degree by the time the interview was conducted, and five were involved in an undergraduate or graduate programme at a Dutch University. The four-year gap in the data collection did not affect the results because we looked at the patterns of everyday use. Technologically the same VoD services were available in each country, but in 2019 mobile use of the services was more common than in 2015. However, since we are focusing here on domestic use, this technical development was not significant.

The interview guide was deductively constructed, drawing on the theoretical framework to which this study belongs. Overall, interviews lasted around 45 to 60 minutes and were audio-taped. The interviews in Germany were conducted in German and the interview quotes included in the manuscript have been translated into English by Mikos. The interviews carried out in the Netherlands were conducted in English. The data collected was analysed by means of a qualitative thematic analysis, a method of data analysis that allows for the systematisation of the interpretative process. Drawing on Braun and Clarke (2006), we applied the six phases of qualitative thematic analysis. Finally, and in relation to the ethics of the investigation, all participants signed a consent form.

RESULTS

To explore how young adult viewers in Germany and in the Netherlands integrate their binge-watching practices into their everyday lives, we have organised the results of the 26 qualitative interviews into the three following themes: 1) media consumption and preferences, which allows us to contextualise and, therefore, reach a better understanding of participants' binge-watching behaviours; 2) integration of television in young adults' lives, where we explore the gratifications people obtain from the consumption of television fiction as well as social viewing practices; and 3) intensive viewing, where we discuss people's critical points of view of their television consumption.

Media consumption and preferences

In Germany, all participants use the internet for personal purposes daily, and all of them hold a VoD subscription, mainly Netflix. Seven of them use the internet for more than four hours per day, while the others use it between two and four hours per day. Internet usage includes shopping, searching for information, listening to music and watching audio-visual content online. Some of the participants regularly go to the cinema to watch movies. As some of them describe, they like the experience of going to the theatre and meeting up with friends. For example, a 24-year-old female participant explains that she would find it interesting to spend an evening watching television series on the big screen at a cinema. All the participants watch television fiction on a regular basis. Moreover, German participants prefer American 'quality' series and American sitcoms over productions from other countries and mainly watch them in the original language. Complex drama series are considered a genre in their own right. With regard to the time of the day to consume television fiction, the evening is the preferred time among young adults, with most of them viewing on weekends, since during the week other activities take priority. Even though all participants live a media-saturated everyday life, they also engage in other leisure pursuits, such as meeting with friends and taking part in outdoor activities. Finally, German participants mainly watch on a TV set in the living room, and some on a TV set in the bedroom or on a laptop when in bed.

In the Netherlands, all interviewees report using the internet for personal purposes on a daily basis. Nine of them explain that they use it for more than three hours per day; this includes, for example, the use of social networks and VoD platforms. Going to the cinema is not firmly embedded in their media diet. For example, nine participants report having been to the cinema fewer than eight times in the last 12 months. Reading books is even less rooted in their media lives. Only three interviewees indicate having read an average of more than one book per month in the last year. Concerning the consumption of television content, most of the participants interviewed in the Netherlands watch television programmes between one to two hours per day on weekdays. Results suggest that having more spare time during the weekends does not necessarily mean an increase in the time they invest in this activity. As some of the participants also explain, engaging in other ventures (e.g., going out) becomes a priority.

Thirteen of the participants living in the Netherlands indicate that they have held a Netflix subscription for the last two to five years. The only participant who does not hold any VoD subscription is a female interviewee from Ukraine, who is not used to paying for these types of services. However, this does not stop her from watching Netflix content (e.g. , *Love, Death and Robots*, Netflix 2019–) available on other platforms. Concerning the preferred television fiction genre, no specific pattern has been identified. All the interviewees like at least two different genres, such as comedy, drama, thriller, sci-fi or action, which they select according to their mood. When it comes to the origin of the series they consume, programmes created in the United Kingdom and the US are the most watched, despite the wide variety on offer on VoD platforms. The consumption of non-English language shows (e.g., Spanish, French) happens among those with a bi-cultural background or non-Dutch nationality. Young adults living in the Netherlands prefer to watch television fiction during the evening, in the living room. Nine prefer to watch the television series on their TV sets, including Netflix series.

Integration of television in young adults' lives

In the Netherlands, five of the interviewees who watch television for around one to two hours a day consider that this medium is an integral part of their everyday lives. This evokes the idea of 'ritualized viewing' (Rubin 1985). Interestingly, a female participant explains that the consumption of television is so rooted in her routine that she even misses it during her holidays:

> It's a very normal part of my day. For example, when I go on vacation for like two or three weeks and you hardly watch any TV, I kind of like miss that about being at home. (female, 30-year-old, the Netherlands)

The way television is embedded in people's everyday rituals becomes very clear from the German interviewees. For example, a German mother explains how important watching television is to her after putting her child to bed:

> The child goes to bed early so that we have the evening for us, and we try to use it for entertainment and relaxation. So it just happens, so ritualised: dinner, news and then we usually decide on two episodes. (female, 32-year-old, Germany)

As the previous quote reflects, watching television is shaped by people's professional lives and other responsibilities. For instance, a German woman reflects on the fact that her professional life leaves her less time to watch series:

> Well, in any case I had a lot of time to see a great number of series, and films too. And that happened, on a very large scale. That is, that I really consumed a great deal in a very short time, both on television and on the internet . . . and now, as a working person so to speak, tied to getting up early, to a personal life in which I now live together with someone else, where I simply don't have the time for it any more . . . But sometimes I wish there were no other obligations and I could just watch episodes for four hours at a time. But unfortunately, it's out of the question, both for personal and for professional reasons. (female, 28-year-old, Germany)

What these participants have in common is the positive experience they obtain from the consumption of television, with relaxation and escapism being the main types of gratification, but also happiness, joy and socialisation. Madill and Goldemeier, in fact, emphasise the power that television fiction has 'to promote interactions with others' (2003, 28). A 32-year-old German woman explains it as follows:

> Because these new, good series, people talk about them a lot, and you have an exchange about them with people. That's another reason I feel like watching them. I want to watch *The Wire* [HBO 2002–8] too some time because people always mention it. So, I just want to see it. I'm actually interested in exploring this genre of the new quality series and kind of catching up. (female, 32-year-old, Germany)

Young viewers draw inspiration from television fiction to cope with issues they deal with in their everyday lives (Lacalle 2015). Results from the present study suggest that the consumption of these types of programmes helps some viewers put their own personal problems into perspective, as the following quotation illustrates:

> When I am really upset about things in my life and then I watch *Grey's Anatomy* [ABC 2005–] it's like 'Oh, wait, things could be much worse' even though it's fiction I will still be, like, this could happen and it is not my life so that it's part of it. (female, 26-year-old, the Netherlands)

Finally, watching television goes beyond the viewing session. Talking to friends about the show and even looking for extra information on the internet are also a part of the viewing experiences of some interviewees. In fact, both word-of-mouth and electronic word-of-mouth are predominant types of entrance flow among interviewees from the Netherlands. For example, a 24-year-old woman explains that she does not pay attention to Netflix's recommendations, but to what other people tell her, and to what she reads online.

Social viewing

In the Netherlands, only those who live with their parents, partners or friends watch television with someone else on a regular basis. In these cases, watching television becomes an everyday ritual that happens mostly before bedtime. Moreover, sharing a mutual interest in the content is pivotal: the social viewing experience is over as soon as the interests diverge. In some cases, a new programme is selected. In others, what was once initiated as a social viewing experience becomes an individual activity. This is different from former viewing rituals when families watched whatever was on television together (Gray 1992; Morley 1986). In these earlier rituals, family members did not agree on content, rather they agreed on having a family activity – watching television together. Sometimes they also agreed to watch certain programmes, mainly signature entertainment shows or television drama series. In the era of streamed content, viewers must figure out whether there is a mutual interest in specific drama series. A 28-year-old woman from Germany explains it as follows:

> The question is 'what he wants to see'. And he has *Breaking Bad* [AMC 2008–13] and, all right, then I give way so that we can watch a series at all. But he's not at all interested in series like *Revenge* [ABC 2011–15] and *Under the Dome* [CBS 2013–15], and so on. So, I have to watch them when he's doing something else. (female, 28-year-old, Germany)

Some participants from the Netherlands report that, when watching television content with someone else, they tend to consume fewer episodes in a row than when they watch alone. In other words, when watching alone participants tend to be more sensitive to cliffhangers. For instance, one female participant (24-year-old) explains that when she is on her own and she watches an episode that has a cliffhanger, she usually continues watching. However, when she is with her partner, and she feels like watching the next episode, they look at each other and conclude that 'no, it's late, we should go to bed'. The awareness of the time spent engaging with television series seems, thus, to increase during physical social viewing, as well as the sense of responsibility. By contrast, another female participant (24-year-old) indicates that she watches more episodes when she is with other people because of the social experience it represents.

Another interesting result that emerged from the data is how separation from one's partner changes viewing habits. For example, participants noted how they stopped watching a specific show after breaking up. For instance, a German couple, both 33 years old, found that their series consumption changed after their separation – while she now watches alone with more focus, he now watches television fiction with friends.

For those interviewees who live alone, watching series on VoD services with someone else is a type of social gathering that needs to be carefully planned. Interestingly, those who in the past would watch television series with relatives (e.g., siblings who now live abroad) try to maintain this ritual. For example, a Dutch female participant (24-year-old) explains that, if she is interested in watching a show that fits within the interests of her sister or mother, she either postpones the watching or re-watches it with them. This tends to happen during the weekend when the sister is back home. Another type of arrangement some siblings implement is to watch series asynchronously, even if they are not physically together. This allows them to discuss the series they both like.

However, waiting for someone else to watch the next episode becomes, for some young adults, a challenge. A 'cheating' behaviour emerges when a physical social viewing is planned, and one of the viewing partners cancels the meeting. For example, an interviewee (19-year-old from the Netherlands) explains how he had planned to watch the *Sense8* (Netflix 2015–18) finale with a friend during a weekend. After the friend's decision to postpone the meeting, he decided to watch the episode on his own. The day he met with his friend, he pretended that he had not watched it.

It is to avoid these types of situations that participants prefer to watch movies, documentaries or series with self-contained episodes (e.g., *Black Mirror* [Channel 4 2011–13; Netflix 2015–]) with people they do not live with. In particular, interviewees identified the following four main reasons: First, those types of cultural products are usually shorter; second, the viewing session is self-contained – it has a very specific beginning and end; third, a lack of attention on the content does not have any future impact as there is no episode to follow; and, fourth, one does not really need to wait for anyone to watch the next episode, as the following two quotations illustrate:

> I was going to watch this series, *Westworld* [HBO 2016–], with some friends and I think you can maybe do two episodes in one day, and after that you get tired of watching, right? So, it is just really hard to find the time for all of you to get together and watch the same show and, with a movie, it's just a one-time thing. (male, 30-year-old, the Netherlands)
>
> I do have a twin sister and we used to watch a lot of TV together and now we still try to do so sometimes, when she is over or I am at her place. Also, my family [. . .] but that is mostly movies [. . .], you know, you do not want to wait for someone to come around to watch another episode. (female, 24-year-old, the Netherlands)

Participants from both countries prefer to discuss serialised television fiction face-to-face. Despite the popularity of so-called social audiences worldwide, data suggest that this is not a popular practice. As a female participant (30-year-old, the Netherlands) argues: 'It feels too private; or it feels like "[w]ho needs to know what I am watching?"' Nonetheless, checking to see what other people share online, for example on Twitter, is a more common practice. Here we see how technological innovations have changed the way viewers discuss television fiction.

Perceptions of intensive viewing

According to the definition given by Merikivi et al. (2019) above that defines binge-watching as viewing more than one episode of the same series in one sitting, all interviewees from Germany and the Netherlands have indulged in an intensive consumption of television fiction at least once in the last 12 months. Some of them have watched whole seasons of series in the space of a few weeks, days, or in one viewing session. Reasons to spend several hours consuming serialised television fiction can be both intrinsic and extrinsic. Identified intrinsic motivations are, for example, establishing a strong identification with the characters, experiencing a high degree of emotional and cognitive participation or dealing with some sort of psychological issue (e.g., depression). Concerning the extrinsic motivations, complex narratives, cliffhangers and even bad weather seem to increase people's chances to indulge in intensive viewing.

Despite the key role that television continues to play in young people's everyday lives, we have observed how critical some of our participants are toward their own viewing habits. In fact, most of the interviewees from the Netherlands tend to detach themselves from the idea of binge-watching due to the negative connotation the concept still carries. Three participants from the Netherlands argue that television is too present in their lives and, consequently, would like to reduce the time spent on this activity. This is the case of, for example, a male participant (25-year-old) who establishes a connection between the high level of television consumption and the rough moments he has been through in the month prior to the interview:

> I think it is now to an extent that I do not want it; [. . .] I definitely want to change. I am aware that it is taking too much energy from me, energy that it could be invested in different things and projects. (male, 25-year-old, the Netherlands)

The collected data also supports the existence of multiple and different personal definitions (Jenner 2016) that viewers have of the concept of binge-watching. These definitions vary according to a wide range of factors such as age and family situation (Horeck et al. 2018), length of episode and genre of the show. These are susceptible to change with the evolution of the viewers' own habits (Castro et al. 2021).

> I am not really a binger I think, so after two or three episodes I am like 'Cool I have had my fix for today and now I can go do other stuff'. [. . .] When I think about 'binging' to me it's like staying in on a Saturday and watching like 8 hours of the same series, and I wouldn't do that. But I do watch the same series every night for 2–3 episodes which you could also consider a binge. But to me binging is like properly staying in and not do anything else until you finish, and that is not something I do. (female, 26-year-old, the Netherlands)

This detachment from the idea of being a binge-watcher is somehow connected with the feeling of guilt among the study's participants. An analysis of the responses obtained in the interviews shows how viewers feel the need to justify themselves by, for instance, emphasising what the weather is like and how these conditions have an impact on their decision-making process.

> So sometimes it's just, it's a rainy Sunday or rainy summer's day and you think: okay I don't have to go out either, let's watch a show. And if we like it, then a few more episodes of it. And then [I have always] such a half-bad conscience: Could I have done something else in that time? Oh no, weather was shit anyway, so it doesn't matter. (female, 34-year-old, Germany)
>
> Sometimes it is a waste of time sitting inside and watching TV, especially when it is 25 degrees outside, and you can still go out or ride your bike or go somewhere else. [. . .] At least I judge people who during a sunny day sit inside and watch TV; so, then, I also think that I should judge myself if I do that. (female, 24-year-old, the Netherlands)

Getting bored, lack of patience or the necessity to engage with something different after having spent some time watching television seems to act as a self-regulator for media engagement. A participant from the Netherlands explains it in the following way: 'I only have patience for two or three episodes in a row; after that, I am really sick of it . . . (laugh) unless I have a hangover' (male, 27-year-old). In other cases, the participants refer to the quality of the programme to pace their viewing consumption.

> You know? Some TV series you want to finish and sometimes you find something so high quality that you kind of want to enjoy a little. It is too good to just consume all in one sitting. (female, 21-year-old, the Netherlands)

Most of our interviewees describe the intense viewing experience in a domestic context. However, on-the-go watching was also mentioned. A 34-year-old female participant from the Netherlands explains how she carefully plans her media consumption for when she commutes for almost three hours by train to visit her parents. For example, she selects light programmes that are available on Netflix to download.

Finally, access to a wide range of content explains the remarkable number of shows that our participants fully watched or started to watch in the six months prior to the interview. In fact, most of them acknowledge being unable to remember the number of shows watched and have to check back, during the interviews, on Netflix's history or other apps some of them use to keep track of the series they consume. Participants from the Netherlands indicate that they have watched 10, 20 or even 30 shows in the semester prior to the interview. Although some participants abandoned some of the shows they started, dropping shows does not represent a common behaviour for two main reasons. First, participants know what they want to watch and, therefore, are selective when choosing a new programme. Second, and related to the previous argument, the investment that people put into viewing the first episodes of a show pushes them to continue watching. 'Why give up now?', asks a Dutch female interviewee (24-year-old). Re-watching shows that one loves also reduces the chances to abandon a series:

> I am not a super adventurous person so, once I have found something I enjoy, I am like 'Ok, cool, that's it, I am enjoying this so . . . I can do it again'. Because I do enjoy it the second time. I watch it or read it or whatever. [. . .] You know that you are gonna enjoy it, so it is not very risky. (female, 26-year-old, the Netherlands)

CONCLUSION

It is well known that, with the popularisation of VoD services, today's viewers are even less dependent on the television schedule; they have expanded their autonomy as well as increased their self-determination. Results from our empirical study suggest that binge-watching is, like linear television (Bury 2017; Chambers 2016; Gauntlett and Hill 1999; Lull 1990; Morley 1986), a domestic activity that happens primarily in the living room in the presence of a TV set.

Viewers shape their television consumption to their personal circumstances and preferences. This way, binge-watching has been considered both as a 'me time' as well as an 'us' activity, when the consumption of a show is shared with partners, family members and, less frequently, friends. The deep immersion into the complex narration of the television fiction shows and the identification with the characters, combined with the technology of streaming services to start the next episode of a television fiction series instantly, allow the experience of 'flow'. Here the combination of technological change (streaming, algorithms) and change in the television market (peak of complex television) which are the basis and prerequisite for binge-watching becomes very apparent.

According to Cohen and Taylor (1992), mass culture and art allow 'escape attempts' from everyday life, a free space for the imagination; and this is applicable to the binge-watching mode of viewing. In general terms, our participants consider consuming television fiction to be a positive experience. They consider it to be a personal leisure-time event from which they relax after a day of work, escape from reality, obtain happiness and socialise. However, results also indicate how critical young people are toward this intensive type of consuming television fiction. In some cases, this goes hand-in-hand with a feeling of guilt and wasting time, that has a long tradition in the history of television. According to Gauntlett and Hill, feeling guilty and wasting time stems

> partly from an internalization of the view that television is an unworthy medium, a banal way to spend time, and the poor relation to reading, listening to music, playing with children, putting up shelves – or any other activity that can be categorized as more mentally or physically challenging, or more sociable. (1999, 121–2)

Our participants compensate for the feeling of guilt and wasting time by labelling binge-watching as a hobby or highlighting the feeling of an imaginary connection to other binge-watchers who are interested in the same series. This sense of collective experience was already evident with radio and television (Chambers 2016, 35) and, today, platforms such as Netflix, which has been conceptualised as a kind of transnational broadcaster (Jenner 2018), is nurturing this sense of collective experience on a global scale.

As noted, our participants tend to discuss serialised content that is offered by streaming services with family members and friends face-to-face. When they are not present, social media may come into play: it is in this way that an individual viewing activity becomes a social activity that is part of everyday life. Finally, participants watched (or started to watch) around 10 to 30 shows in the semester prior to the interview. Despite how carefully they seem to select the content they want to watch, most participants experienced difficulty remembering the shows they had consumed.

This empirical research has shed light on the integration of binge-watching as a domestic consumption practice into young viewers' everyday lives in two European countries. Despite its academic contribution, the study has some limitations. First, the majority of our participants self-identified as female

(69%) and all of our interviewees were well-educated. Future research should construct a more heterogeneous sample. Second, there was a four-year gap between the two periods of data collection in Germany and the Netherlands. Finally, as this study only addresses domestic binge-watching, mobile binge-watching could be a relevant subject for future research.

NOTES

1. See <https://www.broadbandtvnews.com/2019/01/21/39-of-dutch-homes-had-netflix-in-q4-amid-flatter-growth> (last accessed 12 March 2021).
2. See <https://www.broadbandtvnews.com/2019/07/29/research-netflix-growth-slows-in-the-netherlands> (last accessed 12 March 2021).
3. PWC refer to data published by Telecompaper (2019).
4. The impact of social networks (such as Twitter) on the viewing experience has popularised the term 'social audience', which prolongs the life of a text beyond the limits imposed by the act of viewing it as such (Quintas and González 2014).

REFERENCES

Bolin, G. (2014). 'The Death of the Mass Audience Reconsidered: From Mass Communication to Mass Personalisation'. In S. Eichner and E. Prommer (eds), *Fernsehen: Europäische Perspektiven*. Konstanz: UVK, 159-72.

Braun, V. and V. Clarke (2006). 'Using Thematic Analysis in Psychology'. *Qualitative Research in Psychology* 3, 77–101.

Brunsdon, C. (2010). 'Bingeing on Box-Sets: The National and the Digital in Television Crime Drama'. In J. Gripsrud (ed.), *Relocating Television: Television in the Digital Context*. London and New York: Routledge, pp. 63–75.

Bury, R. (2017). *Television 2.0. Viewer and Fan Engagement with Digital TV*. New York: Peter Lang.

Castro, D., J. Rigby, D. Cabral and V. Nisi (2019). 'The Binge-Watcher's Journey: Investigating Motivations, Contexts, and Affective States surrounding Netflix Viewing'. *Convergence* 27(1): 3–20.

Chambers, D. (2016). *Changing Media, Homes and Households: Cultures, Technologies and Meanings*. London and New York: Routledge.

Chambers, D. (2019). 'Emerging Temporalities in the Multiscreen Home'. *Media, Culture and Society*, 41, 1–17.

Cohen, S. and L. Taylor (1992). *Escape Attempts: The Theory and Practice of Resistance to Everyday Life*. New York and London: Routledge.

De Feijter, D., V. Khan and M. van Gisbergen (2016). 'Confessions of a "Guilty" Couch Potato: Understanding and Using Context to Optimize Watching Behaviour'. In *International Conference on Interactive Experiences for TV and Online Video – TVX'16*, Chicago, United States, 22–24 June <doi: 10.1145/2932206.2932216>

Dhaliwal, V., S. Pattheeuws, M. Heeren and J. van der Werf (2018). 'Future of Video: Changing Video Consumption Patterns'. *Outlook: Entertainment & Media Outlook for the Netherlands 2018–2022*. Available at: <https://www.pwc.nl/nl/entertainment-media-

outlook/2018/assets/documents/pwc-entertainment-media-outlook-2018-2022.pdf> (last accessed 14 February 2020).
Frees, B. and W. Koch (2018). 'ARD/ZDF-Onlinestudie 2018: Zuwachs bei medialer Internetnutzung und Kommunikation'. *Media Perspektiven* 9: 398–413.
Gauntlett, D. and A. Hill (1999). *TV Living: Television, Culture and Everyday Life*. London and New York: Routledge.
Gray, A. (1992). *Video Playtime: The Gendering of a Leisure Technology*. London: Routledge.
Hills, M. (2007). 'From the Box in the Corner to the Box on the Shelf'. *New Review of Film and Television Studies* 5(1): 41–60.
Hobson, D. (1982). *Crossroads: The Drama of a Soap Opera*. London: Methuen.
Horeck T., M. Jenner and T. Kendall (2018). 'On Binge-Watching: Nine Critical Propositions. *Critical Studies in Television* 13(4): 499–504.
Jenner, M. (2016). 'Is this TVIV? On Netflix, TVIII and Binge-Watching'. *New Media and Society* 18(2): 1–17.
Jenner, M. (2017). 'Binge-watching: Video-on-demand, Quality-TV and Mainstreaming Fandom'. *International Journal of Cultural Studies* 20(3): 304–20.
Jenner, M. (2018). *Netflix and the Re-Invention of Television*. Cham: Palgrave Macmillan.
Kompare, D. (2006). 'Publishing Flow: DVD Box Sets and the Reconception of Television'. *Television & New Media* 7(4): 335–60.
Lacalle, Ch. (2015). 'Young People and Television Fiction. Reception Analysis'. *Communications* 40(2): 237–55.
Lefebvre, H. (2014). *Critique of Everyday Life* (The One-Volume Edition). London and New York: Verso.
Lull, J. (1990). *Inside Family Viewing: Ethnographic Research on Television's Audiences*. London: Routledge.
Madill, A. and R. Goldmeier (2003). 'Text of Female Desire and of Community'. *International Journal of Cultural Studies* 6(4): 471–94.
McDonald, P. (2007). *Video and DVD Industries*. London: BFI.
Merikivi, J., Bragge, J., Scornavacca, E., and Verhagen, T. (2019). 'Binge-Watching Serialized Video Content: A Transdisciplinary Review'. *Television & New Media* 21(7): 697–711.
Mikos, L. (2016). 'Digital Media Platforms and the Use of TV Content: Binge-watching and Video-on-Demand in Germany'. *Media and Communication* 4(3): 154–61.
Mittell, J. (2015). *Complex TV. The Poetics of Contemporary Television Storytelling*. New York and London: Routledge.
Morley, D. (1986). *Family Television: Cultural Power and Domestic Leisure*. London: Comedia.
Panda, S. and S. C. Pandey (2017). 'Binge-Watching and College Students: Motivations and Outcomes'. *Young Consumers* 18(4): 425–38.
Perks, L. G. (2015). *Media Marathoning: Immersions in Morality*. Lanham, MD: Lexington Books.
Peter, K. (2018). 'You can watch Netflix on any screen you want, but you're probably watching it on a TV'. *Vox*. Available at: <www.vox.com/2018/3/7/17094610/netflix-70-percent-tv-viewing-statistics> (last accessed 3 January 2020).
PWC (n.d.). 'Entertainment & Media Outlook for the Netherlands 2019–2023'. Available at: <https://www.pwc.nl/en/industries/entertainment-media/entertainment-and-media-outlook-for-the-netherlands/tv-and-video.html> (last accessed 14 February 2020).
Quintas, N. and A. González (2014). 'Audiencias activas: Participación de la audiencia social en la televisión' [Active audiences: Social audience participation in television]. *Comunicar* 22: 83–90.
Richter, F. (2018). 'Netflix Users Revert to the Big Screen After Signing Up'. *Statista*. Available at: <https://www.statista.com/chart/13191/netflix-usage-by-device> (last accessed 26 June 2019).

Rubin, A. M. (1985). 'Uses of Daytime Television Soap Operas by College Students'. *Journal of Broadcasting & Electronic Media* 29(3): 241–58.

Rumbucher, J. (2018). „Marktforscher: Netflix überholt Sky in Deutschland bei Abo-Zahlen'. *Blickpunkt: Film*, 15.10.2018. Available at: <http://beta.blickpunktfilm.de/details/434277> (last accessed 29 May 2019).

Scheffer, C. and R. Oemar (2018). 'Ride the new wave of convergence!' *PWC. Outlook. Entertainment & Media Outlook for the Netherlands 2018–2022*. Available at: <https://www.pwc.nl/nl/entertainment-media-outlook/2018/assets/documents/pwc-entertainment-media-outlook-2018-2022.pdf> (last accessed 12 March 2021).

Silverstone, R. (1994). *Television and Everyday Life*. London and New York: Routledge.

Steiner, E. (2017). 'Binge-Watching in Practice. The Rituals, Motives and Feelings of Streaming Video Viewers'. In C. Barker and M. Wiatrowski (eds), *The Age of Netflix: Critical Essays on Steaming Media, Digital Delivery and Instant Access*. Jefferson, NC: McFarland, pp. 141–61.

Steiner, E. and K. Xu (2020). 'Binge-Watching Motivates Change: Uses and Gratifications of Streaming Video Viewers Challenge Traditional TV Research'. *Convergence: The International Journal of Research into New Media Technologies* 26(1) 82–101, <doi: 10.1177/1354856517750365> (last accessed 12 March 2021).

Turner, V. (1982). *From Ritual to Theatre: The Human Seriousness of Play*. New York: Performing Arts Journal Publications.

Williams, R. (1974). *Television: Technology and Cultural Form*. London: Fontana.

Zenith Media (2019). 'Consumers will spend 800 hours suing mobile internet devices this year'. Available at: <https://www.zenithmedia.com/consumers-will-spend-800-hours-using-mobile-internet-devices-this-year> (last accessed 14 February 2020).

Zubayr, C. and H. Gerhard (2019). 'Tendenzen im Zuschauerverhalten. Fernsehgewohnheiten und Fernsehreichweiten im Jahr 2018'. *Media Perspektiven* 3: 90–106.

TV

Black Mirror (2011–), UK: Channel 4, Netflix
Breaking Bad (2008–13), USA: AMC
Crossroads (1964–88), UK: ITV
Grey's Anatomy (2005–), USA: ABC
Into the West (2005), USA: TNT
Love, Death and Robots (2019–), USA: Netflix
Revenge (2011–15), USA: ABC
Sense8 (2015–18), USA: Netflix
Under the Dome (2013–15), USA: CBS
Westworld (2016–), USA: HBO

CHAPTER 9

Binge-Watching Audience Typologies: Conclusion

Lisa Perks, Emil Steiner, Ri Pierce-Grove and Lothar Mikos

Binge-watching was a relatively obscure phenomenon before 2012. Although practised and discussed in niche circles since before the advent of DVDs, it was not until streaming services and broadband internet became more and more ubiquitous that binge-watching received increased media and academic attention. Between 2015 and 2020, researchers have asked many questions about binge-watchers, including why they watch, what motivates them, how engaged they are (or not), and what outcomes they report after the binge-watching experience.

Scholars exploring these questions have found a range of motives, a variety of experiences, a spectrum of engagement, and positively and negatively valenced binge-watching outcomes – some of which are dependent on one another. Why a person binge-watches is strongly tied to what they hope to get out of the experience. What they actually get out of it is tied to what they watch and how they watch it (Castro et al. 2021; Steiner 2017). Our audience part of this book has uncovered additional patterns and structures of binge-watching. To round off the part, we use this chapter to describe audience typologies that shed some light on the why, where, when, with whom, how, and to what end of binge-watching.

MOTIVES

Steiner and Xu (2020) found the following binge-watching motives: 'catching up, relaxation, sense of completion, cultural inclusion, and improved viewing experience' (90). These aligned with finding by Perks (2015), Pittman and Sheehan (2015), and later Panda and Pandey (2017). While some motives, such as relaxation and cultural inclusion, are similar to those of traditional television, others, such as *sense of completion* and *improved viewing experience*, result from the technological affordances of streaming video and high-speed internet. Central to these motives is the issue of control as a motivator, in the sense of using technology to control the viewing experience – catching up, sense of completion. Viewers' desires to express that control – whatever, wherever, whenever – became amplified through binge-watching. Thus, the more you watch, the more control you symbolically express. The extrinsic motivation of cultural inclusion moved in lockstep with the perceived improvements and seasonal bounties of television content associated with Peak TV (Jenner 2019).

ENGAGEMENT

Motives alone cannot explain why people binge-watch. The relationship of their viewing rituals to those motives tells a more complete story. Steiner and Xu (2020) noted that viewers 'differentiated their binge-watching experiences by their levels of attentiveness' (90), which they conceptualised as a Viewer Attentiveness Spectrum (VAS). Viewers seeking relaxation tend to select shows that require less attentiveness than the shows selected by viewers seeking the improved experience (in contrast to linear/appointment viewing) and enhanced narrative transportation and emotional/linguistic engagement. This 'textual appetite' (Perks 2015) drives textual engagement through viewer control of the text and textual control of the viewer. Tukachinsky and Eyal (2018) similarly found that the longer the binge, the greater the intensity of parasocial relationships between viewers and characters. Mikos (2016) found that viewers become accustomed to a series because they engage more intensively with the characters. Concurrently, and ironically, that attentiveness is perceived by viewers, and marketed by Netflix, as 'a disruption of scheduled TV viewing' (Pilipets 2019, 3).

TYPES OF BINGE-VIEWERS BY MOTIVE/ATTENTIVENESS

In a large quantitative study of American binge-viewers, Pittman and Steiner (2021) found two overlapping subtypes across the dimensions of planning, company and engagement: feast-watching and cringe-watching. How and why we binge-watch is the shaper of these subtypes in the synchronicity, or lack of it, between motive, content selection and ritual. The positive feelings associated with feast-watching and the negative feelings associated with cringe-watching were found across genres and are related to how a viewer's experience (how and what is watched) aligns with their motive (why). As Perks (2015) writes, flow has now become viewer-directed and viewer-contained (xxii). Fundamental to all of these is the control to shape one's viewing experience by the entangled relationship of motive, engagement and content selection.

VIEWING PATTERNS

Intentional vs unintentional binge-watching

Merikivi et al. (2019) identified viewer autonomy as a central element of transdisciplinary binge-watching definitions (10). Digital streaming platforms pave the way for viewer agency in terms of *accessing* and *programming* content – affording even more autonomy and ease than DVD box sets or DVRs (see Jenner 2017; Perks 2015). However, the act of bingeing, not just accessing the texts or starting to view, has varying degrees of agency. Binge-watchers report a range of (un)intentionality in their chronologically condensed succession of episodes. Perks (2015) used the phrase 'insulated flow' to capture the 'extended and focused attention on one text' (xxiv) that happens in a streaming binge-watch. Insulated flow is encouraged by narrative features and content-delivery services (queuing up the next one). Continuing to watch can also be attributed to 'self-regulation deficiencies' (Tukachinsky and Eyal 2018), 'impulsivity' (Walton-Pattison, Dombrowski and Presseau 2018), or other internal factors that make it hard to stop watching once the story is rolling.

Perks (2015) found a mix of intentional and unintentional media marathons from her interviewees. Many people 'schedule shifted' – postponing previously scheduled plans or routine obligations to make way for their binges (22). Some of the most common behaviours were postponing sleep or reducing the amount of sleep, de-prioritising eating or food prep (i.e., ordering in instead of cooking) and putting off work. However, many media marathoners were intentional, saving binge-worthy content for a work or school break, or for a break in weekly scheduled TV programming. Those who planned out their binges, Pittman and Sheehan (2015) found, were more likely to be motivated by engagement (considering binge-watching to be more interesting or entertaining than traditional viewing), hedonism (enjoying the sexual or violent content in binge-watched shows), and social factors (connecting with friends over content or feeling less lonely while bingeing).

Bingeing as stable trait vs situational occurrence

The scant evidence on the topic of binge-watching as a stable trait or situational occurrence all gestures in the direction of situational. Riddle et al. (2018)

surveyed over 200 undergraduates, finding that 78% engaged in intentional *and* unintentional binge-watches (2017, 600). Of the 19% who reported only one type of binge-watching, the vast majority were intentional about their viewing (2017, 600). Analysing interviews with adults who media marathoned while going through a health struggle, Perks (2019a) found that the majority of participants 'tapered' their marathon – watching less television and fewer episodes in one sitting – once they started feeling better. She wrote that bingeing 'was not a pathological or fixed pattern; rather, it was a purposeful coping response to unique circumstances and individual cognitive, emotional, and/or physical needs' (31).

Pierce-Grove (2020) found users changing their content preferences as well as bingeing patterns according to circumstances. For example, one interviewee who received word that he would be targeted and blacklisted switched to bingeing content from the country to which he hoped to emigrate. A different interviewee binged narrative content and local sports while at home, but when he left home to bike across the continent, he switched to sporadic watching of non-narrative videos about extreme physical feats. These results show that binge-watching practices are integrated into the demands and rituals of viewers' lives (see Chapter 8 in this volume).

The Covid-19 pandemic brought binge-watching suddenly to prominence as one of the safest pleasures available. The discourse shifted accordingly. In the press, sweeping objections to screen time receded in favour of finer distinctions between 'good' screen time and 'bad' screen time. Millions of healthy people found themselves unexpectedly in the position of Perks's 'health copers'. In order to avoid becoming sick, they had to stay home as much as if they already were. For Perks's participants, binge-watching ebbed naturally when health struggles resolved. It remains to be seen whether that behaviour will play out on a larger scale for the populations who find themselves pinned to their sofas by the needs of public health.

Viewer agency matters, but networks, distributors and streaming services play a role in determining in what direction the binge-watching trend will go. Take, for example, the survey respondent in Perks's chapter who said he 'always binges' and that it was 'tough' to watch *Game of Thrones* (HBO 2011–19) episodes on a weekly release schedule. We expect binge-watching to become a more stable pattern over time, especially if media executives cave in to viewer preferences: As a generation of 'streaming natives' grows up, binge-watching will move toward the new normal of television engagement (see Perks 2015).

Based on qualitative interviews, Steiner (2018) found the following binge-watching subtypes based on rituals that are distinct from what typically have been considered binge-watching: 1) sleep bingeing; 2) speed bingeing; and 3) sports bingeing. Sleep bingeing is described by interviewees as 'watching video on their phones in order to relax in bed at night' (163). While watching TV while falling asleep is not new, what distinguishes this practice is that the content is almost always Low Viewer Attentiveness Spectrum (LVAS) and previously viewed, and viewers often may not actually watch (164). Also, Mikos (2016) found that some viewers prefer binge-watching in bed before falling asleep. Speed viewing is a ritual subtype driven by the motives of catching up and cultural inclusion. Viewers use technologies to speed up the pace at which the show plays, allowing them to consume more quickly (167). Sports bingeing is perhaps the most non-conforming subtype. Because the flow of live television cannot be controlled (at least as far as skipping ahead) by viewers, most scholarship has omitted it from content that can be binge-watched. However, Steiner (2018) found that viewers of tournaments such as US college basketball's March Madness and the World Cup used the term binge to describe their consumption. While these were rare, a follow-up study (Steiner 2020) found that viewers define the components of binge-watching – consumption of multiple episodes that build toward a conclusion during an intense period of time – with the same language as they use to describe the NCAA March Madness basketball tournament.

Solo viewing vs communal viewing

The third viewer engagement pattern of solo versus communal relates to the first two dichotomies or spectra in the viewing patterns section: communal viewing is likely to be both intentional and situational. It is intentional because co-viewing takes planning. It is often situational because of the challenges that planning poses. However, we'll also see that asynchronous binge-watching can be a communal experience.

Mikos and Castro's chapter described binge-watching as 'me time' and an 'us activity' that can be 'shared with partners, family members, and, less frequently, with friends'. Perks (2015) described ritualised marathon viewing for buzz-worthy shows such as *The Walking Dead* (AMC 2010–) and *The L Word* (Showtime 2004–9). Of the participants in Perks's study for this book, 40.8% ($n=49$) reported co-viewing at least one of the two shows they binge-watched. Most often, the co-viewing happened with romantic, cohabitating partners. Sometimes, mutual interest in a new show inspired the viewing. Other times the binge-watchers had a longer relationship with the show. A 28-year-old white woman enjoyed earlier seasons of *Better Call Saul* (AMC 2015–) with her husband. Together, they 'binged the seasons of this show in preparation for the new season coming out'. Co-viewing complications arose for some. A 25-year-old white male participant started binge-watching *Stranger Things* (Netflix 2016–) with his partner, but their stamina didn't align through the season. He reported: 'they fell asleep and I had to finish it so I netflix cheated on them'. Mikos (2016) found that partners with interest in different content sometimes watched their respective favourite series separately, but agreed on common consensus series, usually those that were the subject of much public discussion, that they watched together.

Scheduling complications or an inability to be in the same room while watching isn't necessarily an impediment to bingeing 'together'. Perks (2015) described asynchronous marathoning as a 'shared, but temporally separate, [social] experience' (34), noting that many people binge-watched content that friends or family recommended – and then engaged in lively discussions about it. For binge-watchers going through a health struggle (often homebound or stuck in a hospital), the asynchronous marathon was a productive social opportunity. Perks (2019b) found that many binge-watched content alone that friends, family members and co-workers recommended, thus banking 'social capital' that could be 'realized in the moment *and* stored up for redemption in future social interactions' (323).

The spectrum of solo viewing to co-viewing is more accurately a range of practices that accounts for opportunities to connect with others through many means and temporalities. Many binge-watches are solo enterprises; however, that label doesn't account for the binge-watching inspiration (perhaps a friend's recommendation) and a social aftermath (discussing the show with others in person, online or through other means). Additionally, some motives, such as transportation and cognitive engagement, may lend themselves better to content selections that demand the kind of attentive engagement better suited to solo viewing (Pittman and Steiner 2021).

Alternating vs continuous binge-watching

In an early blog post on binge-watching, Amanda Lotz described herself as occasionally alternating between two series, as one might alternate between a magazine and a novel (Lotz 2014). Pierce-Grove found that behaviour – alternating between watching several shows or types of video content – mirrored in a population of 55 interviews. Some interviewees watched a show continuously, watching straight through a single series from beginning to end, but many viewers interrupted one show with episodes of another over a period of weeks. The presence of a partner tended to influence people toward alternating content, as they switched between shows they enjoyed together and shows that one partner watched alone (Pierce-Grove 2020).

BINGE-WATCHING OUTCOMES

Regret

Binge-watching need not have negative outcomes, but some viewers do experience regret following a prolonged media engagement experience. Perks reported that some 'film and television marathoners felt ashamed of not having anything tangible to show for their time' (2015, 57). Those who anticipated regret, Walton-Pattison et al. found, were less likely to binge-watch (2018). Pittman and Steiner (2021) concluded that 'solo, accidental, and distracted (cringe-watching) predicts increased regret and decreased well-being' (1). It should be noted that they position *accidental* as 'no planning or premeditation was involved so that a viewer's binge motives may not align with content selection' and *distracted* as 'exerting attention in a fashion that inhibits a viewer's attainment of gratification sought' (2).

For others, it was the *quality* of the experience that led to regret (or not). Perks applied the economic term 'sunk costs' to describe how some viewers regretted wasting 'time on a series that was not ultimately pleasurable or entertaining' (Perks 2015, 58). Some people she interviewed knew that they did not enjoy watching the end of their chosen story (*Lost* [ABC 2004–10] earned two mentions), but they kept going just to see how it ended – a dissatisfying experience. This finding dovetails with a participant quote from Steiner's (2017) qualitative study: 'I only feel bad about binge-watching if the show sucks' (155).

After observing that 'the need for completion often led to the longest binges and was often associated with negative feelings' (Steiner 2017, 155), Steiner pursued this line of inquiry quantitatively. Pittman and Steiner 'found that the more participants binged a show out of a cognizant desire for [narrative completion], the less likely they were to regret it' (2019, 10). However, actual narrative completion did not significantly impact regret. The authors propose that '[t]he takeaway here for viewers who want to maximize their binge-watching experiences is to remain relatively cognisant of the process, sporadically asking themselves, "Do I care what happens next? Am I actually enjoying this show?"' (10) Interviewees from Mikos and Castro's study evaluated binge-watching largely as a positive experience and only very few showed regret.

Nostalgia

Nostalgia captures a lingering feeling that connects a previous viewing of a text to a binge-watch. Steiner observed a spectrum of viewer binge-watching attentiveness, finding that '[l]ess attentive bingeing is almost always for relaxation, nostalgia, and distraction' (2017, 151). Those three motivations – relaxation, nostalgia and distraction – accurately map onto Perks's study of media marathoners who went through a health struggle. One participant binged *Mad Men* (AMC 2007–15) following a surgery because: '[I]t's one of my favorite shows, so it was comfortable. And I knew it, and I really didn't have to focus that hard.' He could recover from his surgery while relaxing with a distracting show that he knew he liked. Perks's larger work on media marathoning books, film, and television found that re-engaging familiar texts 'facilitated interactions between the present-day reader and [their] past self' (2015, 53). In other words, people reflected back on what they were doing and who they had been at the time of their first viewing or reading. The experience of nostalgia spins a long thread spanning text, viewer and temporality.

Character engagement

Binge-watching or marathon viewing can encourage viewers to form strong connections with characters and storyworlds, leading to speculation, analysis, reflection and deep appreciation. Tukachinsky and Eyal's marathon viewing study found that '[t]he more back-to-back episodes that viewers consumed, the more they interacted with the characters, reflected upon them, and empathized with them' (2018, 285–6). These viewer/character interactions are signs of parasocial relationships, which refer to feelings of friendship or closeness between viewers and characters (see, for example, Horton and Wohl 1956). When comparing traditional television viewing to marathon viewing, Tukachinsky and Eyal found that marathon viewing was 'related with greater PSR [parasocial relationships]' (2018, 288). Perks observed that these parasocial relationships can lead to parasocial mourning when a text concludes: at the end of a series, media marathoners missed the characters, the storyworlds, and the marathoning experience itself (2015).

DEFINITIONS

Binge-watching discourse has consistently defined binge-watching as multiple episodes watched, rather than multiple hours spent. In a chapter in this volume, Pierce-Grove finds that this emphasis on episodes, rather than time, is mirrored both in how users think about watching and how they watch. Analysis of a large dataset of user viewing histories showed that the more episodes a given season had, the less likely viewers were to complete it. The correlation was stronger than with the number of minutes in a season, and was independent of both the run-time of an individual episode and how highly the show was rated. This suggests that episode boundaries provide viewers with choice points in which they may choose to continue or not, and that the more choice points are presented, the more users drop off.

Qualitative interviews confirmed that viewers thought of episodes, rather than hours, as the units of a binge-watch. They uniformly described their viewing in terms of episodes, and, when planning or negotiating with members of their household for binge-watching time, negotiated for episodes, not hours. We can reasonably conclude that episode boundaries, however arbitrary, delineate the units of a binge-watch for both viewers and scholars.

SUMMARY

Binge-watching is not a homogenous practice. During its period of booming media coverage (2010–15), it was framed as a lengthy, all-consuming experience in which activities of ordinary social life were suspended. But even during this time, cracks and contradictions appeared in the simplistic framing of binge-watching. Viewers and journalists described 'leisurely' binge-watches, absent-minded binge-watches or binge-watches that took up very little time but consumed multiple episodes (Pierce-Grove 2016). Since then, researchers have continued to tease apart the multiple practices that have been bundled together under the rubric 'binge-watching'. We are now prepared to establish a taxonomy of these practices.

Binge-watching types can differ according to motivations and viewing practices, and according to personality, personal circumstances, social relations, and an interest in specific content. Some motives, such as relaxation, nostalgia and cultural inclusion, do not differ very much from classic television engagement. Others, such as a sense of completion and improved viewing engagement, seem to be typical for binge-watching. The main differences in the binge-watching experience typologies can be found between intentional and unintentional viewing, stable trait and situational occurrence, solo viewing and co-viewing, and between alternating and continuous viewing. These different binge-viewing patterns or classifications are ideal-typical, but they can certainly co-exist within individual viewers. The typologies described here show the heterogeneity in cultural practices of binge-watching.

REFERENCES

Castro, D., J. M. Rigby, D. Cabral and V. Nisi (2019). 'The Binge-Watcher's Journey: Investigating Motivations, Contexts, and Affective States Surrounding Netflix Viewing'. *Convergence: The International Journal of Research into New Media Technologies* 25. <doi: 1354856519890856>.

Horton, D. and R. R. Wohl (1956). 'Mass Communication and Para-Social Interaction: Observations on Intimacy at a Distance'. *Psychiatry* 19(3): 215–29.

Jenner, M. (2017). 'Binge-Watching: Video-On-Demand, Quality-TV and Mainstreaming Fandom'. *International Journal of Cultural Studies* 20(3): 304–20.

Jenner, M. (2019). 'Control Issues: Binge-Watching, Channel-Surfing and Cultural Value'. *Participations* 16(2): 298–317.

Lotz, A. (2014). 'Binging isn't quite the word'. *Antenna* (29 October). Available at: <http://blog.commarts.wisc.edu/2014/10/29/binging-isnt-quite-the-word> (last accessed 6 March 2020).

Merikivi, J., J. Bragge, E. Scornavacca and T. Verhagen (2019). 'Binge-Watching Serialized Video Content: A Transdisciplinary Review'. *Television and New Media* 21(7): 697–711.

Mikos, L. (2016). 'Digital Media Platforms and the Use of TV Content: Binge-Watching and Video-on-Demand in Germany'. *Media and Communication* 4(3): 154–161.

Mittell, J. (2015). *Complex TV: The Poetics of Contemporary Television Storytelling*. New York and London: Routledge.

Panda, S. and S. C. Pandey (2017). 'Binge Watching and College Students: Motivations and Outcomes'. *Young Consumers* 18(4): 425–38.

Perks, L. G. (2015) *Media Marathoning: Immersions in Morality*. London: Lexington Books.

Perks, L. G. (2019a). 'Media Marathoning and Health Coping'. *Communication Studies* 70(1): 19–35.

Perks, L. G. (2019b). 'Media Marathoning through Health Struggles: Filling a Social Reservoir'. *Journal of Communication Inquiry* 43(3): 313–32.

Pierce-Grove, R. (2020). 'Binge-Watching: Trait or State?' Unpublished Ph.D. dissertation chapter.

Pierce-Grove, R. (2016). 'Just One More: How Journalists Frame Binge Watching'. *First Monday* 22(1).

Pilipets, E. (2019). 'From Netflix Streaming to Netflix and Chill: The (Dis)Connected Body of Serial Binge-Viewer'. *Social Media + Society*. Advanced online release.

Pittman, M. and K. Sheehan (2015). 'Sprinting a Media Marathon: Uses and Gratifications of Binge-Watching Television through Netflix'. *First Monday* 20(10). Available at: <https://firstmonday.org/ojs/index.php/fm/article/view/6138> (last accessed 2 April 2020).

Pittman, M. and Steiner, E. (2019). 'Transportation or Narrative Completion? Attentiveness during Binge-Watching Moderates Regret'. *Social Sciences* 8(99): 1–14.

Pittman, M. and E. Steiner (2021). 'Distinguishing Feast-Watching from Cringe-Watching: Planned, Social, and Attentive Binge-Watching Predicts Increased Well-Being and Decreased Regret'. *Convergence*. <doi:10.1177/1354856521999183>.

Riddle, K., A. Peebles, C. Davis, F. Xu and E. Schroeder (2018). 'The Addictive Potential of Television Binge Watching: Comparing Intentional and Unintentional Binges'. *Psychology of Popular Media Culture* 7(4): 589–604.

Steiner, E. (2017). 'Binge-Watching in Practice: The Rituals, Motives, and Feelings of Netflix Streaming Video Viewers'. In M. Wiatrowski and C. Barker (eds), *A Netflix Reader: Critical Essays on Streaming Media, Digital Delivery, and Instant Access*. Jefferson, NC: McFarland, pp. 141–61.

Steiner, E. (2018). 'Binge-Watching Killed the Idiot Box: The Changing Identities of Viewers and Television in the Experiential, Streaming Video Age'. Ph.D. dissertation, Temple University, Philadelphia, PA, USA. Retrieved from ProQuest. (10813061).

Steiner, E. (2020, April). 'Binge-Watching March Madness: Live Sports Tournament Consumption as a TV Binge Subtype'. Paper accepted for presentation at the 50th Annual Popular Culture Association Conference, Philadelphia, PA.

Steiner, E. and K. Xu (2020). 'Binge-Watching Motivates Change: Uses and Gratifications of Streaming Video Viewers Challenge Traditional TV Research'. *Convergence*, 26(1): 82–101.

Tukachinsky, R. and K. Eyal (2018). 'The Psychology of Marathon Television Viewing: Antecedents and Viewer Involvement'. *Mass Communication and Society* 21(3): 275–95.

Walton-Pattison, E., S. U. Dombrowski and J. Presseau. (2018). '"Just One More Episode": Frequency and Theoretical Correlates of Television Binge Watching'. *Journal of Health Psychology* 23(1): 17–24.

TV

Better Call Saul (2015–), USA: AMC
Game of Thrones (2011–19), USA: HBO
L Word, The (2004–9), USA: Showtime
Lost (2004–10), USA: ABC
Mad Men (2007–15), USA: AMC
Walking Dead, The (2010–), USA: AMC

PART III

Transnational Bingeing

CHAPTER 10

National, Transnational, Transcultural Media: Netflix – The Culture-Binge

B. G.-Stolz

'Media. I think I have heard of her. Isn't she the one who killed her children?'
'Different woman', said Mr. Nancy. 'Same deal'.

Neil Gaiman, *American Gods*

'EVERYWHERE IS NOW OUR NEIGHBOURHOOD'
(*EXPLORATIONS*, CBC 1960)

With each technological evolution in media, there have been critical voices fearing for ill effects in consumer health, social systems, political stability. In more recent work, Wendy Hui Kyong Chun has pointed out that any sort of habit tied to media is understood as teetering on the addiction side of engagement. One reading of habit is prompting the perpetual technological adaptation that ensures we perceive the same as brand new (Chun 2016). Each innovation restarts what I term a cycle of de-habituation and re-habituation in viewer engagement and consumption practices; in other words, our falling out of use of 'classic' television and into use of all that is today deemed televisual and new. The habits thus may actually not be all that new, even if often discussed as such in academia and public debate. Instead, if looked at closely, they are only perceived as altered, as the elements changed are in effect minuscule and reframe rather than re-invent engagement practices. In step with this cycle of old and new, of interpreting and making tangible a shift of how we meet media, are new voices taking up the debates, isolating the new at times and always inviting a revival of prior key arguments made in regards to the relationship of humans and media. Much of this is inevitably centring on technological determinism and thereby viewer habits tied to how we read technological innovation and interaction or dependency. This is evident, for example, in the recent resurgence of Marshal McLuhan's work, especially visible in media ecology studies, work attempting to revive media specificity, and in media configurations studies that review the inter-dependency and effects-chain of specific media upon each other. Generally there is a cyclical, perceivable rise in technology-based debates, and ongoing 'death of . . .' cries.[1]

Netflix's international growth, global product line and international studio expansion are as valid a site of study for these changes as the other end of the spectrum – hyper-local content, live television, small market production – but as more and more television is produced specifically with both local and global markets in mind, it is that globally available content that underlies the promotion of transculturality which the following considers in its development as communal belonging through binge culture. As windowing practices are coming to an end, scarcity and recency are changing core values. The international trade of media content remains a game of scales and the myth of – or potential for an actual – transcultural media experience offers unprecedented lateral growth (Ball 2016) tied to consumer interaction and value considerations.

Habits, as they are referred to here, are formed around the rhythms of programming, intended by the industries to craft 'appropriate' audiences. Audiences are constructed groupings, shaped by industry expectations and considered appropriate when their members do not turn that dial, push that button or turn off their screens. In other words, appropriate audiences are made of consumers who keep consuming. This is not a habit formed on, by, or in relevance to interfaces. While much work has been done on interfaces (Chun 2016; Jenner 2018; Johnson 2017), for the purposes of this argument there is no relevant difference between zapping with or without a visual interface. De- and re-habituation are concepts I have developed corresponding to the stresses of local versus global content, their audiences (including Foreign Program Adopters (FPA)), (legality of) access, and consumption more broadly speaking. Consumption here is focused on habits formed around concepts of belonging, cultural capital, and the most classic of debates of media: globalisation. There is certainly also an element closely related to binge-viewing more specifically, where a shaping of how we organise our media consumption becomes highly relevant and where habits are valued in relation to our valuing of that consumption. Work such as Dennis Broe's *Birth of the Binge* (2019) identify very briefly a notion of the re-organisation of leisure time in neoliberal capitalism. But the industrial motivations in programming flow, even as discussed through a cultural lens by Raymond Williams, were then as they are now tied to a need to maintain eyes on the screen. Thus, scheduled programming was designed to deliver these just as much as suggestions and auto-play are today. Beyond that, I am interested in the interdependence of audience and industry, the development of social dimensions of the notion of media cultures and how audience identity is constructed through notions of belonging.

Broe identifies a re-organisation of time and content engagement practices as intimately linked with hyper-industrialism in creative industries and, thus, with the exchange of cultural content. Inadvertently, he is connecting bingeing to ongoing debates about the quality of life in a post-digital age. By doing so, Broe's argument makes a case for audience functions in the industrial complex not being given enough importance in studies in various fields of the humanities; something I have been reframing in my own work. We therefore truly need to acknowledge this cyclicality of habit, of de- and re-habituation, falling out of some practices to engage in new ones. This is evident in both the media environments' ecosystems and their scholarly engagement. I argue that much work currently done reviews elements of the 'new age' of media that are repetitions (in more or less successful disguises) rather than actual new developments. That being said, there is much new to be explored, especially in concepts of socio-political investigation and related concepts of belonging, memory and cultural engagement. Shifting our debates may skew the impact upon which we bestow importance in the long run, and ultimately displace Netflix from its highly visible pedestal-position in academic interest and public attention.

To clarify, habit and habitual engagement here are investigated for their impact on sociological dimensions such as concepts of community, nation and culture rather than on the quantity of consumed programming. The medium is not interrogated for its specific technological dimensions or offerings, but for its industry-to-audience pathways that change, as a result, these sociological dimensions by shifting power dynamics, understandings of self, community and globality. The term 'bingeing' conjures specific associations in addition to simple over-consumption: there are notions of undifferentiated, mindless ingestion of content and, if you will, a loss of clearly identifiable 'taste', both where the individual programme's taste is concerned and the taste evidenced through choice by the consumer. As the identity of the subject of consumption loses its intense taste or definition (its sense of the local, its familiarity, moral continuity, etc.), its importance in itself decreases. Still, the habits formed and their effect on engagement and comprehension increase. There is a blending of identities and origins that is enhanced by bingeing not just quantity of hours, but cultures. Cultural meaning, as a result, is shifting. Considering meaning as discourse, information born of specific socio-systems, we may begin to investigate how Netflix's global ambitions and global content screened to its global market relate to binge culture. After all, it is culture, ultimately, that is being binged. But this culture is rendered less distinct, less defined and less detectable in its own right where specificity is concerned. Adjusting to newly shaped viewer habits, Netflix brings you culture that is traded, marketed, made seductively accessible to sell its 'global TV' brand, to entice local audiences, and to sell global citizenship as the service's new cultural capital. This is culture tailored for the binge.

This part has three aims and three chapters including this one, which also functions as its introduction: 1) to identify the relevance of binge studies to the creation, flow and consumption of national content on an international (global) scale; 2) to clarify the key terms, debates and issues in contemporary television studies dealing with international flows of content; and 3) to in itself present three possible and versatile theoretical approaches to investigate the effects of transnational cultural exchange on creative content, affecting audience identities (G.-Stolz), branded national genre (Jenner), and international reception and treatments of narrative (Watts).

It is worth noting here that the international expansion of Netflix and other streaming services is not unlike the shakeout phases of international film in the late 1920s and early 1930s, a case in point for the cyclicality of studies as well as media. While the amount of audio-visual media content and the speed with which it moves across borders and markets has not been matched in the past, it would be problematic not to note the global-markets' history of early film, and its Multiple Language Version Films (MLVs). MLVs were a rather standard practice of ensuring international audiences whilst circumventing licensing restrictions meant to secure cultural protection at the onset of sound film. Especially before dubbing and subtitling practices had been refined, many studios in Europe and America, the two driving forces of 'global' film production and circulation, worked together to reshoot the dialogue sequences in different languages. Both international format television and contemporary deals which Netflix and other global players strike with local outfits in respective markets have dimensions worth critical investigation that are reminiscent of MLV business rationale, production realities, international policy and cultural specificity.[2]

TRANSCULTURALITY, BINGEING AND NETFLIX'S GLOBAL CITIZEN

Transculturalism as a media-relevant model leans on a host of scholarly works (Arslan and Rață 2013). Most importantly for this discussion I build upon three core essentials embedded in Tassinari's work (Cuccioletta 2001):

- transculturalism abandons prior, classic notions of identity shaped by imperialist endeavours rejecting ties to nationalist/national cultures;
- transculturalism often stands in opposition to the nation state and its notions of community and identity
  - transnationalism not only acknowledges the nation state but refers to movement between such states and thus reinscribes their importance as senders/receivers;

- transculturalism is not to be equated with multiculturalism; multi-culturalism celebrates the individual natures of various cultures and equally reinscribes nation-state-based cultural values of individual identities.

That being said, it is important to note that ongoing processes and content are often closer to fulfilment of transculturality in their promotional language and activation of audiences than actual content and industrial practice. Especially the latter remains tethered still to traditional regional boundaries and built on nation states, their geographical limitations and political influences and licences.

I will here simplify and side with the most prevalent academic argument that states that 'nation' is 'entirely modern and entirely constructed'.[3] As such, media studies have often invoked Benedict Anderson's work, built on the central power of media itself, that proclaims: '... the nation [...] is an imagined political community – and imagined as both inherently limited and sovereign' (2006, 6–7). Anderson's argument maintains his validity. Academia tends to discuss media viewers, audiences, and communities as formed, governed, and hierarchically divided through their engagement with media and specific technologies (Anderson 2006). Ernest Gellner (2006) acknowledged a certain distance between the bordered state and the concept of nation (something too often conflated) and Hechter (1995), Herder (Patten 2010) and others see nation building within the state as a form of cultural separation. Let it suffice here to say that debates on nation are varied, complex, contextually bound and ongoing for hundreds of years. Television studies, as a field that discusses national broadcasting, nationalism, transnational trade, the value of national distinctiveness, production systems and content in so much of its contemporary work, has asked remarkably few questions about it and its related meanings in the more recent past. As Netflix and its changes to transnational television flow force the issue more strongly, it seems increasingly pertinent to understand the various ways in which the company builds on notions of a cosmopolitan audience to market itself globally as we will see below.

'National' is by no means required to be directly addressed for it to be a predominant framework organising scholarly, critical and fan-oriented work. 'National' is implied, a backdrop unnamed. US American national industries, no matter their global involvement, are understood as such, yet hardly identified specifically in this way. The focus, when addressing nationhood, marketplace, cultural exchange, by default appears to lie on that which is not national. Scholarship which is concerned with transnational artefacts, cultures and production and which interrogates media's movements from one to another nation in effect reaffirms the nation state as the defining element in its wake. Terms such as international, multinational, global or even multicultural all define their boundary transgressing research, vantage point or subjects precisely by invoking nation as the manifestation worthy to identify against. This is because we expect to have an implied definition ready to apply to the contexts in question, even if those definitions are often vague. This is where transculturalism, and especially its promotion, can function to refocus the studies away from state equating nation. Instead we can explore industry cultures and processes, relationships of power, media makers, media content and media consumers as relating to notions of belonging. This is whether these notions are constructed at the hand of industry or perceived by individuals due to a sense of cultural capital, both often activated by manipulations in the realm of affect. Viewer and creator engagement with international content is tailored to appeal to non-specific cultural markets by maintaining both: cultural odour as point of interest; and a unique selling point (USP). But they also delimit cultural specificity to ensure it will not block textual access.

Delimiting specificity also means selective purchase practices where narrative content is concerned. Stories people can relate to across cultural boundaries most easily travel across national markets and become transnational media. Adrian Athique discusses the value and place of the transnational, placing it in connection with viewers and audiences because content shaped by one cultural background is through trade and perception affected by discursively different communities, their individual participants and new constructs of appropriate audiences. Invested in diasporic communities and audiences, the work focuses on transnational media flow, or better yet, a media exchange (for exchange means not eradication), that is expressed in various clusters of cultural engagement and therefore allows for a distinctive 'zoned' media consumption. Diasporic communities can consume media flows both in cross-cultural and crossover terms, of which Bollywood is an example (Athique 2014). But this should not be understood as a transnational exchange, because it lacks mitigation of content for the new audience; there is no focus on making content accessible to audiences who may hail from a different cultural market.

Considering the realities of media exchange, and the terms of success, it is no surprise that Athique sees content made for crossover exchange as 'defined by the commercial or critical success of a media artefact located in one ethnic culture with a majority audience located in the dominant culture' (Athique 2014, 9).[4] In this chapter's specific context, one may consider the cultural capital of Netflix's (though shifting) productions such as *Typewriter* (Netflix 2019), *Sacred Games* (Netflix 2018–), *Ghoul* (Netflix 2018) and *Jinn* (Netflix 2019), as designed to entice local subscribers in the respective markets. These need to be understood as transnational offerings too, wherein their 'foreignness' is key to their transnational existence, and where we can argue that they add to Netflix's brand as increasingly transcultural.

This chapter cannot cover some of the larger questions of the power dynamics of gatekeeping related to geographic, cultural and national boundaries, key players functioning as the arbiters of taste, or provide an in-depth analysis of transculturality and streaming media, its history, affect and entanglement. Rather, it gives a brief insight to possible vantage points to address these complexities through audience engagement and habit.

DE-HABITUATION, COMMUNAL BELONGING AND LOCAL-NESS – TV ASSUMPTIONS

In the Canadian TV programme *Explorations* (CBC 1956–65), McLuhan said in an interview from 1960: 'The world is now like a continually sounding tribal drum. Where everybody gets the message all the time.' He refers to a medium we now decry as being on its way out: TV. Viewer perceptions of engagement then felt as if all areas of life were permeated by this one home-based, non-mobile screen. Our feelings toward media may thus not have changed all that dramatically, as the same fears and worries for our youth – addiction to media and the power of its message – seem to be surrounding us today as they did then. That being said, few would argue that the pace with which we make use of and access content has visibly changed daily life, and as a result may also affect our sense of communal belonging: newer technological developments and industrial responses to our engagement with them increase agency and therefore a sense of ownership (if access is provided). Much of our willingness to trust the algorithmic process is built on never being more than an arm's length away from it: familiarity breeds acceptance. As Chun puts it in her book *Updating to Remain the Same: Habitual New Media* (2016), reminding us of a long-acknowledged conundrum about media changes; media are most important when their newness has been replaced by their commonness. Community is shaped, according to Anderson (2006), in no small part by sharing knowledge (language, histories, morals, shared values and terminology, etc.) and a sense of ownership and familiarity, a shared commonness of experience. This increases a certain buy-in for consumers and audiences and according to Anderson can be built easily with the help of a uniform medium. That uniformity upon which this original work was built has shifted. How we think of and conceptualise communities is therefore less bound by a geographically regional shared history or knowledge. Media dissemination and reception have changed, region is defined differently, how communities are bordered is less bound by heritage, and how geography impacts on exchange of content is entirely new. I see the move away from geographic boundaries as key to trade in recent years. It is visible in the way in which audiences value foreign content, as argued by academics such as Pia Jensen (2016). This differs substantially from how television scholars found audiences to value such content at the close of the last century (Iwabuchi 2002; La Pastina and Straubhaar 2005; Straubhaar 1991; Tunstall 1994, 2008, and others).

There are underlying political and social norms of international media and television trade, starting with cultural protectionism evidenced in decisions made about subbing or dubbing, content quotas, and financial support for local productions.[5] Cinema is quite global in its earliest trade deals, in part because of its non-existing language component at its onset. For television programming, cultural and language proximity played an important role, visible in the focus of television studies that relate to content trade and cultural exchange as well as television policy. This truly shaped viewing habits, including viewer engagement, and willingness to engage, with content of foreign-language origins, as well as subbing, dubbing or editing practices. English, and to a lesser degree French and Spanish, language markets were perceived by industries to be the least willing to engage with foreign-language content. Jensen, as part of a Danish research group's investigation of Danish Drama's new-found global critical recognition and commercial success, conducted a large-scale participant study that showed 'contemporary audiences (...) continually zooming in and out between the familiar and the strange, and between the local and the global in their engagement with transnational content' (Jensen forthcoming). This identifies a new willingness to playfully engage with content and to investigate the foreign as much as the local, which prior studies had demonstrated as unlikely audience behaviour (Iwabuchi 2002; Lobato 2019; Tunstall 1994, 2008). This is certainly a significant change for audiences from English language markets such as the US and the UK who, traditionally, have not been seen as subtitle- or dubbing-friendly markets in the past, evidenced by a lack of foreign-language licensing and trading (Dwyer et al. 2018).

Ramon Lobato discusses national policies affecting Netflix's expansion and identifies different strains of media scholarship coming together due to changed distribution and exchange flows. He acknowledges the realities of inter-territorial release and distribution modalities – after all, markets, territories, signal area and nation all still play a significant role in shaping the movements and forms of media exchange (2019). He invokes key debates about national identity in its relationship to media, referencing Williams, Iwabuchi, Gillespie and others in his work. As a result, and in line with scholarly work which tries to reframe medium-related terminology, Lobato proposes to focus on different kinds of mobility rather than discussing national vs transnational vs global. When Netflix CEO Reed Hastings exclaims that he is shaping 'the first global television network' (Murgia 2016), it pays to take a moment and question what that means in terms of media mobility: content from where, crafted for whom, moved to where, and for whom?

Foreign Program Adopters need to access international content outside the terms of television windowing practices to gain early access since this determined 'value' in FPA communities online well before social media became a normalised way to engage these debates. Early international mega-successes for niche audiences, such as *Lost* (ABC 2004–10) or *Dexter* (Showtime 2006–13), made this visible in chat forums and community sites such as the now defunct Thefuselage.com, a.k.a. The Fuselage.[6] However, international exchange may often be problematic due to spoiler culture. This is easily traceable through conversations in forums both internationally and nationally during the last seasons of *Dexter*, where FPA exchanged access, but also discussed language barriers that the non-dubbed version posed for many. Significantly, this meant the need to engage with non-subbed or non-dubbed content to access elected programming closer to its release date. And this, at the very least, demanded a comfortable level of English language comprehension. Thus, education entered the equation, only matched by a certain requirement for tech savviness to access the content via servers, P2Ps, through VPNs and DNS proxies. Participation in such activities, I argue, increases cultural capital in international viewing communities, making said early access contain enough value to drive more FPA towards illegally accessing content to circumvent release window delays.[7] The question, then, is whether the accessibility and the trade of content illegally online are enough to put in motion and firmly establish such a large-scale behavioural shift in how industries construct audiences and in how we, as potential audience members, engage with media.

Bringing up again Athique's notion of taste-related consumption of 'foreign' content, the resulting crossover audience relates to such programming based on 'taste' already, clearly invoking Bourdieu (Wallace 2016).[8] This is taste that can be interpreted and understood in this context as cultural capital through early access and, and this is the key, the otherness of the cultural content in question. This cultural capital is a currency in community building and maintenance and, depending on the community, can be influential in crafting a self-identity because it is tied to larger concepts of global citizenship. In a more specific and marginalised sense, this is evidenced by fan communities for Bollywood, who may develop an appreciation of Indian pop culture in a broader sense, or K-Pop listeners who may become interested in Korean identity and history, and Japanophiles who have for a long time included connoisseurs of specific Japanese media outputs such as anime or Japanese horror. What many of these examples share are stories and narrative that tend to have a broad appeal: love stories, song and dance, fear and horror; often generically packaged in a way that is only to a degree foreign to and different from other cultural expressions of similar emotions, stories or life events. To a degree, one may argue that this is the first evidence that affect can be seen at work when connecting to near-universal interpretations of emotions in AV media (Ahmed 2013). Jensen points out that the idea of universal themes is not adopted broadly in academia, but it has merits when widening the idea of cultural proximity – proximity originally built on cultural heritage and language predominantly. Today individual viewers' or target audience's interests, genre concepts and experiences are seen as equally relevant (La Pastina and Straubhaar 2005; Straubhaar 1991). There are arguments in favour of shared human experiences fostering universal themes and narratives. The phrase 'culturally removed – emotionally proximate' (Jensen forthcoming) signifies this quite clearly and appears to apply to Netflix's use of genre and themes embedded in their latest global commissions (and explored further by Jenner in this part). Emotions, in television studies, are sometimes discussed as discourse driven,[9] in other words, affect and attachment are viewed as culturally specific. This does not mean that content is not able to travel on that basis, but that the more foreign a culture is (or the less culturally proximate, to use Straubhaar's terms), the less likely that affect applies, and notions of universal themes or narratives dissipate. That being said, the increased mobility of individuals, and the increased global exchange between individuals via social media outlets, etc., is definitely and visibly fostering an increased cultural approximation. As such, I argue that transculturality has already been (albeit in a less tangible way and with narrower geographic margins), readying audiences through other factors of cultural exchange for decades, and Netflix is making use of this to build its own notion of global television.

One particular Netflix advertisement is built on the game '6 degrees of separation', and was released via its social media feeds such as LinkedIn and soon after discussed in articles by critics and business insiders.[10] The video identified that Netflix users all 'have 6 shows in common', no matter who or where they are. Shows cut across all ages, genders, regional origins and, most importantly, class for all manners of constructed audiences. According to Netflix data, audiences even watch and react to series in the same way at the same point of storytelling (pausing, restarting, binge-watching).[11] The advertisement sells Netflix as a bridge between people, across regional, national, cultural, age, gender, race or class boundaries. A German columnist, when writing about Netflix's first science fiction series, *Sense8* (Netflix 2015–18), used the term Seelen-Kommunismus (soul-communism) (Seibel 2015) to describe the thematic (and affective) politics of the text. In other words, the narrative discusses the emotional connectors between humans leading to a more cerebral connection, a deep and universal understanding and tolerance, which Netflix consumption can bring about. This is, to put it bluntly, cultural capital 2.0, the formation of a better global citizen who understands that we are all the same. This global citizen-ness implies a higher position in the cultural hierarchies of the world. Caitlin Smallwood, VP for Netflix's Data Science and Engineering, spoke in a recent episode of the *Women in Data Science* podcast[12] about data and content at Netflix, and, specifically pointed at the international and even transcultural nature of Netflix's offerings. She argued that those opportunities to engage with international content can result in a more understanding and tolerant, open-minded individual. This further establishes Netflix's underlying marketing strategy, which identifies the individuals who work for the company, the corporate environment created, and the underlying logic of expansion at Netflix: subscribing to or working for/with Netflix both embodies and directly feeds into the assured participation in a global citizenship. Netflix's content is built for the transcultural citizen of tomorrow.

Streaming services and media providers with global ambitions, including but not limited to Amazon (Pilot Season – 'It's in Your Hands'), Netflix ('Anytime. Anywhere. Instantly'), HBO ('It's HBO') embed a sense of exclusivity with 'elite', and more importantly, cosmopolitan audience appeal, marketing still to that constructed 'quality' audience hailed in Robert J. Thompson's work on US television in 1997, still addressed in Newman and Levine's work *Legitimating Television* (2012), and adapted to narrative concepts more specifically but still identifying a specific audience in Jason Mittell's *Complex TV* (2012). The following, however, is less interested in this particular debate of the QTV discussion that focuses on a certain commodity audience (Smythe 2006) and more interested in identify formation as it relates to branding and consumption. As such it discusses how this generates a shifting notion of the national, furthers a brand of transculturalism and feeds an ideal of soul-communism.

BINGEING NATIONAL CONTENT IN INTERNATIONAL MARKETS

Netflix's marketing campaigns work with established parameters of 'quality': respected authors, directors, talent, high budgets, detail-oriented art direction working in 'cinematic' ordained visual styles and complex narratives (Thompson 1997, 13–16), that much is true. Here, then, the now decade-long US television-centric debate may seem appropriate to make an entrance as this does in fact provide an air of legitimacy important to permit the programming to take on cultural capital and produce value, especially at the onset of illegal online exchanges identified as essential in shaping the FPA communities and Netflix's expansion itself. This, however, has somewhat passed, and that fact is essential to the argument here. Binge culture across various borders has eroded much of the definition of content required to create stand-out programming, I argue. Many of the providers offer a broader spectrum of programming tapping into equally broader constructed audiences (accumulative niche = mass audience of scale). As such, we are buying into the marketing strategies and tend to as scholars ignore some of the tell-tale signs of entering a new era of lowest common denominator programming. For Netflix, the cultural capital is paired with melodramatic narrative structures (as discussed in Part IV on narratology in this collection) and branding that identifies the individual viewer as programmer of their own experience, both of which ensure that audiences have opportunities to emotionally attach and then claim that attachment as choice. Announcing, often via the talent involved, that even the creators have agency when working with the provider increases a sense of artistic merit for consumers: writers and producers like Eli Roth have claimed in the past that the creative freedom they enjoy with Netflix is unequalled. A more detailed account was given by the creatives of Miso Film, the production shingle that produced *Rain* (Netflix 2018). The team behind Netflix's Danish thriller series stated at a conference in 2018 in Denmark[13] that they had no dictates, no guidelines, when they had been signed by Netflix. What they also said was that they had a very clear idea of what Netflix wanted, that they had a sense of what Netflix is and what its audience is expecting. That knowledge of international subscribers, the specific 'Netflix audience', may shape the content from the outset because norms and expectations do not have to be transmitted if brand is that well established. This is consumers, talent and content coming together to engage in the Netflix Cultural Moment, the Cultural Binge, the global awakening of television.

POST-DIGITAL BELONGING IN BINGE-MODE

The relationship consumers have with the cultural artefacts, specifically with entertainment media, is changing, but not due to consumption practices tied to a specific medium, or to technological interventions but to an altered understanding. Viewers understand their position and relationship with media differently, acknowledging cultural capital, buying into the myths of ownership and individualism, and seeing the cultural binge as an opportunity to broaden their horizons. As such, some individuals will embrace the thought of global citizenship. Audiences are understood and constructed differently by industries, too. Industries needed to reshape the audience's underlying value, as borders, regions and communities shifted in the post-digital era. The connected notions of taste, even if Netflix invokes the term in its quantum theory, class, or worse, quality, are starting to erode in practice. Yet, the underlying message, picked up as branded sales-pitch remains, is strengthened, and maybe is about to reach its peak. To reiterate Wendy Chun's key points, it is when those that engage with media no longer give that engagement a second thought, when the media or technology is deeply ingrained in daily life, that it is the most powerful. This notion is at the very heart of the concept of post-digital media and without a doubt is why media researchers are forever engaged in asking the same questions, with every new cycle of media evolution, with every new cycle of de- and re-habituation. Little has changed, but everything is new. Netflix makes visible a perfect joining of those elements here noted as relevant to media engagement as shaping identity and self-worth.

Contemporary media content for Netflix and many other global outfits is crafted to appeal to an international audience; it needs to have low entry barriers and provide a marketable human connection, while maintaining a sense of place to feed the transcultural, open-minded, educated viewer who engages purposefully with foreign-made content . . . and can afford the subscription. This set of 'requirements' has direct effects, especially when paired with notions of binge-ability. It does not focus on bingeing quantity in hours, but instead bingeing variety, where cultural diversity is not truly what is on offer and distinctiveness of cultural offerings is eroded. This begets some interesting changes to generic structure, narrative process and storytelling, as well as identifying (through themes) specific genres as clearly successful in generating new and maintaining subscriptions and/or viewers.

Rob Watts is interested in what enables specific content to travel and its reception as both foreign or relatable, and as generating cultural capital. He sees what I above termed foreign program adopters as viewers engaged through a tourist gaze that alters critical engagement with television content nationally and international, aptly pointing out that travel for leisure was always linked to a certain class status, which is now to an extent replicated in viewers' affect built on easy-to-enter but clearly foreign content. The problem addressed above in considering bingeing as something that here erodes specificity can also shift that legitimacy debate, however, leading to a doubted authenticity of the content in question in the long run. Much as travellers now seek authentic experiences away from that which is perceived as staged, this ultimately may lead to a downgrading of Netflix's cultural capital, a process we already see setting in with mounting criticism of Netflix commissioned content. The high-concept strategies behind production and promotion highlight the similarities in content and critics have begun questioning business motives, market needs, etc., and thereby removed a layer of cultural capital. This is affecting the more successful series, such as *13 Reasons Why*, especially in follow-up seasons.

Netflix took over the 2007 young adult novel *13 Reasons Why* in 2015 and released it as a series in 2017. The critical success of the novel was mirrored in the success of the series. Subsequent seasons were increasingly discussed as generated for profit and minimising the power of the original season/novel. Mareike Jenner discusses Netflix programmes that can be understood as coming-of-age stories in a similar vein to *13 Reasons* later in this part. Young adult drama series, often referred to as teen TV, which speak to one of Netflix's key demographics, 14–35-year-old urban viewers, is a genre driven by personal narratives of loss and discovery and navigating the transition between childhood and early adulthood. Stories here often are shaped by highlighting several teens in small cliques, often channelled through the experiences of the odd-one-out lead. Arguably, many cultures experience this transition period in life differently, to different extents of cultural acknowledgement of the same, actual time of living in the transition, yet can still relate to the transition as 'inevitable'. Jenner looks more closely at engaging cultural odour as marker of difference in these series, while maintaining specificity sufficiently low to generate no border barriers for non-native language audiences, as well as considering language admissions by Netflix.

NOTES

1. For recent work focusing on McLuhan and his current role see Anton (2017), Miconi and Serra (2019), and Swartz et al. (2019), amongst others. Especially the fields of media ecology and technology/post-digital studies have re-immersed themselves into debates based on McLuhan's work on Medium and the Global Village.
2. For more on Multiple Language Film see Vincendeau (1998).
3. <http://www.nationalismproject.org/what.htm> (last accessed 8 March 2021).
4. This is markedly different from most readings of Netflix's model. Rajiv Menon (2015) writes: '. . . this global expansion suggests a need for television content that resonates culturally on a transnational scale'. While Netflix's new global audience doesn't share a common site of origin, the shared cultural concerns of dispersed communities provide an important model for thinking about transnational viewership. Much like content that targets diasporic communities, the components of these shows – multiple settings, characters of various national origins, stories about migration and travel – illustrate an interest in audiences defined by their global-mindedness (Menon 2015).
5. Language preference is an often discussed identifier of market value and viability in trade practices in cinema and television trade. There are many country- and/or market-specific writings to identify individual contexts and considerations regarding language policies for audio-visual cultural artefacts, for example Blinn (2008) on the German market, Mereu Keating (2013) on Italy's policies or Vincendeau (1988) on the era of MLVs.
6. This is based on research I conducted in 2013 and 2016 developing the framework for FPA, and mostly focused on German, Dutch and British consumer exchanges online in relation to accessing foreign media content before their national release dates and licence agreements.
7. On a side note it pays to acknowledge that such behaviour is not new for niche fan communities, marginalised or not, and that early access and spoiler culture has now seen a shifted focus to reality television, as corporate media systems have adjusted scripted content accessibility to suit these audiences. A good example of this is Twitter's lively *Survivor* fandom community, which exchanges links and open chat sites focused on English language or subbed international variants of the US franchise of the same name.
8. Bourdieu describes cultural capital as: 'instruments for the appropriation of symbolic wealth socially designated as worthy of being sought and possessed'.
9. For more on this discussion, please review, for example, Lünenborg and Maier (2018), or Cavalcante (2018).
10. For example, see *Forbes* magazine: <https://www.forbes.com/sites/danafeldman/2019/02/13/according-to-netflix-we-all-have-6-shows-in-common/#7eedde05463d> (last accessed April 2019).
11. The video itself has since been removed, but the author has saved a copy. Earlier links include: <https://media.netflix.com/en/company-blog/we-all-have-6-shows-in-common> (originally accessed June 2018).

12. See Garrison (2019).
13. *What Makes Danish TV Drama Series Travel? International TV Drama Conference*. Aarhus, Denmark, Aarhus University, June 2018.

REFERENCES

Ahmed, S. (2013). *The Cultural Politics of Emotion* (2nd edition). Edinburgh: Edinburgh University Press.
Anderson, B. R. (2006). *Imagined Communities: Reflections on the Origin and Spread of Nationalism* (revised edition). London: Verso.
Anton, C. (2017). 'Media Ecological Orientations to Philosophy and Philosophical Problems'. *The Review of Communication* 17(4): 224–39.
Arslan, H. & G. Raţă (2013). *Multicultural Education from Theory to Practice*. Newcastle, NE: Cambridge Scholars Pub.
Athique, A. (2014). 'Transnational Audiences: Geocultural Approaches.' *Continuum* 28(1): 4–17.
Ball, M. (2016). 'Letting it Go: The End of Windowing (and What Comes Next)'. *REDEF Original*. Available at: <https://redef.com/original/letting-it-go-the-end-of-windows-and-what-comes-next> (last accessed September 2016).
Blinn, M. (2008). *The Dubbing Standard: Its History and Efficiency Implications for Film Distributors in the German Film Market*. Freie Universität Berlin. Available at: <https://www.dime-eu.org/files/active/0/BlinnPAPER.pdf> (last accessed March 2021).
Brock, M. L. (2013). 'Beyond Multiculturalism: Invisible Men and Transculturality in *The Human Stain* and *Erasure*', *Cross / Cultures* 167: 159–76.
Broe, D. (2019). *Birth of the Binge*. Detroit, MI: Wayne State University Press.
Cavalcante, A. (2018). 'Affect, Emotion, and Media Audiences: The Case of Resilient Reception'. *Media, Culture & Society* 40(8): 1186–201.
Chun, W. H. K. (2016). *Updating to Remain the Same: Habitual New Media*. Cambridge, MA: MIT Press.
Cuccioletta, D. (2001). 'Multiculturalism or Transculturalism: Towards a Cosmopolitan Citizenship'. *London Journal of Canadian Studies* 17.
Dagnino, A. (2013). 'Transcultural Literature and Contemporary World Literature(s)', *CLCWeb* 15(5).
Dwyer, T. et al. (2018). Comparing Digital Media Industries in South Korea and Australia: The Case of Netflix Take-Up. *International journal of communication (Online)*, p.4553.
Garrison, M. (2019). 'Caitlin Smallwood: Data-Driven Content and the Power of Storytelling'. *Women in Data Science Podcast*. Podcast Audio, 20 February 2019. Available at: <https://engineering.stanford.edu/magazine/article/caitlin-smallwood-data-driven-content-and-power-storytelling> (last accessed April 2019).
Gellner, E. (2006). *Nations and Nationalism*. Malden, MA: Oxford: Blackwell.
Goldsmith, J. (2012). 'Netflix to preem Eli Roth's "Hemlock Grove"'. *Variety*. Available at: <https://variety.com/2012/digital/news/netflix-to-preem-eli-roth-s-hemlock-grove-1118051718> (last accessed May 2016).
Hechter, M. (1995). 'Explaining Nationalist Violence'. *Nations and Nationalism* 1: 53–68. <doi: 10.1111/j.1354-5078.1995.00053.x>
Iwabuchi, K. (2002). *Recentering Globalization: Popular Culture and Japanese Transnationalism*. Durham, NC and London: Duke University Press.

Jenner, M. (2018). *Netflix and the Re-Invention of Television*. Basingstoke: Palgrave Macmillan.
Jensen, P. (forthcoming). 'Far Away, So Close: Sydney-Siders Watching Forbrydelsen, Borgen, and Bron/Broen'. In R. McCulloch and W. Proctor (eds), *Scandinavian Invasion: The Noir Phenomenon and Beyond*. New York: Peter Lang.
Johnson, C. (2017). 'Beyond Catch-Up'. *Critical Studies in Television* 12(2): 121–38.
La Pastina, A. C and J. D. Straubhaar (2005). 'Multiple Proximities between Television Genres and Audiences: The Schism between Telenovelas' Global Distribution and Local Consumption'. *Gazette* 67(3): 271–88.
Lobato, R. (2019). *Netflix Nations: The Geography of Digital Distribution*. New York: New York University Press.
Lünenborg, M. and T. Maier (2018). 'The Turn to Affect and Emotion in Media Studies'. Special issue of *Media and Communication* 6(3): 1–4.
Menon, R. (2015). 'Islands in the Stream: Netflix's new global sensibility'. *LatestNewsWebsite*. Available at: <http://latestnewswebsites.blogspot.com/2016/02/islands-in-stream-netflixs-new-global.html> (last accessed September 2016).
Mereu Keating, C. (2013). '"100% Italian": The Coming of Sound Cinema in Italy and State Regulation on Dubbing'. *California Italian Studies* 4(1). Available at: <https://escholarship.org/uc/item/7f86023v> (last accessed March 2021).
Miconi, A. and M. Serra (2019). 'On the Concept of Medium: An Empirical Study'. *International Journal of Communication (online)*, p. 3444.
Mittell, J. (2015). *Complex TV: The Poetics of Contemporary Television Storytelling*. New York: New York University Press.
Murgia, M. (2016). 'Inside Netflix: How Reed Hastings is building the first global TV network'. *The Telegraph*. Available at: <https://www.telegraph.co.uk/technology/2016/03/26/inside-netflix-how-reed-hastings-is-building-the-first-global-tv/> (last accessed June 2018).
Newman, M. Z. and E. Levine (2012). *Legitimating Television Media Convergence and Cultural Status*. Abingdon and New York: Routledge.
Patten, A. (2010). '"The Most Natural State": Herder and Nationalism'. *History of Political Thought* 31(4): 657–89.
Seibel, S. J. (2015). 'Seelenkommunismus in High End'. *Die Zeit*. Available at: <https://www.zeit.de/kultur/film/2015-06/sense8-netflix-wachowski> (last accessed 1 May 2016).
Smythe, D. (2006). 'On the Audience Commodity and its Work'. In M. G. Durham and D. M. Kellner (eds), *Media and Cultural Studies Keyworks*. Malden, MA: Blackwell Publishing.
Straubhaar, J D. (1991). 'Beyond Media Imperialism: Asymmetrical Interdependence and Cultural Proximity'. *Critical Studies in Mass Communication* 8(1): 39–59.
Swartz, J. et al. (2019). 'Philosophy of Technology: Who Is in the Saddle?' *Journalism & Mass Communication Quarterly* 96(2): 351–66.
Thompson, R. J. (1997). *Television's Second Golden Age: From Hill Street Blues to ER*. Syracuse, NY: Syracuse University Press.
Tunstall, J. (1994). *The Media Are American: Anglo-American Media in the World* (2nd edition). Communication and Society series. London: Constable.
Tunstall, J. (2008). *The Media Were American: U.S. Mass Media in Decline*. New York and Oxford: Oxford University Press.
Vincendeau, G. (1988). 'Hollywood Babel: The Multiple Language Version'. *Screen* 29(2): 24–39.
Wallace, D. (2018). 'Cultural Capital as Whiteness? Examining Logics of Ethno-Racial Representation and Resistance'. *British Journal of Sociology of Education* 39(4): 466–82.

TV

Dexter (2006–13), USA: Showtime
Explorations (1956–65), CN: CBC
Ghoul (2018), IN: Netflix
Hemlock Grove (2013–15), USA: Netflix
Jinn (2019), JO: Netflix
Lost (2004–10), USA: ABC
Rain (2018), DK: Netflix
Sacred Games (2018–), IN: Netflix
13 Reasons Why (2017–), USA: Netflix
Typewriter (2019), IN: Netflix

CHAPTER 11

National TV as Transnational 'Cinematic' Object: How Binge-Consumption Frames the Critical Vocabulary

Robert Watts

Ahead of the second season release of Yorkshire-based crime drama *Happy Valley* (BBC 2014–), series producer Nicola Shindler told *The Hollywood Reporter* that she had been surprised by what she called an 'instant reaction' of acclaim for the programme from audiences and critics in America, where it had been promoted as a binge-worthy 'Netflix Original' on the streaming service's US platform (Ritman 2016). The response was one that Shindler claimed she 'didn't see coming' given that the series 'felt quite local and specific' and was 'never made with an international audience in mind' (Ritman 2016). Indeed, the popular BBC drama's mode of address seems to privilege a national – at times distinctly local – audience, saturated as it is in the names of West Yorkshire villages and towns, regional dialect and idiom, and specific cultural and topical references, often with little to no expositional 'translation' of these details. Unlike other contemporary British crime exports also offering a localised sense of place – such as *Broadchurch* (ITV 2013–17) or *Hinterland/Y Gwyll* (BBC/S4C 2013–) – *Happy Valley* does not seek to align the viewer's gaze with that of an 'outsider' protagonist. Through such a device, local and cultural specificities can be mediated for the non-native viewer. Creator Sally Wainwright has frequently suggested that such specificities are central to a perceived 'authenticity' in her TV work. In the UK press Wainwright positioned *Happy Valley* as a corrective to British crime drama's eagerness to emulate the tropes of popular American series (Anthony 2016). Despite the various cultural and linguistic proximities between the British and American television cultures, the US reception to Wainwright's idiom-rich dialogue would recall the adage of two nations 'divided by a common language': she told British newspaper the *Independent* that in praising the series, US television critics had, more than once, sheepishly admitted to her that they had needed subtitles to follow it (Gilbert 2014).

This chapter considers the role of TV critics in framing such points of national and local difference (as either inconsequential to an overall viewing experience or as specific markers of a text's aesthetic value) and focuses particularly on the impact of binge-consumption on this transnational process of critical positioning. Looking at both *Happy Valley* and *The Fall* (BBC 2013–16) – another BBC series initially produced with a weekly domestic audience in mind and reframed as a 'Netflix Original' in the US – I suggest that Netflix's encouragement of binge-watching lends itself to singular series reviews that take the complete season, rather than the individual episode, as the object of criticism. Such reviews tend to draw more upon the evaluative aesthetics of film criticism – as a mode that considers works as unified wholes – than on traditions of popular TV criticism organised around serialised episodes, appraised as open, 'in-progress' texts, for an imagined national television audience watching along with the critic. In the binge mode, the TV critic typically speaks from a privileged position having accessed the 'complete' text, as with the film critic and the cinematic object. In doing so, they offer what I call a 'big picture' analysis of the serialised drama. In the transnational context, this big picture allows the critic to address points of cultural difference in terms of a broad overview that manages expectations of the relative importance of culturally specific details to the non-native viewer's overall experience.

The rebranding of these BBC series as 'Netflix Originals' came at a particular moment in Netflix's development towards becoming a transnational broadcaster (Jenner 2018) before the two organisations initiated a series of formal co-ventures producing drama specifically oriented towards a transnational audience (Gill 2017; Moore 2017). *The Fall* and *Happy Valley* were both acquired as finished (or 'canned') productions already broadcast weekly in the UK (and which had received 'in-progress' press coverage throughout their runs) before their release as bingeable 'events' in North America, stripped of their BBC imprimatur. As popular national dramas that make distinctly local and national elements a key part of their aesthetic, they provide an opportunity to combine a comparative analysis of the series' transnational critical reception with a consideration of the role of the singular review frame in helping to assimilate, translate or efface their potentially problematic specificities for US audiences.

In looking at how a shift in critical vocabulary might facilitate (and even encourage) the transnational assimilation of textual elements previously deemed as obstructively 'national' in their appeal, I offer two interrelated points of argument. First, that the promotion of binge-watching in some ways feeds into, and extends, the existing legitimation discourses of so-called 'cinematic' TV drama (Newman and Levine 2012), by encouraging an evaluative approach that treats the serialised text as a singular, unified aesthetic object. Second, that the transnational elements of this process can in part be understood through reference to a particular kind of elite 'tourist gaze' (Urry 1990) that critics help to construct, where the mediated experience of difference from the everyday (or from more familiar, expected images of a given setting) becomes – in the big picture evaluation – a point of aesthetic value. Here, a localised address is mobilised and repositioned as a marker of 'authenticity', reframing a text's more exotic elements as points of added value for a more 'discerning' class of viewer.

Before examining some of the transnational variations across both series' critical reception, I will first outline a historical context of the TV review as a form that – in both Britain and America – has been characterised by the lack of any standardised mode of approaching and analysing the television text as an aesthetic object. Anglophone television criticism can be viewed historically as a variable, multimodal discourse that responds to shifts in technology, distribution and the perceived cultural status of television forms. Understanding this inherent variability (throughout history but also across national traditions) can help elucidate the role binge-consumption plays in reshaping aesthetic perceptions of a text as it moves from one national context to another. In both contexts, critical approaches shift back and forth between 'prospective' and 'retrospective' modes (Poole 1984), a distinction imbricated in the longstanding question of TV's assumed place within an aesthetic hierarchy.

FRAMING THE 'CINEMATIC' OBJECT: TV CRITICISM AS A VARIABLE DISCOURSE

The Australian author and critic Clive James, in the introduction to his 2016 book *Play All: A Bingewatcher's Notebook* – an ode to the immersive pleasures of US drama box sets – likened that contemporary mode of television consumption to the embodied cultural experience of movie-going. 'Bingewatching', he added, 'is a night out, even when you spend the whole day in. It's a way of being' (2016, 11). James, in his former role as TV critic for Britain's *Observer* newspaper between 1972 and 1982, had made such pithy aphorisms his stock-in-trade. He was later credited with (and at times maligned for) pioneering a whimsical, impressionistic form of popular TV criticism emulated by British journalists for decades hence (Trelford 2012). Critics working in this 'generalist' mode (Poole 1984) would tend to disavow any claims to specialist knowledge of the medium, instead approaching their reviews as one viewer among many (Rixon 2011). The resultant trend was towards TV criticism as an informal snapshot of an evening's viewing; a wry commentary upon notable moments plucked from the national broadcast flow. It was this mode of 'water-cooler' criticism that the cultural critic Mark Lawson, in the inaugural issue of *Critical Studies in Television* in 2006, argued was becoming unsustainable in the age of transnational box-set culture that James would later celebrate. Lawson argued that the retrospective premise of the generalist criticism – that viewer and critic were, post-transmission, discussing fragments of an ephemeral text that they had both seen – no longer aligned with the modern consumption of drama, a genre where DVDs now afforded texts 'an afterlife equivalent to that of cinema and literature' (2006, 106). Lawson singled out US imports, of which whole seasons were typically available (in some form) to critics in advance of their UK broadcast. As such he argued that these episodic series ought to be considered as unified wholes, recommending the singular season (p)review as a 'lengthy consideration of an event of something the reader may decide to experience themselves' (2006, 106).

Such associations, between the binge-as-event and consumption of the 'higher' arts of cinema or literature, mobilise familiar dynamics of the 'legitimation' of certain TV dramas as something other than (and implicitly superior to) 'mere' broadcast television (Newman and Levine 2012). Scholars have elsewhere noted the discursive links drawn in the popular media between already legitimated forms of 'quality' or 'prestige' television (typically drama) and that which is deemed 'binge-worthy' (Jenner 2015; Pierce-Grove 2017; Tryon 2015). Such discourses work to legitimise the practice of binge-watching itself (whether on DVDs or streaming platforms) as a potential source of cultural capital for consumers, framing it as a more 'socially acceptable' practice than spending the same amount of time with scheduled television (Jenner 2015, 305; c.f. Bourdieu 1984, 1993). The trend towards full-season 'drops' of all episodes of serialised dramas, alongside an industrially managed discourse of 'bingeability', encourages the TV critic to approach full seasons of TV drama as precisely the kind of unified aesthetic object or 'event' that Lawson proposes. Rather than the 'fellow viewer' position adopted by the generalist, the TV critic's relationship with their reader here becomes increasingly akin to that of the film critic, who always speaks from an assumed position of privileged access to the complete text. This changeable relationship between critic, reader and programme reflects the broader historical lack of any consistent critical mode for television, in either the US or the UK.

In an influential essay on the subject in a UK context, Mike Poole develops the idea of popular TV criticism as 'an historically variable discourse' lacking in a consistent tradition or unity of purpose, particularly when contrasted with the more stable and professionalised tradition of film criticism (1984, 42). The latter was seen as operating with a clearer sense of both its object and its audience, tending to address 'a *prospective* audience which it assumes has yet to see the work in question' as opposed to the retrospective mode of the generalist

TV criticism, which carried an 'inscribed sense of television as a closed event, something already too widely circulated to be worth going into in any detail' (1984, 42, emphasis in original). In the US context Amanda Lotz similarly points out that while the earliest television coverage drew on the aesthetic criticism of established arts such as film and theatre, the 'high-art' critics covering the new medium struggled to reconcile the functions and vocabulary of these traditions with the ephemerality of television:

> Unlike the extended run of theatre or film, readers could not use perspectives gained from the critic to elect to view this program, as early television disappeared as soon as it aired. Because it was likely that many newspaper readers did not see the program the critic wrote about, critics' reviews needed to tell a story or provide information in such a way as to make the column meaningful even for those who had not viewed the program. (Lotz 2008, 25)

While the emergence of advance screenings (and later, the rise of VHS and DVD technologies) afforded a more preview-based approach, this did not result in TV criticism coalescing into any one dominant mode. In the US, the preview screenings of the 1970s initially gave rise to a promotional 'junket' culture in which networks – leveraging access to screenings in pursuit of positive coverage – sought to utilise critics as an arm of industry PR (Lotz 2008, 26). This tactic was mitigated by the formation of the Television Critics Association (TCA), through which the US TV critic's role began to professionalise into its own 'beat', characterised by a heightened journalistic rigour and a more industrial focus (2008, 28). British television coverage over this period was broadly split between the promotional function ('capsule' previews of programmes) and the retrospective, first-person 'generalist' mode popularised by James (Rixon 2011), who vocally rejected the notion of cinema-like preview screenings in favour of actually watching 'television' as a communal, ephemeral flow (Ellis 2008). Paul Rixon (2011), in his history of British TV criticism, argues that it is not until the 'quality' discourse emerges around US drama imports and box sets that a more aesthetically oriented 'neo-serious' critical mode noticeably (re)emerges: one that tends to 'focus on text, divorced from the televisual flow', but in doing so leans into more traditional notions of 'legitimate' or 'high' culture familiar from literary and cinematic criticism, such as the privileging of an author figure (2011, 183). Rixon's book traces the distinctions and overlaps between various types of British TV criticism – in both the prospective and retrospective modes – over several decades, and broadly supports Poole's thesis that in being subject to the often conflicting industrial imperatives of TV and journalism, writing about television often resembles 'a discourse in search of an object' (Poole 1984, 47). Lotz, in the

US context, similarly foregrounds TV criticism's continued 'uncertain place relative to other critical traditions' (2008, 20), noting particularly the role of technological and industrial shifts in sustaining this uncertainty.

The turn towards internet distribution – for both journalism and television – shifted the discourse again as online spaces fostered the development of a form of weekly episodic 'recap' criticism that updated the retrospective mode for an era of on-demand abundance and (transnational) online interactivity. The recap mode, which flourished on US-based pop culture sites like *Television Without Pity*, *The AV Club* and *Vulture* (as well as online editions of established publications like the *New York Times*), was viewed by its advocates as a 'sea change' in which serious critics could operate in a direct dialogue with reader-commenters 'as obsessed with a show as they are' (Zoller Seitz 2015, 18–19). The form combined several modes – the social address of a retrospective 'water-cooler' criticism, the textual analysis of earlier aesthetic criticism, and the kind of collective interpretative practices Henry Jenkins (1995) describes as characteristic of online fan communities – whilst reinforcing what Bourdieu (1984) would call the 'aesthetic dispositions' of all involved. As the *AV Club*'s Noel Murray put it in 2010:

> we aren't primarily engaged in telling people whether they should or shouldn't watch a show – because we're usually talking with people who are already watching – we get to kick around symbolism, character development, and real-world connections to what's on the screen, rather than just writing about whether the show is worth a damn. (Murray and Tobias 2010)

The episodic recap-review also emerged as a popular form in the UK press, particularly at *The Guardian*, which was an early mover in this online-only space, launching its TV & Radio blog in 2006 (see Rixon 2019). As a study by Bennett et al. (2010) demonstrated, *The Guardian*'s readership – skewing towards a younger, educated, middle-class demographic – held a particular preference for HBO-style 'quality' drama in their TV consumption, and as such this dedicated episode-by-episode coverage tended to focus primarily on US forms (see Rixon 2019, 240).

This mode of criticism can, to some degree, be viewed as both shaping and responding to a (transnational) context of TV drama's 'legitimation', as an aesthetic object worthy of close analysis. The recap-review typically promotes the idea of the serialised drama as a unified whole, even as it organises itself around an episodic distribution schedule particular to a national context, each review presenting a kind of *in medias res* moment that gestures to an overall aesthetic unity. Critics in the modern 'recap' mode further what Newman and Levine call the 'cinematization' of television by reiterating certain emphases on auteurism and long-form seriality as markers of 'quality' (2012, 5). But they also reassert established televisual logics of episodic segmentation based on weekly national broadcast scheduling, encouraging speculation and discussion about specific plot points, character motivations, passages of dialogue, or intertextual references to broader aspects of popular culture that may require national frames of understanding. So while these online recaps play into binge-culture's favoured logics of the season of television as a self-contained 'packaged text' that can be endlessly revisited from anywhere at any time (Tryon 2015), they also retain some of the countervailing broadcast logics of segmentation, open-ended textuality and specifically located moments of consumption. While this combination favoured US cable networks like HBO who sought to promote 'cinematic' drama but released on an episodic schedule, the latter televisual logics work against Netflix's preferred 'quality' discourse, which aligns the concept of bingeability to the idea of the 'event' drama series as a singular object for transnational consumption, akin to an international cinema release. As this part has outlined, TV criticism's lack of any dominant mode means it tends to accommodate new technologies and consumption norms by shifting its form and vocabulary accordingly, which we see in the subsequent response to Netflix's promotion of binge-consumption.

Chuck Tryon (2015) notes that the 'Netflix Originals' strategy of releasing full seasons as simultaneous 'drops' of all episodes (often with little advance promotion) helps to frame them as '*events* that inspire reviews, op-eds, and essays in a wide range of political, entertainment, and tech industry publications, such as *Slate*, *The Atlantic*, and *Salon*', adding that these articles 'do much of the promotional work for Netflix' (Tryon 2015, 112, my emphasis). As Mareike Jenner outlines in her own chapter in this part, this strategy is inherently transnational, with Netflix texts published in multiple territories simultaneously. The release strategy, then, on one level encourages a generalist approach to television criticism, by removing it from the predictable structures and rhythms of linear (and national) TV and framing it as a news item, an object upon which journalists across various specialisms and modes feel compelled to speak and analyse, while on another level it works to diminish the sense of a programme's consumption as a series of fixed episodic moments, shrinking the series to the singular moment of its (transnational) release, and subsequent question of whether/when viewers are fully 'caught-up'. This puts the onus on TV critics to be ahead of their potential readership, consuming series quickly and condensing reviews into a singular 'big picture' analysis. As the remainder of this chapter outlines, such analyses tend towards more broad, overarching aesthetic evaluations, with less focus on finer details of place and specific social contexts than the 'in-progress' forms of review or recap. For some, including FX president John Landgraf, this shift towards the big picture represents a potential loss, in terms of the relationship between a television text, critics and the audience. Speaking to the critic Emily VanDerWerff in 2018, Landgraf (who as head of a linear TV network obviously holds a particular stake in the issue) said:

> I feel like there's a dialogue between series and their viewers, and writers and critics, when things can be digested and watched. I feel that you as a critic really experience something different if you have the possibility of reflecting, and experiencing it over a ten-week or thirteen-week period of time, versus having to cram it all into a day. (VanDerWerff 2018)

Slate critic Willa Paskin argued elsewhere that binge-watching 'steamrolls flaws' (2015), particularly from the critic's perspective, where discussion of minor points like an actor's awkward performance, moments of clunky dialogue or ineffective sub-plots do not, in the context of the whole, feel significant enough to warrant inclusion in the kind of big picture analysis I describe here. In the remainder of this chapter, I will similarly consider what might be gained, as well as lost, in the shift towards this big picture analysis over the various forms of in-progress review. As noted above, *Happy Valley* and *The Fall*'s rebranding as Netflix Originals came at a particular moment in Netflix's development towards becoming a transnational broadcaster. That they had already aired weekly in the UK before their release as bingeable events in North America presents a specific set of conditions to explore the tension between the various socially embedded 'moments' of the weekly (national) broadcast drama text and its critical mediation into a decontextualised aesthetic object, reframed for (transnational) consumption as a unified, bingeable event, and reviewed for a prospective audience. As I will outline in the next section, that mediation can be understood in terms of the market functions of Netflix's Original branding, but also on a textual level in terms of a reframing of the national television address – into less of an obstacle and more a kind of touristic marker, suggesting an 'authentic' experience of cultural difference.

NATIONAL ADDRESS, TRANSNATIONAL OBJECT: THE 'DISCERNING' VIEWER AS TOURIST

As Karen Petruska and Faye Woods assert, the Netflix's Originals label has – during its expansion into a 'global' producer-distributor – served as a powerful brand marker communicating 'exclusivity and freshness' (2019, 50). It is also a term applied in a deliberately misleading manner to what Petruska and Woods term 'false originals' (2019, 51) – series that, within the logics of national broadcasting systems, would be called imports or acquisitions. In territories where Netflix has acquired exclusive transmission rights, series have been frequently (though inconsistently) labelled Netflix Originals, despite the SVOD (subscription video on demand) having no role in the commissioning, production or financing of the drama before its original transmission. Such a process of reframing texts has long been a feature of the global television trade, allowing for their assimilation into new national contexts, or transnational network identities, in ways that can generate new meanings (Jenner 2018, 201; McCabe 2000, 144; Petruska and Woods 2019, 53). As Catherine Johnson argues in her work on television branding, the channel (or indeed the platform) is a central paratext of television, a frame that works to 'augment, embellish and enrich' the text itself, 'effectively authoring the experience' (2013, 275). During Netflix's initial expansion of its slate of first-run content, the 'false original' label worked to 'appropriate and decontextualise successful foreign content' from its national televisual origins (Petruska and Woods 2019, 53), allowing the company to embellish that slate by reframing existing programmes as new transnational texts, for which it can absorb (however tenuously) some authorial attribution. But in order to successfully decontextualise and reframe 'canned' BBC content, Netflix needed to exercise a degree of curatorial care over which acquired dramas it branded as Original. To avoid undermining the key functions of the term (connoting that 'exclusivity' and 'freshness'), programmes should not be inherently perceived by viewers, or by the critical establishment, as a BBC-authored experience.

Happy Valley and *The Fall* both offer several points of contrast with what US critics have historically associated with British imports. Such associations were shaped by the longstanding relationship between the British public broadcasters and the American PBS Network, which privileged a 'heritage brand' of Britishness – largely characterised by period drama and murder mystery fare – which 'associates Britain with the qualities of elitism, high culture, classic literature, and orderly society' (Selznick 2008, 76). As Elke Weissmann notes, contemporary, regionally specific (particularly Northern) British drama has historically been seen by industry gatekeepers as too 'different' for US audiences, tending to be adapted rather than imported (2012, 57–62). Against these tendencies, *Happy Valley* and *The Fall* both address contemporary social malaise and are each set in a single identifiable present-day location, with particular historical and cultural associations that inflect its construction of narrative and character. Each series shoots on location and flags the specificity of its setting visually and through dialogue and cultural referencing, and by casting actors that reflect the regions' particular cultural, political and class formations. *Happy Valley*, a crime drama set in West Yorkshire's Calderdale Valley, wears such associations with some irony in its title – a reference to the high incidence of drug and alcohol-related problems plaguing the valley's superficially picturesque villages and gentrified market towns, encountered daily by long-suffering police sergeant Catherine Cawood (Sarah Lancashire).

The sexual violence of Belfast serial-killer drama *The Fall* is similarly staged against the city's historical background of decades of political violence ('the Troubles'). Here, London Metropolitan Police Superintendent Stella Gibson (Gillian Anderson) is seconded to Belfast to assist the Police Service of Northern Ireland (PSNI) with what becomes a cat-and-mouse pursuit of local serial killer Paul Spector (Jamie Dornan). As with the troubled bucolic Yorkshire of *Happy Valley*, a certain image of Belfast is foregrounded through specific local details in order to draw thematic or symbolic contrasts: between the psychologies of sectarian violence and gendered violence (all of Spector's victims are women); between gendered and colonial power dynamics (Spector's adversary Gibson arrives from the power centre of London, and Spector himself is later revealed to have been fathered by a British soldier deployed at the height of the Troubles); and between the welcoming tourist gloss of a revitalised city centre and what are depicted as its more dangerous (and still territorial) peripheries.

The following observations are drawn from an analysis of reviews of the first two seasons of both series (across both national contexts), collated through searches of the popular critical aggregators Rotten Tomatoes and Metacritic; the ProQuest and Newsbank Access World News databases; and the online public archives of various national news, trade and culture publications offering regular television coverage. Reflecting the 'variable discourse' outlined above, the various reviews, recaps and other forms of coverage were coded into 'in-progress' and 'big picture' categories. For the US/Netflix release, both series were almost exclusively reviewed in a prospective big picture mode, while the domestic critical reception was far more varied and dispersed across the span of the series' broadcast runs. Across the in-progress domestic coverage, the kinds of specificities of place indicated above were generative of much of the discussion of the two series as representative public service dramas. A UK/Ireland production, *The Fall* aired simultaneously in the UK (on BBC Two) and in the Republic of Ireland (on RTÉ One) and was praised upon its premiere in *The Irish Times* for being 'definitely, intelligently and subtly Belfast' in its cultural referencing (Harrison 2013) and in *The Guardian* for being one of the few modern British dramas to explicitly 'tackle the Troubles' (Lawson 2013). The groundswell of positive responses to *Happy Valley*, meanwhile, were frequently couched within a discussion of writer Sally Wainwright's realistic rendering of not only West Yorkshire dialect and character, but of the small accrual of details that speak 'right to the heart of what it means to be British' (Wyatt 2016). This extended to praising background details such as the prevalence of tea-drinking in almost every scene (Tweedy 2016), prompting the suggestion that 'there is no crisis that can't be solved and no emotion that can't be tempered by a mug of tea . . . this is just what Brits do' (Delgado 2016). The notion of this drama as 'genuine reality television' (Anthony 2016) was reflected in Wainwright's being credited as a significant contributor to a concurrent turnaround in Northern British viewers' sense of being positively represented on the BBC (Creighton 2014).

The domestic in-progress reception for both series was then framed less in terms of an evaluation of a singular aesthetic object, addressed to a prospective consumer, but as part of a wider and ongoing (national) public conversation about authenticity, quality and genre in British television (Frost 2014; Sweet 2013). Critical focus here tended towards the believability of specific plot points, lines of dialogue and performance across the ensemble casts. Points of formal style and aesthetic evaluation, where brought up, were typically entangled with discussions of the social impact and appropriateness of these and numerous other series' depictions of murder and violence, and the BBC's responsibilities to the national public (Dowell 2014). Both Wainwright and *Fall* creator Alan Cubitt defended themselves in the press against criticism of the violence inflicted upon female characters (Brown 2014; Cubitt 2013). After its premiere, the *Daily Mail* published a (characteristically reactionary) review of *The Fall* by sociologist David Wilson, who framed the show's highly aestheticised violence as Hollywood-inspired 'torture porn', insufficiently rooted in British reality, charging that 'BBC2 has brought this genre into the mainstream, beamed into households across the country in the mid-evening and paid for by the license fee' (Wilson 2014). Cubitt dismissed the criticism as missing the point of the show as 'a particular critique of the patriarchy and the way male violence sits in the patriarchy' (Cubitt 2013), an argument in turn dismissed by a *Guardian* TV critic as a particular kind of sophistry masked by 'this veil of classiness, this veneer of BBC2 sophistication' (Cooke 2014). The work of TV critics was thus framed within a very particular national discourse, marked by a tension between domestic ideals of 'public' drama, and excessive aesthetic displays that fell outside of certain implicit parameters of BBC style.

By contrast, US reviews of both series typically addressed a prospective audience, and as such tended towards broader, more spoiler-conscious overviews of plot and theme, with a greater focus on overarching points of style, tone and aesthetic, along with the performance of the leading cast. That *The Fall* was trying to make a feminist statement was largely taken as read in these singular reviews, which from the position of hindsight on the 'complete' text focus their assessment on whether the violence succeeds or satisfies as an aesthetic experience. Rather than being referential to the social/public context, violence here is considered more in terms of innovation and subversion of genre norms, placing it within the particular discursive terms of the US 'quality' drama discourse. In his review of *The Fall* for *The New Republic*, David Thomson declared the series 'a work of great art', noting that despite the series' 300-minute run-time, he completed it 'in one sitting' (Thomson 2013). Neither this review nor those in *The New York Times* (Genzliger 2013) and *Salon* (Paskin 2013) reference the Troubles or explicate Belfast's significance as a contextual background for this story, focusing attention instead on the series' arresting visual style, compelling central performances and bingeability. *Salon* framed the series' 'contemporary cool' approach to the crime genre as compulsive, critic Willa Paskin noting that she 'ate it all up' (Paskin 2013). Thomson's review leans heavily on cinematic frames of reference, offering comparisons to the directorial styles of Scorsese, Hitchcock and Lang while explicitly contrasting the immersive, modern qualities of *The Fall* with 'a certain kind of BBC product' that was 'natural fodder for PBS' (Thomson 2013). Similarly, an early review of *Happy Valley* for *Variety* praised Netflix for its shrewdness in seeking to acquire 'the European dramas that PBS overlooks', suggesting that 'a discriminating crowd in the US can be treated to more than just the requisite detective or costume fare' (Lowry 2014). In her *New Yorker* review, Emily Nussbaum does not reference the BBC at all in regard to *Happy Valley*, the pleasures of which are likened to those of a compelling novel, the violence at its core rendered imaginatively through a careful 'directorial withholding' (Nussbaum 2014). In Alan Sepinwall's *Hitfix* review of *Happy Valley* his admission that, after the harrowing fourth episode he 'had to put the show on hold for a few hours' despite himself, reads like an apology for failing to consume the 'simple, brutally elegant six part story' as a singular event (Sepinwall 2014). Across these big picture US reviews there is an emphasis on both the compulsiveness of the shorter-run series (itself hardly a new trend for British imports) as well as a perceived aesthetic contrast with familiar images of heritage Britishness. Specificities of place, where referenced, are done so obliquely and in terms of their aesthetic (rather than representative) function, seen as providing a 'unique' sense of place that lends vitality to a familiar genre (Greenwald 2014; Ryan 2014). The Originals were seemingly understood to be operating in a different register of 'Britishness' than dramas inherently associated with the BBC in the US, but this understanding did not necessarily lead to any further reflection on the socio-political contexts addressed by the text. Rather, the very fact of such exhibited difference was often an evaluative note in its own right.

In the case of *Happy Valley*, a mode of address that could be assumed to be a potential impediment to transnational appeal (or 'cultural discount') was frequently reframed in the US as a point of added value (or 'cultural markup'), a kind of productive difficulty that would repay the effort of those viewers willing to persevere.[1] Several reviews remark on the series as 'very rooted in a particular time and place' (Ryan 2014), and suggest a particular pleasure in navigating the Yorkshire dialect (or 'Brit-speak') that can be 'difficult to decipher at times' but 'warrant[s] giving your remote's rewind button a workout' (Rackl 2014, c.f. Ryan 2016). *Grantland*'s description of Yorkshire as a place 'where people say "nowt" when they mean to say "nothing"' is a way of suggesting to the reader that this is a text that will require a certain degree of interpretation, the glowing review here implying that viewers' labour will be rewarded (Greenwald 2014). *Happy Valley* is frequently positioned as a potential discovery for 'discerning' or 'discriminating' viewers (Lowry 2014; Ryan 2016); the type of text that will reward certain competencies and a degree of viewer labour, such as the ability to pick up on and interpret local knowledge and dialect from a text that 'doesn't necessarily cater to outsiders' (Renshaw 2016). In this regard the series' US reception was not unlike the British critical reception for Baltimore crime saga *The Wire* (HBO 2002–8), a programme openly embraced for – not despite – a similar degree of untranslated local specificity in its dialogue and cultural referencing, widely taken as a textual marker of 'authenticity' (Brockes 2016; *The Telegraph* 2009). In the latter case, popular critics like Jim Shelley and Charlie Brooker served as early advocates for the series, encouraging British viewers to binge themselves up-to-date through DVD box sets, assuring readers that any initial stumbling blocks in comprehension would be worth confronting. With *Happy Valley*, the US critic plays a similar authenticating role, providing assurance 'from the other side' that the journey will ultimately be enriched by the process of negotiating its more exotic elements. In the case of *The Fall*, the localised elements do not register as intrusive enough to be reframed as a cultural mark-up in the same way and, as a result, the more complex aspects of the series' politics are largely subordinated to a lauding of its formal aesthetics.

Differences between the discursive frameworks of these big picture and in-progress modes of reception can thus be seen as twofold: in part a product of nationally specific discourses, and in part a reflection of weekly linear distribution as generative of an ongoing critical dialogue (a process that binge-consumption works against). The degree to which the national context or the distribution frame prove to be the dominant factor remains difficult to parse, not least due to the continuing variability of the critical mode. What can be said is that as Netflix Originals, these series are decontextualised not just of their production origin but of their assumed social functions, and subsequently specificities of place, depictions of crime and violence, and 'authentic' depictions of idiom and dialect are considered by critics primarily as aesthetic, rather than referential, features. This recalls John Corner's (1995) formulation, in his consideration of the aesthetics and effects of screen violence, of a dialectic between axes of 'referential' and 'poetic' interpretations.[2] Corner sought to explain how television violence might have both a social function (the referential axis provoking 'appropriate' cognitive and affective responses like disgust or sympathy for the victim, as if the violence had been witnessed in everyday life) and an aesthetic function (the poetic axis evoking pleasure, based on an adherence to – or variation from – the norms, rules and expectations of the fictional genre in question) (1995, 148–9). In terms of both the depictions of violence and the 'untranslated' regional specificities, across both series the big picture frame can be seen as helping to suppress the referential axis that connects aesthetics to the immediate social world while strengthening the poetic axis that encourages a more distanced, immanent reading of the text.

So while the legitimating strategy of 'cinematization' is not explicitly in play, the binge frame encourages a similar closing-off of the text from certain contexts that make it 'television', at least in understandings of the term forged within a national broadcast paradigm. The singular, aesthetic-centred analysis activates Bourdieusian dynamics, wherein the positioning of cultural specificities as primarily aesthetic features can be understood in relation to the legitimation discourse, with the critic-as-intermediary linking appreciation of formal complexity (rather than immediate social functions) with the viewer's sense of their own cultural capital. This consumption is still very much marked by its difference from 'regular' television, but here it is the deviation from the assumption (within US television culture) of a universally accessible address – and the resulting sense that this text might not be *for* you – that is here framed as a point of aesthetic value. In one sense this is emblematic of what Bourdieu calls the display of the 'pure gaze', a kind of cultivated disposition towards certain cultural products, formed in opposition to a popular aesthetic, through which the self-appointed 'aesthete' seeks to set themselves apart from 'the common herd' (1984, 23). The transnational variations in *Happy Valley*'s textual status (a mainstream, popular text in the UK; a niche 'discovery' in the US) suggest that it cannot be accounted for simply as an aesthetic object of a homogenous, transnational 'elite' audience demographic. Rather, I argue that what the US critic is constructing here can be usefully viewed as a form of what sociologist John Urry (1990) terms the 'tourist gaze'. Urry draws the link, historically, between the ability to travel and the display of one's social status, and the tourist gaze is constructed around the anticipation of a pleasurable difference from its opposite, from quotidian forms of non-tourist activity (1990, 5). The particular expectations of any given tourist gaze are structured by mediating agents including travel guides, literature, film and television (1990, 2–3). Tourist sites are then constructed around such expectations, with the gazed-upon culture performing anticipated exhibitions of difference, in a process the sociologist Dean MacCannell (1973) calls 'staged authenticity'.

As noted above, US networks had historically constructed a certain expectation of the kinds of cultural difference British television offered, establishing a particular register of Britishness as export-friendly. The notion of an American 'discerning viewer', seeking out British drama beyond the 'requisite' PBS fare, conjures a categorisation of viewers along similar lines to what Donald Redfoot (1984), in his typology of the dimensions of (in)authenticity in touristic travel, called the 'second-order' tourist. Redfoot's 'orders' are, like Urry's gaze, organised according to the expectations and desired outcomes an individual brings to the travel experience. For the first-order tourist, 'expectations are well-formed in advance as to just what one is "supposed" to experience', which are the predictable landmarks and experiences suitably 'authenticated' by guidebooks, tour guides, and holiday brochures (Redfoot 1984, 293). The second-order tourist, conscious of the perceived inauthenticity of that experience, develops conscious strategies to avoid 'mere' tourists. Seeking 'ways to distinguish "real" experiences' from touristic inauthenticity, they 'will likely learn at least a few words of the local language and will stay and eat in places that "only the locals know about"' (1984, 296). The second-order tourist seeks a certain 'tension between participation in an authentic event in the lives of some exotic group, and remaining distinctly an outsider' (1984, 298). Of course, notions of what might be properly considered an 'exotic' experience are themselves shaped by certain 'higher-brow authenticators' within cultural production (1984, 299). In guiding the consumption of a discerning (elite) television viewer, the critic can preserve their own 'privileged status' as a cultural authenticator (Newman and Levine 2012, 7).

In her work on cinema space as a form of touristic spectacle, Amy Corbin sees absorption and immersion as key to the 'activation of touristic instincts', noting that 'tourism is a specific leisure activity, in which you know there is a definite starting and ending time, at which point you return to your "real" world, much like cinema' (2014, 315–16). As an aside, she suggests that the practice of binge-watching television 'could in fact be far more immersive than watching a film on a personal device because of the duration and level of focus' (2014, 320). The binge frame might then be seen as helping to promote a similar tourist gaze as does the cinematic apparatus, encouraging immersion in exhibited difference, with certain forms authenticated by critics as an appropriate object of a more 'discerning' gaze. *Happy Valley*'s 'insider' references may scan as suitably authentic to a foreign 'outsider' (or potentially even to different regional or demographic audiences within the UK) precisely because they are not written with the aim of being universally understood. To the tourist-viewer as outsider, such details might scan as a productive difficulty, connoting authenticity in the sheer fact of their refusal to perform local culture in a more immediately accessible way. It is this register that I argue attracts an elite, transnational tourist gaze. The singular review frame encouraged by binge-consumption shifts emphasis away from specific descriptions of passages of dialogue, regionally specific sub-plots and cultural references, and other details that the weekly episodic recap or episode preview might dwell on and discuss, instead offering a broader view of the series as a kind of event or experience, wherein such details are collapsed into an overall aesthetic judgement of 'authenticity' or a unique 'sense of place'. This dynamic speaks to the question of the separability of national and transnational modes of address in television drama, suggesting that the two are always enmeshed, and in increasingly complex ways.

CONCLUSION

This chapter has built upon existing Anglo-American legitimation discourses of 'cinematic' television by examining how they intersect with shifts in TV drama's transnational flows and emerging critical discourses of bingeability and of the television series as a singular 'event'. The discourse of popular TV critics has always been highly variable, shifting in line with various institutional, technological and cultural changes. Netflix's binge model encourages what I call a singular 'big picture' review that tends to draw on the distanced evaluative aesthetics of film criticism, as contrasted with various forms of 'in-progress' review associated with weekly episodic television, which are more socially embedded. Through a comparative reception analysis, I draw on theories of a tourist gaze to suggest how critics reframe a nationally specific address as an aesthetic marker of authenticity for transnational elite audiences, further feeding the discourse of TV drama as a singular (immersive and personal) moment of consumption rather than an open-ended, dialogic relationship between the text and a specific (collective and socially situated) audience. While such reviews do not necessarily make 'cinematic' the legitimating qualifier, they employ a certain discursive closing-off of the text that similarly emphasises their 'not TV-ness'. This potential impact of the distribution frame must, however, still be considered in relation to the various critical and institutional traditions and discourses into which the text is being received.

Petruska and Woods (2019) point out that the 2010s are likely to represent a transitional moment, and indeed globally operating SVODs and national broadcasters appear set in the subsequent decade to continue jostling over production quotas and distribution rights. The examples of *Happy Valley* and *The Fall*, explored in this chapter, themselves reflect a particular historical juncture in Netflix's development, rather than an illustration of its continuing transnational strategy. The company has since seen the release of self-produced Originals outpace its acquisitions (Hayes 2019), and has also entered into more formal co-ventures with national broadcasters, including the BBC. Limited series such as *Bodyguard* (BBC/Netflix 2018) and *Black Earth Rising* (BBC/Netflix 2018) have remained salient 'watercooler' objects in British in-progress criticism, while clearly being produced with the transnational audience in mind. In a context of continued transformation and flux, it is increasingly difficult to model the flows and parse the 'national' from its transnational contexts. What the examples discussed here do suggest is that we ought to be wary of aligning theoretical models of transnational appeal too closely with the established logics of proximity held by industry gatekeepers, and long-settled assumptions about which localised elements do or do not 'travel'. If anything remains constant here, it is the inherent variability of the discourse of TV criticism – ever uncertain about its object – which remains a powerful mediating tool for industry and critics alike to (re)position forms across an increasingly transnational cultural hierarchy, forging new possibilities for the translation of texts and their elements into constantly negotiated economies of value.

NOTES

1. The notion of the cultural discount is introduced in Hoskins and Mirus (1988). The cultural mark-up is discussed in relation to the transnational reception of Danish drama in Jensen and Waade (2013).
2. Corner borrows these particular terms from two of the 'functions of language' outlined by the linguist Roman Jakobson (1960).

REFERENCES

Anthony, A. (2016). 'Sally Wainwright: The titan of genuine reality television'. *The Guardian*. 7 Feb 2016. Available at: <https://www.theguardian.com/tv-and-radio/2016/feb/07/sally-wainwright-writer-happy-valley-second-series> (last accessed 21 March 2021).

Bennett, T., M. Savage, E. Silva, A. Warde, M. Gayo-Cal and D. Wright (2010). *Culture, Class, Distinction*. New York: Routledge.

Bourdieu, P. (1984). *Distinction: A Social Critique of the Judgement of Taste*. London: Routledge.

Bourdieu, P. (1993). *The Field of Cultural Production: Essays on Art and Literature*. Cambridge: Polity Press.

Brockes, E. (2016). 'Happy Valley has become Britain's version of The Wire'. *The Guardian*. 11 March 2016. Available at: <https://www.theguardian.com/commentisfree/2016/mar/11/happy-valley-quality-drama-sally-wainwright> (last accessed 21 March 2021).

Brown, M. (2014). 'Happy Valley writer: I don't have to apologise for show's violence'. *The Guardian*. 25 May 2014. Available at: <https://www.theguardian.com/tv-and-radio/2014/may/25/happy-valley-bbc-violence-sally-wainwright> (last accessed 21 March 2021).

Cooke, R. (2014). '*The Fall* – misogyny in a veil of classiness?' *The Guardian*. 16 November 2016. Available at: <https://www.theguardian.com/commentisfree/2014/nov/16/the-fall-misogyny-gillian-anderson-tv> (last accessed 21 March 2021).

Corbin, A. (2014). 'Travelling Through Cinema Space: The Film Spectator as Tourist'. *Continuum* 28(3): 314–29.

Corner, J. (1995). *Television Form and Public Address*. London: Edward Arnold.

Creighton, S. (2014). 'Happy Valley and Last Tango in Halifax help North warm to the BBC'. *Daily Mail*. 2 December 2014. Available at: <http://www.dailymail.co.uk/news/article-2856946/Happy-Valley-Tango-Halifax-help-North-warm-BBC-Figures-northern-people-feel-better-represented-corporation-time-living-memory.html> (last accessed 21 March 2021).

Cubitt, A. (2013). 'The Fall's writer Alan Cubitt on women and violence in TV drama'. *The Guardian*. 7 June 2013. Available at: <https://www.theguardian.com/tv-and-radio/2013/jun/07/the-fall-allan-cubitt-women-violence> (last accessed 21 March 2021).

Delgado, K. (2016). 'The crucial role of tea in Happy Valley'. *Radio Times*. 1 March 2016. Available at: <http://www.radiotimes.com/news/2016-03-01/the-crucial-role-of-tea-in-happy-valley/> (last accessed 21 March 2021).

Dowell, B. (2014). 'British TV has too many serial killers says top scriptwriter Andrew Davies' *Radio Times*. 28 March 2014. Available at: <http://www.radiotimes.com/news/2014-03-28/british-tv-has-too-many-serial-killers-says-top-scriptwriter-andrew-davies/> (last accessed 21 March 2021).

Ellis, J. (2008). 'TV Pages'. In B. Franklin (ed.), *Pulling Newspapers Apart: Analysing Print Journalism*. London: Routledge, pp. 231–8.

Frost, V. (2014). 'Have you been watching . . . Happy Valley'. *The Guardian*. 27 May 2014. Available at: <https://www.theguardian.com/tv-and-radio/tvandradioblog/2014/may/27/happy-valley-bbc1-drama-sally-wainwright-sarah-lancashire> (last accessed 21 March 2021).

Genzlinger, N. (2013). 'TV Review: Killing becomes a habit, with madness and method'. *The New York Times*. 10 June 2013. Available at: <https://www.nytimes.com/2013/06/11/arts/television/gillian-anderson-in-the-fall-on-netflix-from-bbc2.html> (last accessed 21 March 2021).

Gilbert, G. (2014). 'Happy Valley and Last Tango in Halifax creator Sally Wainwright on how to create TV gold'. *The Independent*. 13 December 2014. Available at: <https://www.independent.co.uk/arts-entertainment/tv/features/happy-valley-and-last-tango-in-halifax-creator-sally-wainwright-on-how-to-create-tv-gold-9920926.html> (last accessed 21 March 2021).

Gill, J. (2017). 'British drama, global budgets: how co-productions are changing the way TV gets made'. *Radio Times*. 23 March 2017. Available at: <http://www.radiotimes.com/news/2017-03-23/british-drama-global-budgets-how-co-productions-are-changing-the-way-tv-gets-made/> (last accessed 21 March 2021).

Greenwald, A. (2014). 'Brit crime series "Happy Valley" is a good option for when the new network dramas inevitably disappoint you'. *Grantland*. 15 September 2014. Available at: <http://grantland.com/hollywood-prospectus/brit-crime-series-happy-valley-is-a-good-option-for-when-the-new-network-dramas-inevitably-disappoint-you/> (last accessed 21 March 2021).

Harrison, B. (2013). 'TV Review: Gillian Anderson is fired up in "The Fall", but Mr Whicher is getting suspiciously dull'. *The Irish Times*. 18 May 2013. Available at: <https://www.irishtimes.com/culture/tv-radio-web/tv-review-gillian-anderson-is-fired-up-in-the-fall-but-mr-whicher-is-getting-suspiciously-dull-1.1397298> (last accessed 21 March 2021).

Hayes, D. (2019). 'Netflix Reaches Tipping Point As Originals Now Outpace Acquired Titles – Study'. *Deadline*. 21 March 2019. Available at: <https://deadline.com/2019/03/netflix-reaches-tipping-point-as-originals-now-outpace-acquired-titles-study-1202579260/> (last accessed 21 March 2021).

Hoskins, C. and R. Mirus (1988). 'Reasons for the US Dominance of the International Trade in Television Programmes'. *Media, Culture and Society* 10: 499–515.

Jakobson, R. (1960). 'Linguistics and Poetics'. In T. Sebeok (ed.), *Style in Language*. Cambridge, MA: MIT Press, pp. 350–77.

James, C. (2016). *Play All: A Bingewatcher's Notebook*. New Haven: Yale University Press.

Jenkins, H. (1995). '"Do You Enjoy Making the Rest of Us Feel Stupid"? alt.tv.twinpeaks, the Trickster Author, and Viewer Mastery'. In D. Lavery (ed.), *Full of Secrets: Critical Approaches to Twin Peaks*. Detroit, MI: Wayne State University Press, pp. 51–69.

Jenner, M. (2015). 'Binge-Watching: Video-On-Demand, Quality TV and Mainstreaming Fandom'. *International Journal of Cultural Studies* 20(3): 304–20.

Jenner, M. (2018). *Netflix and the Re-invention of Television*. Basingstoke: Palgrave Macmillan.

Jensen, P. M. and A. M. Waade (2013). 'Nordic Noir Challenging "the Language of Advantage": Setting, Light and Language as Production Values in Danish Television Series'. *The Journal of Popular Television* 1(2): 259–65.

Johnson, C. (2013). 'The Authorial Function of the Television Channel'. In D. Johnson and J. Gray (eds), *A Companion to Media Authorship*. Oxford: Wiley-Blackwell, pp. 275–95.

Lawson, M. (2006). 'Why Newspapers Should Stop Publishing TV Reviews'. *Critical Studies in Television* 1(1): 104–7.

Lawson, M. (2013). 'Belfast-set thriller The Fall joins the few dramas to tackle the Troubles'. *The Guardian*. 13 May 2013. Available at: <https://www.theguardian.com/tv-and-radio/tvandradioblog/2013/may/14/the-fall-northern-ireland-troubles> (last accessed 21 March 2021).

Lotz, A. D. (2008). 'On 'Television Criticism': The Pursuit of the Critical Examination of a Popular Art'. *Popular Communication* 6(1): 20–36.

Lowry, B. (2014). 'TV Review: Happy Valley'. *Variety*. 19 August 2014. Available at: <http://variety.com/2014/digital/reviews/tv-review-happy-valley-1201283785/> (last accessed 21 March 2021).

MacCannell, D. (1973). 'Staged Authenticity: Arrangements of Social Space in Tourist Settings'. *American Journal of Sociology* 79(3): 589–603.

McCabe, J. (2000). 'Diagnosing the Alien: Producing Identities, American "Quality" Drama and British Television Culture in the 1990s'. In B. Carson and M. Llewellyn-Jones (eds), *Frames and Fictions on Television: The Politics of Identity Within Drama*. Exeter: Intellect, pp. 141–54.

Moore, K. (2017). 'Netflix has six new BBC coproductions in the works'. *What's on Netflix*. 2 November 2017. Available at: <https://www.whats-on-netflix.com/news/netflix-has-six-new-bbc-co-productions-in-the-works/> (last accessed 21 March 2021).

Murray, N. and S. Tobias (2010). 'How has the culture of TV (and TV watching) changed? *AV Club*. 18 June 2010. Available at: <https://tv.avclub.com/how-has-the-culture-of-tv-and-tv-watching-changed-1798220508> (last accessed 21 March 2021).

Newman, M. Z. and E. Levine (2012). *Legitimating Television: Media Convergence and Cultural Status*. London: Routledge.

Nussbaum, E. (2014). 'Open Secret: Powerful revelations on Happy Valley and Transparent'. *The New Yorker*. 29 September 2014. Available at: <https://www.newyorker.com/magazine/2014/09/29/open-secret> (last accessed 21 March 2021).

Paskin, W. (2013). 'Crime show The Fall is a compendium of contemporary TV cool'. *Salon*. 5 June 2013. Available at: <https://www.salon.com/2013/06/05/crime_show_the_fall_is_a_compendium_of_contemporary_tv_cool/> (last accessed 21 March 2021).

Paskin, W. (2015). 'Binge-watching a show can make you forget about its flaws'. *Slate*. 24 December 2015. Available at: <https://slate.com/culture/2015/12/binge-watching-a-show-can-make-you-forget-about-its-flaws.html> (last accessed 21 March 2021).

Petruska, K. and Woods, F. (2019). 'Travelling Without a Passport: "Original" Streaming Content in the Transatlantic Distribution Ecosystem'. In M. Hills, M. Hilmes and R. Pearson (eds), *Transatlantic Television Drama: Industries, Programs, & Fans*. Oxford: Oxford University Press, pp. 49–67.

Pierce-Grove, R. (2016). 'Just One More: How Journalists Frame Binge Watching'. *First Monday*, 22(1). Available at: <https://doi.org/10.5210/fm.v22i1.7269> (last accessed 21 March 2021).

Poole, M. (1984). 'The Cult of the Generalist: British Television Criticism 1936–83'. *Screen* 25(2): 41–61.

Rackl, L. (2014). 'Lori's List: What to Watch and What to Skip on TV This Week'. *Chicago Sun-Times*. 18 August 2014. Available at: <https://chicago.suntimes.com/2014/8/18/18464887/lori-s-list-what-to-watch-and-what-to-skip-on-tv-this-week-video> (last accessed 21 March 2021).

Redfoot, D. L. (1984). 'Touristic Authenticity, Touristic Angst, and Modern Reality'. *Qualitative Sociology* 7(4): 291–309.

Renshaw, D. (2016) 'It's time to start watching *Happy Valley*'. *Vulture*. 18 March 2016. Available at: <https://www.vulture.com/2016/03/happy-valley-netflix-its-time-to-start-watching.html> (last accessed 21 March 2021).

Ritman, A. (2016) '"Happy Valley" Producer: TV Opening up to "Less Posh British Drama"'. *The Hollywood Reporter*. 16 March 2016. Available at: <http://www.hollywoodreporter.com/news/happy-valley-producer-posh-british-876104> (last accessed 21 March 2021).

Rixon, P. (2011). *TV Critics and Popular Culture: A History of British Television Criticism*. London: I. B. Tauris.

Rixon, P. (2019). 'Contextualizing "Quality" US Television Programs for the United Kingdom'. In M. Hills, M. Hilmes and R. Pearson (eds), *Transatlantic Television Drama: Industries, Programs, & Fans*. Oxford: Oxford University Press, pp. 239–55.

Ryan, M. (2016). 'TV Review: Happy Valley'. *Variety*. 16 March 2016. Available at: <https://variety.com/2016/tv/reviews/happy-valley-review-sarah-lancashire-1201726730/> (last accessed 21 March 2021).

Selznick, B. (2008). *Global Television: Co-Producing Culture*. Philadelphia, PA: Temple University Press.

Sepinwall, A. (2014). 'Netflix's "Happy Valley" a swift, brutal crime story'. *Uproxx*. 11 March 2014. Available at: <http://uproxx.com/sepinwall/review-netflixs-happy-valley-a-swift-brutal-crime-story/> (last accessed 21 March 2021).

Sweet, M. (2013). 'Gillian Anderson's sadistic thriller The Fall feeds our taste for slaughter TV'. *The Telegraph*. 10 May 2013. Available at: <https://www.telegraph.co.uk/culture/tvandradio/10048795/Gillian-Andersons-sadistic-thriller-The-Fall-feeds-our-taste-for-slaughter-on-TV.html> (last accessed 21 March 2021).

The Telegraph (2009). '*The Wire*: Arguably the greatest television programme ever made'. *The Telegraph*. 2 April 2009. Available at: <https://www.telegraph.co.uk/news/uknews/5095500/The-Wire-arguably-the-greatest-television-programme-ever-made.html> (last accessed 21 March 2021).

Thomson, D. (2013). 'The BBC's latest import is modern, chilling and groundbreaking'. *The New Republic*. 2 July 2013. Available at: <https://newrepublic.com/article/113713/fall-bbc-and-netflix-reviewed-david-thomson> (last accessed 21 March 2021).

Trelford, D. (2012). 'How Clive James transformed the role of television critic'. *The Observer*. 24 June 2012. Available at: <https://www.theguardian.com/culture/2012/jun/24/clive-james-tv-critic-donald-trelford> (last accessed 21 March 2021).

Tryon, C. (2015). 'TV Got Better: Netflix's Original Programming Strategies and the On-Demand Television Transition'. *Media Industries Journal* 2(2).

Tweedy, J. (2016). 'There's a cup of TEA in every scene!' *Daily Mail Online*. 2 March 2016. Available at: <http://www.dailymail.co.uk/femail/article-3472552/There-s-cup-TEAscene-Happy-Valley-viewers-Twitter-point-grim-Northern-police-drama-s-obsessionputting-kettle-on.html> (last accessed 21 March 2021).

Urry, J. (1990). *The Tourist Gaze: Leisure and Travel in Contemporary Societies*. London: Sage.

VanDerWerff, E. (2018). 'FX President John Landgraf has been dubbed "the mayor of television". This interview will show you why'. *Vox*. 17 August 2018. Available at: <https://www.vox.com/2018/8/10/17672640/john-landgraf-fx-interview-podcast> (last accessed 21 March 2021).

Weissmann, E. (2012). *Transnational Television Drama: Special Relations and Mutual Influence between the US and UK*. Basingstoke: Palgrave Macmillan.

Wilson, D. (2014). 'Rape fantasies. Sadism. A pin-up killer. A top criminologist says BBC thriller The Fall is . . . the sickest show on TV'. *Daily Mail*. 24 November 2014. Available at: <http://www.dailymail.co.uk/tvshowbiz/article-2846810/Top-criminologist-says-BBCthriller-Fall-sickest-TV.html> (last accessed 21 March 2021).

Wyatt, D. (2016). 'Happy Valley, BBC1 – TV Review: Drama speaks right to the heart of what it means to be British'. *Independent*. 15 March 2016. Available at: <https://www.independent.co.uk/arts-entertainment/tv/reviews/happy-valley-bbc1-tv-review-a-drama-that-speaks-right-to-the-heart-of-what-it-means-to-be-british-a6932886.html> (last accessed 21 March 2021).

Zoller Seitz, M. (2015). *Mad Men Carousel: The Complete Critical Companion*. New York: Abrams.

TV

Bodyguard (2018), UK: BBC, Netflix
Black Earth Rising (2018), UK: BBC, Netflix
Broadchurch (2013–17), UK: ITV
Fall, The (2013–16), UK: BBC
Happy Valley (2014–), UK: BBC
Hinterland/Y Gwyll (2013–), UK: BBC, S4C
Wire, The (2002–8), USA: HBO

CHAPTER 12

Transnationalising Genre: Netflix, Teen Drama and Textual Dimensions in Netflix Transnationalism

Mareike Jenner

In a 2019 commentary in *The Guardian* titled 'Netflix's Sex Education is about as British as a high-school prom', Caspar Salmon heavily criticises the British *Sex Education* (Netflix 2019–) for its general lack of incorporating the 'national' or 'local'. He simplifies complex debates surrounding cultural homogenisation and heterogenisation, instead bringing back an old cultural anxiety, this time in relation to Netflix and its approach to transnational television. As much as debates surrounding what is often called cultural imperialism were common in the 1970s (Lobato 2019; Straubhaar 2007), Netflix's market dominance and its business model of making self-produced originals available in all of its markets at once works to revive some of the debates, as Salmon's criticism shows. This article focuses on the textual politics of Netflix's self-produced originals, especially non-American texts framed via genre conventions predominantly developed in the US television system. A particular focus lies here on how Netflix *transnationalises* genre to make texts more palatable in all its markets. This is done here by discussing two teen drama serials, the British *Sex Education* and the German *How to Sell Drugs Online (Fast)* (Netflix 2019–). The genre conventions of teen drama originate in the US and the countries discussed here have relied heavily on US imports of teen drama to address teen audiences. They also work as examples of how Netflix employs non-American genre texts to position itself transnationally.

Genre studies approaches tend to have a complex relationship with transnational television. Largely, genre studies has dealt with questions of how we define a genre or the analysis of specific genres and the features that define them, as the contributions in *The Television Genre Book* (Creeber 2015) show. Genre theory often seeks to downplay the cultural specifics of the national iterations of the genre in favour of creating inclusive categories. This does not mean that these specificities are unimportant, but it means that genre theory aims to provide definitions that can be applied across cultural contexts. This flexibility and inclusivity can be useful, but it can also serve to downplay the specific histories that shape a genre (see, for example, de Sousa and Trültzsch-Wijnen 2016). There is a visible shift with the recommendation system Netflix uses and its privileging of self-produced originals. Within the context of Netflix, genre has largely been analysed in relation to the initial reliance of the company's recommendation algorithm on categories of genre, as laid out in an article by Alexis C. Madrigal in *The Atlantic* in January 2014 and later explored by scholars such as Ed Finn (2017). What Madrigal describes is not just a system of genre, however, but one of micro-genres where a range of characteristics are tagged, such as actors, tone or themes. This suggests that the individualised taste profiles the algorithm builds focus on more minute criteria than genre. Thus, as Netflix has accumulated more information about its subscribers and expanded, it has come to rely less on genre and more on individual taste structures. However, genre, sub-genre and micro-genre have remained important aspects in the organisation of tags. On Netflix, the descriptions for self-produced originals do not mention language and texts are often not tagged according to this (though they are tagged according to national context, i.e., British cinema, Canadian television, etc.). Netflix provides English-language dubbing for its self-produced originals and automatically plays trailers in the language the account holder usually consumes content in. Thus, non-American texts are recommended alongside American productions. While this de-emphasising of language is not unusual for countries that rely heavily on imports and dubbing, it is less common for English language countries. Further, as described later, the texts themselves work to remove the local. As such, the transnationalisation of television genre purported by Netflix goes further than established genre categories.

Discussions surrounding transnational television trade have often focused on questions of cultural hegemonisation and problems of cultural imperialism through (predominantly US) imports versus issues of domestication of texts into national television landscapes and through various alterations, such as editing or translation (see, for example, Appadurai 1996; Buonanno 2008, 85–118; Lobato 2019; Straubhaar 2007). It is hardly unusual for television to be constructed in a way that makes it easily 'exportable' to foreign markets. Denise Bielby and C. Lee Harrington argue:

> . . . while TV producers do not traditionally create programming solely for the export market, in the current economic climate they are motivated to develop programs and program concepts that speak to *both* local and global audiences. [. . .] One way local-global connections are manifested is through strategic efforts to internationalize (or deculturize)

narrative content to enhance portability across cultural borders. (2008, 89, italics in the original)

The authors identify more ways in which these connections are made, such as textual properties, integration of different languages and programming decisions. Harrington and Bielby point to the importance of genre in transnational contexts. However, Netflix and its function as transnational broadcaster heightens genre's importance in textual structures. Netflix's publication models and the lack of a traditional schedule create different conditions.[1] The important shift Netflix brings with it is the publication of all its texts at the same time in all of the markets it operates in. This shift is not to be underestimated: several texts are designed to be easily exportable and therefore aim to address themes that are considered 'universal' across multiple cultural spheres. Netflix's self-produced originals aim to be transnational *from the outset*, rather than to operate in one domestic market before being exported. They may not aim to address all cultural spheres to the same extent, but as becomes obvious on a textual level, they heavily emphasise a certain level of 'universality'. Sabina Mihelj explores what she terms 'grammars of nationhood', a term that describes the different ways in which nationalism is inherent and expressed in national media systems and the texts produced in them (2011, 70–92). I have previously inverted her concept to suggest the term 'grammar of transnationalism': this describes the ways in which texts, and specifically Netflix self-produced originals, aim to appeal to a transnational sensibility. This grammar of transnationalism suggests the use of textual characteristics that appeal in multiple markets (though hardly universally or globally) (Jenner 2018, 219–40). I have described some of the elements of this as genre, aesthetics, value systems and themes, and efforts towards linguistic diversity, especially in American texts that pre-dated wider efforts in translation by Netflix (via subtitles or dubbing). An example of this is the way *Stranger Things* (Netflix 2016–) employs the conventions of the fantasy genre to underplay national history and culture, and to emphasise the transnational language of Hollywood cinema (see Couldry 2012, 160). Another example is the way *Orange is the New Black* (Netflix 2013–19) engages with internationally (but in no way globally) shared values of anti-sexism, anti-racism and anti-homophobia, as laid out in the UN Human Rights Convention. This article explores the aspect of genre in more detail, focusing particularly on thematic and aesthetic concerns of the contemporary teen genre. Yet, other aspects of the grammar of transnationalism are important in these texts, too. The focus here lies on the comparison of two Netflix series published in 2019, a few months apart, *Sex Education*, published on 11 January, and *How to Sell Drugs . . .*, published on 31 May. The fact that the two series were published in such close succession suggests that they did not influence each other (as the latter series was already in production when the earlier one was published).

Yet, they are similar in significant aspects that are indicative of the ways in which Netflix employs genre to enable transnational communication. The teen genre is an interesting case study with which to explore this, as, in Western countries, the genre has been dominated by American imports and, therefore, local conventions have often developed in reference to the US genre.

NETFLIX AND THE TEEN GENRE

The teen genre, as an umbrella genre, is directed predominantly at teenage and young adult audiences. The teen genre is broadly divided into two strands: music television and scripted teen television.[2] The latter is the category described here, with a specific focus on the scripted teen drama serial (here shortened to teen drama) or teen soap, to use two synonymous terms (as opposed to teen sitcom or scripted reality TV).[3] This is not to say that the different branches of the genre do not overlap and interact in significant ways, as described throughout this section. I will outline the structural conventions of the teen drama series here and will then move on to describe how Netflix has used the genre. To understand the teen genre on Netflix, I use Karen Petruska and Faye Woods's terminology of the 'false original' and the 'self-produced original'. This helps divide content into categories of licensed and commissioned original productions (2019, 51). For the teen genre, this distinction is relevant as Netflix continues to reap the reputational promises of successful teen dramas like *Riverdale* (CBS 2017–), for which it is the distributor in a number of countries, seeking to attract and bind younger viewers to the platform. Its initial reliance on false originals has shifted into more and more self-produced original films and TV series. The self-produced teen dramas are often not American, positioning Netflix as a platform that enables transnational communication across countries while remaining indebted to American genre conventions.

To explore these conventions, I will move on to outline the teen drama genre, using the structural approach. In 1975, Douglas Pye suggested a list of textual criteria to determine (film) genre. He posits a list of local conventions that determine genre conventions: Plot, Other Structural Features, Characters, Time/Space, Iconography, Themes.

Pye's list makes a good starting point, but elements such as narrative structures and soundtrack, both in film and television, also deserve to be considered. What Pye's structuralist approach also neglects is the sub-genres at work: the two dominant sub-genres, supernatural teen drama and teen soap, can vary widely. Though the themes are similar, the narrative modes are different. A brief comparison of *Buffy the Vampire Slayer* (The WB 1997–2003; UPN 2001–3) and *Dawson's Creek* (The WB 1998–2003), which ran on the same network at roughly the same time, often scheduled on the same night, serves well as an example. Both have homosexual main characters, but the narrative mode requires a much more melodramatic coming out for Jack (Kerr Smith) on *Dawson's Creek*, where far-reaching family conflicts and detailed debates among friends are spread across a mid-season double episode (02/14 'To Be or Not to Be . . .' and 02/15 '. . . That is the Question'). Meanwhile, Willow's (Alyson Hannigan) coming out on *Buffy* is much more subdued, as more immediate concerns about Willow's werewolf-ex-boyfriend become central (04/19 'New Moon Rising').

More recently, teen thrillers have developed with series such as *Pretty Little Liars* (ABC 2010–7), *Riverdale*, *Baby* (Netflix 2018–) or *Elite* (*Élite*, Netflix 2018–). This structuralist perspective on genre is limiting in the sense that it reduces complex discourses that are at the intersection of audience reception and definitions, industry and technological discourses, and cultural discourses and histories to purely textual characteristics. Hence, the work of theorists such as Jane Feuer (1992) and later Jason Mittell (2004) on discursive approaches that highlight the interplay of audience and reception, industry, and textual structures is important. These discursive approaches recognise that some genre texts are more easily understood via one discourse than the other: for example, 'cult' TV is better understood via audience discourses than textual while the development of music television heavily hinges on industry discourses. As Valerie Wee (2010) outlines, industrial discourses are highly relevant to the development of teen drama and, thus, the genre's relevance for strategies of companies such as Fox or the WB (later The CW) cannot be underestimated. This highlights the importance of considering the interplay between different discourses. With these caveats in mind, Pye's list is still helpful in outlining the general structure of genre texts, particularly in the transnational context.

The advantage of the structuralist approach is its 'transportability' across cultures while acknowledging how some elements may be de-emphasised or changed, depending on national traditions. In teen television, the addition of texts focused more on the supernatural have shifted plot structures immensely. However, though the genre tends to be united on themes (as discussed below), there is less unity on plots than may be expected. Stories are usually focused on teen characters as they move through various events to build an adult identity, but the narrative tools that frame these plots (such as comedy or melodrama) are less unified. Other Structural Features may link to the daytime setting in teen soaps and the night-time setting in supernatural teen dramas or the common middle-class/upper-class divide that dominates many teen soaps. For teen drama, soundtrack is crucial as it operates as a guide to the particular time and offers relatively quick characterisation. American teen drama has often served to further marketing for contemporary rock and pop bands. Rachel Moseley (2015, 39) credits *The OC* (Fox 2003–7) with having helped launch the career of The Killers, whereas *One Tree Hill* (The CW 2003–12) featured the lead singer of Fall Out Boy for several episodes. The publication of the DVDs of *Beverly Hills 90210* (Fox 1990–2000) was significantly held up over a dispute over royalties with bands like R.E.M., before distributors settled on replacing the music entirely, pointing to how relevant contemporary music is in the genre.[4] Characters are a group of teenagers, often starting out at the age of 15 or 16, though some teen soaps follow these characters through further education and adulthood. Importantly, teen dramas trace the relationships of teenagers amongst each other. This sets the genre apart from a majority of sitcoms and dramas that depict family relationships and feature teenagers as part of this family, such as *The Fresh Prince of Bel Air* (NBC 1990–6) or *Gilmore Girls* (The CW 2000–7). In fact, parents, with few exceptions (normally one couple within each series), are often absent or appear as marginal characters (see Banks 2004). The time is usually contemporary and common spaces are the school and the family homes of main characters, in American teen soaps often the family kitchen. Many teen dramas also involve clubs as regular 'hangout' spots. Supernatural teen dramas also often include libraries or other research facilities. Iconography highlights rich colour schemes, as well as images of locations such as school. The school cafeteria, hallways and lockers take on a particular importance, here. Supernatural teen dramas include images of monsters, whereas teen soaps are often centred around wealth and show a number of fetishised objects, such as cars. As this suggests, particularly the American teen soap tends to focus on the social inequality between the super-rich and the middle class. While massive wealth is, thus, visually fetishised, middle-class families are positioned as places of moderation and idealised value systems. *Beverly Hills 90210* sets the template, but series such as *One Tree Hill*, *The OC* or *Gossip Girl* (CBS 2007–12) have expanded on this. Furthermore, as Moseley argues, the thematic focus of teen drama is:

> . . . the 'teen problem', including questions of identity, love, sex and romance, high-school hierarchies and family relationships, but also, in the process, on the teenager as problem, as a figure both troubled and troubling and in need of education and guidance. (2015, 40)

Yet, the focus is less the family in which this guidance is given, but, as mentioned above, the relationships between teens that allow for the exploration of boundaries.

Netflix's approach to the teen genre has remained relatively uneven since it has started to commission self-produced originals. This is at least partly due to the affordances of algorithmic culture and the need for texts to be 'taggable'. Netflix initially desired to associate itself with American 'quality' television and 'adult' themes, for example through series such as *House of Cards* (Netflix

2013–18). Implicit in this is a relatively vague idea of the negative associations a teen soap such as *Beverly Hills 90210* might suggest as the service was only starting to introduce itself to a broader audience. In line with its emphasis on adult themes, Netflix's approach to the teen genre went via the horror genre. One of its earliest in-house series was *Hemlock Grove* (Netflix 2013–16), a graphic horror series created by Eli Roth, which featured teenagers as central characters. *Hemlock Grove* was generally overshadowed by the critical success of *House of Cards* and *Orange is the New Black* and the critical attention given to Season 4 of *Arrested Development* (Fox 2003–6; Netflix 2013–).

In terms of its self-produced originals, Netflix's first foray into teen soaps was via *Degrassi: Next Class* (Netflix 2016–), a continuation of previous iterations of the successful Canadian franchise. The series draws on a rich series memory of its own, with *Degrassi High* (CT 1987–91) premiering in 1987. Elana Levine, in an article discussing the global–local dimensions of the 2001 iteration *Degrassi: The Next Generation* (CTV 2001–15), identifies a specifically Canadian identity within the series by analysing it from an industry studies perspective (Levine 2009). Since, in its American iteration, the teen soap is often remarkable for the whiteness of its main characters, *Degrassi*'s discussion of race and its refusal to cast people of colour as Other stands out. Its approach to racial diversity also explains much about Netflix's use of the franchise. As I have argued before, the success of *Orange is the New Black* appears to have guided much of Netflix's approach to its self-produced originals by highlighting female leads, representation of queer identities and racial diversity. This kind of 'Netflix diversity' (similar to the 'Netflix Feminism' Havas and Horeck describe in the final part of this volume) plays into (American) liberal value systems, highlighting American histories that lead to specific emphases in the representation of women, particularly women of colour, and African Americans (Jenner 2018, 161–82).[5] It also speaks to the value systems inherent in the grammars of transnationalism and the way these link to interpretations of Human Rights shared across Western countries. The *Degrassi* franchise's approach to racial diversity may be specifically Canadian in the sense that racial histories are clearly embedded in Canadian history, but it also fits within a wider 'Netflix diversity', even extending this to include explicitly non-American racial identities. *On My Block* (Netflix 2018–), which focuses on young Hispanic American teenagers, follows this template quite closely, with teenage characters who are working class and racially marginalised. This is furthered in the Spanish *Elite*, with its foregrounding of institutional Orientalism and Islamophobia through Muslim character Nadia (Mina El Hammani). Netflix's strand of teen rom-com films also works well within these parameters. *Sierra Burgess is a Loser* (Samuels 2018), *Dumplin'* (Fletcher 2018), *Tall Girl* (Stewart 2019) and others all feature female leads and debate teenage angst, often surrounding body image issues in (usually white) teenage girls.

As its first American teen drama, *13 Reasons Why* (Netflix 2017–) aimed to address a teen audience by focusing on teen characters. Though heavily indebted to the American 'quality' TV tradition of innovative narrative structures and cinematic aesthetics (see Dunleavy 2018), the series' first season displayed a thematic focus rare for the genre. In this respect, it can be compared to *Breaking Bad* (AMC 2008–13), a series invested with the 'quality' TV label, which is focused on one specific issue: the criminal pursuits of its main character. This focus often happens at the expense of other storylines. *Breaking Bad* also functions as an important reference point as the international (same-day) distribution of its final season in 2013 happened through Netflix in the UK and Ireland, a deal that helped establish the company as transnational television (Dent 2013). Several genre texts have explored serious issues such as teen suicide and sexual assault, often through the more melodramatic soap structures. Yet, individual episodes usually mix melodramatic storylines with those more focused on comedy. Veronica Mars's (Kristin Bell) sarcastic voice-over often lightens the thematic focus on her own sexual assault and the murder of her friend Lily (Amanda Seyfried) in *Veronica Mars* (UPN 2004–6; The CW 2007; Hulu 2019). In this regard, *13 Reasons Why* remains an exception in the way it frames sexual assault as not one singular event that leads to suicide, but rather a continued experience. In its second and third seasons, the series often becomes more conventional as a teen drama, though its tone remains relatively serious. Within a month of the publication of *13 Reasons Why*, *Dear White People* (Netflix 2017–), another Netflix self-produced original, was published. The series operates on the fringes of what could be described as teen drama: *Dear White People* is set on a college campus, thus featuring young adults living away from the family and its restrictions, rather than teenagers. Similar to *13 Reasons Why*, it remains focused on one issue, in this case, race relations on a fictional US college campus. This means that *13 Reasons Why* and *Dear White People* are taggable across genres, functioning both as 'quality' television and teen series (see also Jenner 2019, 311). This focus is enabled by the narrative structures of both series that foreground binge-ability: in its first season, the narrative of *13 Reasons Why* is framed by 13 cassette tapes recorded by Hannah (Katherine Langford), who lists a harrowing series of instances of sexual harassment and assault that lead to her suicide. The framing of her suicide and ever-escalating sexual assault as a mystery propels the narrative forward, inviting viewers to binge the series (see also Horeck 2019). Later seasons involve more storylines and focus on more violent instances of sexual assault but nevertheless remain focused on the issue. *Dear White People* uses voice-overs, flashbacks and non-linear narrative structure. The non-linear structure can produce instances of enigmas where later episodes give more context to events happening in the background of other episodes.[6] These series are very different for a range of reasons but remarkable for remaining focused on one specific issue, highlighting its complexity.

TRANSNATIONALISING GENRE: *SEX EDUCATION* AND *HOW TO SELL DRUGS ONLINE (FAST)*

Netflix's non-English language teen series include the Spanish *Elite* and the Italian *Baby*, which both draw on established themes of the genre, especially regarding social inequality and the fetishisation of wealth. They follow the narrative mode of the teen thriller by drawing on predecessors like *Pretty Little Liars*. The year 2019 saw more non-American iterations of the genre in the form of *Sex Education* and *How to Sell Drugs . . .* that drew on a range of traditions and served to transnationalise the genre. The transnationalisation of genre on Netflix is raised here in order to explore how genre conventions are used in the production of non-American Netflix texts, and thus enable transnational communication. The tradition that both *Sex Education* and *How to Sell Drugs . . .* draw on is American. However, this does not mean that the local conventions of the American iteration of the genre are somehow universal, rather that the massive international success of series like *Beverly Hills 90210*, *Dawson's Creek* or *The OC* has made the conventions these texts employ internationally recognisable. Using the American genre conventions as a template, the structuralist approach is used here to explore how *Sex Education* and *How to Sell Drugs . . .* negotiate their allegiance to the American genre tradition and position Netflix as transnational television.

The British tradition of teen drama is, as Moseley puts it, 'more uneven [. . .] than its US counterpart' (2015, 41). Teen-centred dramas have been as varied as *Hollyoaks* (Channel 4 1995–), *As If* (Channel 4 2001–4), *Skins* (Channel 4, 2007–13), *Hex* (Sky 2004–5) and *The Inbetweeners* (E4 2008–10), each indebted to different traditions of storytelling. Yet, some broader characteristics can be identified. While the US tradition tends to highlight social inequality, often visually fetishising displays of massive wealth in opposition to more moderate middle-class families, British series tend to focus on middle-class and working-class families without emphasising social inequality as theme. As Moseley argues, series are often underpinned by a realist paradigm, featuring swearing and discussion of masturbation, often for comedic effect. This tradition is carried on in *Sex Education*, which puts themes of sex at its centre, again often highlighting its more embarrassing aspects for comedic effect. Yet, the 'uneven' nature of the genre also appears to lie in a refusal to follow established American genre templates and, instead, highlight the local. This is linked to the requirements of British television for representation as well as an insistence on regional identity, often expressed via accents. On German television, it is the Public Service Broadcasting channels that also carry the responsibility of representation of different regions, though this engagement usually takes place in a different manner. The German tradition of teen drama is dominated by imports, often from the US. The soap *Gute Zeiten, Schlechte Zeiten* ('Good Times, Bad

Times') (RTL 1992–), which focused on young adults, was launched in 1992 on commercial channel RTL. In the 1980s, the tradition of the so-called 'Weihnachtsserie', a format of mini-series in the run-up to Christmas targeting children and teenagers, featured a few dramas that focused on teen characters, such as the enormously successful *Anna* (ZDF 1987) or *Ron & Tanja* (ZDF 1990). However, the genre has been dominated by American imports and music television channels, such as MTV or Viva. The lack of clearly recognisable national traditions makes drawing on US genre conventions a relatively obvious choice. As such, neither *Sex Education* nor *How to Sell Drugs* . . . operates within a well-established national genre framework, even though the UK has a more robust tradition of this than Germany. *Sex Education* remains indebted to the UK tradition through its frank discussion of sex, but many British genre predecessors such as *The Inbetweeners* have, arguably, relied more on cringe-worthy humour. *How to Sell Drugs* . . . is loosely based on the story of German teenager Maximilian S. and his online drug trade. Yet, the series avoids a realist mode of storytelling through stylistic means such as fast editing or direct address.

Genre, on a transnational level, is a complex negotiation of different national traditions and the traditions of domesticated imports. As Mihelj argues:

> Global standardization and homogenization, therefore, does not imply an obliteration of difference. To the contrary, [. . .] globalization requires – and in fact thrives on – differences, but constructs and organizes them in uniform ways. (2011, 29)

Thus, the transnationalisation suggested here is a complicated negotiation of the local and the transnational, though the context of texts that are transnational from the outset also means that they need to function within recognisable genre structures. Very simply put, neither *Sex Education* nor *How to Sell Drugs* . . . aims to simply copy an American genre template. Yet, within the structures of Netflix's recommendation algorithm, these texts need to be taggable as part of specific genre, sub-genre and micro-genre traditions, emulating a specific tone and style within these genres (see Alexander 2016; Arnold 2016). The use of dubbing into English (with American accents and in some cases done by the actors of the original version themselves) has made it easier for non-English language texts within the transnational Netflix ecology. Still, even countries with strong domestic productions (such as the UK and Germany) may only produce one or two self-produced originals for Netflix per year, usually with seasons of around ten episodes. In the case of *Sex Education*, this is reduced to eight 45-minute episodes while *How to Sell Drugs* . . . only has six 30-minute episodes in their respective first seasons. This context may make it more worthwhile for non-American Netflix texts to transnationalise genre by de-emphasising the local.

In terms of plot, both *Sex Education* and *How to Sell Drugs*... challenge existing (American) genre conventions. However, this challenge plays out in remarkably similar ways that suggest the establishment of a new sub-genre. Both series play on familiar underdog stories by focusing on young male characters who turn to somewhat illicit and unusual businesses: a version of sex therapy provided by students for students, and an online drug trade, respectively. Otis (Asa Butterfield) in *Sex Education* and Moritz (Maximilian Mundt) in *How to Sell Drugs*... engage in these practices to impress teenage girls, both of whom are blonde and fit comfortably within contemporary beauty ideals for teenage girls. Both become often so engrossed in their courtships that they neglect other relationships, especially with their (male) best friends. The relationship with their best friends is heavily emphasised within these series. Both series also focus on one specific issue, similar to the way in which *13 Reasons Why* and *Dear White People* draw on *Breaking Bad*-style 'quality' television to formulate their bingeability.

The characters of Otis and Moritz both fit a traditional concept of the 'geek' within the genre typology, visually recognisable through a vintage striped jacket (Otis in red, orange and white and Moritz in different blue tones and white). Their haircuts are almost defiant of contemporary beauty standards for men, and both are often juxtaposed with more muscular male teenagers. Otis's sex therapy business is run with Maeve (Emma Mackey), and Moritz begins to trade drugs to win back his ex-girlfriend Lisa (Lena Klenke). Otis and Moritz are both accompanied by their childhood best friends who, to put it reductively, both fit into a broad category of 'diversity'. Otis's best friend Eric (Ncuti Gatwa) is a queer black teenager who participates in the sex therapy only marginally. However, his own storyline surrounding his negotiation of sexual identity features prominently. Moritz's best friend Lenny (Danilo Klamber) develops much of the online infrastructure for the drug trade and often collaborates with Moritz against his will. Lenny uses a wheelchair as a consequence of a fatal disease and the first season makes clear that he may die within the next two years. Diversity is an insufficiently broad concept, and the comparison of Eric and Lenny makes this especially clear as the storylines they dominate are distinct and their challenges different, in many respects, even opposite. Yet, the important point here is that both characters significantly challenge a norm of white, heterosexual, able-bodied, and middle-class masculinity of teenagers within the genre. This, of course, fits into a broader concept of Netflix diversity, as discussed above.

In these series there is a visible tendency to avoid any national specificity that would require long-winded explanations. School systems are a particularly important part of this. Though not offering detailed outlines, the tradition of American teen drama and films has created at least a passing understanding of the American school system for most viewers. Highlighting the distinctions, not only in terms of educational policy but also in terms of available facilities (lockers, cafeteria, swimming pools) would require lengthy explanations that are also of limited relevance to the narrative. Thus, place, or rather its denial, becomes an important factor in the transnationalisation of genre in these series. Language, and its role within often English-language national contexts, is of particular importance, here. As Robert Watts points out in his chapter in this part, language can often signal a certain level of 'authenticity' that works well within transnational marketing discourses. For most UK texts, the linguistic 'default' is what the British call a 'posh' accent. Common for most British television drama as well as film, it has become the language of UK exports. For *Sex Education*, which is filmed in Wales, the 'posh' accent of its stars works to suggest a lack of regional specificity (never mind Welsh national identity), instead highlighting a general Britishness (or rather, Englishness). This points to the necessity for the series to appeal more broadly than within a UK context, instead addressing audiences who have no desire or need to engage with issues of regional specificity. Though streaming in the UK is (at the time of writing) governed by EU media policy, there is no requirement to represent regional identities (or minority languages, as would be the case in Wales) within each country in the same way Public Service Broadcasting is required to do. On German television, the use of 'Hochdeutsch' (High German) is common, no matter where a programme is set. *How to Sell Drugs . . .* describes its place as the fictional town of Rinseln, with a population of 28,734, of whom about two-thirds have online access ('Life's not Fair, Get Used to It', 01/02). The series integrates scenes in Dutch, suggesting that Rinseln is located close to the German-Dutch border, but gives no further information.[7] The series mostly settles on Moritz's and Lisa's desire to 'get out' of the town, a sentiment that is shared by a large number of characters in teen dramas set in a small town. The linguistic world is expanded on, as the teenagers of the series are fluent in English as a 'standard' language of the internet widely integrated in their colloquialisms and even text exchanges. The fact that the English-language dubbing was provided by the original German-language actors in Season 1 (including their German accents) works to lend even more authenticity to this. *How to Sell Drugs . . .* thematically emphasises the transnationalism inherent in online culture. Though this seems more relevant for the two main characters and their goal to sell illegal drugs online, significant parts of this online culture are linked to much less nefarious online behaviours such as reading and sharing on social media. In the representation of the local, there is little outside of the national language to suggest place in *Sex Education* and *How to Sell Drugs . . .*

Perhaps the most significant addition to genre conventions over the last five years is the visualisation of online culture to represent the world that teenagers inhabit. Of course, teen dramas are not the only ones that feature text bubbles to signify text messages or computer screens, but this feature has become almost integral to the genre, driving plots in teen films like *Sierra Burgess is a Loser*. The transnational nature of online culture makes its visualisation, perhaps, better suited than other genre conventions to signify the transnationalisation of the teen genre. Especially in *How to Sell Drugs . . .*, the use of English language in written online communication comes to signify its relevance to wider transnational teen culture. Other visual features employed by both texts are the broad-striped vintage jackets Moritz and Otis wear to signify their geek status (as mentioned above). Further, both series feature the school and the main characters' homes (predominantly kitchen and teen bedroom) prominently. In showing the school, both series highlight lockers in school hallways, even though these are not of prominent usage in the British and German school systems. It may be this element that most strongly invokes the reliance of the genre on American genre predecessors and the transnational nature of its visual language. Visually, both series avoid giving too much specificity in terms of place. *Sex Education* has flyover shots of woods, signifying its rural setting. *How to Sell Drugs . . .* establishes some national specificity by showing letterboxes quite prominently, but, again, avoids being too specific outside of the national.

There is a thematic link to *The OC* and its emphasis on male characters. The focus in both series on male friendship and a geek male character's pursuit of a 'popular' girl (though this category is reformulated in both series) is highly reminiscent of the storylines surrounding Seth (Adam Brody) in *The OC*. Yet, the narrative focus mentioned above means that both *How to Sell Drugs . . .* and *Sex Education* tie fewer storylines together and have smaller main casts. Both series deal with the subversive behaviour engaged in by the main characters, the significant difference being that selling drugs is illegal, while giving advice on sex is not. The behaviour, however, is not sanctioned by official authorities such as teachers or parents, even though there is a general acceptance that teenagers will take drugs and have sex. For example, *How to Sell Drugs . . .* justifies Lisa's (and other character's) drug consumption with her home life and a general anxiety about her future. The choice to take or abstain from drugs is seen as part of forming a moral identity, often in relation to home life. Moritz and Lenny both grapple with the morality of selling drugs linked with the capitalist implications of selling an inferior product (and less so moral questions of the conditions under which drugs are manufactured). Moritz is treated as an anti-hero who is pushed into his actions by love (much like Otis) and pressures his best friend to go along. However, they do largely abstain from drugs themselves. The search for adult identities is universalised here and taken to mean sexual as well as moral. It is also linked to capitalist systems, establishing the desire and ability to build businesses as (supposedly) universally desirable.

CONCLUSION: TRANSNATIONALISING GENRE

The issue here is not merely the transnational use of genre conventions. As texts cross national borders, it becomes hardly remarkable that they influence each other on a transnational level. The dominance of US imports within the genre also makes it unsurprising that its local conventions are adopted elsewhere, particularly in Western countries. Since, as Rick Altman (1999, 13–29) pointed out about film, genre functions as a means of communication between industry and audience, it makes sense that its language is adopted as universal by Netflix. Yet, what is remarkable is how these local conventions operate as a grammar of transnationalism on Netflix. A significant feature here is the de-nationalisation of texts by removing the local. For *Sex Education*, this means removing the regionality of accents and minority language (Welsh). In both series, the institutional specificities in the form of school systems are removed: while both series are set in schools, there is no real suggestion of what grade the characters are in or what kinds of exams they are likely to take – not even in the passing manner common for scripted television. Meanwhile, the imagery of lockers and the school setting remains important, no matter how common their use in national schools actually is. The visualisation of online culture by showing text messages or websites on screen stands in for a supposedly universal teen experience. In *How to Sell Drugs . . .* the dominance of English in coding and online culture in general also serves to momentarily bridge language gaps (though translation in different languages is provided as well). This call to the universal offered through genre conventions means that, structurally, *Sex Education* and *How to Sell Drugs . . .* serve as vehicles for transnational communication beyond American imports.

The transnationalisation of genre serves to highlight the position of Netflix as transnational broadcaster as well as the role of genre as a means of transnational communication. Perhaps the most significant addition Netflix offers to the transnational television landscape on a textual level is the design of texts that are transnational from the outset. This means that they are available in all of the markets in which Netflix operates with different translation options. But it also means that they have to operate within an algorithmic category that Netflix recognises, such as genre, and have to thematically, aesthetically and tonally align with texts that already exist. This offers non-American texts an opportunity to align with each other to find common ground through existing generic structure and, thus, effectively transnationalise genre. While this may also pose questions about cultural homogenisation, it is important not to revert back to anxieties surrounding imports, but to recognise the ways in which individual texts negotiate the local and the transnational. Genre studies and a focus on the transnationalisation of genre in the context of Netflix provides opportunities to explore these complex negotiations as transnational, rather than only in relation to American contexts.

NOTES

1. The lack of a traditional schedule does not mean that content is unscheduled or that viewers are not nudged towards specific viewing behaviours, such as binge-watching (see Jenner 2018).
2. Music television is often discussed in different terms than teen TV, for example as sub-genres of contemporary reality TV (see Hill 2015; Kavka 2012).
3. It is not unusual for genre studies to have several terms encompassing the same meanings. Similarly, in crime genre, the terms 'mystery' and 'whodunit' describe the same kind of story.
4. The most reliable sources to confirm this today are fan blogs. See: <http://coldbananas.com/2010/02/television/on-the-beverly-hills-90210-dvds-the-song-doesnt-remain-the-same-and-thats-a-problem/> (last accessed 19 March 2021); and <http://blog.thecaptainsofindustry.com/beverly-hills-90210/9-0-2-1-easy/>(last accessed 19 March 2021) and subreddits, largely because R.E.M.'s song 'Losing my Religion' featured memorably in the depiction of the romantic relationship between characters Dylan (Luke Perry) and Brenda (Shannon Doherty). The author's personal VHS collection also confirms this.
5. This is also visible in Netflix's reaction to the international Black Lives Matter protests in 2020: the company responded by creating a Black Lives Matter category, which includes several self-produced documentaries, series and films, as well as licensed content. Netflix even licensed a range of sitcoms featuring African American casts, like *Girlfriends* (UPN 2000–6; CBS 2006–8), *Moesha* (Nickelodeon 1996–2001) or *Sister, Sister* (ABC 1994–5, WB 1995–9).
6. Tom Hemingway explores these 'mini-cliffhangers' further in his chapter on comedy and narrative structure in this volume.
7. Scenes between the German and Dutch characters are in English and the Dutch remains intact in the dubbing (subtitles specify language) to retain the sense of 'foreignness' suggested in these scenes. The case on which the story is loosely based took place in Leipzig, which is a city located in eastern Germany whereas the Dutch border is at the opposite end of the country.

REFERENCES

Alexander, N. (2016). 'Catered to Your Future Self: Netflix's 'Predictive Personalization' and the Mathematization of Taste'. In K. McDonald and D. Smith-Rowsey, D. (eds), *The Netflix Effect: Technology and Entertainment in the 21st Century*. New York: Bloomsbury Academic, pp. 81–97.

Altman, R. (1999). *Film/Genre*. London: BFI.

Appadurai, A. (1996). *Modernity at Large: Cultural Dimensions of Globalization*. Minneapolis, MN: University of Minnesota Press.

Arnold, S. (2016). 'Netflix and the Myth of Choice/Participation/Autonomy'. In K. McDonald and D. Smith-Rowsey (eds), *The Netflix Effect: Technology and Entertainment in the 21st Century*. New York: Bloomsbury Academic, pp. 49–62.

Banks, M. (2004). 'A Boy for all Planets: Roswell, Smallville and the Teen Male Melodrama'. In G. Davis and K. Dickinson (eds), *Teen TV: Genre, Consumption and Identity*. London: BFI, pp. 17–28.

Bielby, D. and C. L. Harrington (2008). *Global TV: Exporting Television and Culture in the World Market*. New York; London: New York University Press.

Buonanno, M. (2008). *The Age of Television Experiences and Theories*, edited by Jennifer Radice. Bristol: Intellect.

Couldry, N. (2012). *Media, Society, World: Social Theory and Digital Media Practice*. Cambridge: Cambridge: Polity.

Creeber, G. (2015). *The Television Genre Book* (3rd edition). London: Palgrave.

Dent, S. (2013). 'Final Breaking Bad Season to Air on Netflix UK Right After US Broadcast'. *Engadget*. 26 July 2013. Available at: <https://www.engadget.com/2013/07/26/breaking-bad-netflix-uk-right-after-broadcast/?guccounter=1&guce_referrer=aHR0cHM6Ly9 3d3cuZ29vZ2xlLmNvLnVrLw&guce_referrer_sig=AQAAALYUDiaqPCZDqDZUS zgLN5XRkQvuFcr9-u5LvQHp8kb3OaTmiwpoCKEpgUFUiGNhyF8iAv64KrCf9z sOqVl2oShX2iHCKhKmjl8FPAxQhIR-QGjMvYMS4Rg9oxMvyV_wCoWsqcW2_ KVpxDJbAFuD1J7QDsKFNsRyjY9dh2jxW2R1> (last accessed 15 January 2020).

De Sousa, W. and S. Trültzsch-Wijnen (2016). 'Watching the Hobbit in Two European Countries: The Views of Younger Audiences and Readers in Austria and Portugal'. *Participations* 13(2): 469–95.

Dunleavy, T. (2018) *Complex Serial Drama and Multiplatform Television*. London: Routledge.

Feuer, J. (1992). 'Genre Study and Television'. In R. C. Allen (ed.), *Channels of Discourse, Reassembled*. London: Routledge, pp. 138–60.

Finn, E. (2017). *What Algorithms Want: Imagination in the Age of Computing*. Cambridge, MA: MIT Press.

Gillan, J. (2015). *Television Brandcasting: The Return of the Content-Promotion Hybrid*. New York; London: Routledge.

GrahamFunke. (2008). '9-0-2-1-Easy'. 7 September 2008. Available at: <http://blog.thecaptainsofindustry.com/beverly-hills-90210/9-0-2-1-easy/> (last accessed 19 March 2021).

Hanson, J. (2010). 'On the "Beverly Hills, 90210" DVDs, the Song Doesn't Remain the Same (and That's a Problem) (TV Commentary)'. 10 February 2010. Available at: <http://coldbananas.com/2010/02/television/on-the-beverly-hills-90210-dvds-the-song-doesnt-remain-the-same-and-thats-a-problem/> (last accessed 19 March 2021).

Hill, A. (2015). *Reality TV*. Abingdon: Routledge.

Horeck, T. (2019). 'Streaming Sexual Violence: Binge-Watching Netflix's 13 Reasons Why'. *Participations* 16(2): 144–66. Available at: <https://www.participations.org/Volume%2016/Issue%202/9.pdf> (last accessed 19 March 2021).

Jenner, M. (2018). *Netflix and the Re-Invention of Television*. Basingstoke: Palgrave Macmillan.

Jenner, M. (2019). 'Control Issues: Binge-Watching, Channel-Surfing and Cultural Value'. *Participations* 16(2): 298–317.

Kavka, M. (2012). *Reality TV*. Edinburgh: Edinburgh University Press.

Levine, E. (2009). 'National Television, Global Market: Canada's Degrassi: The Next Generation'. *Media, Culture & Society* 31(4): 515–31.

Lobato, R. (2019). *Netflix Nations: The Geography of Digital Distribution*. New York: New York University Press.

Madrigal, A. C. (2014). 'How Netflix Reverse Engineered Hollywood'. *The Atlantic*. Available at: <https://www.theatlantic.com/technology/archive/2014/01/how-netflix-reverse-engineered-hollywood/282679/> (last accessed 19 March 2021).

McKinley, E. G. (1997). *Beverly Hills, 90210: Television, Gender, and Identity*. Philadelphia: University of Pennsylvania Press.

Mihelj, S. (2011). *Media Nations: Communicating Belonging and Exclusion in the Modern World*. Basingstoke: Palgrave Macmillan.

Mittell, J. (2004). *Genre and Television: From Cop Shows to Cartoons in American Culture*. New York; London: Routledge.

Moseley, R. (2015). 'Teen Drama'. In G. Creeber (ed.), *The Television Genre Book*. London: BFI, pp. 38–41.
Petruska, K. and F. Woods (2019). 'Traveling without a Passport: "Original" Streaming Content in the Transatlantic Distribution Ecosystem'. In M. Hills, M. Hilmes and R. Pearson (eds), *Transatlantic Television Drama: Industries, Programs, & Fans*. Oxford: Oxford University Press, pp. 49–67.
Pye, D. (1975). 'Genre and Movies'. *Movie* 20: 29–43.
Straubhaar, J. D. (2007). *World Television: From Global to Local*. Thousand Oaks, CA: Sage Publications.
Wee, V. (2010). *Teen Media: Hollywood and the Youth Market in the Digital Age*. Jefferson, NC: McFarland & Co.

TV

13 Reasons Why (2017–), USA: Netflix
Anna (1987), GER: ZDF
Arrested Development (2003–), USA: Fox, Netflix
As If (2001–4) UK: Channel 4
Baby (2018–) IT: Netflix
Beverly Hills 90210 (1990–2000), USA: Fox
Breaking Bad (2008–13), USA: AMC
Buffy the Vampire Slayer (1997–2003), USA: The WB, UPN
Dawson's Creek (1998–2003), USA: The WB
Dear White People (2017–), USA: Netflix
Degrassi High (1987–91), CN: CTV
Degrassi: Next Class (2016–), CN: Netflix
Degrassi: The Next Generation (2001–15), CN: CTV
Elite (*Élite*, 2018–), ES: Netflix
Fresh Prince of Bel Air, The (1990–6), USA: NBC
Gilmore Girls (2000–7), USA: The CW
Girlfriends (2000–6): USA: UPN, CBS
Gossip Girl (2007–12), USA: CBS
Gute Zeiten, Schlechte Zeiten (1992–), GER: RTL
Hemlock Grove (2013–16), USA: Netflix
Hex (2004–5), UK: Sky
Hollyoaks (1995–), UK: Channel 4
House of Cards (2013–18), USA: Netflix
How to Sell Drugs Online (Fast) (2019–), GER: Netflix
Inbetweeners, The (2008–10), UK: E4
Moesha (1996–2001), USA: Nickelodeon
OC, The (2003–7), USA: Fox
On My Block (2018–), USA: Netflix
One Tree Hill (2003–12), USA: The CW
Orange is the New Black (2013–19), USA: Netflix
Pretty Little Liars (2010–17), USA: ABC
Riverdale (2017–), USA: CBS
Ron & Tanja (1990), GER: ZDF
Sex Education (2019–), UK: Netflix
Sister, Sister (1994–9), USA: ABC, WB

Skins (2007–13), UK: Channel 4
Stranger Things, (2016–), USA: Netflix
Veronica Mars (2004–), USA: UPN, The CW, Hulu

FILM

Fletcher, A. (2018) *Dumplin'*. USA: COTA Films
Samuels, I. (2018) *Sierra Burgess is a Loser*. USA: Black Label Media
Stewart, N. (2019) *Tall Girl*. USA: Wonderland Sound and Vision

CHAPTER 13

Transnational Bingeing: Conclusion

B. G.-Stolz, Robert Watts and Mareike Jenner

This section brought together different ways to think about television in the context of current shifts to television content, circulation and culture in an increasingly global marketplace. Netflix and its re-organisation of national television programming re-negotiates cultural content under the headings 'national' and 'transnational', building itself to be what its CEO called a 'global television network' (Lobato 2019). In this section, the question of what the concept of the 'national' means, in this particular media environment, is approached through a focus on Netflix and its marketing strategies, textual structures and critical reception. Netflix's early emphasis on 'bingeability', and a simultaneous publication model to appeal to transnational markets, has been viewed as part of a re-organisation of television (see Jenner 2018). While other transnational streaming services – most notably Amazon – engage in similar strategies, Netflix's insistence upon itself as 'the first global TV network' (Murgia 2016), alongside a notable effacing of national elements in the promotion of its Originals, speaks to its centrality in a broader re-negotiation of TV's national functions. The chapters here have examined how this re-negotiation intersects with existing ideas of genre and public service; notions of common culture and shared value systems; and analytical frameworks of media consumption based on entrenched boundaries – of medium, of nation – all of which demand rethinking in turn.

Often, the rhetoric surrounding these shifts in television culture is structured by opposing categories of 'global' and 'national', which can obscure the degree to which these processes occur between or beyond these two poles, or encompass both simultaneously. In his book on geo-blocking, *Locked Out*, Evan Elkins (2019) discusses the geographical and even geopolitical hierarchies implicit in the practice in which content is unavailable to users in 'foreign' markets (meaning markets where the content is not licensed). Netflix's self-produced Originals are available across borders, making it easy for viewers to continue where they left off, even when they cross national boundaries. In his article on 'The Myth of Televisual Ubiquity', Mark Stewart (2016) describes how such affordances, while real in specific cases, also contribute to a wider popular discourse of global accessibility and abundance for television that reinforces the marketing imperatives of specific distributors (including Netflix). Roman Lobato (2019) also describes the various ways in which Netflix restricts access via geo-blocking to some of its catalogues while making its self-produced Originals freely available. Thus on the one hand Netflix masks its reinforcement of global cultural hierarchies with promotional tactics like the false Original that sustain the myth of ubiquity, while on the other it works to eliminate those hierarchies in relation to distribution of its own self-produced Originals. Yet, this model of distribution requires mediation on a textual level, via journalistic reception, and on the level of broader understandings of transnational culture.

B. G.-Stolz's article on the transcultural offers an opportunity both to reframe the concepts of the national in their application to internationally traded and circulated content and to identify the falsity of transculturalism as a marketing strategy that results in an erosion of cultural specificity. The concept is in no way limited to Netflix, and certainly is not built on a new approach to texts generated for international exchange, but identifies a re-negotiation of relationships between texts, industries, markets and audiences, one built predominantly on affect. The transcultural operates as a mode of production that is *above* distinctions of national culture because it invites this erosion as a basis for cultural global enlightenment. As such, its acknowledgement and celebration of different national cultural programming leads inevitably to an erosion of the same.

Watts argues that the binge-watching frame can, in some circumstances, work to ease the transnational assimilation of public service-originated content that is marked by the sense of a distinctly national address. Focusing on how transatlantic television critics frame local details in reviews of Netflix's British false originals, he suggests that the singular full-season review encouraged by the binge model promotes a more touristic mode of engagement with textual displays of local and cultural specificity. Here, the encounter with the local is collapsed into a more generalised notion of viewers experiencing an authentic 'sense of place' that is discussed in aesthetic terms, rather than the socially representative terms of much of these series' domestic broadcast reception. The texts are positioned accordingly by critics as 'discoveries' for a more niche, elite audience.

Jenner engages with genre as a vehicle to make transnational communication possible on Netflix, functioning as part of a Netflix-specific 'grammar of transnationalism'. She highlights genre as a framework to understand how Netflix texts can function as vehicles for transnational communication. In this, she particularly considers the algorithmic structures of Netflix and the ways in which genre tags position series as 'quality' TV and teen drama, often disregarding language, as texts are automatically played in the language the account holder normally uses, and translation (often dubbing) is provided. As such, the bingeability of the text, the 'binge model' (the publication of texts at the same time across all markets in which Netflix operates) and the algorithmic nature of streaming all work together to bring the transnationality of genre to the forefront.

For both Watts and Jenner, the denial of place becomes particularly important, for both the false and self-produced Originals. Watts discusses the ways in which false Originals are reframed as more or less place-less in the American reception of British programmes. What stands out is the fact that while these programmes are perceived as markedly local and specific in their UK context, these details of place are muted into a more generic sense of locality or 'authenticity' in their transatlantic reception. Similarly, Jenner finds that the self-produced teen dramas that Netflix publishes largely rely on de-emphasising place by avoiding local accents or giving detailed information about setting. Both processes reflect the promotion of what G. Stolz calls a 'transcultural media experience', despite very different renderings of the 'national' on the level of the text. In the first instance, national specificities remain highly visible but are de-emphasised in the transnational reception process, or translated into the terms of a more elite (transcultural) mode of consumption. In the latter case, national and local specificities are either excluded from the text from the outset or rendered in a way that will resonate with existing transnational cultural discourses. The transcultural encompasses these policies of reception and texts. It gives us a vocabulary to think about shifts in global television cultures, in which globalisation changes how texts are structured and operate.

Of course, the cultural hierarchies Elkins discusses remain in place, as several streaming platforms, such as Hulu, and 'foreign' Netflix or Amazon catalogues remain geo-blocked and, thus, inaccessible. Several of the players in the so-called 'streaming wars' have made content available in more than one market at the same time. Yet, this will likely lead to different systems of exclusion as few viewers, no matter where they are geographically located, will have the financial capital to subscribe to all these services at once. In the meantime, however, this section has provided new insights into the way bingeability and Netflix interlink to rethink how transnational television operates as cultural property.

REFERENCES

Elkins, E. (2019). *Locked Out: Regional Restrictions in Digital Entertainment Culture*. New York: New York University Press.
Jenner, M. (2018). *Netflix and the Re-Invention of Television*. Basingstoke: Palgrave Macmillan.
Lobato, R. (2019). *Netflix Nations*. New York: New York University Press.
Murgia, M. (2016). 'Inside Netflix: How Reed Hastings is building the first global TV network'. *The Telegraph*. 26 March 2016. Available at: <https://www.telegraph.co.uk/technology/2016/03/26/inside-netflix-how-reed-hastings-is-building-the-first-global-tv/> (last accessed 20 March 2021).
Stewart, M. (2016). 'The Myth of Televisual Ubiquity'. *Television & New Media* 17(8): 691–705.

PART IV

Binge-Watching Narratives

CHAPTER 14

Digressions and Recaps: The Bingeable Narrative

Lynn Kozak and Martin Zeller-Jacques

Stranger Things (Netflix 2016–) has arguably been Netflix's most successful original show, arriving on the back of an enormous international advertising campaign, and occasioning extensive online discussion on its release. Its first season surpassed *House of Cards* (Netflix 2013–18) in terms of viewership (Lawson 2016), while the third season's release prompted the usually secretive Netflix to boast about its viewership numbers on 8 July, just four days after its release:

> @Stranger Things 3 is breaking Netflix records! 40.7 million household accounts have been watching the show since its July 4 global launch – more than any other film or series in its first four days. And 18.2 million have already finished the entire season. (NetflixUS 2019a)

This tweet significantly highlights not only *Stranger Things*' huge third-season audience but also how much of that audience had 'binged' the season. Two of Netflix's key metrics for determining a show's success are 'survivability' – how many viewers who watch the first few episodes of a show continue to watch the rest – and '28 day viewership' – how many viewers watch through a whole series within a month of starting it (Adalian 2018). While industry professionals, critics and scholars can argue about the precise definitions of what constitutes a binge (see Jenner 2016, 265), any reasonable definition of the term must end up somewhere in the vicinity of 'watching a lot of a show in a short space of time', and that is exactly what Netflix is measuring when it applies the metrics of 'survivability' and '28 day viewership'. Finishing *Stranger Things 3* in fewer than four days means that audience members were watching at least two hour-long episodes each day. Netflix asserts here that the speed at which more than a third of the show's audience watched the season is in itself a metric of the show's success. In other words, Netflix brags about *Stranger Things*' bingeable narrative.

Critics, likewise, spoke of *Stranger Things*' brisk and easy narrative pace, from the advent of the first season. Emily Nussbaum (2016) praised its 'astoundingly efficient storytelling' and 'eight hours that pass in a blink', while Emily VanDerWerff (2016) admitted her own binge-watching of the show: 'I watched all eight hours of *Stranger Things* within a 24-hour period, and when I was done, I found myself hankering to go back and start over from the very beginning . . .'. *Collider* named it one of the best shows of the year, and also pointed towards its length and pace: 'By running just 8 episodes, *Stranger Things* manages to be lean and mean, feeling almost like an exceptionally long movie rather than a series of installments. The show was made for binge watching . . .' (Valentine 2016).

Following Hudelet's argument that we need close analysis to understand how technology might be affecting television aesthetics (2020), we believe that only close reading can explain just how, and if, *Stranger Things*' narrative fulfils these claims of bingeability. This chapter will look specifically at how standalone episodes and narrative redundancies work in *Stranger Things*, so as to re-examine both industrial and scholarly assertions of how the season-drop is changing televisual narrative form.

Early on in the post-2000s boom in premium cable dramas, Kristin Thompson (2003) similarly applied textual scrutiny to some of the HBO dramas which were being celebrated at the time. Although she noted that HBO touted the creative and practical freedom afforded to its showrunners as a distinguishing feature of its dramas, her analysis of the narrative structures of two of its original series, *Sex and the City* (HBO 1998–2004) and *The Sopranos* (HBO 1999–2007), showed relatively little formal experimentation at the level of episode structure. Thompson's intervention in the debate around high-end television narrative was relatively early and uncommon in terms of the way it provided, however briefly, a formal structural analysis of television dramas. It gestured towards a path which remains largely untaken in contemporary television scholarship, presumably because structural analyses of serial television narratives are both extraordinarily time-consuming, and because choosing any one programme to devote such time to necessarily begs the question of why that programme above any other. Yet streaming television and the Netflix 'season-drop' invites textual analysis more than ever before, because, as Jenner puts it:

> The practice of binge-watching implies not only viewers' desire for autonomy in scheduling when they want to watch what, but also a wish for a 'pure' text (as Jacobs [2011] terms it) that is distinctively not part of the television flow. (2016, 266)

Despite this, there have been few before this part's contributors who have sought to examine streaming programmes through close textual analysis, even when asserting those programmes' narrative innovations. Robyn Warhol's (2014) chapter on *House of Cards*, *Orange is the New Black* (Netflix 2013–19) and *Arrested Development* (Fox 2003–6; Netflix 2013–) looks for signs of structural changes in the new Netflix narrative model. She argues that features such as the lack of 'Previously On' segments, *House of Cards*' supposed near-elimination of diegetic retelling, *Orange is the New Black*'s strong temporal play and flashback-based character development, and *Arrested Development*'s chronological experimentation all emerge as *more* possible because of the show's delivery format in full, bingeable seasons. Jenner makes similar assertions about *Arrested Development*'s discourse time (2016, 266–7). Chuck Tryon agrees with this premise of innovation in 'bingeable narratives', asserting that the 'season-drop' enables:

> (1) more attentive viewing practices as binge viewers are assumed to be more familiar with previous episodes of a show and, as a result (2) more innovative storytelling practices because a show's creators can assume that those viewers will be more likely to remember subtle details. (2015, 110)

Yet this emphasis on the season collapses the distinction between season-drop streaming shows and so-called 'quality' cable shows: while Warhol points to each show's 'idiosyncracies born of the streaming format', for the dramas, at least, 'neither is fundamentally different in structure from the serials that have preceded it in the genre that has come to be called "quality TV"' (2014, 146). And '[i]f one of serial form's hallmarks is its perceived addictiveness, then quality-TV serials are the ideal vehicle for Netflix's business model' (2014, 149). In other words, Netflix adopted a 'quality television' approach to its programming that was already going strong (Horeck, Jenner and Kendall 2018, 501). O'Sullivan has argued that the shift towards a 'thirteen episode uninterrupted sequence' (2010, 60) as the key unit of television drama narration has led to an increasingly dense, poetic form of television narrative which rewards close reading at the level of structural analysis. Smith completely collapses the binge-watching model and that of weekly quality television serials, discussing 'season plots' on both HBO and Netflix, as creators for both platforms 'similarly conceive of the season, rather than the episode, as a primary narrative unit' (2018, 94), and concludes that:

> Narrative designers working on Netflix and HBO series instead often take the opportunity to implement season-spanning storylines (often referred to as 'season arcs') that accumulate slow gradual build-ups

throughout the duration of a season. *A season's relative shortness and continuous frequency of transmission (or simultaneous release of episodes) raises the chances of viewers 'keeping up with' intricate season-length storylines, as the format lessens the demand placed on viewers to keep track of what has occurred previously in the narrative.* (93, our emphasis)

This quote suggests that both the Netflix and HBO models share the season as the primary narrative unit, as well as that season being short, whatever its delivery mode. These two features clearly link with Warhol's and Tryon's earlier assertions and align with Netflix producers' claims that the season-drop presents a more unified, condensed narrative that requires fewer redundancies than standard television.

In the sections that follow, we directly address these two claims. Through close readings of *Stranger Things*, we question what a stand-alone episode like 'Chapter Seven: The Lost Sister' (02/07) says about the season as a narrative unit, as well as how *Stranger Things* uses narrative recall strategies within its condensed form. We apply these tools of structural textual analysis as a check against producers, distributors and executives behind so-called bingeable television setting the terms of the aesthetic debate around it, as they have the most to gain from audiences believing those claims.

STAND-ALONE EPISODES

Among the most persistent claims made about streaming television, both by Netflix itself and by the creatives responsible for producing it, is that these shows are 'one long movie' or are 'novelistic' in their conception and structure. *Stranger Things* explicitly signals both forms in its presentation, with each season's title resembling a film title (*Stranger Things 2*, *Stranger Things 3*) and each episode given a 'chapter' title (i.e., 'Chapter One: The Vanishing of Will Byers'). Netflix has been explicitly positioning its programmes this way since it began producing them. In Kevin Spacey's MacTaggart Lecture at the Edinburgh Television Festival, which he used as a pitch event for the new wave of Netflix Originals which would define the platform's first attempts at made-to-order bingeable television, he asked: 'Is 13 hours watched as one cinematic whole really any different than a FILM?' (Spacey 2013). Just as we see scholars elevating the Netflix model alongside the HBO model above traditional television, this rhetorical positioning of television series as 'one long movie' was also a feature of earlier waves of high-end television. Such rhetoric has become sufficiently commonplace among television critics and creatives discussing streaming television to engender its own backlash. (See, for example, Sepinwall 2015 and VanArendonk 2017a). These claims are typical of the discourses of legitimation which, according to Newman and Levine (2012), have long worked to shape the reception of contemporary television. In their words, the most 'ubiquitous legitimating strategy is cinematization: [in which] certain kinds of television and certain modes of experiencing television content are aligned with movies and the experience of movies' (2012, 5). While much of their discussion of cinematisation focuses on the valorisation of the televisual image as 'cinematic', there is an equally pervasive strain of critical and creative discourse which also describes television storytelling in terms of its relationship to cinema. Baker argues that Netflix describes its original dramas as 'cinematic' or 'novelistic' in order to 'recuperate the negative tinge of the term "binge-viewing"' (2017, 46).

This strain of thinking overlaps with a discourse which has been present in discussions of digital television since long before the advent of streaming television. Just as the practice of the season-drop exempts many 'made for bingeing' shows from the ordinary 'flow' of traditional broadcast television, Jason Jacobs has argued that

> Digital television is promoted and to an increasing extent consumed, at least in part, in terms of its ability to purify the connective tissue of the schedule, to remove the adverts, the promotional material and other pollution that gets in the way of the 'pure' text. (2011, 257)

The notion of the television text as 'pure' underpins a significant strain of journalistic, fan and critical discourse which centres around the text as a singular expression of an auteur/showrunner's personal vision, and which is implicitly, and sometimes explicitly, understood as an inviolate whole with a single central narrative.

However, it is our contention that the television text – even the season-dropped, made-for-bingeing television text – is far from pure and inviolate. Indeed, like earlier forms of television narrative, it is, in Sean O'Sullivan's memorable phrase, 'broken on purpose' (2010). Examining an earlier era of such notionally inviolate texts, O'Sullivan suggested that 'we need to think not of patterns but of exceptions' (2010, 66), in his discussion of the way the episode 'That's My Dog' (04/05), in which David (Michael C. Hall) is abducted, breaks up the episodic norms and the seasonal narrative of *Six Feet Under* (HBO 2001–5). O'Sullivan argues that within contemporary drama serials, where the season has emerged as the dominant narrative unit through which to understand the way the narrative is structured, the presence of variations, breaks or caesuras in the narrative is especially significant. In this same spirit, we want to examine one such caesura in *Stranger Things*: the Season Two episode, 'The Lost Sister'. We follow VanArendonk's assertion that episodes like this one, which stand to interrupt the narrative momentum and cohesion of their seasons, draw on pre-bingeing forms of television narrative in order to reinscribe a form of structured flow within the text (2019, 78).

While 'The Lost Sister' is a particularly apt example of the kind of in-built pause we wish to discuss, it is far from the only one. Indeed, many of Netflix's made-for-bingeing serials have incorporated a similar pause, and in a similar place within their season arc. The opening season of *House of Cards*, for example, contains an episode which takes place almost entirely in Frank's old military school, and more recently, the first season of *The Punisher* (Netflix 2017–19) incorporates a Rashomon-like episode which explores the central character's actions from the perspective of various bystanders just a few episodes before the conclusion of the season. These episodes represent a narrative strategy which does several things simultaneously. First, they break the plot-centric flow of each of their respective series, pausing the progress of the action and directing the audience's focus to events which at least appear tangential to the plot of the rest of the narrative. Second, they tend to operate in ways which draw sharp attention to the way their stories are being told, sometimes incorporating novel narrative devices, sometimes new locations, and nearly always creating a significant moment of suspense as the central narrative is left suspended until these episodes are resolved (cf. VanArendonk 2019, 77–9). Finally, they create a sense of structure within the overarching season narrative, creating natural act-breaks which help to guide the viewers in how to approach the text.

'The Lost Sister' follows immediately on from the episode, 'The Spy', in which Will's possession by the Mind Flayer leads to the slaughter of a troop of soldiers, and which ends with the main characters and their various adult protectors about to be attacked by a mass of demo-dogs. Rather than resolving this cliffhanger, 'The Lost Sister' works to produce what O'Sullivan calls a 'procedural shock' (2010, 66), subverting the expectations created by the series' forward-driving hermeneutic in order to demarcate the episode as special and separate. Instead of returning to Hawkins to witness the fate of Eleven's (also known as El, Millie Bobbie Brown) friends, 'The Lost Sister' opens on a series of flashing images, which recall the ones El saw several episodes earlier when attempting to reconnect with her long-lost mother Terry (Aimee Mullins). These images of El's life in captivity, and of another young girl held captive there, strobe by rapidly as we hear her mother reciting a garbled array of words which seem to relate to them. We then cut to El removing her blindfold and explaining her vision to her aunt. The rest of the episode deals with El tracking down the girl from her vision with the help of her own psychic powers and the documents her mother left behind. This removes her far from the scene of her friends' adventures, taking her all the way into Chicago. While this diversion feels significantly different to what has come immediately before, it pays off a narrative thread which opened the second season. The cold open to the second season of *Stranger Things* shows us Kali (Linnea Berthelson) – the 'Lost Sister' of the title – leading a gang of misfits in flight from Pittsburgh, and then displaying psychic powers and a numerical tattoo which implicitly connect her to El. Apart from that initial glimpse of Kali, however, we have seen nothing of these characters throughout the rest of the series, and the episode's immediate connection to the plot unfolding in Hawkins remains somewhat unclear. The episode ultimately functions as a test of character for El, as the young girl explores how far she is willing to go in order to seek restitution for what was done to her as a child. And while much of the attention paid to this episode in the popular press focused on the ways in which it seemed to postpone or pervert the narrative momentum of what had come before, this kind of interlude – effectively a training sequence in which the hero of the story comes to understand and develop her powers – has plenty of precedents in shorter, more obviously linear narratives. The ostentatious 'narrativity' of the episode also stands out from the general run of episodes in *Stranger Things*. The starkness of its cold open, rapid changes of setting and a narrative trajectory which pulls us ever further from the danger beneath Hawkins all help to activate what Jason Mittell has called the 'operational aesthetic' (2006, 35), borrowing a term from Neil Harris. Central to the operation of 'narrative complexity', for Mittell, the 'operational aesthetic' refers to the moments in which television calls attention to the process of its own storytelling, encouraging the viewer to speculate as much about how the story will link together the various strands it is producing as upon what exactly will happen.

This appeal to the operational aesthetic is significant both in its own right and in its timing within the wider narrative. On the first level, it operates as one of the show's claims for 'complexity' or 'quality', values which are important parts of Netflix's brand, and which its made-for-bingeing television series are designed to bolster. And, if we assume all viewers are watching these programmes in long-term binges, then the narrative diversion might end up feeling jarring, but is unlikely to be confusing. Although we haven't seen the character of Kali since the opening scene of the season, the show gives us ample glimpses of someone who might well be (and indeed does turn out to be) Kali. The mystery of El's 'lost sister' is hardly the driving force of the season, but it is nevertheless one of the mysteries which the show sustains throughout the second season.

On the second level, this episode creates a natural stopping-place – a moment for consideration, and for slowing down the pace of the narrative. In this way, it recalls any number of earlier, more conventionally broadcast television dramas, which utilise similar 'stand-alone' episodes to break up the flow of the narrative. For example, in 'The Weight of the World' (05/21), the penultimate episode of Season 5 of *Buffy the Vampire Slayer* (The WB 1997–2001; UPN 2001–3), Buffy suffers a moment of despair, and an entire episode passes with her friends trying to awaken her from a comatose state so that she can actually go and fight the season's central villain.

While action-oriented series like *BtVS* and *Stranger Things* typically organise their seasons around a central antagonist and rely on narrative momentum towards a climactic confrontation between the hero(es) and the villain (see Mittell 2015, 19), individual episodes may work to accelerate, retard or simply complicate the journey towards that confrontation. If the final conflict between hero and villain is destined to arrive near the end of the season, then after a certain point, the job of individual episodes is not so much to progress towards that conflict as to forestall it until the moment at which it is deemed appropriate. Greg Smith (2008) has argued that this use of character-centric drama to motivate individual episodes which do not advance the larger plot is one of structuring tensions of episodic television narratives. Drawing on Barthes's terminology, he sees such character-led episodes as providing the hermeneutic (plot) code for a single episode, while also contributing to the semic (contextual/character) code for the narratives of entire series. For Smith, this lets individual episodes achieve 'resolution without progress' (2008, 85), an apparent contradiction which is built into the structure of long-form episodic television dramas.

Yet the critical/creative discourse of bingeable television as 'one long movie' positions it separately from conventional forms of television, and its episodic detours and delays are often received differently. This is part of what has led to the complaints of a phenomenon sometimes referred to as 'Netflix bloat' (see Sepinwall 2018; VanArendonk 2017b), wherein Netflix shows outstay their 'natural' welcome by padding out their episode numbers with 'filler' episodes. At the back of such a conception, however, is another set of assumptions about what constitutes a natural length or structure for a made-for-bingeing television show – effectively, another discourse of textual purity. This view of these shows assumes that they are the proverbial '13 hour movies' of Spacey's Edinburgh speech, and thus, that they are unified, plot-driven narratives. However, these 'stand-alone' episodes demonstrate that, in fact, these shows are anything but unified. Indeed, they incorporate episodes designed to create narrative speculation which does not advance the plot, and to direct viewer attention away from the resolution of the central storyline and towards ancillary characters. Both of these functions find their roots in the norms of earlier ages and practices of television, rather than in the digitally driven, textually pure construct of the made-for-bingeing television text. Nor is this the only way in which bingeable television narratives adopt and adapt the strategies of earlier forms of television storytelling. The next section of this piece examines another dissonance between the critical conversation around these shows – which often praises them for avoiding the textual redundancies and expository dialogue of earlier forms of television narrative – and their actual narrative practices, which make frequent use of these and other strategies of narrative recapping.

NARRATIVE RECAPPING

Narrative recall strategies provide a useful analytical lens for the bingeable narrative because the season-drop model challenges every assumption we have about television's so-called 'mechanics of memory'. Michael Newman's work on television poetics, dating to before streaming services, sees the 'repetitiveness of prime-time series storytelling' as 'a commercial function of making the narrative easily comprehended even by viewers who watch sporadically, or only pay partial attention, or who miss part of an episode when the phone rings or the baby cries' (2006, 19; cf. Mittell 2010: 79). Mittell understands this constraint on prime-time television as producing a number of 'storytelling conventions', including the following recall strategies: 1) diegetic retelling – character dialogue that recalls past narrative events; 2) voice-over narration; 3) flashbacks (Mittell 2010, 82–9). In his 2015 book *Complex TV*, Mittell again revisits television recall strategies with 'diegetic retelling', as well as pointing to 'more subtle visual cues such as objects, setting, or shot composition' which 'can serve a similar function to activate long-term memories' (2015, 182). He then points to two, sometimes competing, motivations between television's reliance on recall strategies. On the one hand, these recall strategies can be linked to developing and maintaining so-called 'complex' narratives; on the other hand, they are inextricably linked to television's traditional distribution model of weekly episodes with long in-between season breaks.

As we have discussed, Netflix challenges both assumptions, self-fashioning its programming as both HBO-style 'quality' television, with short seasons and season arcs, while pioneering a season-drop model that eliminates forced weekly gaps between episodes, along with the likelihood of someone missing an episode. As mentioned above, scholars argue that these changes should in theory remove, or greatly lessen, the audience's memory burden, and allow for new formal possibilities, with Warhol turning specifically to recall strategies:

> Netflix can experiment with . . . radical changes in storytelling . . . for *House of Cards*, the main formal departure from traditional serialized programs is the complete lack of recapping, exposition, and contextualization. Not only does *House of Cards* eschew the usual 'previously on' montage that story-arc-based programs typically include in order to remind viewers about previous plot details, the dialogue also includes very little of the expository conversation that serials have traditionally depended upon to help audiences catch up. (2014, 149–50)

While the elimination of 'previously on' segments is interesting, we want to focus exclusively on the diegetic changes that Warhol lists here, which deviate from the kind of repetition that both Newman and Mittell discuss. Burroughs sees something similar in looking at *House of Cards*: '*House of Cards* does not use recaps, redundancy, or "tells" within the text or narrative (again mimicking the "quality" conventions of HBO)' (2019, 7). Both Warhol and Burroughs clearly and pejoratively link redundancy with traditional North American television, which they place beneath so-called 'quality' television like HBO and Netflix's *House of Cards*. This ignores the significant aesthetic and affective possibilities that repetition allows. Mittell, discussing repetition in the pilot of *Veronica Mars* (UPN 2004–6), links it to 'narrative pleasure', and says one repetition in particular 'calls attention to the programme's well-crafted storytelling' (2015, 80). For Newman, too, 'Redundancy functions not only to make stories comprehensible but, more importantly, to make stories more interesting and to deepen our experience by appealing to our emotions' (2006, 20). This leaves us with two interconnected questions: first, does the season-drop model actually allow a new kind of narrative form, free from traditional recall strategies, and, if so, what are the affective or aesthetic implications of that difference?

If *Stranger Things* boasts an unusually bingeable narrative, we might expect it to follow Warhol's and Burrough's claims about *House of Cards* and eschew the kind of narrative recall strategies that are endemic to traditional North American television shows. Close reading, however, reveals the opposite. In fact, we would even go so far to say that part of the reason *Stranger Things* feels so 'efficient' and bingeable comes down to its extraordinary reliance on narrative recall strategies. Its density of recall strategies, using several different types for several different previous narrative elements, allows the viewer to retain an enormous amount of narrative information as they move forward through the story. Even more so, each episode, even the stand-alone episode of 'The Lost Sister', ties into previous episodes in a way that absolutely aligns *Stranger Things* with other television shows.

To consider how *Stranger Things* uses narrative recall strategies, it is useful to return to Mittell's list of recall strategy types (2010; 2015, in italics here), and to expand on it, using popular press discourses around 'callbacks': *1) diegetic retelling; 2) voice-over narration; 3) flashbacks; 4) repeated emphasis on an object; 5) repeated emphasis on a setting; 6) repeated shot composition*; 7) repeated musical cue; 8) repeated costume element; 9) repeated language; 10) fulfilled predicted action; 11) repeated scenario; 12) returning characters. This list demands further refinement (cf. Kozak forthcoming), but it gives us a starting point for considering the types of recall strategy that *Stranger Things* uses.

Where Warhol (2014) and Burroughs (2019) claim that *House of Cards* does not use diegetic retelling, *Stranger Things* uses it in its first few minutes. The first scene opens on the four protagonists playing Dungeons and Dragon.

Will (Noah Schnapp) rolls the dice to fight the Demogorgon, and loses, just as Mike's mom Karen (Cara Buono) interrupts and Mike (Finn Wolfhard) runs up the stairs. As the boys disperse, Lucas (Caleb McLaughlin) tells Will that his throw didn't count because Mike didn't see it, but as they get ready to leave, Will pulls Mike aside and tells him that the Demogorgon got him. So something as simple as a dice-throw is diegetically retold twice in just the few minutes after it happened, while what Will tells Mike also becomes a prediction for fulfilled action: it's the very next beat sequence where Will vanishes into the Upside-Down; the Demogorgon does get Will, after all. And of course, Will's honesty not only speaks volumes about his character, but also foreshadows the party's credo that 'Friends don't lie'.

This kind of immediate and quick repetition, through complex combinations of recall strategies, is everywhere in the pilot. After the sequence that shows Will's disappearance, the show introduces Hawkins's Chief of Police Jim Hopper (David Harbour) waking up shirtless on a couch, a child's drawing on the wall, surrounded by Schlitz cans: the sequence follows him through his morning routine of smoking, showering, shaving, taking pills and another swig of Schlitz beer. The Schlitz cans also serve to specify time and place. The next sequence cuts to Will's mother, Joyce (Winona Ryder), and brother, Jonathan (Charlie Heaton), making breakfast and realising that Will is not there. Joyce says that he was 'at the Wheelers'; the show cuts to the Wheelers, establishing them as Mike's family, as Joyce calls there to see if Will is with them. Karen says no; Joyce suggests that Will went to school early. The next beat shows Lucas, Dustin (Gaten Matarazzo) and Mike going to school; they too don't see Will, and so repeat Joyce's statement that Will must have gone to school early. Three beats later, Hopper arrives at the police station, and Florence (Susan Shalhoub Larkin) tells him 'you look like hell, chief. While you were drinking or sleeping . . . Joyce Byers's son is missing'. This short line diegetically retells details that we have both seen and heard, from the Chief's bad habits, to his role, to the fact that Will is missing, and we are still less than twenty minutes into the first episode.

Let's turn now to 'The Lost Sister', *Stranger Things*' 'stand-alone episode' that we discussed above. The episode's cold open deviates from that of other episodes in that it does not directly repeat or continue the action from the previous episode's final beat. Nevertheless, it directly repeats an earlier scene – from Episode 5 – and seemingly picks up at the same time, with Eleven wearing the same outfit and seated in the same place as she psychically experiences the same flashback-montage from her mother. As the montage closes to reveal Eleven, we understand that not only is this scene a direct call-back to the scene from Episode 5, but that it also contains numerous repeated elements that situate us within the narrative – Eleven removing her blindfold, her nose bleeding, the television showing static in the background – and which are all repeated elements that convey Eleven's use of her psychic powers. At the same time, Eleven's outfit of overalls and Hopper's shirt is a costume element that ties back to several other episodes in this season, and one which will remain significant throughout the episode.

The next beat diegetically retells the montage, as Eleven tells her aunt Becky (Amy Steimetz) that her mom kept showing her the girl in the rainbow room: throughout this conversation, Eleven flashes back to the montage to images of the girl and the rainbow room. The visual cue of the girl's image then finds a new iteration outside of the psychic space, as Becky gives Eleven a file of missing kids that her mother kept, which contains an image of the girl, with the headline 'Indian girl goes missing from London'. This strategy of reduplicating a visual cue in a different medium parallels the main storyline's use of visual cues around the Mindflayer in the second season, starting with Will's vision of it (02/01); then showing up in his drawing of it (02/02; 02/03; 02/04; 02/05; 02/06); Joyce's finding the image on a video (02/03); Joyce's drawing of it (02/03; 02/04); and finally, pictures of Will's drawing of the monster (02/06; 02/08): 'The Lost Sister' is actually the only second-season episode that does not have a visual cue of the monster. Eleven tries and fails to find the girl using the image in the next beat, only to succeed with the image in the beat after that: Eleven then grasps the image as she makes her way to Chicago; and holds the image in her hand as she claims that she used it to find Kali, the other girl, when she encounters her friends. Finally, Kali herself holds the image when she reminds her friends that Eleven was able to find her using only the image. So this narrative information of what the girl looks like and how Eleven uses that knowledge to find her is repeated throughout the episode, often through a combination of visual cues and diegetic retelling.

This combination of flashbacks, visual cues and diegetic retelling also appears frequently throughout the episode to recall significant narrative events from previous episodes. Unsurprisingly, given the episode's aforementioned central theme of testing Eleven's character, these significant narrative events revolve around Eleven's developing powers, as well as her relationships in Hawkins – especially with Hopper as a newfound father figure. The most extensive of these scenes is where Eleven 'trains' her powers with Kali's help, where Kali offers a series of diegetic retellings about Eleven that are confirmed through Eleven's subjective flashbacks to earlier episodes. After telling Kali's crew, 'I've killed', with a flashback of her killing the orderlies (01/03) and soldiers (01/08), Eleven is taken outside by Kali who tells her to move a train. When El says she can't, Kali reminds her that 'Last night you told me you lifted a van once', which prompts El to have a subjective flashback of that scene (01/07). Kali tells her to focus on something that angers her: El flashes back to seeing Mike and Max talking (02/03). Kali tells her to 'dig deeper. Your whole life you've been lied to'; Eleven flashes back to Hop telling Eleven that her mother wasn't around anymore (02/03). Kali continues: 'you've been in prison'; Eleven flashes back to being locked up (01/01); to Hop yelling at her not to walk away from him and unplugging the TV, and her telekinetically breaking the cottage's windows (02/04). When Kali says: 'the bad men took away your home, your mother', Eleven flashes back to scenes of Terry being dragged away from her, as Jane (02/04; 02/05). As Kali says 'they stole your life', Eleven flashes back to Dr Martin Brenner (Matthew Modine) and her seeing the Demogorgon in the drowning pool (01/06). The sequence ends with Eleven moving the train, to everyone's cheers, which in itself is a callback to her moving the van (01/07), the flashback that started the sequence.

Eleven's flashbacks to Hopper in this sequence are played on with different recall strategies throughout the episode, again in combination with diegetic retelling, but also including costume elements and repeated language: she wears his shirt throughout the first half of the episode (and significantly picks it up again towards the end as she chooses to return home); Kali confirms that Eleven has been with 'this policeman' for 327 days (cf. 326 days in Hop and Eleven's conversation, 02/03); when Kali tells Eleven, 'I think your mother sent you here for a reason, I think that you're home', Eleven repeats, 'home?' in the same way she did when Hop told her she was home in his cabin (02/03); later in the episode, Kali tells her own story, relating it to her understanding of Eleven: 'I found a place to hide. A family. A home. Just like you and your policeman.' Eleven herself subjectively flashes back to the scene in which Hop tells her that the cabin is her home as she clutches his shirt towards the end of the episode, which prompts her to go into the void and see Hop there, in a direct repeat of the closing beats from the previous episode (02/06). Seeing Hop in danger at the lab, along with Mike, Eleven decides to leave Kali and her crew, telling a woman on the bus back into Indiana: 'I'm going to my friends. I'm going home.'

With these recall strategies, *Stranger Things*' stand-alone episode 'The Lost Sister' presents a lovely paradox: a trip away from Hawkins and its characters that reminds us why that place and those people have become 'home', for Eleven and for us, the audience. The episode presents a chance to reflect on and to re-invest in that place and those characters at precisely the moment they are most imperilled, and so sets up a conclusion that both Eleven and the audience return to with renewed imperative. And the episode accomplishes this not because it contributes to a 'pure' television text with a consistent forward-driving plot, but precisely because of the ways in which it both separates itself from and works to recall the rest of the series of which it forms a part.

CONCLUSION

We started our discussion of *Stranger Things*' bingeable narrative with reference to Netflix's boast about *Stranger Things 3*'s audience numbers and bingeing speed, but we should also note the show's marketing prowess. Adebisi Adewusi concludes his discussion of *Stranger Things*' marketing approach on *PostFunnel*, a marketing strategy website, by saying:

> 'Stranger Things' has undoubtedly made cultural waves, and Netflix is riding that popularity all the way to the bank. Instead of creating great content and calling it a day, the streaming platform folded the show into various other verticals, formed partnerships, and made sure location wouldn't become a barrier wherever users wanted to watch the show. Maybe it was the marketing push that sent this show into our pop culture canon? (2019)

Numerous other critics have also commented on *Stranger Things*' successful use of product placement, brand partnerships and marketing strategies (Powers 2019; Rodriguez 2019; Walpert 2018). We point to this because *Stranger Things* is not just 'great content', after all, but part of a profitable business model. When Disney Plus announced that its new streaming service would be delivering content on a week-by-week basis, prompting rumours that Netflix might do the same, Twitter went into panic mode. Netflix simply replied: 'we're not changing' (NetflixUs 2019b). As Netflix continues to offer season-drop shows within an increasingly diverse subscription video on demand (SVOD) landscape, we can only imagine that it will become even more adamant that its model offers something new and different in terms of televisual narrative.

Scholarship often reinforces such commercial claims. The tendency towards broad generalisations about television storytelling, which is so visible in the critical and creative discourse around these shows, is one which academic writing on television narrative is in a unique position to correct. We have shown through this close analysis of just two narrative features of a single show how rich close textual analysis can be for challenging assertions and assumptions around changing televisual forms (cf. Hudelet 2020; VanArendonk 2019). While *Stranger Things* clothes itself in cinematic and novelistic discourses, it shows clear formal alignments with its television predecessors. And while scholars, critics and producers alike might suggest that the season-drop model produces a more unified narrative that requires fewer narrative redundancies, *Stranger Things*' use of a stand-alone episode like 'The Lost Sister', as well as several types of diegetic recapping strategy, suggests otherwise. It is only through close textual reading that the continuities and contrasts between the narrative norms of streaming-era television drama can be adequately explored. And though this work is only a preliminary step in this direction, it points towards the narrative forms of made-for-bingeing television being much more heavily indebted to the narrative forms of the older modes of television drama than they tend to announce.

REFERENCES

Adalian, J. (2018). 'Inside the Binge Factory'. *Vulture*. Available at: <https://www.vulture.com/2018/06/how-netflix-swallowed-tv-industry.html> (last accessed 27 August 2019).

Adewusi, A. (2019). '4 Marketing Lessons From "Stranger Things"'. *PostFunnel*. Available at: <https://postfunnel.com/4-marketing-lessons-from-stranger-things/> (last accessed 26 February 2020).

Baker, D. (2017). 'Terms of Excess: Binge-Viewing as Epic-Viewing in the Netflix Era'. In C. Barker and M. Wiatrowski (eds), *The Age of Netflix: Critical Essays on Streaming Media, Digital Delivery and Instant Access*. Jefferson, NC: McFarland.

Buonanno, M. (2019). 'Seriality: Development and Disruption in the Contemporary Medial and Cultural Environment'. *Critical Studies in Television* 14(2): 187–203.

Burroughs, B. (2019). 'House of Netflix: Streaming Media and Digital Lore'. *Popular Communication* 17(1): 1–17.

Horeck, T., M. Jenner and T. Kendall (2018). 'On Binge-Watching: Nine Critical Propositions'. *Critical Studies in Television* 13(4): 499–504.

Hudelet, A. (2020). 'Dealing with Long Duration: TV Series, Aesthetics and Close Analysis'. *InMedia: The French Journal of Media Studies* (8.1). Available at: <https://journals.openedition.org/inmedia/1931> (last accessed 21 January 2021).

Kozak, L. (forthcoming). 'Re-considering Epic and TV'. In M. Boni and T. Carrier-Lafleur (eds), *Intervalles sériels, sens public*. Available at: <http://sens-public.org/articles/1477> (last accessed 29 March 2021).

Jacobs, J. (2011). 'Television, Interrupted: Pollution or Aesthetic'. In J. Bennett and N. Strange (eds), *Television as Digital Media*. Durham, NC: Duke University Press, pp. 255–80.

Jenner, M. (2016). 'Is this TVIV? On Netflix, TVIII and Binge-Watching'. *New Media & Society* 18(2): 257–73.

Jenner, M. (2018). *Netflix and the Reinvention of Television*. Basingstoke: Palgrave Macmillan.

Lawson, M. (2016). 'Nostalgic Nightmares: How Netflix made *Stranger Things* a Watercooler Smash'. *The Guardian*. 5 August 2016. Available at: <https://www.theguardian.com/tv-and-radio/2016/aug/05/netflix-hit-stranger-things-highlights-tvs-trend-for-nostalgia> (last accessed 17 December 2019).

Mittell, J. (2006). 'Narrative Complexity in Contemporary American Television'. *The Velvet Light Trap* 58: 29–40.

Mittell, J. (2010). 'Previously On: Prime Time Serials and the Mechanics of Memory'. In M. Grishakova and M.-L. Ryan, *Intermediality and Storytelling*. Berlin, New York: De Gruyter, pp. 78–98.

Mittell, J. (2015). *Complex TV: The Poetics of Contemporary Television Storytelling*. New York and London: New York University Press.

Nelson, R. (2007). *State of Play: Contemporary 'High-End' TV Drama*. Manchester and New York: Manchester University Press.

NetflixUS (2019a). Available at: <https://twitter.com/netflix/status/1148359444188712960?ref_src=twsrc%5Etfw%7Ctwcamp%5Etweetembed%7Ctwterm%5E1148359444188712960&ref_url=https%3A%2F%2Fwww.vanityfair.com%2Fhollywood%2F2019%2F07%2Fstranger-things-3-ratings-netflix> (last accessed 17 December 2019).

NetflixUS (2019b). Available at: <https://twitter.com/netflix/status/1168998974507945990?ref_src=twsrc%5Etfw%7Ctwcamp%5Etweetembed%7Ctwterm%5E1168998974507945990&ref_url=https%3A%2F%2Fbgr.com%2F2019%2F09%2F04%2Fnetflix-assures-fans-its-most-binge-able-shows-wont-switch-to-weekly-release-schedules%2F> (last accessed 26 February 2020).

Newman, M. (2006). 'From Beats to Arcs: Toward a Poetics of Television Narrative'. *The Velvet Light Trap* 58(1): 16–28.
Newman, M. and E. Levine (2012). *Legitimating Television: Media Convergence and Cultural Status*. London and New York: Routledge.
Nussbaum, E. (2016). '*Stranger Things* and *The Get Down*'. *The New Yorker*. 22 August 2016. Available at: <https://www.newyorker.com/magazine/2016/08/22/stranger-things-and-the-get-down-reviews> (last accessed 17 December 2019).
O'Sullivan, S. (2010). 'Broken on Purpose: Serial Television and the Season'. *Storyworlds: A Journal of Narrative Studies* 2: 59–77.
Powers, K. (2019). 'Product Visibility in "Stranger Things 3" Valued at $15 Million'. *American Marketing Association*. Available at: <https://www.ama.org/marketing-news/product-placement-in-stranger-things-3-valued-at-15-million/> (last accessed 26 February 2020).
Prudom, L. (2018). 'Netflix boss explains why some shows have pacing issues'. *IGN*. 30 July 2018. Available at: <https://uk.ign.com/articles/2018/07/29/netflix-marvel-series-pacing-issues-spinoffs-daughters-of-the-dragon> (last accessed 22 September 2019).
Rodriguez, A. (2019). 'What Netflix's strategy for "Stranger Things" season 3 tells us about its evolving marketing ambitions'. *Business Insider*. 15 July 2019. Available at: <https://www.businessinsider.com/what-stranger-things-says-about-netflix-marketing-strategy-2019-7> (last accessed 26 February 2020).
Sepinwall, A. (2015). 'Why your TV show doesn't have to be a novel: In defense of the episode'. *Uproxx*. Available at: <https://uproxx.com/sepinwall/why-your-tv-show-doesnt-have-to-be-a-novel-in-defense-of-the-episode/> (last accessed 11 April 2019).
Sepinwall, A. (2018). 'Why Netflix Dramas Sag Midseason – and How they're Fixing It'. *Rolling Stone*. 18 August 2018. Available at: <https://www.rollingstone.com/tv/tv-features/why-netflix-dramas-sag-midseason-cindy-holland-interview-707986/> (last accessed 22 September 2019).
Smith, G. (2008). 'A Case of Cold Feet: Serial Narration and the Character Arc'. *Journal of British Cinema and Television* 3(1): 82–94.
Smith, A. (2018). *Storytelling Industries: Narrative Production in the 21st Century*. Basingstoke: Palgrave Macmillan.
Spacey, K. (2013). 'Kevin Spacey: James MacTaggart Memorial Lecture in Full'. *The Telegraph*. 22 August, 2013. Available at: <https://www.telegraph.co.uk/culture/tvandradio/10260895/Kevin-Spacey-James-MacTaggart-Memorial-Lecture-in-full.html> (last accessed 22 September 2019.
Thompson, K. (2003). *Storytelling in Film and Television*. Cambridge, MA and London: Harvard University Press.
Tryon, C. (2015). 'TV Got Better: Netflix's Original Programming Strategies and Binge Viewing'. *Media Industries Journal* 2(2): 104–16.
Valentine, E. (2016). 'Why *Stranger Things* is one of the best tv shows of the year'. *Collider*. 22 July 2016. Available at: <http://collider.com/stranger-things-best-tv-shows-2016/> (last accessed 17 December 2019).
VanArendonk, K. (2017a). 'Why are we so sure "Prestige" TV looks like a 10-hour movie?' *Vulture*. 28 March 2017. Available at: <https://www.vulture.com/2017/03/prestige-tv-why-are-we-sure-it-looks-like-a-10-hour-movie.html?wpsrc=nymag> (last accessed 11 April 2019).
VanArendonk, K. (2017b). '7 Netflix shows that are too dang long'. *Vulture*. 21 April 2017. Available at: <https://www.vulture.com/2017/04/netflix-shows-too-dang-long.html> (last accessed 21 September 2019).
VanArendonk, K. (2019). 'Theorizing the Television Episode'. *Narrative* 27(1): 65–82.

VanDerWerff, E. (2016). '*Stranger Things*, Netflix's scary new drama, is only made stronger by its flaws'. *Vox*. 8 August 2016. Available at: <https://www.vox.com/2016/7/17/12201098/stranger-things-review-netflix-winona-ryder> (last accessed 17 December 2019).

Walpert, J. (2018). '11 Supernatural Ways "Stranger Things" Has Turned Marketing Upside Down'. *Entrepreneur*. Available at: <https://www.entrepreneur.com/article/307086> (last accessed 26 February 2020).

Warhol, R. (2014). 'Binge Watching: How Netflix Original Programs are Changing Serial Form'. *Literature in Wissenschaft und Unterricht* 47(1/2): 145–58.

FILM

Kershner, I. (1980) *Star Wars: Episode V – The Empire Strikes Back*. USA: Lucasfilm

TV

Arrested Development (2003–), USA: Netflix
Buffy the Vampire Slayer (1997–2001, 2003), USA: WB, UPN
Good Wife, The (2009–16), USA: CBS
Orange is the New Black (2013–19), USA: Netflix
Punisher, The (2017–19), USA: Netflix
Sex and the City (1998–2004), USA: HBO
Six Feet Under (2001–5), USA: HBO
Sopranos, The (1999–2007), USA: HBO
Stranger Things (2016–), USA: Netflix
Veronica Mars (2004–6), USA: UPN

CHAPTER 15

'Next Episode in 5 . . .' – Binge-Watching and Narrative in Streaming Television Comedy

Tom Hemingway

This chapter will argue that original comedy programmes created for streaming services have adapted their narrative structure in a number of ways to better suit the presumed viewing habits of their audience. This will be demonstrated through an analysis of two Netflix original comedies, the fourth season of *Arrested Development* (Fox 2003–6; Netflix 2013–) and *Love* (Netflix 2016–18). I will apply a text-based methodological approach to this study in order to underline the extent to which these narrative changes not only affect the overall structure of the texts but have also resulted in changes to comedic style as a consequence of the rise in popularity of binge-watching. As argued throughout this collection, the practice of binge-watching isn't new. It was first made possible when VHS tapes were introduced into the market, and later DVDs. Writing in 2010, Charlotte Brunsdon noted: 'The impressive speed with which the DVD has penetrated the domestic has been accompanied by the adoption of new metaphors to describe home DVD viewing'. For Brunsdon, 'most notable has been the emergence of the somatic metaphor of "bingeing" to describe the domestic viewing of multiple episodes sequentially' (2010, 64–5). However, in both academic and wider social discourse, this term is now most frequently associated with the rise in popularity of online streaming platforms such as Netflix and Amazon Video. In their edited collection *The Netflix Effect*, Kevin McDonald and Daniel Smith-Rowsey note how Netflix 'has somehow triggered an insatiable appetite to consume more' and has therefore 'become inextricably intertwined with the phenomenon known as binge-watching' (2016, 8), enabled by the company's decision to release entire seasons of their original programmes at once rather than individual episodes on a week-by-week basis. The episodes I'm analysing in this chapter have been created specifically with the intention of being streamed on a platform different to that of traditional broadcast and/or scheduled television. They are what Karen Petruska and Faye Woods call 'self-produced Originals', meaning they have been commissioned by Netflix (2018, 51).

My decision to focus on comedy texts comes partly from the relative lack of critical attention academia has paid to the genre when compared to other types of programming. Writing in 2005, television comedy scholar Brett Mills noted, '[t]elevision is seen to be a low cultural form compared to, say literature and art, and the same holds true for comedy; combine the two and you're left with one of the most maligned cultural forms' (2005, 153) – a judgement reflected by the general 'paucity of work in the field' (2015, 89). When the area of research is narrowed to focus exclusively on comedy programmes created for streaming services, there is a notable lack of academic scholarship examining the aesthetics of these programmes.

The most popular permutation of the television comedy genre, the sitcom, is known for its frequent ability to re-set and return to a state of equilibrium at the end of each episode. Discussing the narrative architecture of sitcoms, Jane Feuer believes 'the episodic format forces us to return to the familiar status quo with which each week's episode began' (2015, 99). Even the most idiosyncratic and ground-breaking examples, such as a show like *Seinfeld* (NBC 1989–98), feature episodes which are, for the most part, self-contained. This structure is almost opposed to the demands of 'bingeability' that a platform like Netflix demands from its texts, as explored throughout this section. Thus, an analysis of how an almost supremely televisual genre (see Jenner 2018, 146) like the sitcom operates in the context of streaming reveals much of how the television text is re-configured as bingeable. The two comedy programmes examined in this chapter have taken different approaches towards their narrative and comedic style which appear to offer suggestions on how the genre can work when episodes are being created by streaming services for a binge-watching audience.

ARRESTED DEVELOPMENT

In spite of its original run as a broadcast show in the mid-2000s, *Arrested Development* is a particularly useful case study as a result of its move to Netflix in 2013, following a seven-year hiatus. This long gap and shift to a new company also marked a significant change to the programme's narrative and comedic style. The fact that the show has three seasons of broadcast episodes to reference as a point of comparison only serves to underline the structural and comedic changes that took place in its move to an online streaming platform. The fourth season of *Arrested Development* was the first set of episodes that were made available to stream exclusively on Netflix. They premiered on 26 May

2013 after the show was cancelled in 2006 by the Fox network. The show is created by Mitchell Hurwitz who oversaw writing and production on both the broadcast original and the later Netflix seasons. In the years between its cancellation by Fox and renewal by Netflix, many of the programme's ensemble, such as Michael Cera and Jason Bateman, had become internationally recognised stars. Cera appeared in numerous successful comedies during the late 2000s such as *Superbad* (Mottola 2007) and *Juno* (Reitman 2007). Bateman also starred in *Juno* as well as *Horrible Bosses* (Gordon 2011) and the superhero comedy *Hancock* (Berg 2008). The show had also amassed a large cult following, arguably strengthened by its untimely cancellation, which led to speculation regarding a possible feature film revival of the programme before Netflix commissioned a set of fifteen new episodes. A 2013 article from *Vulture* claimed the show's fandom was one of the instigating factors for its Netflix revival, stating

> *Arrested Development* is not the only show to have inspired feverish loyalty—it's a spirit shared by countless fans who have had their favorite shows cut short in years past . . . But the Arrested Development cult was different: more crazed, more committed, and ultimately more powerful. (Leitch 2013)

The narrative of *Arrested Development* is massively convoluted and 'exhibits a playful approach to seriality . . . [by] employing frequent flashbacks, callbacks and foreshadowing' (Vermeulen and Whitfield 2013, 105). One could describe its original premise as being focused on the exploits of the dysfunctional Bluth family who are plagued with financial misfortune and numerous run-ins with the law after the patriarch, George Sr (Jeffrey Tambor), is imprisoned as a result of tax evasion. It is left to Michael (Jason Bateman), with his young son, George Michael (Michael Cera), in tow, to hold together what remains of the failing Bluth business empire despite their extended family continuing to indulge in the lavish lifestyle they're accustomed to. The broadcast seasons of the show use this as their overarching narrative whilst still being able to feature smaller, contained narratives within individual episodes. The show's handheld visual style and offbeat comedy may have signalled a break from the sitcoms of the 1980s and 1990s, but in many ways its narrativisation is surprisingly similar to that of innumerable broadcast sitcoms. Similar to, for example, *The Middle* (ABC 2009–18), it has an A and a B storyline, and each episode remains relatively self-contained. Each episode is structured into three acts, which are punctuated by ad breaks. Its narrative focus is the biological family (see also Hartley 2015; Mills 2015). Despite this, as discussed below, the series also diverts from this structure in significant ways, making it more akin to the American version of *The Office* (NBC 2005–13), which premiered on NBC the year before *Arrested Development* was cancelled. Netflix, however, utilised the instant availability of the entire fourth season to create a more intricate narrative which was dependent on viewing multiple episodes of the show consecutively to establish a sense of narrative cohesion.

Arrested Development originally found its fanbase through its use of multiple running jokes and catchphrases, moving at such a pace that many of the gags aren't recognisable as such until they've already passed the viewer by. A fan-made website, *Arrested Development Wiki*, is dedicated to cataloguing every character appearance, piece of trivia, catchphrase and recurring gag from across the show's five seasons, presuming that most viewers will not have caught on to this. In his 2013 book, *Complex TV*, Jason Mittell recognised that 'Complex comedies such as *Arrested Development* encourage the rewind and freeze-frame power of DVDs to catch split-second visual gags and to pause the frantic pace to recover from laughter', acknowledging that 'this type of viewing was fully enabled during the Netflix-distributed fourth season, as all viewers had even more control of the screen time than they did on the broadcast original' (Mittell 2015, 38). Since its first revival season, Netflix has produced two more seasons that have been met with a mixed response in contrast to the critical praise heaped upon the show's original three-season run. The first season won multiple Emmys for outstanding comedy writing, directing, and Best Series in 2004. In 2007, before the revival, *Arrested Development* was listed as one of the greatest TV shows of all time by *Time* magazine. In contrast, the most recent season holds a mixed 55% rating on critical aggregate site *Rotten Tomatoes*, compared to the first season's unanimously positive 100% rating. These later streaming episodes of the show are the ones that will be my primary focus in this chapter, but it is first necessary to establish some of the original stylistic traits from the broadcast seasons in order to discuss how its narrative and comedic style has been transformed to achieve bingeability.

The broadcast episodes of the show do not feature some of the traditional and most common markers of sitcom television such as canned laughter on the soundtrack or the three-camera setup. Instead, they employ handheld camera work which became increasingly popular in the mid-2000s through its use on shows like *The Office* and *Parks and Recreation* (NBC 2009–15). Timotheus Vermeulen and James Whitfield note how the show's 'mobile handheld cameras, forever reframing the action through rapid movements and sudden zooms, together with its rough editing style and voice-over narration give the sitcom a quasi-documentary feel' (2013, 105), invoking Mills's term 'comedy vérité' (2009, 128). The show also featured a long-running plot which progressed over the original three seasons. In this regard, *Arrested Development* provided a template for later sitcoms such as the multiple-season-spanning romance between Jim (John Krasinski) and Pam (Jenna Fischer) in *The Office* or the mystery at the heart of *How I Met Your Mother* (CBS 2005–14): the question of how main character Ted (Josh Radnor) met the mother of his children. Furthermore,

Arrested Development was self-reflexive about its relationship to generic sitcom tropes, often subverting the tradition of a closed narrative which has always reset and returned to a state of equilibrium by the start of each episode. In its early seasons, this was achieved through a running gag where the narrator (voiced, and eventually played, by Ron Howard) teases the events of the next week's episode. One example of the 'on the next *Arrested Development* . . .' teaser from the episode 'Bringing Up Buster' (01/03) includes aspiring actor Tobias (David Cross) receiving a bad review of his play in the paper before cutting to the character sobbing in the shower screaming 'WHY?!' This joke concludes a sub-plot from this specific episode. The very existence of this segment also serves to clue the viewer into realising that the show is diverging from the norm to some degree and helps to prepare them for its extended overarching narrative regarding the business deals of the Bluth family.

As previously stated, the comedic style of the show relies heavily on running gags and demands a high level of attention from its viewers for the jokes to land successfully. This isn't to say the show can't be watched and found amusing based on the premise of some of its episodes and the scenarios contained within them. Sitcoms like *Everybody Loves Raymond* (CBS 1996–2005) also rely on running gags and the jokes become more enjoyable if viewers are already familiar with the family dynamics. However, *Arrested Development* adds a layer of exaggeration and absurdity. For example, the ambition of psychiatrist Tobias to join the Blue Man Group frequently features him covered head-to-toe in blue paint as he prepares to audition, arguably an absurd image, which is repeated throughout the season. However, the frequent appearance of blue paint smudges around various doorknobs and on the walls of the house, often inconspicuously present in the background of numerous shots, for the rest of the season offers one example of how the show extends a joke beyond its initial punchline to reward the attentive viewer, as can be seen during the episode 'Sad Sack' (02/05) when George Michael opens the fridge only to find the residue of blue paint smudged across his fingers. Furthermore, the changeable nature of the visual gag extends beyond the running gags of its sitcom contemporaries.

As well as allowing viewers to fast-forward, pause and rewind with relative ease, the fourth season's distribution on Netflix also marked a distinct shift in how the show approached narrative structure and its comedy on the whole. Rather than create narratives which involved a consistent interplay between its ensemble cast, the fourth season gave each member of the Bluth family their own episode. Moreover, these Netflix episodes most notably contrasted with the original series with regards to their increasingly complex and convoluted plot. This is supported by Mareike Jenner who states

> While seasons 1–3 of *Arrested Development* already rejected the familiar sitcom formula, relying on complex jokes . . . that easily extend beyond

one episode or even season, season 4 complicates the matter further by developing an even more complex narrative structure. (2016, 266)

Outlining his intentions for the season, Hurwitz stated, 'The goal was that by the end of the season, a unified story of cause and effect would emerge for the viewer – full of surprises about how the Bluths were responsible for most of the misery they had endured' (2018). The season encouraged, and even required, binge-watching through its jigsaw-puzzle approach, where the whole of the story was presented out of order and incomplete, only forming a full picture once the viewer had watched all fifteen episodes. Jenner states, 'the individual storylines intersect at varying points, leaving "mini-cliffhangers" in the middle of episodes' (2016, 266) rather than at the end, and notes how 'the season seems to mostly function as a way to "teach" audiences how to watch Netflix in the long term' (2016, 267). This 'teaching' can be extended to the ways in which the show itself sometimes resembles the platform's interface during the Netflix-produced seasons. Whenever an episode moves back-and-forth in time, the screen becomes a slideshow of images from throughout the season with a timeline at the bottom displaying 'then' and 'now'. In between the timeline is a little red marker being dragged to wherever necessary for the timeline of that particular episode. Because the show is constantly moving back-and-forth through time in these later seasons and is therefore employing this visual technique on a recurring basis, the viewer will become accustomed to this image as one that is associated with rewinding or fast-forwarding. It is certainly no accident that the graphic resembles Netflix's own interface and would help provide new users with a type of unconscious digital training to navigate their way around the platform and its shows.

In the fourth season, the further the viewer progresses through its narrative, the more the show's disparate elements begin to fit together, forming a whole, and therefore allowing the show to add complexity to its jokes. Mittell cites *Arrested Development* in his discussion of 'narrative special effects', where a programme 'flexes its storytelling muscles to confound and amaze a viewer' (2015, 43). For Mittell, these moments call attention to 'the narration's construction and [are] asking us to marvel at how the writers pulled it off' (2015, 43–4). The way plot information is provided (and just as importantly withheld and segmented) through the show's narrative becomes one of its main sources of comedy, much in the same way it has previously used recurring visual gags and one-liners. Therefore, in the move to streaming television, *Arrested Development* presents a clear shift from a type of visual and verbal comedy.

Moving away from the 'running gag' structure described above, the series develops towards a narrative-dependent style of comedy. The convoluted nature of the narrative and its use of narrative special effects also means that an understanding of the show's comedy is reliant to a large extent on the act of binge-watching its episodes. One example of this can be found in the way the viewers are shown a meeting between Michael and G.O.B. (Will Arnett) at the abandoned Bluth family home in the fourth season's opening episode, 'Flight of the Phoenix' (04/01). When the characters first run into each other in the Bluth house, the narrator comments that '[n]either had expected to see each other after some . . . recent unpleasantness'. This is echoed in the dialogue when G.O.B. tells Michael, 'I didn't expect to be seeing you again after the . . . unpleasantness', briefly pausing much like the narrator before the final word. At this point, the episode is only four minutes in, and the repeated references to the 'unpleasantness' between the characters appear to be completely self-aware, signalling to the viewers that there is clearly more to the story and that the full details will be revealed later. This promise of narrative satisfaction is a driving force of the comedy in this season, as Michael and G.O.B. run into each other periodically in subsequent episodes, baiting the viewer who is patiently waiting for the pieces of the story to fit together. Later in this sequence, Michael admits to feeling ashamed for something he's done but refuses to tell G.O.B. the specifics. A teasing and inquisitive G.O.B. says, 'Bad example – if you were ashamed of being in love with a man, suddenly discovered these new feelings, then I might say something like, "Homo much?"' Out of context, this seems like an oddly specific and nonsensical line but is recontextualised for viewers later through the revelation that G.O.B. believes himself to be romantically involved with rival magician Tony Wonder (Ben Stiller). Michael goes on to say that he did something he wishes he could forget and that G.O.B. has no idea how he could feel, to which G.O.B. replies, '[w]ell if you're talking about doing something embarrassing with a woman, then no I don't', once more hinting prematurely (for the viewer) at his bisexuality. This leads to the final mystery established during this scene from the first episode when someone runs down the staircase in the ostensibly empty house during Michael and G.O.B.'s conversation. The viewer is only shown their feet and legs in this first instance and has to wait for eleven episodes for the reveal of the face belonging to the pair of legs. Here, bingeing is almost necessary in order to remember the information required to appreciate the show's 'narrative pyrotechnics' (Mittell 2015, 43).

When comparing the broadcast episodes of *Arrested Development* alongside those created for Netflix, it becomes clear that the comedy isn't necessarily emerging from what is told to the viewer (via character dialogue and catchphrases) but rather how it is told narratively. This not only changes the show on a structural level but also transforms the style of the comedy to better suit a binge-watching experience.

LOVE

A more recent Netflix original series, *Love*, ostensibly offers an alternative approach towards constructing a bingeable narrative in the way it details the courtship of its two central characters, Gus (Paul Rust) and Mickey (Gillian Jacobs). The show was created by director/producer Judd Apatow, along with one of its leading stars, Paul Rust, and writer/producer Lesley Arfin, upon whom the character of Mickey is loosely based. The topics and themes addressed by *Love* meet the expectations of a typical Apatow project. All his feature film work as a director and producer is focused to various degrees on romance, courtship, sex and marriage, and *Love* is no different. Yet, because of television's long-form serial nature, more time is invested in exploring the minutiae of these topics. Despite seasons of *Love* being released once a year for three consecutive years, the show only charts the first six months of Mickey and Gus's relationship over an accumulated running time of roughly seventeen hours.

An important concept to introduce here in relation to the difference between broadcast television and streaming television is Christine Geraghty's discussion of unrecorded existence, which she relates to serial programming and the soap opera. Geraghty states, '[t]he characters in a serial, when abandoned at the end of an episode, pursue an "unrecorded existence" until the next one begins' (1981, 10). Despite the fact that the existence of these characters is unrecorded when the show isn't on air, for Geraghty, this doesn't mean that the viewer is unable to imagine what they might be doing in their daily lives. On the contrary, Geraghty believes that as viewers 'we are aware that day-to-day life has continued in our absence' (1981, 10). This narrative sensation of unrecorded existence isn't strictly limited to the soap opera and can increasingly be applied to narratively complex programmes across various genres. The awareness of an existence outside of what is recorded and broadcast can often be related to the familiarity viewers feel regarding characters in serial programmes. In some cases, Geraghty notes, 'significant days in the outside world such as bank holidays or special anniversaries are referred to and celebrated on the right day' (1981, 10), which creates a further sense of familiarity and identification with the characters represented on screen. However, this storytelling device has become increasingly difficult to maintain in the move towards streaming as there is no specified broadcast slot for programmes and viewers are free to choose the speed at which they watch the episodes. Programmes such as *Sense8* (Netflix 2015–18) and *BoJack Horseman* (Netflix 2014–20) have produced Christmas specials, but whether these episodes were watched on the day of release, or even during the winter season, is uncertain.

Remarkably, the narrative of *Love* leaves almost no unrecorded time/unrecorded existence between its episodes. In many cases, an episode will end at night, and the next episode will begin the following morning, but this time in which characters sleep is the full extent of unrecorded time within the series – at least for the main characters. Specifics regarding the preceding episode are rarely referred to explicitly or in great detail. Because of this, I argue that the show encourages the viewer to watch its episodes much more quickly than they would if the episodes were broadcast in a weekly schedule on network television. This is supported by Tanya Horeck's *CST* blog post about the show where she observes, 'I found myself immediately clicking on the "play next episode" button before the credits had even finished' (2016). In the first three episodes, that is, over a three-week period on broadcast television, the narrative only covers a few days in the diegesis of *Love*. The viewer is alerted to this fact during the second season episode, 'Shrooms' (02/04, the 14th episode overall), where Gus mentions that he first met Bertie three weeks earlier when helping to move furniture into Mickey's house. However, in real time it had been just over a year since the first season was released on Netflix. In some cases, there is even an overlap of time in the show, which further links and closes the time gap between episodes. The show's first episode, 'It Begins' (01/01), concludes with Mickey arguing with a shop clerk before Gus steps in to help out. At the start of the next episode, we are shown Gus shopping in the store and overhearing the argument between Mickey and the shop clerk; a short sequence which eventually leads into the footage the viewer has already seen, continuing further with the story. This technique creates a sense of the show as providing a detailed examination of both characters from their individual perspectives as well as documenting many of the moments which lead to their meeting. The important moments in their relationship, such as the first meeting, first kiss, and so forth are often lingered on, forming the end of one episode and the beginning of another. An example of this can be found at the end of the episode 'First Date' (01/05), where Mickey first kisses Gus in his car, and then at the start of the following episode, 'Andy' (01/06), which begins with Gus sat in his car after the kiss and even has him repeat the same line from the end of the previous episode. The way in which *Love* uses techniques such as multiple perspectives and overlapping narratives also has much in common with the fourth season of *Arrested Development* and indicates some shared goals in the structuring of their narratives.

In her discussion of unrecorded existence, Geraghty comments that whilst the viewer is aware that day-to-day life occurs between episodes, 'the problem we left at the end of the previous episode has still to be resolved' (1981, 10). *Love* sidesteps this narrative convention of serial programming. For example, if an episode is about a road trip, a date or a concert, the event will always be fully depicted in the episode with no cliffhangers provided to entice the viewer to keep watching. This relates back to Jenner's comments about the fourth season of *Arrested Development* where any cliffhangers take place in the middle of an episode, encouraging the viewer to watch multiple episodes at a time in order to find a sense of narrative cohesion. Despite this, Geraghty's comments about unresolved problems still apply to *Love* in terms of the long-term emotional struggles which the characters have to overcome. Mickey's sex and love addiction, as well as her problems with drugs and alcohol, are covered throughout each season of the show. Gus's irrational outbursts of anger and struggle to reconcile moments from his past with his current situation are hinted at in the first two seasons but only explored in depth in the show's final set of episodes. Aside from the way in which the show uses time, these character problems and the way in which the show explores them slowly, revealing a little more each episode, work as another narrative technique designed to encourage bingeing.

CONCLUSION

Both *Arrested Development* and *Love* show experimentation with narrative structures in order to reconcile the comedy format with the imperative of bingeability on Netflix. These case studies offer ways of approaching narrative that break from previously established norms and consistently engage with time in a way that has not been explored in the comedy television genre. Both shows also flaunt their unconventional narrative style in ways which recall Mittell's discussion of narrative special effects: as shown above, both shows rely heavily on narrative enigmas or mini-cliffhangers positioned in the middle of an episode rather than at the end. What propels the narrative forward to encourage binge-watching is often the promise that these will be resolved later on. Other than in broadcast television, 'later on' can mean almost a whole season later, as viewers are expected to continue watching several hours of a series in a row. Broadcast sitcoms like *The Office* may rely on series memory and develop storylines over several seasons (as with the courtship and romance between Jim and Pam). However, each episode is self-contained, and that week's storyline is resolved. Meanwhile, neither *Love* nor *Arrested Development* strive for any such resolution, but, instead, constantly promise a resolution in later episodes, which often only serves to pose more questions. Sitcoms, as a genre that is highly televisual, serve as an important case study to explore the reconfiguration of television narrative during a period in which the medium shifts more towards bingeability. The lack of unrecorded existence in *Love* or the shift in the narrative structure of *Arrested Development* are highly indicative of the way in which digital streaming influences content. One question that remains is how this influences more traditionally televisual examples of Netflix sitcoms, from *The Ranch* (Netflix 2016–) to *Alexa & Katie* (Netflix 2018–). What this analysis has shown, however, is one way in which the comedy genre can function on digital streaming platforms.

REFERENCES

Brunsdon, C. (2010). 'Bingeing on Box-Sets: The National and the Digital in Television Crime Drama'. In J. Gripsrud (ed.), *Relocating Television: Television in the Digital Context.* Oxford: Routledge, pp. 63–75.

Feuer, J. (2015). 'The Unruly Woman Sitcom'. In G. Creeber (ed.), *The Television Genre Book – 3rd Edition.* London: BFI, pp. 99.

Geraghty, C. (1981). 'Continuous Serial – A Definition'. In R. Dyer (ed.), *Coronation Street.* London: BFI, pp. 9–26.

Gripsrud, J. (ed.) (2010). *Relocating Television: Television in the Digital Context.* Oxford: Routledge.

Hartley, J. (2015). 'Situation Comedy, Part 1'. In G. Creeber (ed.), *The Television Genre Book – 3rd Edition.* London: BFI, pp. 96–8.

Horeck, T. (2016). 'On Not Feeling the Love: Rom-Com Sexism and Binge-Watching'. *CST Online.* March 2016. Available at: <https://cstonline.net/on-not-feeling-the-love-rom-com-sexism-and-binge-watching-by-tanya-horeck> (last accessed 19 January 2020).

Hurwitz, M. (2018). *Twitter.* 1 May. Available at: <https://twitter.com/arresteddev/status/991361672605523971> (last accessed 8 September 2019).

Jenner, M. (2016). 'Is this TVIV? On Netflix, TVIII and Binge-Watching'. *New Media and Society* 18(2): 257–73.

Jenner, M. (2018). *Netflix and the Re-invention of Television.* Cham: Palgrave Macmillan.

Leitch, W. (2013). 'The Persistent Cult of *Arrested Development*'. *Vulture.* May 2013. Available at: <https://www.vulture.com/2013/05/arrested-developments-persistent-cult.html> (last accessed 23 March 2021).

Lotz, A. (2007). *The Television Will Be Revolutionized.* New York: New York University Press.

McDonald, K. and D. Smith-Rowsey (eds) (2016). 'Introduction'. In K. McDonald and D. Smith-Rowsey, *The Netflix Effect: Technology and Entertainment in the 21st Century.* London: Bloomsbury Academic, pp. 1–12.

Mills, B. (2005). *Television Sitcom.* London: BFI.

Mills, B. (2009). *The Sitcom.* Edinburgh: Edinburgh University Press.

Mills, B. (2015). 'Studying Comedy'. In G. Creeber (ed.), *The Television Genre Book – 3rd Edition.* London: BFI, pp. 89–90.

Mittell, J. (2015). *Complex TV: The Poetics of Contemporary Television Storytelling.* New York: New York University Press.

Petruska, K. and F. Woods (2019). 'Traveling without a Passport: "Original" Streaming Content in the Transatlantic Distribution Ecosystem'. In M. Hills, M. Hilmes and R. Pearson (eds), *Transatlantic Television Drama: Industries, Programs, & Fans.* Oxford: Oxford University Press, pp. 49–67.

Vermeulen, T. and J. Whitfield (2013). 'Arrested Developments: Towards an Aesthetic of the Contemporary US Sitcom'. In J. Jacobs and S. Peacock (eds), *Television Aesthetics and Style.* New York: Bloomsbury Academic, pp. 103–11.

TV

Alexa & Katie (2018–), USA: Netflix
Arrested Development (2003–), USA: Fox, Netflix
BoJack Horseman (2014–20), USA: Netflix

Everybody Loves Raymond (1996–2005), USA: CBS
How I Met Your Mother (2005–14), USA: CBS
Love (2016–18), USA: Netflix
Middle, The (2009–18), USA: ABC
Office, The (2005–13), USA: NBC
Parks and Recreation (2009–15), USA: NBC
Ranch, The (2016–), USA: Netflix
Seinfeld (1989–98), USA: NBC
Sense8 (2015–18), USA: Netflix

FILM

Berg, P. (2008) *Hancock*. USA: Columbia Pictures
Gordon, S. (2011) *Horrible Bosses*. USA: Warner Bros. Pictures
Mottola, G. (2007) *Superbad*. USA: Columbia Pictures/The Apatow Company
Reitman, J. (2008) *Juno*. USA: Fox Searchlight Pictures

CHAPTER 16

The Bingeable Ms Gilmore: A Comparative Analysis of Narrative Structure in Broadcast TV Show *Gilmore Girls* and Netflix Original Show *Gilmore Girls: A Year in the Life*

Orcun Can

On 8 June 2016, online streaming platform Netflix issued a press release titled 'Netflix & Binge'. The press release focused on a so-called 'binge-scale' that placed different television genres on a spectrum in terms of how much time Netflix users spent 'bingeing' them. In a short statement on methodology, the company stated that the data was derived from Netflix users who had finished at least one season of a show between October 2015 and May 2016. Netflix claimed that 100 shows across more than 190 countries had been analysed to construct the 'binge-scale'. The scale represents which television genres were 'devoured' – watched for more than two hours in one sitting on average – and which genres were 'savoured' – watched for less than two hours in one sitting on average (Dwyer 2016). The accuracy and reliability of the binge-scale is debatable. As Netflix is a billion-dollar company, it is expected that the data released will be in favour of corporate interests. Even so, the existence of this 'binge-scale' is noteworthy as it demonstrates that Netflix actively tries to establish a connection between binge-watching and genre; bingeability and narrative form.

Only months after presenting the binge-scale, Netflix released *Gilmore Girls: A Year in the Life* (2016). The SVOD platform already had the broadcast television show *Gilmore Girls* (2000–7),[1] in its library in many territories. The two shows supposedly belong in the middle of the binge-scale as dramatic comedies, yet two iterations of the story reveal differences in narrative form. With this consideration, this chapter sets out to analyse the narrative structure of two televisual shows: *Gilmore Girls*, a broadcast television show and *Gilmore*

Girls: A Year in the Life, its Netflix Original successor. The differences and similarities in narrative form are explored through a formal structural analysis of both shows. By employing a formal structural analytical model called the Serialised Televisual Narrative Analysis (STNA) Model to look at narrative units in detail, this chapter aims to explore the question of why the shows feel different. While *Gilmore Girls* and *Gilmore Girls: A Year in the Life* display similar narrative structures, the all-in-one-released latter series reveals a more closed narrative. The broadcast TV show, on the other hand, exhibits sporadically recurring events and existents, leading to frequent use of plot twists and cliffhangers. The analysis further shows that there is a significant difference in the volume of narrative elements that are introduced in one episode. While the abundance and scarcity, the frequency and irregularity of these elements provide an insight into narrative possibilities in the Netflix environment, these findings also reveal how narrative form may impact the show's ease of consecutive viewing – its bingeability. Finally, the analytical model also provides an understanding of what are the narrative characteristics of shows that are revived in a non-broadcast television environment.

DEFINITIONS AND METHODOLOGY

To break the narrative down to its individual elements, this study uses a formal structural analysis. To make meaningful analysis and provide an insightful comparison, a common ground is needed on which the two shows can be examined. The aim of the model used here is to translate the episodic content of two shows to a common comparable dataset. In order to devise this model, Barthes's approach to structural analysis has been followed, and Seymour Chatman's categorisation of narrative structure has been used (1978, 26). As per Chatman's taxonomy, narrative comprises two parts: story (content) and discourse (expression). The form of content consists of the existents – the settings and characters in the story – and the events – the actions and happenings surrounding the existents. The analytical model breaks down the form of content into serial narratives.

The model is called the Serialised Televisual Narrative Analysis (STNA) Model. While the model does not look at a text's bingeability specifically, it is used to analyse multiple consecutive episodes of a TV show or any serialised televisual narrative, which are seen next to each other. Hence, the STNA Model can be used to look at a bingeable number of episodes together. The model breaks down consecutive episodes of TV shows in terms of whether each event or existent appears at a certain point in the story.

The elements of narrative structure are put on the vertical Y-axis of the diagram in the following order: characters, settings, happenings and actions.

Actions in the model are defined as actions performed by one or more characters. Happenings refer to 'events that happen to one or more characters, or the state or condition that a character or multiple characters are in. For instance, 'Rory has trouble getting used to Chilton' – the private school she attends – is listed as a 'happening' and 'Rory studies for Chilton' is listed as an 'action'. Both events recur over the course of episodes and move the narrative forward, but while the former refers to the character's state, the latter refers directly to an action performed by that character. Finally, a notes section is included at the end of the vertical axis to mark elements in the narrative that cannot be categorised into forms of content but are significant in how narrative is relayed. These notes demonstrate commercial gaps, title credits, recap of events and flashback scenes.

The horizontal X-axis shows the linear discourse time – the duration of the episode. All episodes are put into the same diagram consecutively to emphasise the seriality of the narrative. In order to be able to locate where exactly in an episode any given element is present, story 'beats' are used as the smallest units of time in television storytelling. As Michael Newman explains, television writers' 'first task is to "break" the story into a moment-by-moment outline, or "beat-sheet" . . . the story only takes shape when they begin to think of it as a series of moments' (2006, 18). Beats were preferred as the smallest unit of episodes over scenes as one scene can have multiple beats. Each beat in an episode signals a change in the story: change in setting, addition of a new character, a new action or happening taking place.

The X-axis tracks discourse time using two different sets of markers. The first one tracks the actual duration of the episode – how many minutes and seconds into the episode did this beat occur – and the second one tracks the number of beats. The beats are marked with the number of the episode, followed by the number of the corresponding beat. For instance, 'Beat 1.12' refers to the 12th beat of the first episode, and this specific beat can be found 18 minutes 55 seconds into the first episode of *Gilmore Girls*.

In order to determine which elements seen on screen are going to be put into the STNA Model and to better determine the points in the story where beats change, a set of questions is asked every time a new event or existent emerges:

- Does the event/existent recur?
- Does the event/existent move the story forward and/or develop into any other event?
- Does the event/existent help reveal a character trait or motivation?
- Does the event/existent foreshadow or recap another event/existent?

If the answer to any of these questions is 'yes', then the event/existent is put into the diagram, and a beat change is noted. All events and existents are listed in descending order of importance. Every event and existent that appears in any beat is marked on the diagram.

Chatman divides events into two groups: kernel (major) and satellite (minor) events (1978).[2] Newman also refers to the industry terminology of A plots, and B and C plots accordingly in declining order of narrative significance (2006, 18). It should be noted that the STNA Model does not categorise the events hierarchically, and does not make a distinction between major and minor events for two reasons: Firstly, the model should be able to demonstrate the prominence of any event after data on entire episode(s) is collected rather than presuming the momentousness of the element as it is recorded. Secondly, following on from Jason Mittell's notion of narrative complexity, contemporary television 'employs a range of serial techniques, with the underlying assumption that a series is a cumulative narrative that builds over time, rather than resetting back to a steady-state equilibrium at the end of every episode,' (2015, 18). Therefore, it is also inappropriate to presume the impact any event will have on the narrative since its cumulative recurrence may change its significance.

GILMORE V. GILMORE

The two shows analysed for this chapter have been chosen partly because of their curious nature. *Gilmore Girls*, the broadcast TV show that originally aired as one episode per week, is reported to be one of the most bingeable TV shows (Lyons 2016; Tang and Aminosharei 2016a; VanArendonk 2016). In fact, it has been reported that a reason for Netflix's decision to revive the series was seeing the interest the show got after the company added *Gilmore Girls* to its catalogue for the first time in 2014 in many territories (Yahr 2016). Yet its successor, *Gilmore Girls: A Year in the Life*, which was developed for and released by Netflix with all episodes published simultaneously, is hard to put on Netflix's binge-scale, with its episodes running for 84–100 minutes each. Each episode covers the span of a quarter of a year in story time and the large number of events and existents sometimes appear too inconsequential for the development of the story (Tiffany 2016).

Gilmore Girls tells the story of mother and daughter Lorelai and Rory Gilmore, played by Lauren Graham and Alexis Bledel, as they go through life. Starting off from when Rory is in high school, the show takes the viewer all the way through Rory's graduation from the university, Lorelai's union with Luke Danes (Scott Patterson) and a healed relationship with her parents – Rory's grandparents – Richard and Emily Gilmore (Edward Herrmann and Kelly Bishop) through seven seasons. *Gilmore Girls: A Year in the Life* picks up almost a decade after the broadcast series' finale, focusing on how all three generations of Gilmore women are navigating the current stage of their lives. Emily Gilmore is trying to move on after her husband's death; Lorelai Gilmore is trying to figure out what she wants from life and from her partner Luke; and Rory Gilmore is in a quest to disentangle the chaos that her life has become. Both shows were created by Amy Sherman-Palladino who also served as showrunner except for the final season of *Gilmore Girls*.

The first four episodes of *Gilmore Girls* and the first two episodes of *Gilmore Girls: A Year in the Life* were analysed using the STNA Model for the purposes of this chapter. The number of episodes included in the analysis was determined in order to examine a similar running time across multiple episodes in each show. The first four episodes of *Gilmore Girls* amount to a total of 173 minutes, while the first two episodes of *Gilmore Girls: A Year in the Life* add up to 179 minutes of running time.

The analytical model revealed that both shows had a similar narrative structure in terms of how and when they introduce their main events and existents as well as the number of main events and existents – based on how frequently they appear. This is noteworthy but not entirely surprising since the Netflix show's resemblance to the original show was praised by fans and TV critics alike (Chaney 2016; Radnor 2016; Sims 2016).

A more interesting aspect of the narrative in both shows is the number of beats in a single episode. *Gilmore Girls*' first four episodes have 23, 26, 21 and 23 beats respectively for episode running times of 42–3 minutes. Newman points out that television networks typically dislike beats that are longer than two to three script pages – one script page being equivalent to one minute of screen time – and therefore television writers rarely write beats that are longer than two minutes (2006, 17). Hence, a typical one-hour show usually has between 20 and 40 beats with an average of 25 beats per episode. Newman further explains that the two-minute beat pattern stems from a concern surrounding audience attention: hence, storylines ideally develop unpredictably to keep viewers from changing the channel (2006, 18). *Gilmore Girls* follows this formula. The analysis shows that beats seldom exceed two to three minutes. However, *Gilmore Girls* was famous for its dialogue-heavy scripts, amounting to 80 pages per episode in contrast to a typical 45-page script (Grady 2016). Because of this, beats in *Gilmore Girls* frequently contain multiple events and characters.

Gilmore Girls: A Year in the Life has the signature fast-paced dialogue structure, but while the first episode has a running time of 91 minutes – twice as long as the first episode of *Gilmore Girls* – it only has 31 beats, a mere 30% more than its broadcast counterpart. More than half of the beats in the episode last longer than two minutes. Twelve beats were more than three minutes in length, and three of those beats were around six minutes, the longest beat lasting close to seven minutes in duration. The second episode has a running time of 88 minutes and 32 beats. The majority of beats last longer than two minutes, with the longest beat going over six minutes.

So how is *Gilmore Girls: A Year in the Life* able to use longer beats? A potential explanation for this may be the absence of gaps. As Sean O'Sullivan argues (2006, 119–22), the viewer of a television show has 'old knowledge' of the televisual text from previous episodes and previous seasons, and 'new knowledge' from the episode that is watched momentarily. In between these two types of knowledge, the audience is left in a state of 'between'. This state of 'betweenness' can be between two episodes, between two seasons or even on commercial breaks between two acts of the television show, where the new knowledge has already become old knowledge, and newer knowledge is not yet accessible. Perhaps the smallest units of gaps in television are the commercial breaks and the fades-to-black that accompany them. As Newman suggests, broadcast television shows typically consist of four acts, divided by a commercial break,[3] each having approximately six beats (2006, 18). This way, networks' demand to hold the attention of viewers is spread throughout the gaps in commercial breaks. As O'Sullivan points out, audiences spend this time speculating about and adding to the story they engage with (2006).

In the case of Netflix, the omission of commercial breaks means there is no 'between' space during an episode. In fact, even the 'between' space between two episodes is minimised with the utilisation of a post-play function in the 'continue watching . . .' interface that automatically plays the next episode. I argue that the absence of commercial breaks enables serial narratives to have more flexibility in terms of the number and duration of beats and acts. *Gilmore Girls* creator Amy Sherman-Palladino emphasises this flexibility of setting the pace in an interview with the Writers Guild of America about her television series *The Marvelous Mrs. Maisel*, which was streamed on Amazon Prime Video (Amazon 2017–):

> It's so amazing to not have to think about – to not have the argument about – act breaks. Because on Gilmore, the act breaks were all about selling soap. You know, you've got to meet that act break so you can sell some tampons. It just felt like the marketing department runs network television, so we are finally in the place where the creative rules all. They don't even want to see a title sequence. They just want the story to start and keep going. As far as end time, whatever time works for the story. Some are a little longer, some are a little shorter. (Hoey 2018)

Sherman-Palladino's creative sovereignty also manifests itself in how many narrative elements are fit into beats. *Gilmore Girls: A Year in the Life* uses more characters in a single beat and beats often include more events. It might even be argued that this results in an excess of existents. The first episode of the Netflix Original introduces us to a total of 22 characters – three of them new to the *Gilmore Girls* universe – while the first episode of the broadcast TV version introduces 12. The number of characters introduced seems proportionate to the duration of episodes if we compare them individually. However, the second episodes in both shows introduce another group of characters – 10 characters in *Gilmore Girls* Episode 2 and 11 characters in *Gilmore Girls: A Year in the Life* Episode 2. The broadcast television show only adds a single additional character during the remaining two episodes. In a way, both iterations of the show utilise similar amounts of time to establish their most prominent characters.

The same can be said about the settings. The first episode of *Gilmore Girls* had seven settings introduced while its Netflix iteration had twelve settings in its first episode. It takes four episodes for the broadcast TV show to reach the same number of settings. *Gilmore Girls: A Year in the Life* introduces eleven more settings in its second episode. In 84 minutes, the viewer is exposed to the same number of narrative elements that *Gilmore Girls* has in its first four episodes (169 minutes). By the time Episode 2 ends, the Netflix Original has introduced 41% more characters and 91% more settings across 67% fewer beats.

On the other hand, the abundance of existents does not reflect the number of events in the Netflix Original show. Both iterations of the show had 17 events in their first episode. The broadcast TV show comprised 13, 13 and 17 events respectively for the next three episodes while the Netflix Original's second episode had a total of 21 events. The broadcast television show introduced new events in its subsequent episodes and omitted some that had been seen before. For instance, only five out of the 13 events of Episode 2 were introduced in the first episode, whereas half of the events in the second episode of the Netflix show were already introduced earlier. Combined with the fact that *Gilmore Girls: A Year in the Life* uses longer beats, it can be argued that the Netflix show uses its longer running time to elaborate its plot, devoting more discourse time to each action and happening.

Recurrence of existents, both in terms of characters and settings, was apparent in both shows. The fictional town of Stars Hollow, Lorelai's House, the Gilmore Residence and Luke's Diner are significant settings in both iterations of the show. Characters frequently revisit these settings, and different events unfold there at different times in the narrative. In fact, part of the broadcast show's greatest appeal seems to be this recurrence. As Nojan Aminosharei reflects, '. . . I like to come home and "turn on" Stars Hollow so that I feel like I'm catching snippets of the town's life as I live my own. Like I'm just there. It's oddly comforting' (Tang and Aminosharei 2016b). As discussed later, evoking a sense of familiarity is central in the Netflix show too. David Sims raises the point that in *Gilmore Girls: A Year in the Life*

Every member of the show's cast, regular and recurring, pops back up for at least a scene or two, and Stars Hollow remains essentially the same as it ever was, even if everyone's added a few wrinkles in the intervening decade. Lorelai is still running her Dragonfly Inn, is still living in the same house, and has settled down with her long-time love interest Luke [Scott Patterson]. (Sims 2016)

The diagrams for both shows demonstrate the frequent reappearance of the same settings and characters.

While both shows emphasise recurrence, there is a difference between the two. *Gilmore Girls*' use of existents is more intermittent. For example, one of the major plot points of the first episode is Rory's admission to the prestigious Chilton High School. The second episode focuses on her first days at Chilton, and the school is used as the setting for a large part of the episode. The third episode has a central plot point about Chilton too. Rory needs to pick a sport to play at school and, on her grandmother's insistence, spends a day golfing with her grandfather. While Chilton plays a role in the episode, it is not seen in a single beat as a setting until the next episode comes along. Characters associated with Chilton, such as Rory's classmates or teachers, are also absent from the episode. Another major event in the first episode, Rory's encounter with Dean (Jared Padalecki) and their interaction, is also presented in an inconsistent pattern. The new transfer student to Stars Hollow High School gets a crush on Rory and is presented as the love interest of the main character. However, while the characters and their interaction influence the pilot episode's narrative arc, we do not see the character of Dean again until Episode 5. Not only is the existent missing, but mention of him is limited as well. He is only mentioned once in the fourth episode when Lane (Keiko Agena) – Rory's best friend from Stars Hollow – updates Rory on her old school and casually mentions that 'this guy' asked about her. The show hints at the significance of some characters and settings but does not guarantee when they will next appear. The Gilmore Residence, Luke's Diner and the Independence Inn appear frequently, but irregularly. Characters such as Miss Patty (Liz Torres) and Paris Geller (Liza Weil) appear often, but sporadically. This results in cliffhanger moments that propel the narrative forward.

Gilmore Girls: A Year in the Life does not follow this irregular pattern of appearance. Settings such as Lorelai's House and the Gilmore Residence appear in each episode while other settings such as Doose's Market, Kim's Antiques or – in a later episode – Chilton are only visited once. As for characters, apart from the Gilmores, Luke Danes and a few supporting characters, many are shown only once or twice. These include two of Rory's three love interests and Lorelai's best friend Sookie (Melissa McCarthy). Even when these characters take up more screen time, it does not necessarily mean that they contribute to kernel events or the A plotlines. For instance, Stars Hollow mayor Taylor Doose (Michael Winters) appears several times in the first episode and interacts with other characters. Yet, his interaction is limited to a plotline on building a new sewer system in the town: Other characters make references to his ambition for a new sewer system too; but none of the main characters play an active role in his sewer system plans, the sewer system storyline does not move the narrative forward, and his lobbying for a new system has no impact on any major characters' motivation, nor does it develop another action or happening in the narrative. It does reveal Doose's character traits and demonstrates the dynamics of Stars Hollow town, but it is not clear why the audience needs this much exposure to Doose's peculiarities. The broadcast television show displays many quirky minor plots like these, but they are usually used to accentuate the main characters' features or dilemmas. In a smaller number of episodes and a shorter total running time, one can expect smaller numbers of minor events – satellite events or B and C plotlines – but that does not seem to be the case in *Gilmore Girls: A Year in the Life*.

The freedom to use inconsequential events and existents is an affordance of *Gilmore Girls: A Year in the Life* that its broadcast TV predecessor does not have. The Netflix Original's first episode contains long shots of Stars Hollow town troubadour singing about seasons of the year – also the titles of each episode. Similar scenes in the broadcast television show would either connect the town troubadour to another action or happening, or use it as scene transition, cutting to a new beat after a few seconds of singing. Another episode contains a rather long scene where Rory, her love interest Logan (Matt Czuchry) and their college friends perform a steampunk-inspired dance number to a rendition of the Beatles' 'With a Little Help from My Friends'. Some of these elements do not serve to move the story forward. As discussed below, as sequel, the show heavily refers to its predecessor and rewards the fans of the show who already have 'old knowledge' from earlier seasons. For instance, the second episode of the Netflix show introduces Kirk's second short film. Kirk's short film was a fan favourite gimmick of the broadcast show, so while the short film is inconsequential to everything else in the narrative, it works as a nod to fans, because it reverts back to 'old knowledge' of *Gilmore Girls* for fans who have seen Kirk's first short film.

Not all of these trivial scenes serve the same purpose, though. One episode has a recurrent event of preparations for a Stars Hollow musical with full songs. While the broadcast television show always showed the town participating in different performance activities, the performers of the musical are not familiar characters and the musical plotline does not move the story forward. The abundance of seemingly inconsequential events and existents alienated some viewers such as *The Verge*'s Kaitlyn Tiffany, who argues that presumed creative freedom by Netflix might not be beneficial for storytelling.

> Netflix has a reputation for giving its content creators complete freedom, so it's retroactively clear that the family-friendly constraints of Gilmore Girls' primetime network days actually helped the team rein in some gaudier impulses. Aesthetic restrictions may have made the Palladinos double down on wit and sparkle in their writing – something they all but abandoned in the revival. (Tiffany 2016)

In the absence of 'aesthetic restrictions' and 'constraints of primetime network', *Gilmore Girls: A Year in the Life* displays a more closed narrative than its predecessor. For example, Lorelai's contemplations about conceiving another child, a major plotline that comes up around the middle of the first episode, unfold and resolve in one half of the first episode and do not seep into the next one. In fact, apart from the three major plotlines that each generation of Gilmores follow and which run through all four episodes – Emily coping with Richard Gilmore's death; the chaos of Rory's life; and Lorelai's questioning of her existence – most plotlines seem to be self-contained.

Gilmore Girls, on the other hand, introduces plotlines that run for various lengths. Lorelai and Sookie's ambition to run their own inn is introduced in the very first episode, but their dreams are only realised in the finale of Season 4. The plotline even makes a comeback in the Netflix show with Lorelai's aspiration to expand the inn. Another recurring plotline in the first episodes of the show is Rory's struggle to adapt to a new and more competitive environment at Chilton High School. This plotline recurs for the first few episodes and is resolved by the end of the fourth episode.

THE REVIVAL OF *GILMORE GIRLS*

The differences in narrative elements between the two shows should not only be attributed to the fact that *Gilmore Girls: A Year in the Life* is a Netflix Original show with all episodes released simultaneously. It is not the same show; it is not the next season of *Gilmore Girls*; it is the 'televisual afterlife' of the original show. The televisual afterlife tends to happen in three different forms; derivative afterlives such as reboots or spin-offs of shows, repetitive afterlives such as reruns of the shows, and renewed afterlives such as reunion shows and revival shows (Loock 2017). Kathleen Loock and Ryan Lizardi both categorise *Gilmore Girls: A Year in the Life* as a revival show (Lizardi 2017; Loock 2017), arguing that it is a renewed form of televisual afterlife. The fact that it is a revival show mandates particularities in narrative form. Ryan Lizardi argues that the show is neither a remake that retells the story nor a reunion that seeks to answer the fan service question of what characters are doing now, but a revival – a *zombie show* as he defines it – that carries the story forward after nine years (2017, 381). He maintains that streaming services 'leverage a certain kind of nostalgic longing – melancholia – through encouraging binge consumption of, and access to, both the original and revived series' (2017, 380). Arguably, this brings a duality to the narrative form of *Gilmore Girls: A Year in the Life* between references to the broadcast show such as obligatory appearances from characters – for example Rory's first boyfriend Dean – and use of familiar settings such as the town meetings of Stars Hollow on one side; and the introduction of new events and existents to move the story forward on the other. Hence, the narrative constantly needs to strike a balance between nostalgia and future, familiarity and possibility. Loock argues that this brings new dynamics to the narrative:

> On the level of text, the revival needs to maintain narrative continuity with the past series while its premise must nonetheless warrant an entire new season (or more) . . . Revivals must address the historical lapse of time and adjust to changes in prevailing televisual aesthetics and norms of representation, which often involve complex negotiations between the nostalgic referent and its revived counterpart. (2017, 304–5)

While *Gilmore Girls: A Year in the* Life adjusts to these complex negotiations on the narrative level, the subscription-video-on-demand (SVOD) platform Netflix also negotiates on an outer level. Sarah Kozloff calls this outermost layer of narrative the super-narrative level, referring to television networks having ultimate narrative power through the use of their schedules (1987). While the content on Netflix does not play on a schedule, the SVOD platform arguably still holds super-narrative powers through the use of its interface, and it uses the interface to adjust to the negotiations of a revival show. As the provider of the content, on a super-narrative level Netflix's catalogue shows new episodes as a separate entry, a self-contained show called *Gilmore Girls: A Year in the Life*. Furthermore, until late 2019, the four available episodes were categorised as Season 1.[4] Neither Amy Sherman-Palladino nor Netflix officials have given any news about a possible new season, yet neither party has publicly denied the possibility of further seasons either. In fact, when Sherman-Palladino signed a deal with Amazon to develop original content for Amazon Prime, a special clause was put into the contract to allow her to develop any further *Gilmore Girls*-related projects with Netflix (Ausiello 2017).

The prospect of further episodes is also signalled at the narrative level. While *Gilmore Girls: A Year in the Life* displays a closed narrative with fewer cliffhangers than its predecessor, it ends on a major cliffhanger that both serves as a nostalgia moment for fans and a segue into future storylines. In an exchange between Lorelai and Rory, the final dialogue of the show is as follows:

Rory: Mom?
Lorelai: Yeah?
Rory: I'm pregnant.

The revival show ends with this new knowledge of Rory's pregnancy. The viewers are left in an indefinite 'between' state in which to speculate who might be the father. By the time viewers finish the new show, four episodes of *Gilmore Girls: A Year in the Life* become old knowledge, and an implicit promise of new knowledge is given.

CONCLUSION

Gilmore Girls: A Year in the Life displays a peculiar form that arguably impacts its bingeability. As was pointed out earlier in the chapter, viewers are sated with the same number of existents in half the time in the Netflix iteration of the show compared to the original broadcast version. Days after the show was released, it was reported that nearly 6 million people started watching the show and 80% – almost 5 million people – finished the show in three days (O'Connell 2016). While *Gilmore Girls* and *Gilmore Girls: A Year in the Life* reveal similar narrative structures, the all-in-one-released latter exhibits a more closed story with an absence of gaps and scarcity of cliffhangers, whereas the former offers sporadically recurring events and existents, making use of plot twists and cliffhangers. The volume of events and existents that are introduced in one episode as well as the frequency and irregularity of these elements of narrative may affect the show's bingeability. Moreover, I maintain that narrative form in *Gilmore Girls: A Year in the Life* is not only different because it is a Netflix Original show, but also because it is a revival show that operates inside Netflix. Yet, I argue that the all-in-one-release model and omission of commercial breaks does not change televisual narratives uni-dimensionally, but opens up a vast range of narrative possibilities that can be explored and examined using the STNA Model. Roland Barthes put forward that a common analytical model helps distinguish between various narrative texts (Barthes and Duisit 1975, 237). If the environment of an SVOD platform facilitates different approaches to narrative forms, then a common analytical model will be instrumental in translating overarching stories told over several episodes into singular, linear representations of the narrative. Through this common model, different shows can be analysed to map out the limitations and liberties in narrative afforded by Netflix. Hence, the evolution of serial storytelling can be chronicled.

NOTES

1. The show debuted on the WB network in 2000 and moved to the CW network in 2006 for its final season.
2. Chatman notes that kernels are narrative moments that are 'branching points which force a movement into one of two (or more) possible paths' and contends that taking out a kernel event from the story would disturb the logic of the plot. Satellite events are minor plot events that 'entail no choice but are solely the workings-out of the choices made at the kernels' (1978, 53–4).
3. Newman's argument of four acts divided by a commercial break applies to US television networks. In most countries, acts in television narratives are determined by the number of commercial breaks an episode of the show has.
4. As of January 2020, *Gilmore Girls: A Year in the Life* is seen as a 'limited series' and the mention of 'Season 1' has gone.

REFERENCES

Ausiello, M. (2017). 'A Second Gilmore Girls Revival at Netflix? Team Palladino's New Amazon Deal Contains a Big Clue'. Available at: <https://tvline.com/2017/09/26/gilmore-girls-second-revival-netflix-amy-sherman-palladino/> (last accessed 19 September 2019).

Barthes, R. & Duisit, L. (1975). 'An Introduction to the Structural Analysis of Narrative'. *New Literary History* 6(2): 237–72.

Chaney, J. (2016). 'Gilmore Girls: A Year in the Life Review: The Girls Are Back in Town'. Available at: <https://www.vulture.com/2016/11/gilmore-girls-a-year-in-the-life-tv-review.html> (last accessed 19 September 2019).

Chatman, S. B. (1978). *Story and Discourse: Narrative Structure in Fiction and Film*. Ithaca, NY: Cornell University Press.

Dwyer, E. (2016). 'Netflix & Binge: New Binge Scale Reveals TV Series We Devour and Those We Savor'. Available at: <https://media.netflix.com/en/press-releases/netflix-binge-new-binge-scale-reveals-tv-series-we-devour-and-those-we-savor-1> (last accessed 18 September 2019).

Grady, C. (2016). 'Why everyone on Gilmore Girls talks a mile a minute'. Available at: <https://www.vox.com/culture/2016/11/22/13554566/gilmore-girls-fast-talking-explained (last accessed 19 September 2019).

Hoey, M. (2018). 'A Stand-up Woman'. Available at: <https://www.wga.org/writers-room/features-columns/the-craft/2018/amy-sherman-palladino-daniel-palladino-the-marvelous-mrs-maisel> (last accessed 19 September 2019).

Kozloff, S. (1987). 'Narrative Theory and Television'. In *Channels of Discourse, Reassembled Television and Contemporary Criticism*. London: Routledge, pp. 52–76.

Lizardi, R. (2017). 'Mourning and Melancholia: Conflicting Approaches to Reviving Gilmore Girls One Season at a Time'. *Television & New Media* 19(4): 379–95.

Loock, K. (2017). 'American TV Series Revivals: Introduction'. *Television & New Media* 19(4): 299–309.

Lyons, S. (2016). 'Your Complete Guide to Binge-Watching "Gilmore Girls"'. Available at: <https://www.hercampus.com/culture/entertainment/your-complete-guide-binge-watching-gilmore-girls> (last accessed 19 September 2019).

Mittell, J. (2015). *Complex TV: The Poetics of Contemporary Television Storytelling*. New York: New York University Press.

Newman, M. Z. (2006). 'From Beats to Arcs: Toward a Poetics of Television Narrative'. *The Velvet Light Trap* 58(1): 16–28.

O'Connell, M. (2016). '"Gilmore Girls" Revival Appears to Be a Huge Ratings Hit for Netflix'. Available at: <https://www.hollywoodreporter.com/live-feed/gilmore-girls-netflix-ratings-third-biggest-2016-951967> (last accessed 19 September 2019).

O'Sullivan, S. (2006). 'Old, New, Borrowed, Blue: Deadwood and Serial Fiction'. In D. Lavery (ed.), *Reading Deadwood: A Western to Swear By*. London: I. B. Tauris, pp. 115–29.

Radnor, A. (2016). 'Gilmore Girls: A Year in the Life Review – A Beautifully Wrapped Gift'. Available at: <https://www.theguardian.com/tv-and-radio/2016/nov/25/gilmore-girls-a-year-in-the-life-review-a-beautifully-wrapped-gift> (last accessed 19 September 2019).

Sims, D. (2016). '"Gilmore Girls: A Year in the Life" Is a Rare TV Revival That Works'. Available at: <https://www.theatlantic.com/entertainment/archive/2016/11/gilmore-girls-a-year-in-the-life-review/508580/> (last accessed 19 September 2019).

Tang, E. and N. Aminosharei (2016a). 'Two Gilmore Girls Virgins Watched Every Single Season of the Cult Show'. Available at: <https://www.elle.com/culture/movies-tv/a41067/gilmore-girls-virgins-3/> (last accessed 19 September 2019).

Tang, E. and N. Aminosharei (2016b). 'What Do Our Gilmore Girls Virgins Think of Seasons 3 and 4?' Available at: <https://www.elle.com/culture/movies-tv/a40958/revisiting-gilmore-girls-pt-2/> (last accessed 19 September 2019).

Tiffany, K. (2016). 'The New Gilmore Girls is Weirdly Hostile Toward Fans, Women, and Storytelling in General. Available at: <https://www.theverge.com/2016/11/28/13765088/gilmore-girls-year-in-the-life-review-netflix> (last accessed 19 September 2019).

VanArendonk, K. (2016). 'The Best Way to Binge-Watch Gilmore Girls'. Available at: <https://www.vulture.com/2016/11/best-way-to-binge-watch-gilmore-girls.html (last accessed 19 September 2019).

Yahr, E. (2016). '"Gilmore Girls" revival: How a TV Reboot Goes From Idea to Reality'. Available at: <https://www.washingtonpost.com/lifestyle/style/gilmore-girls-revival-how-a-tv-reboot-goes-from-idea-to-reality/2016/11/03/5c241150-94d3-11e6-bb29-bf2701dbe0a3_story.html> (last accessed 19 September 2019).

TV

Arrested Development (2003–6; 2013–), USA: Fox, Netflix
Black Mirror (2011–13; 2015–), UK: Channel 4, Netflix
Black Mirror: Bandersnatch (2018), UK: Netflix
Full House (1987–95), USA: ABC
Fuller House (2017–19), USA: Netflix
Gilmore Girls (2000–7), USA: The CW
Gilmore Girls: A Year in the Life (2016), USA: Netflix
The Marvelous Mrs. Maisel (2017–), USA: Amazon

CHAPTER 17

Netflix Feminism: Binge-Watching Rape Culture in *Unbreakable Kimmy Schmidt* and *Unbelievable*

Júlia Havas and Tanya Horeck

As the world's most famous online streaming service, Netflix has gained a certain cultural cachet through showcasing the work of women and minorities as actors and showrunners (Bucciferro 2019; Marghitu 2019).[1] In its marketing and self-publicity on social media sites such as Twitter, Netflix strategically promotes itself as 'feminist TV'. Of course, as noted elsewhere in this collection, it is not only its content that marks Netflix out as different: it is the online delivery of entire seasons of TV in one go, and its directive to audiences to binge-watch its offerings. As CEO Reed Hastings said in 2011, 'Netflix's brand for TV shows is really about binge viewing. It is . . . to just get hooked and watch episode after episode. It's addictive, it's exciting, it's different' (cited in D'Souza 2019).

In this chapter, we examine the extent to which Netflix's bingeable programming strategy and its effect on serialised narrative structures open up new avenues for interrogating rape culture in popular storytelling. As a term that refers to how patriarchal culture normalises and rationalises sexual violence, the concept of 'rape culture' is not new (Mendes, Ringrose and Keller 2019, 6–8). However, as Sarah Banet-Weiser notes: 'Though feminists have long used the term and concept "rape culture" . . . it began to circulate with frequency in the popular media in the first decade of the twenty-first century' (2018, 54–5). As Katherine Bryne and Julie Anne Taddeo discuss in a recent essay on rape in period TV drama, plotlines involving sexual violence may have long been present on TV, but they are 'especially visible now in the aftermath of the #MeToo and #TimesUp movements' (2019, 380). Although such increased visibility is without doubt significant, it is important to explore what kinds of political affordances and opportunities are opened up through the new attention paid to sexual violence. As feminist philosopher Linda Alcoff contends in her book

Rape and Resistance, the key question now is: 'How can we take advantage of the new focus on rape and sexual violence to push toward more understanding and effective resistance?' (2018, 23).

In this chapter, we focus on two salient Netflix series that attempt to find new ways of televisually representing rape and post-traumatic recovery from rape: *Unbreakable Kimmy Schmidt* (2015–19) and *Unbelievable* (2019). While generically the shows are very different, with one a comedy and the other a crime drama, *Kimmy* and *Unbelievable* both subvert generic conventions to challenge audience expectations of rape narratives. Both series are striking examples of what we dub 'Netflix feminism': programmes that speak to the company's effort to brand itself as concerned with feminist issues via production background and content. Although *Kimmy* launched two years before the Harvey Weinstein scandal and the emergence of the #MeToo movement, the show's ongoing thematic engagement regarding what it means to survive sexual harassment and assault resonates within the current cultural context of abuse testimonies and stories of survival. Indeed, the show's producers acknowledge that they began to lean into the theme more heavily following the rise of the #MeToo movement (Watkins 2019). *Unbelievable* was released in September 2019 to critical acclaim and rapturous online response. Adapted from a 2015 Pulitzer prize-winning ProPublica and The Marshall Project article, 'An Unbelievable Story of Rape', by journalists T. Christian Miller and Ken Armstrong, *Unbelievable* is a limited series of eight episodes that focuses on two female detectives and their attempt to catch a serial rapist. Although the idea for the adaptation emerged before #MeToo and focuses on a real-life case from 2008, the series is reflective of the context of its release in its commitment to rectifying the social and representational treatment of rape. *Unbelievable* acts as a corrective in two important ways: firstly, it demonstrates how *not* to deal with rape cases by showing a more compassionate way for police to proceed and, secondly, it works to revise sensationalised depictions of sexualised violence in Hollywood crime films and TV shows through its sensitive and self-conscious handling of the subject matter.

Feminist television scholars have explored the potential of the serial form for an extended examination of socially significant issues (Berridge 2011; Feuer 1984; Modleski 1979). Unlike episodic TV, in which, as Susan Berridge notes, the 'sexual violence storyline is introduced, explored and "resolved" all within the episode's timeslot, without extending into subsequent instalments' (2011, 467), the continuous serial potentially enables a more in-depth, sustained treatment of rape as a social problem tied to normative constructions of gender (Berridge 2017).[2] How *Kimmy* and *Unbelievable* address rape culture is closely tied to their use of the serialised format and its links to the practice of binge-watching. In the case of *Kimmy*, discussion has focused on how the series 'mines comedy out of sexual abuse' (Rosenberg 2015) and creates a bingeable, entertaining show out of such grim subject matter. *Kimmy* was initially commissioned for NBC but was deemed too dark for a network show; the producers have said that Netflix was a more suitable home, with the streaming service allowing them to be more daring in their comedic treatment of certain dark themes (Iannucci 2015). Aesthetic freedom from 'broadcast constraints like running time, lead-ins and time slot competition' (Lewis 2019) is also regularly invoked in producer interviews; a freedom which, as co-producer Tina Fey insists, also involves the usefulness of bingeability and serialisation for creative and thematic purposes.[3] In the case of *Unbelievable*, scriptwriter Susannah Grant has said that she initially thought it could be a film before deciding on the long-form, full-drop release format: '[I] pretty quickly figured out that there is enough there to really warrant eight full hours and there is a propulsive enough story that people will continue watching' (cited in Kilkenny 2019).

In focusing on two different generic examples of Netflix series dealing with rape, we explore the ways in which they mine the affordances of the platform's much-touted binge-watching formula to explore and criticise both rape culture and the established tropes of narrativising rape culture.[4] Further, as we will show, a number of recurring themes and narrative approaches reverberate across the two programmes despite their generic and tonal differences. Both series gain their narrative propulsion from serialised and immersive explorations of rape culture and of female anger, at the same time intertextually critiquing well-worn narrative devices through a strategic de-centring of white masculinities and the use of casting and star cameos. References to popular forms of narrativising rape, like the true crime genre or the police procedural, are also central to both series' attempts to revise dominant cultural scripts. Finally, we argue for the importance of exploring how these narrative practices feed into Netflix's brand of 'feminist TV' since these series exist, both on a textual and extra-textual level, within the platform's own promoted 'pioneering' and 'iconoclastic' media universe,[5] to the extent that they explicitly invoke and speak to the content and gender politics of other Netflix series.

UNBREAKABLE KIMMY SCHMIDT

In this section we consider how the focus on rape culture and especially the psychological aftermath of sexual violence works in the bingeable comedy mode; i.e., how this focus is couched in an overdetermined comedy aesthetic, how it utilises bingeable serialised storytelling, and how all this relates to cultural ideals around tastefulness and responsibility in addressing sexual violence and survivor psychology.

Kimmy revolves around the life of 30-year-old Kimmy Schmidt (Ellie Kemper), who was kidnapped at the age of fourteen in rural Indiana by cult leader Richard Wayne Gary Wayne aka the Reverend (Jon Hamm), and who is rescued by law enforcement at the beginning of the series. The Reverend kept Kimmy and three other women in an underground bunker for fifteen years, and manipulated them into believing they were the last survivors in a post-apocalyptic world. In the first episode, Kimmy starts a new life in New York City. The ensemble cast includes Kimmy's roommate and aspiring actor Titus Andromedon (Titus Burgess), her employer, the rich housewife (then divorcé) Jacqueline (Jane Krakowski) and her elderly landlady Lillian (Carol Kane). The series updates the 'rural woman in the city' premise by heightening its stakes: Kimmy is not simply from the American Midwest but lived in complete isolation from the outside world, and was sexually and otherwise abused, throughout her teenage and young adult life. Psychological impacts of this isolation and abuse and the effects of rape culture on its targets are central themes in *Kimmy*. Even its cartoon-esque and bright iconography, a seemingly counterintuitive aesthetic choice, forms a key part of the series' focus on survivor psychology since these visuals reflect Kimmy's stunted mental state as trauma survivor permanently stuck in a pre-adolescent, child-like phase.

Given the relative proliferation of the 'sexual violence as social ill' trope in post-#MeToo television, it is useful to couch *Kimmy*'s engagement with it in existing literature on media representations of rape, to explore some recurring characteristics. A key theme in scholarly analysis is the rape's and rapist's symbolic narrative function as stand-in for patriarchal systems of oppression. The field's leading experts such as Lisa Cuklanz, Sujata Moorti, Sarah Projansky, Karen Boyle, Tanya Horeck and Susan Berridge agree that rape as symbol fulfils a fundamental role in storytelling traditions. As Horeck shows, mediatisations of rape entail a conspicuous paradox by claiming to speak to 'public' ideas around sexual and gendered mores through depicting this most 'private' of crimes against the body (2004, 4). Scholars studying televisual representations of rape agree that up until the 2000s sexual violence had been overwhelmingly portrayed as an individualised, personal concern, and that series dealing with rape had negotiated the portrayal of heterosexual masculinities by inserting idealised male characters into rape narratives who function as feminist correctives to violent male behaviour. As Berridge writes, rape in these series is 'presented as an aberration of an otherwise functioning patriarchy' (2011, 479). Both Berridge and Boyle (2008) argue that teen-targeted network programmes like *Buffy the Vampire Slayer* (The WB 1997–2001; UPN 2001–3) and *Veronica Mars* (UPN 2004–6; The CW 2007; Hulu 2019) start to puncture this representational trend by centralising sympathetic male protagonists who themselves commit sexual violence. These portrayals are also embedded in concurrently emerging discourses around television complexity, a concept championed by TV scholar Jason Mittell (2015a). According to this, 'complex' televisual narrative formats (those merging episodic and serialised narration) allow for more complex (morally and psychologically layered) character portrayals than before – such as an initially sympathetic male character who is also a rapist. Such portrayals become even more widespread in the 'quality TV' era and with the advent of the complex (male) antihero (Mittell 2015b).

Portrayals of fictional rapists continue to shift in the streaming era, affecting their symbolic place both in the complex narrative and in the series' articulation of rape's public function, via highlighting socially dominant white male characters' systemic and specific culpability. Female-centric series such as *Kimmy*, along with others like *Jessica Jones* (Netflix 2015–19) or *Big Little Lies* (HBO 2017–), explicitly revolve around the quasi-mythologised monstrosity of a sexually and otherwise abusive, but also charismatic, white male villain, and tie his figure to deeply entrenched social systems of gendered abuse and entitlement. Especially in *Kimmy* and *Jessica Jones*, no redeeming qualities or psychological layering are offered in this figure's portrayal; for instance, the narratives avoid excavating backstories that could relativise or explain his motivations.

In *Kimmy*, the Reverend's figure remains emphatically static in his villainous misogyny, portrayed as a mixture of ominous and risible, upending the notion of (male) character complexity. This stands in notable contrast to Kimmy's (and other central characters') serialised psychological development. Further, the overdetermined simplicity of the misogynist's risible monstrousness reverberates in the series in a way that merges serialisation and episodic storytelling. Throughout the series' four seasons, several episodes introduce one-off storylines in which a specific type of authoritative white male figure attempts to sabotage Kimmy's or her friends' ambitions and is exposed as villainous, a buffoon, a fraud, or all of the above. The comedy uses episodic storytelling to cumulatively present, then tear down and ridicule iterations of toxic (and often incompetent) masculinity in power. Their toxicity as symbolic patriarchal figure is reiterated in narrative trajectories, dialogue and via gross-out physical comedy. A selection of these includes a GED[6] teacher, Kimmy's stepfather who is also a bumbling policeman, Kimmy's entitled rich boyfriend, Jacqueline's businessman husband, a Dr Phil-like TV therapist, a celebrity plastic surgeon, or a SoulCycle trainer exposed as a fraud. Critical reception has noted the relentlessness of this aspect of *Kimmy*'s comedy (e.g., Coates 2015), and the series itself comments upon it in a Season 2 storyline in which Jacqueline muses to herself about her latest love interest: '[h]e's the only decent straight white man in the entire universe'. In the bingeable and serialised context, this curiously cumulative portrayal of a rigid type of mediatised identity (i.e., toxic masculinity) becomes especially striking, given that the series otherwise traffics in exploring racial, gendered, sexual, national, class etc. identities as cultural constructs and as such always in flux and open to re-interpretation. But if this deconstructivist fluidity of identity is a central concern for *Kimmy*, then it is noticeably absent for privileged masculinities, which are rendered fixed by their multiplied villainy, yet provide continued fodder for satire. The combination of episodic and serialised misogyny then outlines a culture organised by and shot through with a system of gendered oppression wherever Kimmy and her friends turn; a key additive in the binge narrative's engine (or, a driver of the narrative propulsion that Grant describes above) is precisely the question of what new iterations of misogyny this oppressive system may offer next for the protagonists.

The series' episodic-yet-serialised portrayal of toxic masculinity is further underlined by the usage of star cameos for these villainous male characters (e.g., the celebrity surgeon is played by Martin Short, the television therapist by Jeff Goldblum, the SoulCycle trainer by Nick Kroll), since extra-textual significance is gained from the contrast between these actors' star texts and their characters' association with toxic male power, most conspicuously in Jon Hamm's casting as the Reverend. A meta-textual source of humour is the transparency between the repulsive Reverend and Hamm's star persona defined by his role as the mythical and über-masculine Don Draper in *Mad Men* (AMC 2007–15), a series canonised as a landmark of male-centred complex television and male anti-heroism. Prestige TV's 'complex white male character in crisis' trope (Lotz 2014; Martin 20134; Mittell 2015b) has dominated cable television since the late 1990s and continues to be a touchstone of discussions around prestige television's gendered character portrayals. Therefore, the Reverend's pointed repulsiveness in this equally pointedly gynocentric series has meta-textual ambitions to speak to this television culture through Hamm's presence.

The satire of toxic masculinity serves yet another function for *Kimmy*, by helping negotiate the contradiction between theme and tone in the series' premise. In the following, we turn to this apparent contradiction and examine the issue of *Kimmy*'s position in bingeable television culture as a comedy about a rape survivor. According to critical consensus, exemplified by *New Yorker* writer Emily Nussbaum's article 'Candy Girl' (2015), *Kimmy*'s singularity is rooted in its telegraphed adherence to cartoon-esque and chipper comedy aesthetics tinged with a dark, sarcastic tone. In the TV landscape of the 2010s, the heroine's and storyworld's extreme cuteness and childishness (yellows, pinks, and purples dominate the series' colour palette) also mark this out as prestige comedy, where the contrast between theme and tone provides the uniqueness necessary for cultural clout. *Kimmy*'s generic exceptionality comes from prevalent cultural links between dark subject matter and tonal appropriateness; i.e., from the idea that embedding a serious issue like sexual violence in comedy is inherently incongruent, even offensive. Indeed, the themes the series focalises – the gendered emotional labour of dealing with post-traumatic stress disorder, sexual violence, and grappling with patriarchal oppression – are more readily associated with the traditions of melodrama and crime drama. *Kimmy* navigates this tricky cultural position by displaying in full force the signifiers of bingeable 'quality' comedy. This involves the serialised narrative treatment of PTSD psychology, the sustained satire of gender and race politics, and the equally sustained meta-commentary on the received wisdoms and cultural assumptions around narrativising this subject.

Even in the environment of streaming, the idea of a 'rape comedy' is still in apparent need of careful management, presumably due to concerns that in patriarchal cultures, a 'rape comedy' or 'rape joke' overwhelmingly functions as expression of gendered aggression toward victims. The taboo of the comedy treatment of sexual violence highlights the firmly defined cultural boundaries shaping the aesthetic channels through which rape and sexual violence can be respectfully represented, despite, as noted earlier, rape being a fundamental trope of human storytelling onto which context-specific social anxieties about gender are projected. As meta-textual 'quality' comedy, *Kimmy* comments on this incongruence and the ways it plays out in the cultural industries. In the fourth season, Kimmy has an epiphany about writing a children's fantasy book aimed at boys, with a mission to educate them about gendered violence and treating girls as human beings. When she takes the idea to a publisher, he shuts it down: '[p]eople see you as a mole woman [the nickname the media gave her and the other abductees] and my job is to keep you in that box. This is a business and nobody's ever gonna buy your children's book'. He wants her to write a dark memoir enumerating harrowing details of her experience instead, and even proposes a book cover with the title 'Tunnels of Terror: The Super Sad Story of Kimmy Schmidt'. Both the grim cover art and the title send up the true crime genre, which often thematises sexual violence against women and is considered female-targeted media (Tuttle 2019). The genre is popular in various media forms: the book industry, American podcast culture, and Netflix itself via its prominent true crime documentary line-up like *The Keepers* (2017), *Making a Murderer* (2015; 2018–) or *Amanda Knox* (2016). *Kimmy*'s mockery comes full circle in the special episode 'Party Monster: Scratching the Surface' (Season 4, Episode 3), a satire of *Making a Murderer*'s aesthetics and gender politics. The show thus signals its awareness of culturally viable and established aesthetic avenues of narrativising sexual violence against women, and the self-referentiality becomes even more pronounced in light of *Kimmy*'s own candy-coloured visual aesthetics and its producers' repeated claims that a key cohort of their audience is adolescent children (Adams 2019). As such, even in the show's meta-textual admission, the scarce cultural precedence of a comedy on sexual violence and the assumed moral panic around it means that this connection is treated with special care. This is where bingeable serialisation emerges as a narrative means to manage the potential discrepancy between tone and topic.

In regard to serialisation, it is crucial that *Kimmy* focuses on temporal and psychological aftermaths of sexual violence (even though flashback scenes to the bunker recur almost every episode), this way avoiding visual representations of rape which are a particularly contentious issue in the theme's discussions (Projansky 2001, 19). It is arguably possible to watch the series and ignore the fact that Kimmy is a victim of years-long sexual abuse since it contains no visual depictions of physical contact, let alone sexual abuse, between the Reverend and the four women. Nonetheless, ample narrative stress highlights this aspect of the Reverend's abuse both via Kimmy's character psychology and via her and the other survivors' dialogue. Yet, this putatively curious omission of visual representations of rape has led to a critical discourse pondering whether this is a rape survivor narrative at all, culminating in articles written about Episode 3 of the third season in which the word 'rape' was first uttered by a character and supposedly laid these debates to rest (see, e.g., Lindsay 2017; Miller 2017). In other words, verbal confirmation to the fact of rape seems to have been needed in lieu of visual representation. *Kimmy* inverts the cultural fascination with representing rape through posing the problem of how to *not* represent rape visually in a comedy format while narrativising rape culture. The seeming elimination of the problem by concentrating on rape survivor psychology is, in the show's logic, more fitting with serialised comedy. The long-term characterisation of the PTSD-addled rape survivor both in its physical and mental aspects provides plenty of running jokes, couched in therapeutic narratives of self-examination and resilience. Recurring themes are physical manifestations of Kimmy's PTSD, for instance, the Season 2 storyline of her intermittent and grotesquely loud burping, which serves as a serialised exploration of affective meaning: the burps are not simply comic since they signal Kimmy's repressed emotional disturbance, which the narrative gradually excavates. This is serialised burping then, its narrative-affective importance set up in the season's opening sequence when Kimmy emits the first loud belch, then recurring periodically to signal both vulgar humour and narrative enigma. Bingeability negotiates the burp joke's low-culture vulgarity and potential offensiveness by imbuing it with relevance for the Big Story's larger fabric, in this case for the serialised affective-therapeutic narrative. Casting Fey as the therapist who helps Kimmy place the burps in medical discourse by calling them 'peristalsis' indicates the extra-textual significance given to them. Fey's presence as (diegetically) nurturing caregiver and (extra-diegetically) feminist authorly/authority figure linking fiction and production context together telegraph the care with which the topic is handled, thus helping reconcile the tricky theme and the 'light' comedy environment. The burp storyline's scatological humour, an example of *Kimmy*'s serialised comedy around the psychological-physical effects of years of sustained abuse, throws into sharp relief assumptions of tone, appropriateness and offence around the 'rape joke', especially the question of physical humour and slapstick.

An overarching source of slapstick comedy is Kimmy's hyperbolic physical strength, a further example of the series' strategic negotiation of comedy, serialisation and affect. For instance, Kimmy tends to involuntarily hit or fight potential boyfriends in intimate situations, a recurring gag that serves not only as slapstick joke but a sign of her sexual violence-induced PTSD, and her lack of ability to control its physical symptoms. But the running gag of Kimmy's bodily strength as uncontrolled aggression shifts in the series' fourth season, serving for the first time not as illustration of her unprocessed sexual trauma but to address the stupidity of men's rights activism, this way re-purposed as public service against misogyny. A scene in which Kimmy meets a men's rights activist who argues that '[m]en are strong, so they look after women. Women are weak so they can only take care of children' culminates in Kimmy defeating him in arm wrestling, then repeatedly smashing his head against a table, the implication being that reasoned dialogue is pointless here. The serialised stress on Kimmy's extraordinary physical strength blurs the line between physicality used as slapstick, sign of trauma, and controlled and righteous aggression toward oppressors. The scene also speaks to the discourses around feminist rage that have emerged in the post-#MeToo media environment, and which we discuss in more detail in the next section.

In the following section on *Unbelievable*, we turn from comedy to the serialised crime drama to continue exploring the ways in which bingeable narratives can potentially upend entrenched genre tropes around narrativising rape culture.

UNBELIEVABLE

Described as 'revolutionary' in its depiction of rape (Blake 2019), Netflix's *Unbelievable* was welcomed as a series that pays special attention to the female victim's experience. Helmed by showrunner Susannah Grant,[6] the series' production process was significant in shaping its survivor-centred focus. Before the release of *Unbelievable*, Netflix worked in conjunction with the American anti-sexual violence organisation Rainn (Rape, Abuse and Incest National Network), which helped to 'provide resources and information for viewers' (Rainn 2019). Going beyond the tokenistic inclusion of helpline numbers, *Unbelievable* speaks to 'the need for sensitive, survivor-centred interviewing and support throughout the criminal justice process', as noted by Keeli Sorensen, Rainn's Vice President of Victim Services (cited in Rainn 2019). Additionally, the real-life rape victim whose story is the basis for the series (and who has retained anonymity) was an executive producer and helped during production (cited in Dibdin 2019).

Where *Kimmy* builds up its fictional exploration of post-trauma over the course of four seasons, *Unbelievable* delivers its dramatisation of a real-life rape case in a powerful burst of eight episodes. It tactically deploys the bingeable

Netflix format in the service of a feminist revision of TV crime drama and its tropes of misogynistic violence. Indeed, showrunner Grant notes that the modus operandi of streaming TV and its strategy of full-drop release enables different storytelling choices and 'changes how the viewer consumes' the final product (cited in Dibdin 2019). Working with information from Netflix that audiences tend to watch 'in two-episode bites', Grant thought about 'the first part of the story as a two-hour chapter' and wrote the story differently than she would have for a network television series (cited in Dibdin 2019). In other words, the release of all the episodes at once enabled Grant to plot the show differently and to narrativise the rape in such a way that would maximise what they wanted to convey to viewers about how rape should – and should not – be handled, both procedurally and narratively.

The first episode, which is just under an hour long, tells the true story of 18-year-old white woman Marie Adler[7] (Kaitlyn Dever), who is raped in her apartment. Marie is a vulnerable young woman who has been in foster care most of her life; she reports her rape to the police, but they question so-called inconsistencies in her story and challenge the appropriateness of her reactions post-assault. In the end, she is brow-beaten into retracting her confession by two middle-aged white male officers. There are brief, subjective flashbacks to the attack, but Marie's trauma is more significantly made palpable in how the camera focuses on her embodied responses to the terrible interrogation scenes and the community vilification that occurs after the assault. Episode 1 ends with a cliffhanger, as Marie, alone and ostracised by her community, climbs atop a bridge and contemplates suicide.

Next episode in five-four-three-two-one: Episode 2 begins with Marie deciding not to jump. In this episode viewers meet the two female detectives who will ultimately help Marie: Karen Duvall (Merritt Wever) and Grace Rasmussen (Toni Collette). From this point on, the series shifts between two timelines and two locations: 2008 in Washington as Marie tries to deal with life post-assault, and 2011 in Colorado as Duvall and Rasmussen try to identify and capture a serial rapist. The question of when these two storylines will meet up, and when –and if – Marie will be rescued and redeemed by the two female detectives shapes the narrative impetus of the series.

In Episode 2, viewers are introduced to another rape victim, 22-year-old Amber Stevenson (Danielle Macdonald), but this time, we are shown a much different, more sensitive way of handling the investigation, through the detective work of Karen Duvall. Following immediately on the heels of the first episode, as enabled by the binge-watching format, this second instalment serves to correct the excruciatingly ignorant and bullying behaviour of the male police officers that viewers have just witnessed: by contrast, Detective Duvall handles her interview with the young victim in a gentle and supportive manner that shows an understanding of how trauma works. This is a different, feminist order of things: both in terms of the revision of police procedure that plays out at the level of content, and in regard to the formal representational strategies the series uses to narrate violence. Crucially, the horror of what happened to Amber is refracted through the intelligent and supportive female detective who conveys the bravery, strength and resilience of the victim. Duvall is thorough and meticulous: many scenes show her demanding the same level of professionalism from her male juniors, as she multi-tasks and shares co-parenting duties with her police officer husband.

In his review of *Unbelievable* in *The Guardian*, Adrian Horton suggests that the second episode 'could be a high-budget training video for sexual assault investigators' (2019). Netflix highlights the educational thrust of the series in a two-minute promotional video about Episode 1 of *Unbelievable*, produced in conjunction with Rainn. Serving to instruct viewers on how to proceed with (binge-) watching *Unbelievable*, the clip describes the pilot episode as 'incredibly hard to watch . . . And maybe it should be'. In other words, it is only after experiencing the negative affect of the first episode that viewers can move forward to the next one, and fully appreciate the paradigm shift to a feminist epistemology of rape. With its self-conscious address to an imagined binge-viewer who watches episodes in pairs (or more), the second episode of *Unbelievable* is, to borrow Horton's words, 'a portrait in how things should be – how serious sexual assault cases should be taken, how crucial it is to listen to victims' (2019). If, as Mareike Jenner has suggested, it has always been part of Netflix's strategy to teach its viewers how to binge-watch its offerings (2016, 264), then with *Unbelievable* that training is yoked to feminist pedagogical and political ends. In its pointed pedagogical switch between damaging ways of dealing with rape and more socially just methods, *Unbelievable* produces a politically immersive viewing experience designed to interrogate rape culture.

By making careful, critical use of the full-drop release format to focus attention on female victims of violence, *Unbelievable* is speaking back to TV crime dramas, and also to recent true crime series, which, as discussed, have been both popularised (think *Making a Murderer*) and sent up (think *Kimmy*) by Netflix itself. In addition to the central story of Marie, the episodes of *Unbelievable* spend time exploring the experiences of other victims of the serial rapist. Where so many TV crime dramas and long-form true crime series sensationally depend on, only to then elide, the figure of the 'lost girl' who, in the dominant terms of these shows, is invariably young, beautiful, and white, it is significant that the victims in *Unbelievable* are of different ages, classes, races and body types. As noted by Detective Grace Rasmussen, what they all have in common is that they are women who live alone. Because the series is dealing with a serial rapist, and not a murderer, the victims are alive and are able to speak for themselves (rather than appearing as ghostly figures only to be accessed through lurid crime-scene photos).

Outrage over violence against women and the systemic forces that underpin it is what drives the series. In her essay, 'Fuck the Patriarchy: Towards an Intersectional Politics of Irreverent Rage' (2019), Helen Wood explores the value of the word 'fuck' in Anglophone feminist political protest (610) and argues for a 'category of "irreverent rage" that might be politically productive in the current climate' (611). Instead of turning rage destructively inwards, against the self, this 'irreverent rage' is turned outwards, 'precisely to publicly trouble regulatory power' (611). We suggest that rage in both *Unbelievable* and *Kimmy* functions productively in the way discussed by Wood, with the political charge of these series 'fuelled by an affectively viral media landscape' (613) and given critical momentum through the binge-watching format even despite, and within, the two series' distinctively different genre contexts.

The curse 'fuck' in *Unbelievable* is used self-consciously and tactically, as at the very end of Episode 6, when Rasmussen responds with 'Holy fuck!' to the discovery that the suspect, Chris McCarthy (Blake Ellis), has a brother and that there are now two suspects. Play next episode and Episode 7 begins with Duvall, the quieter (and more religious-minded) of the two detectives, blurting out 'What the fuck?' when Grace tells her the news that there is another suspect. As a kind of sound bridge across episodes, Duvall's and Rasmussen's 'fucks' satisfyingly resound in the current cultural milieu and its exposure of gendered power and sexual harassment and violence. However, it is not just a cheap or hollow cursing-for-cursing's sake: the outrage of the two women is focused and political. There are key set-piece displays of anger in *Unbelievable*, in which the female detectives rail against the injustices of male violence against women. Where *Kimmy*'s outrage manifests itself physically, in *Unbelievable* female anger is expressed in impassioned speeches. The first major speech is in Episode 3 and is delivered by Karen Duvall, the more mild-mannered of the two detectives. Her anger is borne out of her empathy for the victim, Amber Stevenson, and her frustration over the slowness of the investigation and the processing of rape kits. When her cowed male junior complains that she doesn't have to yell at him, an incensed Duvall responds with a speech acknowledging the depth of trauma that victims 'carry with them forever, like a bullet in the spine' – a description that, in its visceral physicality, conveys the long-term psychological effects of experiencing rape and evokes *Kimmy*'s thematic concerns and character portrayals.

Grace Rasmussen, the fierier and swearier of the two detectives, delivers a passionate speech in Episode 5, when male FBI agent Taggart challenges their theory that the serial rapist could potentially be a police officer because of his apparent knowledge of police investigation work. In response to Taggart's claim that the TV crime drama *CSI: Crime Scene Investigation* (CBS, 2000–15) has 'turned a generation of American TV viewers into crime scene experts', and that the rapist could therefore be anyone, Grace becomes furious:

Cops beat up their partners at two to four times the rate of the general population, add to that, prior acts of violence against women are the biggest predictor of whether a man will commit sexual assault and our suspect's better-than-*CSI* knowledge of the police investigation procedure . . . You'd be a fucking idiot not to pursue it [the line of enquiry that the rapist could be a cop].

For Grace, the key issue is accountability, and she refers to data about wife-beating cops to back up her arguments. As she argues, outrage is important: there is a need to acknowledge that the system is 'supremely fucked up'. Karen quietly suggests that anger does not do anything to 'un-fuck it'. The series could be said to endorse Karen's viewpoint by showing the time and diligence it takes to capture assailants; nonetheless, focused political anger is what powers *Unbelievable*'s attempt to educate audiences about the need to un-fuck how the criminal justice system handles rape cases and how popular culture represents them.

It is one of the series' greatest achievements that the serial rapist is never made a focal point – even as the narrative momentum and suspense derives from the race to catch him. The audience never sees things from his perspective, and he is never glorified or rendered mysterious in any way. Even when he shares his 'take' on his own crimes after he is finally captured, it is not presented in any kind of dramatic, revelatory way; the two female detectives watch it on a video on a laptop that they pause and shut off when they tire of watching (which can be viewed as a quiet reference to the power of user-directed viewing). It is *their* take that we care about. In other words, there is no Hannibal Lecterisation of the male criminal here: there is no characterisation of him as a fascinating evil sage who holds forth on the workings of the criminal mind, similar to *Kimmy*'s strategy of rendering toxic masculinity banal and ridiculous. *Unbelievable* also avoids the trap of sexualising or eroticising the male criminal. It is true that his is the only body shown naked in the entire series, but this is in order to render him banal, not exotic. Shortly after he is captured, McCarthy is ordered to strip naked as DNA evidence is captured from his body. The sequence is cross-cut with shots of Karen Duvall looking at the pink Sony camera found in McCarthy's bedroom, the one he stole from a victim and used to take photos as part of his abuse of the women. On-screen flashes of a camera's light evoke this abuse, but it is the camera's flash on the rapist's naked body that makes *him* the source of visual humiliation, not his victims. A long shot at the sequence's end shows McCarthy standing alone in the middle of his cell, his fleshy white body exposed as pitiful and commonplace. In this regard, *Unbelievable* stands in pointed contrast to other recent crime series such as *The Fall* (BBC 2013–16), which eroticise the male serial killer. Indeed, *The Fall* devotes an extraordinary amount of screen time to serial killer Paul

Spector (played by handsome former Calvin Klein underwear model, Jamie Dornan), with the camera lovingly roving over his sculpted body; moreover, the 'cat and mouse' chase between him and female detective Stella Gibson (Gillian Anderson) is heavily sexualised. Indeed, one of the more disturbing side effects of *The Fall*, whether intentional or not, is that serial killer Paul Spector (as played by the chiselled Dornan) had a cult of adoring female fans on social media (Brennan 2016).

The casting in *Unbelievable* is relevant in other ways too. For example, there is extra-textual significance to the decision to cast Brooke Smith – the actress who played Catherine Martin, the young woman held captive in a well by serial killer Buffalo Bill in horror classic *Silence of the Lambs* (Demme 1991; a film that is now part of Netflix UK's catalogue) – in the role of Marie's court-appointed therapist, Dara. Where *Kimmy*'s casting of well-known actors in the roles of toxic male characters derives its charge from these actors playing against type, here the resonance comes from Smith's previous association with the role of a smart and resilient young female victim. Smith's appearance in Episode 7 can be read as part of *Unbelievable*'s wider attempt to rework mainstream depictions of rape (in addition to *Silence of the Lambs*, there are visual and thematic references to the rape film *The Accused* [Kaplan 1988]) across its eight episodes.

In the eighth and final episode of *Unbelievable* Marie confronts the white male cop who botched the investigation of her case and went so far as to charge her with false reporting of a crime. She tells him: 'Next time, do better'. Contrite and ashamed, the male police officer hangs his head in mea culpa. The portrayal of the repentant police officer is all the more effective for not showing him as wicked or villainous: his incompetency is much duller than that and is based on unexamined and insidious cultural assumptions about the nature of rape as a crime.[8] That Marie has her moment to call him out and demand accountability is deeply satisfying and harks back to another scene, from the penultimate episode, in which Grace Rasmussen sends the same police officer the photos the rapist took of Marie, thereby offering irrefutable evidence that there was indeed a rape. While Grace calmly waits on the phone for his response, viewers are given his reaction shot of stunned and guilty recognition at how wrong he got it. 'F***ing unbelievable' is the phrase that came to mind when we watched this scene (and others), and indeed this is the reaction the series seeks to solicit. It is not just that Marie Adler was not believed; it is that the patriarchal criminal justice system is seriously flawed and needs to be turned on its head. The series uses the compressed binge-viewing format to produce social outrage and to suture viewers into its intensely focused and politicised critique of rape culture.

In a review that discusses the experience of watching *Unbelievable* as a full-drop release series, US TV critic Emily Todd VanDerWerff points to the value of the streaming service as a venue for telling this particular story. It is worth quoting VanDerWerff at length:

> [I]magine that *Unbelievable* was airing on traditional television, where it wouldn't immediately roll over to episode two once episode one's credits started to roll. Imagine having to sit with the weight of what happened to Marie for a full week. It might be artistically fulfilling, but it might also cause the sense that you never want to return to the series to grow and grow . . . I have issues with the way that Netflix's binge-watching model too often turns its shows into one big mass, instead of a series of distinct episodes, but there are times when the strongest thing to do is simply push forward, into the next episode. *Unbelievable* needs to be excruciating and infuriating but also watchable. And the platform where it airs might be the only place where it can accomplish that goal. (2019)

Here, VanDerWerff is gesturing towards the critical potential of the binge model and the significant affective relation it can forge between the unwatchable and the watchable. In a digital era of ubiquitous images of violence, what is paramount is the issue of not only what to watch but '*how* to watch' (Baer et al. 2019, 15, my emphasis). Taking advantage of what Jenner, following Lisa Glebatis Perks, refers to as the 'insulated flow' of binge-watching (Jenner 2018, 126), *Unbelievable* guides its viewers 'from one episode to the next' (2018, 115), productively using its management of viewer attention to produce a better cultural understanding of rape narratives.

Elsewhere in her work on true crime, Horeck has examined the ways in which the Netflix bingeable format produces strong affective responses in viewers in ways that work to evacuate crime of its social dimensions (Horeck 2019a). She has called for a feminist true crime that captures the collective and intersectional dimensions of crime, and that intervenes in meaningful ways in public discourses of sexual violence and social justice in the streaming era. *Unbelievable* is an important example of a series that repurposes true crime and uses the serialised devices of the red herring and the cliffhanger in order to hook viewers into its political interrogation of a system that fails women. In the final episode, the two timelines and the two narratives, of Marie Adler and of Karen Duvall and Grace Rasmussen, finally meet when Marie phones Karen to say thank you to the two women for looking out for her and 'making things right'. The final image of the series is of Marie in her jeep driving down the highway, the wind blowing her hair. Significantly, then, the series offers more than just critique: it leaves viewers with an understanding of how things should – and could – be handled differently and better.

CONCLUSION: NETFLIX FEMINISM

During Women's History month in 2017, the digital entertainment company *Refinery29* ran the following feature article: 'Netflix feminist shows to binge watch this month'. Instructing its young female readership to '[l]et those golden specks of empowerment make their way onto your computer screen', the piece pronounced that 'the streaming service is home to multitudes of bingeable TV shows that portray smart, brave, funny, flawed, and utterly relatable women' (Nicolaou 2017). As further indication of Netflix's feminist credentials, it was noted that its so-called feminist shows, which include *Orange is the New Black*, *GLOW* (2017–) and *Grace and Frankie* (2015–), pass 'the Bechdel test with flying colors' (Nicolaou 2017). The suggestion here, as in other recent listicles on 'top' feminist Netflix shows to binge-watch, is that through the intensive consumption of these popular series, one can be schooled in feminism. Further indicating the platform's purported pioneering role in bringing about a new era of television feminism *and* a new viewing model, is the praise that *Orange is the New Black*, one of Netflix's inaugural self-produced programmes, received upon its seventh season closure in 2019. When *New York Times* critic James Poniewozik declared that '*Orange is the New Black* taught us what Netflix was for', he identified two ways in which the series was a landmark in television culture: not only was it 'the first series to show us how streaming TV would really work and to teach us how to watch it' but also, it inaugurated 'the next era [which] would be open to a wider range of identity, color, sexual orientation and life experience', which for him is indivisible from the narrative affordances of bingeable TV (Poniewozik 2019b). Drawing correlations between Netflix fandom, consumption through binge-watching, and feminism, these articles bring into relief the idea of 'Netflix feminism'. Both *Kimmy* and *Unbelievable* speak to Netflix feminism and the company's self-branding as a pioneer of feminist activism.

Netflix series are designed for the affective connections of the online world. Therefore, the kinds of attachments and affordances opened up by the viral circulation of shows such as *Kimmy* and *Unbelievable* need to be considered. As we mentioned in our discussion of *Unbelievable*, Netflix's use of online promotional clips works to frame *Unbelievable* as a difficult, yet socially necessary series and instructs viewers on how to proceed with (binge-)watching it. Netflix's short promotional video about Episode 1 of *Unbelievable*, which circulated on social media sites such as Facebook and Twitter, hails a socially concerned viewer who, upon completing the eight-episode-long Netflix series, will be better informed about the 'right – and the wrong way to talk to victims of sexual violence'.[9] The clip, which directs viewers to Rainn and crisis resources, is illuminating for the ways in which it constructs and consolidates Netflix's promotion of its brand as 'Do Good TV' (Ouellette 2012). 'You Are Not Alone' is the clip's final message before the branded interface appears: 'Unbelievable now streaming on Netflix'.

Netflix's second-person mode of address in this clip is part of a wider social media promotional strategy by which the streaming corporation makes viewers feel that they are on-trend in their viewing habits and are part of a wider affective community of binge-watchers. In its press releases, tweets and trailers, Netflix deploys a form of personal address that interpellates the viewer as a knowing and active social agent. Digital media theorist Wendy Hui Kyong Chun observes that 'new media relentlessly emphasizes you' and indeed, Netflix's emphasis on YOU is central to its promotion of itself as a user-directed, interactive service (Chun 2016, 3). What needs to be unpacked further in this regard are the affective, ideological and economic dimensions of Netflix's attempt to brand itself as 'woke' TV.[11] As Poniewozik writes:

> Netflix . . . likes to present itself on social media as having a personality and a playful voice. It doesn't just want your patronage; it wants a relationship. It wants to be your TV buddy you spend time with. It wants to assure you that it loves the TV that you love, the better for you to transfer some of your affection toward its #brand. (2019a)

Interactivity, playfulness and social commentary characterise *Kimmy*'s online promotion as well, most prominently through the opening sequence's online presence. The sequence, an interview by the local news channel with a neighbour living near the bunker where the abducted women were found, was, within the series' fictional world, edited together and auto-turned into an earworm of a hip-hop beat, spoofing 'songify' culture (Rich 2015). Apart from the theme song video, Netflix has also circulated the 'original' online, i.e., the unedited and un-songified version of the interview, which provided added meanings to the song's initial upbeat exclamations about 'unbreakable' women (the line 'females are strong as hell' is a recurring catchphrase in both fandom and promotion). As it turns out from the unedited version, the neighbour's use of the word 'unbreakable' has less to do with the women and more with a pair of sunglasses he has just found and which can be bent without breaking. In other words, this extra joke works both as mockery of the neighbour's character and as a rather convoluted (but in the show's hyper-referential world, fitting) admission of the way these women become turned into media images of female toughness and resilience. Given Kimmy's four-season long character trajectory, the series complicates this trope by explicating in detail the ways in which she is a deeply broken (psychologically scarred), while resilient, person.

Unbreakable, unbelievable: both of these titles gain their promotional strength from the contradictoriness of the notions they reference, emerging through Netflix's promotional materials, the programmes' own narrative devices, and viewer affect. For *Unbelievable*, this refers to both societal incredulity towards the testimonies of victims of sexual assault and also an incredulous viewer, outraged about what they see happening on screen (constantly being reminded of the 'based on a true story' backdrop). For *Kimmy*, 'unbreakable' blends together the media prominence of individualised female resilience and the critique of this notion through Kimmy's story. In their own ways, the two titles tap into questions of gendered social power: who can (is socially sanctioned) to break whom and believe whom. Both titles suggest something outside the norm, thus provoking incredulity – even though rape is one of the most widespread and normalised acts of violence, its ubiquity perpetuated not least by the media, as is so poignantly revealed by the #MeToo movement. To put it bluntly, the series express the opposite of their titles' signification: women are breakable, and rape is believable.

The two shows' wordplay around their titles taps into current discourses about female toughness and believing women, which also helps Netflix establish its 'woke' brand through bingeability and online promotional tie-ins with its direct address to media-savvy and feminised audiences. These audiences are, as Sarah Arnold (2016) argues, identified as a key target demographic through the company's datafication of viewer response via the interface recommendation system, and are thus enclosed in Netflix's gynocentric online sphere.

To point to the links between the commercial/profit imperatives of Netflix's streaming service and its strategic deployment of ideas of community and social responsibility is not to malign or discount its promotion of socially and politically motivated programming. Instead, it is to critically reflect on Netflix's brand identity and its investment in an imagined viewer whose consumption through binge-watching is seen to be socially justified through the civic worth of its programming. Bearing in mind Roopali Mukherjee's and Sarah Banet-Weiser's point that politics is always bound up with consumerism and it is therefore important not to resort to 'binary thinking that separate(s) consumption practice from political struggles' (2012, 13), it is crucial to examine the relationship between binge-watching, as Netflix's preferred mode of consumption, and cultural processes of meaning-making around rape culture.

NOTES

1. As Claudia Bucciferro cautions, there are caveats to Netflix's progressiveness. It is important to remember that Netflix is, above all, a profit-making company and that it 'still carries plenty of masculinist content. It is possible to have a viewing profile that includes only action movies, gritty series, and erotica, all featuring tough men (who are mostly heterosexual, cisgender, and white) in leading roles, with plotlines that support a patriarchal order' (2019, 3).

2. Berridge (2017) discusses the potential for the serialised form to uncover the dynamics of rape culture in relation to the first season of Netflix's controversial teen drama *13 Reasons Why*. Horeck (2019b) has written on the later seasons of the series, arguing that they ultimately end up reinforcing the forms of harm they profess to challenge.
3. Red Carpet Report (2015). Available at: <https://www.youtube.com/watch?v=DR4Wmd B7ZoY&feature=youtu.be> (last accessed 23 March 2021).
4. After we completed this chapter, British actor, writer and showrunner Michaela Coel released her 12-episode-long series exploring issues of sex and consent, *I May Destroy You* (2020). Coel's series centres the black woman's (and man's) intersectional experience of sexual assault. According to Coel, she turned down an attractive Netflix offer because she wanted to retain control over her copyright (Gonzales 2020). She published the series instead on BBC One and BBC iPlayer in the UK, and HBO in the US. In light of what we are arguing in this chapter, it is significant to note that HBO released one episode per week of *I May Destroy You*, while the BBC released two episodes per week. In interviews, Coel has stated that she wanted viewers to sit with the episodes before watching the next (Ibekwe 2020). As Caetlin Benson-Allott has suggested, *I May Destroy You* is thus different to shows such as *Unbelievable*, in that it 'allows its spectator the time to recover between installments. Not only does each episode hit with an intensity that discourages rapid consumption, but many emphasize character growth between episodes that might otherwise be lost on viewers' (2020, 103). (It is worth noting here that similar discourses surrounded Hulu series *The Handmaid's Tale*'s (2017–) weekly release strategy around its first and second seasons, framing the programme as resistant to bingeability since it is supposedly 'a tough show to watch' due to its depiction of a dystopian misogynist society [Ha, Crook and Perez 2018].) While we do not have the space here to analyse this issue in detail, the above discourses around *I May Destroy You*'s release strategy signal that there is increasing discussion around the value of binge-watching versus weekly broadcasting/ release for narrating rape. We suggest that neither mode of narration carries inherently fixed ideological attributes, as these are shaped by a number of factors (among them the companies' promotional and branding strategies in a competitive streaming environment, producers' professed ideological and ethical intent, audiences' varied responses, and public discourses about rape and audience engagement).
5. 'Pioneering' and 'iconoclastic' are the adjectives that Netflix CEO Reed Hastings applied to *Orange is the New Black* (Netflix, 2013–19) in 2015, speaking to that series' (at the time) unusual gender politics and generic uncategorisability (Zuckerman 2015).
6. General Equivalency Diploma, an adult education certificate in the US.
7. While Grant is generally credited as the showrunner, *Unbelievable* was co-created by Michael Chabon and Ayelet Waldman and has a large team of executive producers including Katie Couric, Lisa Cholodenko and the real-life rape survivor listed in the credits as 'Marie'.
8. 'Marie' is the middle name of the actual rape victim; Adler is a fictionalised last name given to the character in the Netflix drama.
9. Susannah Grant has said she did not envision the male police officer as 'a bad man'. Rather, it is a 'systemic problem, a cultural problem' regarding 'misapprehensions' about sexual assault as a crime (cited in Dibdin 2019).
10. Netflix's promotional clip (made in conjunction with Rainn) can be found at the following link: <https://www.facebook.com/watch/?v=1196602357208804&external_log_id=f31b77 27406a7a7b09adcfb1dc2be937&q=Episode%201%20of%20Unbelievable> (last accessed 21 March 2021).
11. The Merriam-Webster Dictionary defines 'woke' as a 'slang term that is easing into the mainstream from some varieties of a dialect called African American Vernacular English'.

Originating in reference to awareness of racial injustice in particular, it is 'increasingly used as a byword for social awareness'. For the full definition please see: <https://www.merriam-webster.com/words-at-play/woke-meaning-origin> (last accessed 23 March 2021). For a discussion of how Netflix brands itself as 'woke' as part of a wider business strategy, please see Angus (2019). See Francesca Sobande for an academic analysis of 'how and why ideas regarding "intersectional" approaches to feminism and black activism are drawn on in marketing content related to the concept of being "woke"' (2019, 1).

REFERENCES

Adams, E. (2019). 'Tina Fey and Robert Carlock on the end of *Unbreakable Kimmy Schmidt*'. *TV Club*. 21 January. Available at: <https://tv.avclub.com/tina-fey-and-robert-carlock-on-the-end-of-unbreakable-k-1831730551> (last accessed 23 March 2021).
Alcoff, L. (2018). *Rape and Resistance: Understanding the Complexities of Sexual Violence*. Cambridge: Polity Press.
Angus, H. (2019). 'Netflix Isn't Your Woke Friend; They're a Brand'. *Medium*. 21 April. Available at: <https://haaniyah.medium.com/netflix-isnt-your-woke-friend-they-re-a-brand-69250ab3623e> (last accessed 23 March 2021).
Arnold, S. (2016). 'Netflix and the Myth of Choice/Participation/Autonomy'. In K. McDonald and D. Smith-Rowsey (eds), *The Netflix Effect: Technology and Entertainment in the 21st Century*. New York: Bloomsbury.
Baer, N., M. Hennefeld, L. Horak and G. Iversen (eds) (2019). *Unwatchable*. New Brunswick, NJ: Rutgers University Press.
Banet-Weiser, S. (2018). *Empowered: Popular Feminism and Popular Misogyny*. Durham, NC: Duke University Press.
Benson-Allott, C. (2020). '*I May Destroy You* Reinvents Rape Television'. *Film Quarterly* 74(2): 100–5.
Berridge, S. (2011). 'Personal Problems and Women's Issues: Episodic Sexual Violence Narratives in US Teen Drama Series'. *Feminist Media Studies* 11(4): 467–81.
Berridge, S. (2017). 'Teenage Boys' "Intrusion" and Sexual Violence in *13 Reasons Why* (Netflix 2017)'. *CST online*. Available at: <https://cstonline.net/teenage-boys-intrusion-and-sexual-violence-in-13-reasons-why-netflix-2017-by-susan-berridge/> (last accessed 2 November 2018).
Blake, M. (2019). 'How Netflix's *Unbelievable* created its revolutionary depiction of rape'. *LA Times*. 3 October. Available at: <https://www.latimes.com/entertainment-arts/tv/story/2019-10-03/unbelievable-netflix-rape-representation> (last accessed 23 March 2021).
Brennan, S. (2016). '"Paul Spector can drown me in the bath anytime:' The Fall fans continue to go wild for Jamie Dornan's character even though he's a serial murderer'. *The Daily Mail*, October 21. Available at: <https://www.dailymail.co.uk/femail/article-3858940/The-Fall-fans-continue-wild-Jamie-Dornan-s-serial-killer.html> (last accessed 23 March 2021).
Bryne, K. and J. Taddeo. (2019). 'Calling #TimesUp on the TV Period Drama Rape Narrative'. *Critical Studies in Television* 14(3): 379–98.
Bucciferro, C. (2019). 'Women and Netflix: Disrupting Traditional Boundaries between Television and Film'. *Feminist Media Studies* 19(7): 1053–6.
Chun, W. (2016). *Updating to Remain the Same: Habitual New Media*. Cambridge, MA: The MIT Press.
Coates, T. (2015). 'Tina Fey and Race: 'Unbreakable Kimmy Schmidt' Has A Straight, White Male Problem'. *Decider*. 15 May. Available at: <http://decider.com/2015/03/10/tina-fey-race-unbreakable-kimmy-schmidt/> (last accessed 23 March 2021).

Dibdin, E. (2019). '*Unbelievable* Showrunner Susannah Grant Breaks Down the Choices That Made the Show So Powerful'. *Harpers Bazaar*. 30 September. Available at: <https://www.harpersbazaar.com/culture/film-tv/a29093906/unbelievable-netflix-susannah-grant-interview/> (last accessed 23 March 2021).

D'Souza, D. (2019). 'Netflix Doesn't Want to Talk About Binge-Watching'. *Investopedia*. 18 May. Available at: <https://www.investopedia.com/tech/netflix-obsessed-binge-watching-and-its-problem/> (last accessed 23 March 2021).

Feuer, J. (1984). 'Melodrama, Serial Form and Television Today'. *Screen* 25(1): 4–16.

Gonzales, E. (2020). 'Michaela Coel Turned Down Netflix's $1 Million Dollar Offer for *I May Destroy You*'. *Harper's Bazaar*. 7 July. Available at: <https://www.harpersbazaar.com/culture/film-tv/a33234332/michaela-coel-turned-down-netflix-deal/> (last accessed 23 March 2021).

Ha, A., J. Crook, and S. Perez. (2018). 'Original Content Podcast: 'The Handmaid's Tale' Is Even More Intense in Season Two'. *TechCrunch*. 28 April. Available at: <https://social.techcrunch.com/2018/04/28/original-content-handmaids-tale/> (last accessed 23 March 2021).

Havas, J. (2017). 'Tina Fey: "Quality" Comedy and the Body of the Female Comedy Author'. In L. Mizejewski and V. Sturtevant (eds), *Hysterical! Women in American Comedy*. Austin, TX: University of Texas Press, pp. 347–78.

Horeck, T. (2004). *Public Rape: Representing Violation in Fiction and Film*. London/New York: Routledge.

Horeck, T. (2019a). *Justice on Demand: True Crime in the Digital Streaming Era*. Detroit, MI: Wayne State University Press.

Horeck, T. (2019b). 'Streaming Sexual Violence: Binge-Watching Netflix's *13 Reasons Why*'. *Participations: Journal of Audience & Reception Studies* 16(2). Available at: <https://www.participations.org/Volume%2016/Issue%202/9.pdf> (last accessed 23 March 2021).

Horton, A. (2019). 'Unbelievable: the quiet power of Netflix's fact-based rape drama'. *The Guardian*. 17 September. Available at: <https://www.theguardian.com/tv-and-radio/2019/sep/16/unbelievable-quiet-power-netflix-drama> (last accessed 23 March 2021).

Iannucci, R. (2015). '*Unbreakable Kimmy Schmidt* Team on Netflix Move, F-Bombs, *30 Rock* Vibe'. *TVLine*. 7 January. Available at: <https://tvline.com/2015/01/07/unbreakable-kimmy-schmidt-netflix-spoilers-tina-fey/> (last accessed 23 March 2021).

Ibekwe, D. (2020). 'Michaela Coel: "TV is unforgiving – but I'm built for this"'. *Screen Daily*. 3 June. Available at: <https://www.screendaily.com/features/michaela-coel-tv-is-unforgiving-but-im-built-for-this/5150313.article> (last accessed 23 March 2021).

Jenner, M. (2016). 'Is this TVIV? On Netflix, TVIII and binge-watching'. *New Media & Society* 18(2): 257–73.

Jenner, M. (2018). *Netflix and the Reinvention of Television*. Basingstoke: Palgrave Macmillan.

Kilkenny, K. (2019). 'How a Pulitzer-Prize Winning Investigation Became Netflix's Unbelievable'. *The Hollywood Reporter*. 13 September. Available at: <https://www.hollywoodreporter.com/live-feed/how-a-pulitzer-prize-winning-investigation-became-netflixs-unbelievable-1239342> (last accessed 23 March 2021).

Lewis, H. (2019). '"Kimmy Schmidt": Tina Fey and Robert Carlock on Thinking Behind Finale's Happy Endings'. *Hollywood Reporter*. 28 January. Available at: <https://www.hollywoodreporter.com/live-feed/kimmy-schmidt-tina-fey-robert-carlock-interview-final-season-1180121> (last accessed 23 March 2021).

Lindsay, K. (2017). 'Why Did It Take *Unbreakable Kimmy Schmidt* 3 Seasons to Talk About Sexual Assault?' *Refinery29*. 22 May. Available at: <https://www.refinery29.com/en-us/2017/05/155648/unbreakable-kimmy-schmidt-season-3-sexual-assault> (last accessed 23 March 2021).

Lotz, A. D. (2014). *Cable Guys: Television and Masculinities in the 21st Century*. New York: New York University Press.

Marghitu, S. (2019). 'Independent Women: From Film to Television'. *Feminist Media Studies* 19(7): 1050–3.

Martin, B. (2013). *Difficult Men: From The Sopranos and The Wire to Mad Men and Breaking Bad*. London: Faber & Faber.

Mendes, K., J. Ringrose and J. Keller (2019). *Digital Feminist Activism: Girls and Women Fight Back Against Rape Culture*. Oxford: Oxford University Press.

Miller, C. T. and K. Armstrong (2015). 'An Unbelievable Story of Rape'. *Propublica*. 16 December. Available at: <https://www.propublica.org/article/false-rape-accusations-an-unbelievable-story> (last accessed 23 March 2021).

Miller, L. S. (2017). '"Unbreakable Kimmy Schmidt" Season 3 Finally Used the Word "Rape": Why It's a Big Deal'. *IndieWire.com*. 22 May. Available at: <https://www.indiewire.com/2017/05/unbreakable-kimmy-schmidt-rape-season-3-spoilers-1201829912/> (last accessed 23 March 2021).

Mittell, J. (2015a). *Complex TV: The Poetics of Contemporary Television Storytelling*. New York: New York University Press.

Mittell, J. (2015b). 'Lengthy Interactions with Hideous Men: Walter White and the Serial Poetics of Television Antiheroes'. In R.E. Pearson and A. N. Smith (eds), *Storytelling in the Media Convergence Age: Exploring Screen Narratives*. Basingstoke: New York: Palgrave Macmillan, pp. 74–92.

Mizejewski, L. (2014). *Pretty/funny: Women Comedians and Body Politics*. Austin, TX: University of Texas Press, pp. 59–91.

Modleski, T. (1979). 'The Search for Tomorrow in Today's Soap Operas: Notes on a Feminine Narrative Form'. *Film Quarterly* 33(1): 12–21.

Moorti, S. (2002). *Color of Rape: Gender and Race in Television's Public Spheres*. Albany, NY: State University of New York Press.

Mukherjee, R. and S. Banet-Weiser (2012). 'Introduction: Commodity Activism in Neoliberal Times'. In R. Mukherjee and S. Banet-Weiser (eds), *Commodity Activism: Cultural Resistance in Neoliberal Times*. New York/London: New York University Press, pp. 1–17.

Nicolaou, E. (2017). 'Netflix's Most Feminist Shows to Binge-Watch This Month'. *Refinery29*. 21 June. Available at: <https://www.refinery29.com/en-gb/2017/03/160350/best-feminist-shows-on-netflix> (last accessed 23 March 2021).

Nussbaum, E. (2015). 'Candy Girl'. *The New Yorker*. 30 March. Available at: <http://www.newyorker.com/magazine/2015/03/30/candy-girl> (last accessed 23 March 2021).

Ouellette, L. (2012). 'Citizen Brand: ABC and the Do Good Turn in US Television'. In R. Mukherjee and S. Banet-Weiser (eds), *Commodity Activism: Cultural Resistance in Neoliberal Times*. New York/London: New York University Press, pp. 57–75.

Poniewozik, J. (2019a). '"One Day at a Time" and Why Netflix is Not Your Friend'. *The New York Times*. 14 March. Available at: <https://www.nytimes.com/2019/03/14/arts/television/one-day-at-a-time-canceled-netflix.html> (last accessed 23 March 2021).

Poniewozik, J. (2019b). '"Orange is the New Black" Taught Us What Netflix Was For'. *NYTimes.com*. 17 July. Available at: <https://www.nytimes.com/2019/07/17/arts/television/orange-is-the-new-black-final-season.html> (last accessed 23 March 2021).

Projansky, S. (2001). *Watching Rape: Film and Television in Postfeminist Culture*. New York: New York University Press.

Rainn (2019). 'Rainn Teams Up with Netflix on Limited Series Unbelievable'. 25 September. Available at: <https://www.rainn.org/news/rainn-teams-netflix-limited-series-unbelievable> (last accessed 23 March 2021).

Red Carpet Report on Mingle Media TV (2015). 'Tina Fey at Netflix's *Unbreakable Kimmy Schmidt* FYC Event'. Video recording, YouTube, viewed 24 September 2019. Available at: <https://www.youtube.com/watch?v=DR4WmdB7ZoY&feature=youtu.be> (last accessed 23 March 2021).

Rich, K. (2015). 'Why you Can't Get the *Unbreakable Kimmy Schmidt* Song Out of Your Head'. *Vanity Fair*. 10 March. Available at: <https://www.vanityfair.com/hollywood/2015/03/unbreakable-kimmy-schmidt-theme-song> (last accessed 23 March 2021).

Rosenberg, A. (2015). '"Unbreakable Kimmy Schmidt" Mines Comedy Out of Sexual Abuse'. *Washington Post*. 10 March. Available at: <https://www.washingtonpost.com/news/act-four/wp/2015/03/10/unbreakable-kimmy-schmidt-mines-comedy-out-of-sexual-abuse/> (last accessed 23 March 2021).

Sobande, F. (2019). 'Woke-Washing: 'Intersectional' Femvertising and Branding 'Woke' Bravery'. *European Journal of Marketing*. Available at: <http://orca.cf.ac.uk/126357/7/Woke-washing%20-%20%27Intersectional%27%20femvertising%20and%20branding%20%27woke%27%20bravery%20%28Francesca%20Sobande%29%20%28PDF%29.pdf> (last accessed 23 March 2021).

Tryon, C. (2015). 'TV Got Better: Netflix's Original Programming Strategies and Binge Viewing'. *Media Industries*, 2(2). Available at: <https://quod.lib.umich.edu/m/mij/15031809.0002.206/--tv-got-better-netflixs-original-programming-strategies?rgn=main;view=fulltext> (last accessed 23 March 2021).

Tuttle, K. (2019). 'Why Do Women Love True Crime?' *The New York Times*. July 16. Available at: <https://www.nytimes.com/2019/07/16/books/review/kate-tuttle-true-crime-women.html> (last accessed 23 March 2021).

VanDerWerff, E. (2019). 'How Netflix's Unbelievable turns a true story about rape into challenging, must-watch TV'. *Vox*. 15 September. Available at: <https://www.vox.com/culture/2019/9/15/20861707/unbelievable-netflix-review-episode-1-recap> (last accessed 23 March 2021).

Watkins, G. (2019). 'Why *Unbreakable Kimmy Schmidt* Tackled #MeToo With a Puppet Penis'. *Vulture*. February 11. Available at: <https://www.vulture.com/2019/02/kimmy-schmidt-mr-frumpus-puppet-penis.html> (last accessed 23 March 2021).

Wood, H. (2019). 'Fuck the Patriarchy: Towards an Intersectional Politics of Irreverent Rage'. *Feminist Media Studies* 19(4): 609–15.

Zuckerman, E. (2015). '*Orange is the New Black* Will Be Considered a Drama at The Emmys'. *Entertainment Weekly*. 20 March. Available at: <https://ew.com/article/2015/03/20/orange-new-black-will-be-drama-emmys/> (last accessed 23 March 2021).

TV

13 Reasons Why (2017–), USA: Netflix.
Big Little Lies (2017–), USA: HBO
Buffy the Vampire Slayer (1997–2003), USA: WB, UPN
CSI: Crime Scene Investigation (2000–15) USA: CBS
Fall, The (2013–16), UK/Ireland: BBC
GLOW (2017–), USA: Netflix
Grace and Frankie (2015–), USA: Netflix
Handmaid's Tale, The (2017–), USA: Hulu
Jessica Jones (2015–19), USA: Netflix
Keepers, The (2017), USA: Netflix

Mad Men (2007–15), USA: AMC
Making a Murderer (2015, 2018), USA: Netflix
Orange is the New Black (2013–19), USA: Netflix
Unbelievable (2019), USA: Netflix
Unbreakable Kimmy Schmidt (2015–19), USA: Netflix
Veronica Mars (2004–), USA: UPN, The CW, Hulu

FILM

Blackhurst, R. and McGinn, B. (2016) *Amanda Knox*. USA: Plus Pictures
Demme, J. (1991) *Silence of the Lambs*. USA: Strong Heart/Demme Production
Kaplan, J. (1988) *The Accused*. USA: Paramount Pictures

CHAPTER 18

Bingeing Narratives: Conclusion

Lynn Kozak and Martin Zeller-Jacques, Tom Hemingway, Orcun Can, Júlia Havas and Tanya Horeck

The emergence of binge-watching as one of the defining logics of the SVOD era of television presents a challenge to the scholar of television narrative. As a practice of television audiences, binge-watching seems resistant to textual analysis. However, as television producers and distributors attempt to distinguish their programming in the crowded SVOD marketplace, they have begun to claim that they are producing their shows in ways which facilitate or encourage bingeing. The chapters in this part of the collection interrogate those claims by examining the narrative structures of 'made-for-bingeing' television programmes on Netflix. Collectively, we explore both the continuities and the developments of television form which characterise bingeable television in the SVOD era.

The centre of our approach is the investigation of a claim often made in trade discourse, publicity and journalism around streaming television: that television made in the season-dropped, bingeable format offers a qualitatively different form of television storytelling than conventional scheduled television. As the title of a 2015 *New York Times* article by TV critic James Poniewozik puts it: 'Streaming TV Isn't Just a New Way to Watch: It's a New Genre'. According to Poniewozik, the practice of full-drop release has generated 'new conventions and aesthetics' that 'we're just starting to figure out' (2015). Indeed, Poniewozik goes so far as to suggest that: 'More so than any recent innovation in TV, streaming has the potential, even the likelihood, to create an entirely new genre of narrative . . .' (2015). This part on Netflix and narrative evaluates such claims and explores the narrative mechanics of TV series designed for user-directed, bingeable viewing. While CEO Reed Hastings might claim that Netflix's full-drop release strategy has 'improved' television (cited in

Sharf 2018), to what extent are the narrative dynamics of bingeable TV any different from those of linear television?

The 'quality' turn which crystallised around HBO in the 2000s occasioned similar claims that new scheduling and commissioning practices were leading to different forms of television storytelling (McCabe and Akass 2007; Nelson 2007). While such claims had some basis in fact, they were also part of the strategies of legitimation (Newman and Levine 2012) undertaken by the new players driving changes in the television industry. This makes it doubly important for scholars to regard claims of narrative distinction with a critical eye, lest we allow press releases and popular journalism to set the terms of the discussion around television narrative.

In the introductory essay to this part, Lynn Kozak's and Martin Zeller-Jacques's exploration of 'The Bingeable Narrative' examines the Netflix original *Stranger Things* (Netflix 2016–). Responding to critical claims about textual 'purity' (Jacobs 2011) as a defining feature of bingeable television, the first half of the chapter explores the narrative impact occasioned by the violation of that purity in the form of the stand-alone episode, 'The Lost Sister' (2:8). The second half of the chapter interrogates claims about the supposed lack of narrative redundancy in made-for-bingeing television, and demonstrates that various forms of redundancy are essential to the storytelling in the *Stranger Things*.

Tom Hemingway's chapter compares two texts available for streaming on Netflix, *Arrested Development*'s (Fox 2003–6; Netflix 2013–) fourth season and *Love* (Netflix 2016–18). These case studies offer ways of approaching narratives which break from the previously established norms of broadcast television comedy. Both shows demonstrate different ways in which the comedy genre has been able to adapt its narrative structure to suit the binge-watching practices encouraged by streaming services. The chapter's engagement with bingeability is on a strictly textual level, building on Jenner's previous work (2016) regarding *Arrested Development*'s complex narrative structure. It then moves on to explore *Love*'s irregular use of temporality. The chapter points toward future areas of research in the audience response to these texts and by noting that there are, in fact, a small number of comedy programmes on Netflix which adhere to the traditional style associated with innumerable broadcast sitcoms. It would be interesting to examine how these programmes, *The Ranch* (Netflix 2016–) and *Alexa & Katie* (Netflix 2018–), fit alongside other Netflix original comedies in an expanded version of this study.

Orcun Can introduces a new analytical model to examine so-called bingeable narratives. Breaking down consecutive episodes to their formal structural elements, the Serialised Televisual Narrative Analysis (STNA) Model presents overarching narratives in multiple episodes as a single, linear dataset. His chapter offers a comparative analysis of the broadcast TV show *Gilmore Girls*

(The CW 2000–7) and the Netflix Original *Gilmore Girls: A Year in the Life* (Netflix 2016) using the STNA Model. By exploring narrative possibilities afforded in an SVOD environment and investigating how televisual afterlives take shape on Netflix, Can argues that the omission of commercial breaks enables a variety of changes in the narrative form of televisual serials in Netflix.

In 'Netflix Feminism: Binge-Watching Rape Culture in *Unbreakable Kimmy Schmidt* (Netflix 2015–19) and *Unbelievable* (Netflix 2019)', Júlia Havas and Tanya Horeck examine the political potential of Netflix's bingeable programming strategy for narrating rape. Focusing on two Netflix series that attempt to find new ways of televisually representing rape and post-traumatic recovery from rape – *Unbreakable Kimmy Schmidt* and *Unbelievable* – Havas and Horeck reflect on how these series represent what the authors refer to as 'Netflix feminism'. While *Kimmy* is a comedy and *Unbelievable* a crime drama, both series mine the affordances of Netflix's much-touted binge-watching formula and its use of serialised narrative structures to explore and criticise both rape culture and the established tropes of narrativising rape culture. Havas and Horeck commend the feminist innovation of these two series, but they also point to the need to think critically about how Netflix deploys an idea of itself as a feminist company in relation to its self-branding strategies as a pioneer of what has been referred to as 'woke' media culture.

While there is not one set formula or template that Netflix uses for its bingeable narratives, these chapters demonstrate that its business model of full-drop release has led to certain significant shifts and trends in narrative form, storytelling and temporality. At the same time, this work across genres also emphasises where streaming TV has merely innovated on or adopted historical television forms. Textual analysis gives all these chapters the critical leverage to push back against commercial claims of the 'new'.

REFERENCES

Jacobs, J. (2011). 'Television, Interrupted: Pollution or Aesthetic'. In J. Bennett and N. Strange (eds), *Television as Digital Media*. Durham, NC: Duke University Press, pp. 255–80.

Jenner, M. (2016). 'Is This TVIV? On Netflix, TVIII and Binge-Watching'. *New Media & Society* 18(2): 257–73.

Jenner, M. (2018). *Netflix and the Reinvention of Television*. Basingstoke: Palgrave Macmillan.

McCabe, J. and K. Akass (eds). (2007). *Quality TV: Contemporary American Television and Beyond*. London and New York: I. B. Tauris.

Nelson, R. (2007). *State of Play: Contemporary 'High-End' TV Drama*. Manchester and New York: Manchester University Press.

Newman, M. and E. Levine (2012). *Legitimating Television: Media Convergence and Cultural Status*. London and New York: Routledge.

Poniewozik, J. (2015). 'Streaming TV Isn't Just a New Way to Watch: It's a New Genre'. *The New York Times*. 16 December. Available at: <https://www.nytimes.com/2015/12/20/

arts/television/streaming-tv-isnt-just-a-new-way-to-watch-its-a-new-genre.html> (last accessed 23 March 2021).

Sharf, Z. (2018). 'Netflix CEO Says Company Has "Improved Television" and Is Concentrating More on Original TV Than Film for a Reason'. *Indiewire*. 30 April. Available at: <https://www.indiewire.com/2018/04/netflix-reed-hastings-improved-television-1201959008/> (last accessed 23 March 2021).

T V

Alexa & Katie (2018–), USA: Netflix
Arrested Development (2003–6; 2013–), USA: Fox, Netflix
Gilmore Girls (2000–7), USA: The CW
Gilmore Girls: A Year in the Life (2016), USA: Netflix
Love (2016–18), USA: Netflix
Ranch, The (2016–), USA: Netflix
Stranger Things (2016–), USA: Netflix
Unbelievable (2019), USA: Netflix
Unbreakable Kimmy Schmidt (2015–19), USA: Netflix

Index

addiction, 12–13, 30–2, 50–1, 60, 71–4, 76–7, 145, 151, 233
affect, 75, 98, 118, 150–4, 157, 202, 224, 247, 257, 267
  affective, 34, 41, 43–5, 53, 56, 61, 82, 154, 174, 216, 257–8, 260, 264–6
algorithm, 2, 11, 112, 115, 127, 184, 192
  algorithmic, 151, 188, 196, 203
Arrested Development (2003–), USA: Netflix, 189, 209, 224–30, 232–3, 275
attention, 2, 12, 15, 24, 28–9, 35, 44, 59, 65, 70, 74, 82–3, 85, 88, 90–2, 94, 106, 115–17, 122–3, 131, 133, 137, 147, 173, 189, 212–16, 225, 228–9, 240–1, 250, 258, 260, 264

BBC, 10, 27, 162–3, 170–3, 177
beat, 166, 217–19, 238–44, 262, 266
behaviour, 1, 11, 13, 24, 60, 70, 72, 88, 91–3, 98, 105–6, 108–9, 123, 126, 134, 136, 152, 195, 253, 259

bingeable, 1, 9, 15, 23, 163, 169, 208–10, 214–16, 219, 225, 231, 237, 239, 250, 252, 254–6, 258, 264–5, 274–6
bingeability, 10, 14–15, 165, 168, 173, 177, 190, 193, 201, 203, 208, 225, 227, 233, 236–7, 247, 252, 257, 267, 275
Black Mirror (2011–19), UK: Channel 4, Netflix, 45–6, 51–4, 104, 123
BoJack Horseman (2015–20), USA: Netflix, 45, 47, 50–2, 55, 231
brand, 42, 68, 145, 147, 150, 155–6, 169–70, 213, 220, 250–2, 265–7
  branding, 67–8, 77, 155, 169–70, 265, 276
  rebranding, 5, 163, 169
Breaking Bad (2008–13), USA: AMC, 42, 76, 104, 122, 190, 193
Brunsdon, Charlotte, 12–13, 31, 113, 224
Buffy the Vampire Slayer (1997–2003), USA: UPN, The CW, 186–7, 213, 253

Bury, Rhiannon, 11, 13, 59–60, 85, 89, 115
'buzz', 12, 135

catch-up, 23, 30, 42, 53, 56, 59
character, 43, 47, 55, 60, 66, 69, 72–3, 76, 94, 124, 127, 132, 138, 167–8, 170–2, 186–90, 192–6, 209, 212–19, 227–8, 230–3, 237–8, 240–6, 253–5, 257, 261, 263, 266
cinematic, 9, 70, 74–5, 155, 163, 166, 168, 173, 176–7, 190, 210–11, 220
cognitive, 82–4, 89, 91–5, 124, 134, 136, 174
comedy, 15, 48, 54, 70, 104, 120, 187, 190, 224–30, 233, 251–2, 254–8, 275–6
communal, 16, 113, 135, 146, 151, 166
completion, 42–4, 51, 53, 56, 87, 90, 99–100, 102, 104–6, 109, 116, 131–2, 137, 139
Covid-19, 15–16, 134
CSI: Crime Scene Investigation (2000–15) USA: CBS, 10, 261–2

demographics, 12, 83–4, 88, 157
digital, 2, 5, 10–12, 24, 26, 34, 36, 59, 61, 71, 95, 115, 117, 133, 211, 214, 229, 233, 264–6
  digitalisation, 115
  post-digital, 147, 156
  pre-digital, 27
diversity, 4, 10, 13, 157, 185, 189, 193
Doctor Who (1963–), UK: BBC, 6, 104

emotions, 72, 107, 153–4, 216
  emotional, 42–3, 50, 52, 54, 56, 72, 89, 92, 124, 132, 134, 154, 233, 255, 257

engagement, 5–6, 11, 30, 33, 35, 41, 50, 56, 60, 67, 82, 87, 89–90, 92, 95, 112, 125, 131–6, 139, 145, 147, 149–52, 156–7, 191, 202, 251, 253, 275
entrance flow, 115, 122
episodic, 59, 101, 165, 167–8, 176–7, 211, 214, 225, 237, 251, 253–5
epistemology, 260
everyday, 41, 50, 56, 83–4, 89, 101, 112–22, 124, 127, 164, 174

Fall, The (2013–16), UK: BBC, 163, 169–74, 177, 262–3
fandom, 1, 13, 23–6, 28–33, 35, 41–4, 59–60, 74, 226, 26–6
fannish, 25, 29–30, 33–5, 40, 43, 56–7, 59–60
feminism, 189, 251, 265, 276
flashback, 190, 209, 217–19, 238, 256
flow, 28, 41–2, 68, 90, 98–9, 108, 115–16, 122, 127, 133, 135, 146, 148–50, 152, 165–6, 177, 208, 211–13, 264
Friends (1994–2004), USA: NBC, 9, 104

Game of Thrones (2011–19), USA: HBO, 76, 85–6, 90–1, 104–6, 134
gender, 84, 118, 154, 251–2, 256
  gendered, 24, 51, 57, 171, 253–6, 261, 267
genre, 14–15, 26, 44, 61, 76, 82–3, 88, 92–5, 106, 119–21, 125, 132, 148, 154, 157, 165, 172–4, 183–96, 201, 203, 209, 225, 231, 233, 236, 252, 256, 258, 261, 274–6
  generic, 83, 94, 153, 157, 196, 203, 228, 251–2, 255

Gilmore Girls (2000–7), USA: The CW, 15, 188, 236–47, 275
Gilmore Girls: A Year in the Life (2016), USA: Netflix, 15, 236–7, 239–47, 276

habits, 3, 67, 73, 82, 84, 98–9, 109, 113–14, 116, 122, 124–5, 145–7, 151–2, 217, 224, 266
  habitual, 101, 147, 151
HBO, 2, 9–10, 73, 86, 117, 155, 167–8, 208–10, 215–16, 275
health, 13, 54, 65, 76, 100, 134, 136, 137, 145
  unhealthy, 60, 66, 68
history, 1–2, 4, 6, 10–11, 13, 27, 40, 65, 67, 75, 100, 126–7, 148, 151, 153, 164, 166, 185, 189, 265
Horeck, Tanya, 15, 90, 189, 232, 253, 264, 276
House of Cards (2013–18), USA: Netflix, 3, 11, 42, 45, 56, 74, 104, 188–9, 207, 209, 212, 215–16
Hulu, 10, 70, 72, 203

inequality, 188, 191
innovation, 124, 145–6, 172, 209, 274, 276
insulated flow, 98–9, 115, 133, 264
interactive, 2, 266

Jenkins, Henry, 24–5, 27–8, 42, 53, 167

language, 3–5, 12, 24, 29–32, 34–5, 66, 71, 119–20, 135, 148–9, 151–3, 158, 162, 176, 184–5, 191–2, 194–6, 203, 216, 219
linear, 5, 7, 9–11, 41, 108, 117–18, 126, 132, 168–9, 174, 213, 238, 247, 275
  non-linear, 10, 190

local, 4, 7–8, 14, 16, 42, 117, 134, 146–8, 150, 152, 162–4, 171, 174, 176–7, 183–4, 186, 189, 191–2, 194, 196, 202–3, 266
Lost (2004–10), USA: ABC, 10, 137, 153
Lotz, Amanda, 11, 40, 136, 166

Mad Men (2007–15), USA: AMC, 137, 255
marathon, 9, 12–13, 23–4, 27–35, 42, 51, 55, 59–61, 82, 99, 134–6, 138
marketing, 2–6, 9–11, 14, 48, 66, 98, 155, 187, 194, 201–2, 220, 241, 250
mass communication, 112
mass culture, 114, 127
mass media, 67, 69
Merikivi, Jani, 41, 43, 83, 92, 112, 124, 133
metrics, 207
Mittell, Jason, 155, 187, 213, 215–16, 227, 229, 233, 239, 253
multiple screens, 86–7

narrative arc, 51, 243
narrative complexity, 9–10, 213, 239
narrative structures, 1, 3, 14–15, 54, 155, 186, 190, 208, 233, 237, 247, 250, 274, 276
narrative time, 15, 106
national, 4, 11, 14–16, 40, 113, 148–50, 152, 154–5, 162–5, 167–72, 174–7, 183–5, 187, 192–6, 201–3, 254, 258
Newman, Michael Z., 155, 167, 211, 215–16, 238–41

INDEX 281

online, 3, 4, 10–11, 14, 32, 44, 61, 70, 74, 117, 119, 122, 124, 136, 152–3, 155, 167–8, 171, 183, 192–6, 207, 224–5, 236, 250–1, 265–7
Orange is the New Black (2013–19), USA: Netflix, 11, 47, 74, 86, 90, 104, 185, 189, 209, 265

parasocial, 132, 138
participation, 24, 28, 30, 33–4, 41, 43–4, 60, 124, 153, 155, 176
   participants, 15, 57, 83–4, 83–95, 98–9, 101–2, 106, 108–9, 118–27, 134–5, 137, 152
   participatory, 40, 42–4, 48, 56
Perks, Lisa Glebatis, 12–14, 16, 42, 48, 50, 53, 55, 98–9, 106, 115, 131, 133–8, 264
plot, 43, 55, 83, 107–8, 168, 172, 186–7, 193, 195, 209, 212–15, 219, 227–9, 237, 239, 243–4, 247, 259
   sub-plot, 169, 176, 228
popular culture, 168, 262
power, 4–6, 51, 69, 94, 121, 147, 149–51, 157, 171, 212–13, 217–18, 227, 246, 254–5, 261–2, 267
   empower, 66, 78, 265
   powerful, 9, 75, 156, 169, 177, 226, 258
press, 25, 43, 68, 134, 162–3, 167, 172, 213, 216, 236, 266, 275
public, 25, 32, 35, 41, 50, 61, 66–7, 69–70, 117, 134–5, 145, 147, 170–2, 191, 194, 201–2, 253–4, 258, 264
publication, 8, 14, 25–6, 33, 112, 167–8, 171, 185, 188, 190, 201, 203

'quality', 2, 4, 9, 16, 28, 31, 52–4, 61, 67, 69, 74, 92, 95, 109, 119, 121, 125, 137, 147, 155–6, 165–8, 172, 188, 190, 193, 203, 209, 213, 215–16, 254, 256, 275

race, 57, 84, 154, 189–90, 256, 260, 262
rape, 15, 250–64, 267, 276
recap, 15, 167–8, 171, 176, 238
recommendation, 112, 136, 184, 192, 267
Reddit, 13, 35, 40, 44–5, 55–7, 59–61
release, 23, 43–6, 48–9, 51–3, 56, 59–60, 74, 85, 134, 152–4, 157, 162–3, 168–9, 171, 177, 207, 210, 224, 231–2, 236–7, 239, 245, 247, 251–2, 258–60, 263, 266, 274–6
repetition, 7, 108, 147, 216–17
review, 14–15, 34, 44, 52, 83, 100, 112–14, 146–7, 163–9, 171–3, 176–7, 202, 228, 260, 263
re-watch, 8–9, 24, 30, 33–4, 53–4, 56, 60, 86, 90, 94, 105–6, 123, 126
Russian Doll (2019–), USA: Netflix, 45, 47, 86, 90

schedule, 4–5, 7–8, 10–11, 24–5, 27–8, 30, 35, 41–4, 50, 53, 91, 94–5, 106–7, 114, 126, 132–4, 146, 165, 167–8, 185, 187, 211, 225, 232, 246, 274
social, 4, 16, 30, 35, 42–3, 50, 59, 66–7, 70, 72, 85, 87–9, 114–17, 119, 121–4, 127, 133, 136, 139, 145, 147, 152, 165, 167–70, 172, 174–5, 177, 188, 191, 202, 224, 251, 253–4, 256, 260, 263–7

social media, 34, 43, 74, 83, 89, 95, 102, 127, 152, 154, 194, 250, 263, 265–6
Sopranos, The (1999–2007), USA: HBO, 9, 208
spectrum, 83, 90, 92, 131–2, 135–7, 146, 155, 236
speed, 89, 100, 132, 134–5, 148, 207, 220, 224, 231
Star Trek (1967–9), USA: NBC, 23, 25–6, 28–31, 42
Starsky and Hutch (1975–9), USA: ABC, 9, 23, 25–7, 30–3, 60
storytelling, 10, 13, 15, 98, 154, 157, 191–2, 208–9, 211, 213–16, 220, 229, 231, 238, 244, 247, 250, 252–4, 256, 259, 274–6
Stranger Things (2016–), USA: Netflix, 14, 16, 45–6, 86, 90–1, 104–5, 135, 207–8, 210–11, 213–14, 216–17, 219–20, 275
SVOD, 59, 170, 177, 220, 236, 246–7, 274, 276

taste, 67, 147, 150, 153, 156, 184
television culture, 3, 5, 7, 10, 12–13, 16, 67, 162, 175, 201, 203, 255, 265
theme, 1, 7, 11, 40, 45, 52, 60, 69, 90–1, 108, 119, 153–4, 157, 172, 184–9, 191, 218, 231, 251–3, 255, 257, 266

thematic, 70, 108, 118, 154, 171, 185, 188, 190, 194–6, 251–2, 261, 263
13 Reasons Why (2017–), USA: Netflix, 157, 190, 193
timeline, 3, 229, 259, 264
time-shifting, 4, 8, 24, 91
transcultural, 14, 16, 146, 148–51, 154–5, 157, 202–3
transnational, 1, 10, 14, 16, 127, 148–50, 152, 163–5, 167–70, 173, 175–8, 183–7, 190–2, 194–6, 201–3
twentieth century, 5, 65–6, 69–72, 76–7
Twitter, 35, 59, 124, 220, 250, 265
tweet, 35, 207, 266

VanDerWerff, Emily, 169, 208, 263–4
Veronica Mars (2004–), USA: UPN, The CW, Hulu, 190, 216, 253
voice-over, 71–3, 75–6, 190, 215–16

Walking Dead, The (2010–), USA: AMC, 42, 104, 135
Williams, Raymond, 146, 152
Wire, The (2004–8), USA: HBO, 10, 121, 174
'woke', 72, 266–7, 276

YouTube, 101, 106, 117